SEPARATE WORLDS

Charles had desperately wanted a happy, trouble-free marriage. But in his search for a young, untrained bride, he had been swept off his feet. His ego had been boosted by the beautiful young teenager who was so plainly in love with him. The marriage he had planned for so long had disintegrated into a marriage of convenience, exactly what he had feared would happen. He knew he had to find a way out of the mess he was in and to take charge of his life again. He didn't know how.

Diana, meanwhile, knew exactly where the marriage was heading. For the rocks. She had spurned her husband and usurped his position as the nation's favorite royal. She now realized that she could behave very much as she liked and get away with it. The fact that the marriage hadn't worked did not mean her life was going to end there. She had her two sons, her charity work, and her looks, and she was determined to enjoy her position, her privileges, and her power.

DIANA

A PRINCESS AND
HER TROUBLED MARRIAGE

NICHOLAS DAVIES

BANTAM BOOKS
NEW YORK • TORONTO • LONDON • SYDNEY • AUCKLAND

DIANA

*A Bantam Book / published by arrangement with
Carol Publishing Group*

PUBLISHING HISTORY
*Birch Lane Press edition published 1992
Bantam edition / January 1993*

ISBN 0-553-56255-X

Published simultaneously in the United States and Canada

*Bantam Books are published by Bantam Books, a division of Bantam
Doubleday Dell Publishing Group, Inc. Its trademark, consisting of the
words "Bantam Books" and the portrayal of a rooster, is Registered in
U.S. Patent and Trademark Office and in other countries. Marca
Registrada. Bantam Books, 666 Fifth Avenue, New York, New York
10103.*

PRINTED IN THE UNITED STATES OF AMERICA

OPM   0 9 8 7 6 5 4 3 2 1

Contents

Author's Note

English forms of address, having evolved over centuries, are complicated. According to Buckingham Palace, the title of the wife of the Prince of Wales is the Princess of Wales, not Princess Diana. According to Debrett's, if a daughter of a peer marries a peer, she takes her husband's rank, but if she marries the eldest or younger son of a peer, she ranks either according to her own inherent precedence (i.e., as the daughter of her father) or according to that of her husband, whichever happens to be the higher, no matter what the courtesy title may be.

That is, the daughter of a duke, marquess, or earl bears the title "Lady" before her Christian name and surname. If Lady Diana Spencer had married a commoner, John Smith, she would have become Lady Diana Smith. But when she married a man who outranked her father, she took her husband's title and so became the Princess of Wales.

Since, however, the term "Princess Diana" has passed into the vernacular, at least in America, it has been used throughout this book.

1

Separate Tables, Separate Lives

Princess Diana strode through her spacious apartment in Kensington Palace giving orders to those around her. She told Nanny Wallace that Harry would need looking after because she would be out late. She asked her lady-in-waiting, Anne Beckwith-Smith, to check through her speech for later that day, and then explained that her hairdresser should arrive by ten o'clock at the latest.

She wore an old tracksuit and running shoes, her hair pushed up inside her baseball hat. Like any other young mother who had just been out jogging after a morning swim, Diana looked fit and healthy. She wore no makeup.

The phone rang and someone called out, "It's for you, Ma'am," and Diana, with a smile, disappeared into the quiet of the study to take the call. She seemed relaxed, with no hint of stress or strain. A young woman, a secretary needing to know about some appointments, walked into the room looking for the Princess and was told she would return later.

Diana appeared friendly and firm, brimful of confidence. There was no doubt she was in total command of everything that went on in Kensington Palace. No one mentioned "HRH"—the Prince of Wales, her husband of ten years and heir to the throne.

One hundred miles away in Gloucestershire, Prince Charles was at his own home, Highgrove. That evening he sat in the drawing room with his close friend of many years, Camilla Parker Bowles. Having had dinner together, they chatted and listened to classical music. Charles seemed relaxed and happy, and Camilla appeared very much at home in the Prince's house.

It is January 1992.

Just two months earlier, in November 1991, near the time of his forty-third birthday, the Prince of Wales told his most trusted friends that to all intents and purposes his marriage to Princess Diana was "over." Though by royal tradition there could hardly be a divorce, the famed couple were "separated," in reality, if not in law, living separate lives, at separate tables, in separate beds.

For some time his friends had seen the writing on the wall for Charles and Diana. They knew there was little, or nothing, they could do to save the marriage.

On a Saturday morning in November, Charles discussed his situation with a friend, one of Britain's premier dukes: "Charles was very sad but he felt he had to tell someone. He kept slowly shaking his head, unable to understand where it had all gone wrong. I asked him if he was sure there was no way the marriage could be rekindled, kept alive. No, he believed that events between the two of them had gone too far. There was no going back. There was no way to make it work."

The Prince and the Princess have been going their separate ways in their private lives for some time. Only now the estrangement had hardened into a true, lasting break. During that time there had been an increasing conflict between their public duties and responsibilities. Stories emerged from Kensington Palace, their country estate in Gloucestershire, and from "friends" that, far from dovetailing their lives and their duties, they appeared to be going out of their way to treat each other as rivals, both for the attention of the media and the nation itself. As if the United Kingdom would some day have two royal heads—a King and a Queen who barely spoke to one another.

The 1990s were a far cry from the early years of their marriage. Friends remember the glory days when Charles and Diana were obviously in love—when they became engaged; when the shy Diana was besotted by her Prince; when the entire world watched the fairy-tale wedding. They recall dinner parties where wine was flowing and the atmosphere was happy and relaxed. Diana would give her husband a kiss as she passed. He would hold her hand comfortingly, reassuring her that he would always be at her side to give her the confidence she then lacked.

But those supper parties, those friendly barbecues on summer evenings, stopped some years ago. Most could not remember when they had last been invited to an "at home" dinner party thrown by Charles and Diana.

The friends had discounted the trials of their first few months of married life as natural. The very young Diana had just settled into her new, restricted surroundings. Many of the earlier difficulties were put down to the fact that Diana was just twenty when she married Charles, who was thirteen years her senior, and had no experience with responsibility. They all felt assured, as did the Royal Family, that in time Diana would settle happily into her role as Princess of Wales.

When Prince William was born in 1982, there was rejoicing. The arrival of an heir to the throne would surely help cement the relationship; the royal couple would now settle down to a normal married life. But somehow it didn't happen. The arrival of Harry in 1984 was also greeted as another sign that the marriage was safe, the first awkward years behind them. But again their friends saw that, far from growing closer together, Charles and Diana were drifting farther apart.

When they married, Diana was shy, immature, a lonely girl from a broken home, a teenager who was happy looking after babies in a kindergarten, young, loving, and beautiful, someone who would be the perfect foil to the Prince of Wales, the action man who played international polo, skied down dangerous mountains, piloted warplanes, captained Royal Navy ships, parachuted from the sky—dashing, fearless, and brave, and yet a man who put his royal duties above all else.

The bachelor Prince had been popular with the nation as a whole, particularly the women. The great majority believed him honest, sincere, and hard-working, a dutiful son who would make a good husband, father, and future King. By the time he was thirty, however, many people said it was time for the world's most eligible bachelor to settle down, stop his romancing of good-looking, long-legged blond beauties, and get married.

The nation believed his choice could not have been better. They admired Charles for choosing an unspoiled innocent, a pure, virginal young teacher, and they took Diana to their hearts, unreservedly. Those in the know of course realized Diana was a blue blood, from aristocratic stock, her breeding impeccable.

The nation believed that a fairy-tale marriage lay ahead. The Queen and her courtiers crossed their fingers and hoped the marriage would work out.

It hasn't.

Friendly royal watchers like to put up a happy, glossy front for the split couple, sometimes offering a Pollyanna-ish portrait. In her recent book, *Charles and Diana: Portrait of a Marriage*, author Penny Junor claimed: "Charles and Diana have a marriage that works for them. Given the pressure they have had to live with and the difficulties they have had, it is something of a miracle, but there is no doubt their union is strong and permanent and that they love one another very deeply . . . their relationship is all the better for periods apart—as are dozens of relationships."

Another is the romantic novelist Barbara Cartland, the mother of Raine Spencer, who became the second wife of Diana's father, Earl Spencer. In July 1991, she wrote: "Diana was someone so unusual, so perfect for Prince Charles's needs . . . she was everything people wanted in their future Queen. . . . Diana was like a lovely flower, opening its petals to the sun, and every day she seems more beautiful, more charming, more compassionate and more feminine."

Barbara Cartland went on with her encomium: "What is more important than anything else, I think, is that she is the Fairy-tale Princess in that her life until she married was blameless. She had no flirtations or love affairs that were sniggered over. . . . She was everything a man could want as a wife and exactly the right person for Prince Charles.

"Of course, now that they have been married for ten years, there are the usual articles in the press, sniggers in the gossip columns, that they are having difficulties and are not as happy as they were," Miss Cartland continued. "This is absolute nonsense. . . . I am absolutely convinced that the love which started their marriage will continue to grow."

Diana herself tries to put a good face on the tragic situation. "The truth about our separate lives is very simple," she recently told a friend. "My husband and I get about two thousand invitations to visit different places every six months, so we have to be apart a fair bit. But don't worry about me, my marriage is fine. I have never been happier."

Few people close to the couple believe this obfuscation. In fact, their marriage exists in name only, and while Charles and Diana have now reached a truce, it came only after she had plumbed the depths of despair in early 1986. She was desperately unhappy at home, totally at her wit's end, and seeing no possible happiness for herself in the years to come. She believed her marriage was a sham, she was convinced Charles had stopped loving her, and she often wondered whether he had indeed ever really loved her.

Diana would throw herself onto her bed at home in Kensington Palace and cry with frustration, sadness, and sometimes anger; she would often cry herself to sleep at night as she lay alone in her bed.

She could not understand how she had been so very, very happy with Charles and he had spurned her love, seemingly indifferent now to the way she felt, to what she did, to anything about her life. She remembered their early days together, when everything was so wonderful and happy—and now her life seemed so pointless.

Diana felt that life was not worth living. No one seemed to love her, no one wanted her; even Wills and Harry seemed happiest with their nanny.

One night, in a fit of desperation and loneliness, she went to the cupboard where she kept her medication. Hardly realizing what she was doing, Diana took a bottle of paracetemol, emptied a handful of the pills into her hand, and pushed them into her mouth. She took a glass of water and swallowed them. She had no idea how many pills she took. Then she went to her room . . . and waited.

But since nothing seemed to happen, she began to realize the enormity of what she had done. The thought of Wills and Harry alone in the world came rushing into her mind, and she knew she had to undo what she had just done. She went to the bathroom and made herself violently sick, determined to throw up all the pills she had taken.

It was the turning point of Diana's life.

Diana immediately phoned Charles and told him what she had done. He was thunderstruck, but he acted instantly. He called a doctor and told him to go to Kensington Palace on an urgent mission, only hinting at what had happened. Diana was examined by the doctor, but she was in no danger. She had successfully vomited all the pills.

In retrospect, Diana realizes that her overdose was a desperate cri de coeur to Prince Charles to prove to him that she was indeed in such an emotional state about her life and marriage that the only way out had seemed to be to end it all. But she knows it was never her intention to really attempt suicide: she had never consciously taken the decision to end her life. And she never has.

It was after this episode that Diana knew she had to

come to terms with her life with Charles. What she didn't know was how she was going to do that. She had to change her life, find a role for herself, throw herself into her children—for she knew that, for all intents and purposes, she had lost Charles and his love. But she also knew there was no escape from the marriage. Legal separation would never be tolerated and divorce, of course, was impossible. She had been told that before she married, and she had agreed.

Six years later she is still facing that reality, and there is little or no affection between them. They now lead separate lives most of the time and spend most of their days and nights in separate homes. They had had their own sets of friends and different interests. Whenever the couple ate together, barely a word was spoken between them. All of England seemed to become intensely concerned about the relationship between Charles and Diana.

At Christmastime in 1991, Diana, for the first time since she married, sent out personal Christmas cards to friends signed simply, "Lots of love, Diana." Although the front of the card featured a new family photo, there was no mention of Charles in the message. That is most unusual and certainly a break in protocol for the Royal Family. By sending cards signed only by herself, Diana was making a statement unofficially informing her friends that she was now totally on her own.

They both accepted that they have a job to do, and they get on with it for the inflexibility of the monarchy requires that they remain compulsory companions for life. But when they are forced to perform royal duties together, their body language reveals all. Inevitably, they turn away from each other. The chemistry has totally disappeared.

Two telling incidents occurred in February 1992 during Charles and Diana's official six-day tour of India. Charles had just played a game of polo and scored a hat trick; Diana was presenting the prizes. Charles went to kiss her on the cheek, as he has done many times in the past after a match. But it was not to be. Deliberately, Diana turned away, and a hundred cameras caught the inelegant moment as Charles seemed to kiss the back of her neck.

It was a conscious movement on Diana's part. She wished to show the world that she no longer welcomed those photo opportunities which purported to demonstrate that their marriage was still okay. It appears Diana wants people to know the truth.

Earlier in the tour, Charles had illustrated his view of the current state of their marriage. Twelve years ago, while still a bachelor, Charles had visited the Taj Mahal, the shrine to love, and promised to return one day to share its magic with his wife-to-be. But he did not keep the pledge when the opportunity arose that February. Instead, Diana went alone to see the splendor of the monument on the banks of the sacred river in Agra. Charles, meanwhile, was taking part in the rather less romantic Indo-British Industrialists' Forum in Delhi. On this occasion, Charles, it seemed, was saying the love and romance had gone from their marriage. Nothing was left but joyless duty.

No more does Charles call, "Over here, darling," and proudly propel his wife toward the crowd, delighted at their pleasure in seeing her. Diana once had a way of making Charles laugh, for example, stretching out her upturned hand on which she had scrawled the words "Smile, Daddy." There are no such jokes anymore.

The rumors that have emerged during the past ten years about their stormy relationship are basically accurate. The tales of Diana, distraught, unhappy, and alone in her world of palaces and privileges, were, to a great extent, true. The fearful shouting matches—including Diana's use of four-letter epithets—which took place in private did occur. Charles's jealousy of Diana's love affair with the British people confused and consumed him, and his decision to live a life separate from her and the children began to take shape in the late 1980s when he felt there was very little, if anything, left between him and Diana.

The papering over of their separation is part of the British royal way of life. Charles and Diana are living a sham, but the Queen is adamant that, above all else, all members of what she likes to call "The Firm" are expected to be the embodiment of stability, to uphold the finer virtues of family life, the home, and responsible parenthood, if only for appearance's sake. The Queen believes in it implicitly, especially when one-third of all marriages in Britain end in divorce, and one-quarter of all live births are to young women out of wedlock.

The state of Charles and Diana's marriage was one of the prime reasons the Queen clearly indicated in her Christmas broadcast of 1991 that she intended to continue as monarch until her death. With just twenty-six words the Queen, then aged sixty-six, put a halt to the mounting speculation that she might abdicate. At the same time, she put a damper on the hopes of those who would like Prince Charles to become King before he is in his dotage.

The Queen knows that she can totally trust Charles to uphold the monarchy and carry out his duties no matter what happens in his private life. But she is not sure she can trust Diana. Diana was not brought up with the same sense of obedience and duty, and the Queen has seen that the Princess is extremely willful and quite capable of rebelling, going her own way, leading her own life, even to the extent of risking her reputation and her husband's by spending time with eligible young men.

The Queen would be distraught if she should abdicate in favor of Charles and then watch helplessly as Charles and Diana fight openly while nominally a bastion of family life in Britain.

What concerns the Queen even more is the possibility that Diana might take rebellion further and announce publicly that she is living apart from her husband, in exactly the same way Diana's mother, Frances, announced to a shocked world in 1967 that she was living apart from her husband, Viscount Johnny Althorp.*

Such an announcement would be an unmitigated catastrophe for the monarchy. It would plunge the country into a constitutional crisis that would pose the greatest threat to the future of the British monarchy since the abdication of King Edward VIII in December 1936. For if Diana did

---

* Johnny is Earl Spencer's baptismal name.

formalize their present private separation, Charles would find it all but impossible to take the religious vows at his coronation as King and head of the Church of England, thereby precluding his accession to the throne.

If those events did indeed unfold, then the throne would pass directly to young Prince William, who would become monarch on the death, or abdication, of the Queen. And if the Queen should die before William reached the age of twenty-one, then Prince Charles would act as regent, ruling in the name of his son until he reached his majority.

The entire situation is complicated by two factors: Diana's growing popularity and the decline of support of the British monarchy among the young.

Diana's rise in popularity has been remarkable. Not a "royal" by birth, she has succeeded in capturing the hearts of the British people to an astonishing degree and put every other member of the Royal Family in the shade. In terms of popularity she has usurped Prince Charles's position as the darling of the nation. She knows and revels in it.

A 1991 Gallup poll revealed Diana was the favorite royal with 22 percent of the nation, almost twice as many as in a 1988 survey. Prince Charles, first in the earlier poll, had been pushed by Diana to joint second place with his sister Princess Anne, both with 15 percent. The Queen Mother, now ninety, was next with 14 percent and the Queen with 12 percent. (The remaining 22 percent is dotted around the rest of the Royal Family, all with just a few points each.)

In just three years Diana's popularity has leapt, while Charles's has plummeted. In those years Diana has taken control of her life, is seen to be a good, caring, and loving mother to her two sons, and has become the most respected royal because of the enormous amount of charitable work she undertakes. Equally important, she has emerged as the undisputed power in Kensington Palace. Charles, for his part, had virtually abandoned his London home for the calm and privacy of a country life at Highgrove.

In January 1992, another poll, by the *Daily Express*, showed Diana had further increased her popularity as the nation's favorite royal, with 29 percent of the votes. The Queen and Princess Anne both scored 15 percent, while Charles had sunk to just 10 percent. Diana was also voted the "most fun" royal by 42 percent, while Charles scored a rather miserable 6 percent. Diana also scored 38 percent as setting a good example, while Charles scored 29 percent. Only 7 percent thought Diana was snobbish, whereas 13 percent thought Charles was. "Which royal was the rudest?" Diana scored a zero.

The rise of Diana in prestige, power, and popularity seems unbelievable when anyone looks at those early photographs of the shy young woman, hardly able to hold her head up for the cameras, seeking the protection and confidence of the man of her dreams, Prince Charles.

Now she has emerged, at the age of thirty, a *strong* woman in every sense of the word, oozing confidence, strikingly beautiful, and far more in command of her life than the man whose position in the hearts of the nation she has usurped, her own husband, the man destined to be King. If Charles should ever become King, Britons will have a very headstrong, determined woman as their Queen.

It is accepted that the British monarchy today is under greater stress than since Edward VIII's abdication. Criticisms of the Royal Family's cost, life-style, and relevance have never been sharper. Some believe the monarchy is under threat partly because of Britain's move toward full European union, partly because of the obsessive media coverage of the glamorous Princess Diana, but also because Charles and Diana's marriage has seemingly failed.

A Gallup poll in July 1991 found that 22 percent did not think Britain needs a monarchy—nearly a quarter of the population professing itself republican. The next distressing figure was that the young who now seek an end to the monarchy, 60 percent, said they felt little or no affection for the Royal Family. Equally disturbing, 51 percent disagreed with the proposition that the Royal Family provided a good example of family life, once one of the greatest strengths of the monarchy. The Queen's sister, Princess Margaret, and her daughter, Princess Anne, and now her second son, Prince Andrew, have both suffered broken marriages, and it is no wonder the Queen is concerned that the same fate could befall her son and heir.

The Gallup poll identified Diana's principal qualities as her charm, her caring nature, and her fashion sense. Very few were prepared to describe her as arrogant, patronizing, or snobbish. But the public is realistic about her in some ways: Few thought she was intellectual, and one in ten described her unkindly as "empty-headed."

One question the Gallup poll did not ask: How well will Diana cope with bringing up the two Princes on her own, as a royal single mother? So far, Diana seems to be taking it in her stride.

During the past few years Diana has increasingly taken over responsibility for her two sons. Her relationship with them both has always been loving and, for the British Royal Family, remarkably physical and open. There have been many unprecedented public displays of affection shown by Diana. Indeed, it is one of the things the British people admire about her. Until Diana, it was most unusual for members of the Royal Family to show any affection in public, and from reports, it appears the Queen's own four children were shown little parental affection when growing up.

Now Diana is seen queuing at McDonald's for burgers and chips with her sons, stopping at motorway cafés eating a small salad while the boys tuck into fast-food snacks and a detective stands guard nearby.

It was no gimmick, no photo opportunity. Dressed in a baseball jacket, Diana took her sons for the short walk from the palace, followed by a detective, and stood in line like everyone else. Recognized by the McDonald's manager, she refused to let the staff whisk them to the front of the line. Di put a finger to her lips and whispered "Shh" when manager Joe Wireko came over to say hello. After ordering two burgers, chips, and apple pie, the four left the restaurant and walked back home.

. . .

If there can be father surrogates to heirs to the throne, Diana's male friends might fill that role.

The Queen's fears that Diana might increasingly be seen and rumored about with eligible men has become a full reality. In fact, her two boys have built up a relationship with one of Diana's close friends, the handsome Life Guard officer who commanded a tank squadron in the 1991 Gulf War, Major James Hewitt, thirty-four. James has not only helped teach the boys to ride, he has spent many hours helping Diana overcome her nervousness on horseback (ever since she had a bad fall from her pony in childhood, she has disliked riding). Despite efforts by Prince Charles, the Queen, and others who have tried to help Diana, Hewitt is in fact the only person who has succeeded in giving Diana the confidence to enjoy riding.

Both William and Harry think a lot of James. Once when James fell while playing polo, William was the first person on the scene. The youngster ran onto the pitch shouting: "James! James! Are you all right? Did you hurt yourself?"

At the time, Major Hewitt was stationed at Combermere Barracks near Windsor, and Diana used to drive over for riding lessons with him at the barracks. At first Jamie gave her his own surefooted mount, Gruden II, to help ease her nervousness. Then the two of them would go out alone together for rides through romantic Windsor Great Park. But the more Diana saw of Jamie, the more she preferred going to Windsor to ride. Sometimes Diana would even leave her sons at the barracks to mess about in the tanks while she went off with Jamie for an hour's ride.

Throughout 1989 and 1990, Diana saw more of James. They were constantly on the phone to each other. They went out together in London, to parties, to supper, and to restaurants, as Diana sought for company in her loneliness. She gave him presents, including a diamond-studded tiepin and a gold-and-silver alarm clock from the Queen's jewelers, Asprey. The gifts would arrive with a handwritten note from Diana, signed "Dibbs," James's pet name for the Princess. During the Gulf War, Diana would wake as early as five A.M. to hear the latest radio and television reports of the fighting, fearful that anything should have happened to "my James."

Jamie Hewitt was the only man who attended her thirtieth birthday celebration in July 1991, a private tea party at Kensington Palace which she held with Prince Harry and her great friend and lady-in-waiting, Anne Beckwith-Smith. For Harry's sake, Diana had a cake with candles and jelly and ice cream. William could not be there because he was away at boarding school. Charles stayed at Highgrove that day, raising eyebrows throughout the land. It gave more credence to rumors of their separation and caused everyone to question seriously the state of the royal marriage.

Diana first met Jamie when she presented a silver cup to him as captain of the victorious polo team in the summer of 1989. At the time, he had been going steady for four years with a girl who bears an uncanny resemblance to Diana, a beautiful and wealthy heiress, Emma Stewardson, a member of the famous Losely ice cream family.

Emma spoke about Jamie's affection for Diana, claiming she lost her man to a princess: "How could I compete with the Princess of Wales? Diana is beautiful, fabulously rich, and she lives in a completely different world from mine.

"Jamie told me all about it one evening in the summer of 1990. We went to a pub near my home, a cottage not far from Diana's country home, Highgrove. He told me that Diana had become a friend of his, a very close friend. He told me he was infatuated with her but realized she was married and nothing could come of such a relationship. He seemed to think it wouldn't damage our relationship. Even during the Gulf War he would send me wonderful love letters.

"I think Jamie is infatuated with the Princess. I feel sure he was carried away by the glamour of the Princess's world. So I wrote to Jamie's father, warning him that Jamie seemed to be getting carried away by his infatuation, but he told me that I should mind my own bloody business. I still hope that we can get together when this is over. He has always made me go weak at the knees."

Those who see the copper-haired major and Diana together say there is a definite chemistry between the two. Diana was attracted by the way he always blushed when they met, something she did when she was younger. James Hewitt, however, is seen by the general public as a dashing, ice-cool tank commander who distinguished himself with his leadership and tactics during the Gulf battles.

A member of the Royal Family commented, "There is indeed a special relationship between the two of them. And they do see a lot of each other."

James Hewitt is not the only handsome young man to have found favor with Diana in the past few years. The first was Philip Dunne, then a twenty-eight-year-old Old Etonian who was nicknamed Superman because, when wearing glasses, he bears an uncanny resemblance to Clark Kent as portrayed by actor Christopher Reeve. Diana and Dunne first got to know each other in 1986 when Dunne attended parties Diana went to with Fergie and other young people. Diana then invited the fun-loving banker, who was then with S. G. Warburg, to join her and Charles as part of a skiing party at Wolfgang, near Klosters, in early 1987.

Dunne accepted the royal invitation to Switzerland. At night he and Diana, with other young people, would go out to discotheques and restaurants while Charles, who has never liked such entertainment, would remain at the chalet. Diana and Dunne would spend the evening dancing together, often wildly, whatever the music dictated. That included close, "smoochy" numbers as well as funky music and rock 'n' roll. Always, Diana was seen with a great smile on her face, obviously enjoying herself.

The second evening, after skiing, everyone joined in a party, playing games and charades. At the end of the evening, while playing hide-and-seek, Diana hid in the bottom of a large chest of drawers pretending to be asleep. She called out that the first person to kiss her would become a prince. It was Philip Dunne who found her, and kissed her, long and full on the lips. But after a couple of days Dunne flew home to England, alone. He confided to friends that the atmosphere in the chalet was so tense he thought it wise to leave.

A month later Diana went to stay with Philip Dunne at his family's private estate, Gatley Park, near Leominster, Herefordshire. Eyebrows were raised because the weekend Diana was there, Philip Dunne's parents were away skiing in the French Alps. For the wife of the Prince of Wales to accept an invitation to spend a weekend at the home of a handsome young bachelor is unheard of in royal circles. That Diana agreed to go revealed to Charles, and everyone else, that the Princess didn't mind what people said, or that she was deliberately making a fool of Charles. Or, what worried the Queen, that Diana was boldly indicating that she believed she was free to act as she wished, and damn the consequences.

Rumor being what it is in Britain (as in the United States), gossip about the Princess and Dunne escalated. But when a book about Diana was published in 1988, Philip Dunne took great objection to his being mentioned and demanded that certain interpretations of his friendship with Diana be deleted.

A few months later, in June 1987, Charles and Diana had one of their rare public rows at a top society bash, the wedding reception of Lord "Bunter" Worcester and a beautiful actress named Tracy Ward. Diana spent most of the evening dancing with Philip. During one dance, she kissed him on the cheek and ran her fingers through his hair. Prince Charles, obviously annoyed, had long conversations with one of his old flames, Anna Wallace, to whom he had once proposed marriage. But much of the evening he spent watching Diana dance. At last, Charles went up to Diana, who was still dancing with Dunne, and said: "I'm leaving. Don't you think you should come too?"

Diana just laughed. "No. I'm enjoying myself; I'm going to stay," she said.

Charles turned and walked straight out of the reception into his car and was driven away. Diana continued to dance as though nothing had happened. She didn't leave the reception until dawn. Once again, it was an appalling insult to Charles, proving that Diana simply didn't care that others saw how she treated her husband. Her manner toward her husband, the Prince of Wales, was more than rude; she was ridiculing him, treating him with derision, if not contempt. Charles was deeply hurt and he would not forget.

During that same wedding reception Prince Andrew stepped into the royal row over Diana's flirtation with Dunne when he delivered an indignant "hands off" ultimatum to Dunne through a mutual friend. In an astonishing public scene, Andrew buttonholed financial whiz kid Justin Frewen and said: "Tell Philip to leave Di alone."

Diana showed off her open friendship with the "hunky" Dunne when he accepted her invitation to ride down the course with her in the royal carriage procession before racing began at Royal Ascot. In social circles, to appear in that procession is considered a great honor. Diana could have done nothing more to show the aristocrats of England and the media that Philip Dunne was indeed a close and privileged friend. It was another of Diana's many rebellious gestures, all aimed at those who dared to criticize her or her choice of friends.

Diana and Philip met secretly in the home of a mutual friend, Major David Waterhouse, in London's Pimlico district. At one of those meetings Diana told Dunne that the Queen's advisers suggested she be more discreet and think seriously about her relationship with Dunne. Dunne himself was advised by friends, more bluntly, to "cool" his relationship with the Princess of Wales. He was left in no doubt that it would be in his best interests to end the relationship. Diana wanted to continue seeing Dunne, but in the end he rebuffed her.

Dunne always knew there could be no future with Diana. The warning suggested that his career prospects in the narrow banking world of the City of London could suffer if he was seen becoming too close to the Princess of Wales. Two years later, in February 1989, Philip Dunne married Domenica Fraser, daughter of former Rolls-Royce and Lazard Brothers chairman Sir Ian Fraser. One of the guests was Prince Diana, who jetted in from New York only hours before the church wedding at London's Brompton Oratory. Charles, who had thoroughly disapproved of Diana's fling with Dunne, did not attend. He went hunting instead.

As Diana's involvement with Dunne ended, another relationship with another handsome man began. This man was the same Guards officer who had loaned Diana his home for her secret meetings with Dunne, thirty-year-old Major David Waterhouse. A friend of Lord Linley (the elder son of Princess Margaret and Lord Snowden) and Fergie, Waterhouse is a nephew of the Duke of Marlborough. He began escorting Diana to parties and rock concerts in 1987 and has remained friends with her ever since.

As David Waterhouse and Diana grew closer, they went to parties, had dinner dates, were seen together at the theatre, the ballet, the cinema. Diana would sometimes be out with David while Charles remained at Kensington Palace carrying out royal duties such as entertaining foreign leaders. As the Princess of Wales, Diana would be expected to attend these occasions, but she began making excuses not to do so, preferring to go out on the town with her younger friends.

The two continued to see each other throughout 1988 and 1989, with Waterhouse escorting Diana to many private functions. Nearly always, he parted from her with a kiss.

Sometimes, Diana has told her friends, her relationships with dashing young men is misunderstood by the media. She has maintained that is only her way of being escorted to events which Charles doesn't want to attend. Diana hates going alone because she feels so exposed and embarrassed when on her own at informal parties, dinners, and suppers. She likes to have a man with her.

Going out to discos and fun evenings is her way of letting off steam, she has explained. The Royal Family likes to relax, she argues, by riding around a royal estate or deer stalking. She likes to do so at discos, pop concerts, and supper parties with friends of her own age. Naively, she asks: "Is there anything wrong with that?"

Diana is always in the glare of the limelight. She is the person whom the public loves to see on television and in the newspapers and magazines, day after day, week after week. Conversely, Charles still undertakes all his royal engagements and duties and remains quite popular in Britain. But the nation is not entirely aware of the private life he is living in the quiet of Gloucestershire, far from the paparazzi and the public gaze.

While Diana has been mixing with a number of young bachelors, Prince Charles has turned for solace, support, and affection to the girl he first fell in love with—Camilla Shand (her maiden name)—twenty years before. From the moment he met Camilla, Charles knew that she was his ideal mate. They got on superbly together, they shared all the same interests, they spent hours talking together. They joked and laughed and shared the same sense of humor. She loved the country and country life, just as Charles has always loved it.

But at that time Charles was a young man of twenty-three about to go to sea with the Royal Navy, and marriage was a million miles away from his mind. Camilla was a society debutante and enjoying life with the young men about London in the early 1970s. One was the handsome Andrew Parker Bowles, an officer in the Brigade of Guards, a good friend of Charles's, and ten years older than both Charles and Camilla.

Six months after Charles went to sea, Camilla married her cavalry officer. Today, to a great extent, Camilla has taken over Diana's role. And today Charles knows that Camilla is the person with whom he had truly wanted to share his life, the person that he now wishes were his wife, the Princess of Wales, the future Queen of England.

Camilla spends days and nights at Highgrove whenever Charles is at his country house, which has become his principal home. She hosts dinners and lunches for Charles, sits beside him at table, organizes his personal life, checks the menus and the guest lists, organizes the staff, kitchen, and the chefs. Most important, she is the only person Charles allows inside his walled vegetable garden. Indeed, Charles only permits Diana and his own two sons to enter the garden on special occasions, which are infrequent.

Camilla is a woman of some character and undoubted strength. She is much quieter than Diana, more mature, more understanding of Charles's character and personality. She has studied his wishes and needs and appreciates the sort of life that Charles prefers to lead. No arguments or rows are reported when Camilla is at Highgrove. Yet when Diana takes the children there on weekends to visit their father, the stories of fighting and turbulence emerge.

Charles and Camilla enjoy hunting, horses, dogs, and the country life. With Camilla, Charles has the life he would truly love, that of a wealthy country squire. Charles relishes that existence, far from the hurly-burly of London, which he does not enjoy, and far from the woman who has usurped his place at Kensington Palace and, in many respects, his position as head of the family.

Camilla lives just fifteen miles away from Highgrove in beautiful Middlewick House in Wiltshire, where she stables her beloved horses. Like Charles, she prefers to spend most of her time in the country, while husband Andrew stays most weeks in London, returning to the country on weekends.

Camilla is always ready to comfort the Prince of Wales. The evening Charles was discharged from the hospital after breaking his arm in a polo fall, he went immediately to Highgrove to convalesce. Within the hour, Camilla arrived to care for the injured Prince. She was escorted by a police bodyguard to Highgrove for dinner—on the eve of Diana's twenty-ninth birthday.

Many believe that Andrew Parker Bowles should be jealous, if not enraged, by his wife's close friendship with the Prince of Wales. Those who know him well, however, reveal that Andrew recognizes that Charles needs someone like Camilla who can understand and relate to him, comfort and cherish him in his loneliness. He also sees there is a certain mutual attraction, compatability, and great intimacy between them. As a fellow officer in the Brigade of Guards, he believes he should accommodate the role his wife is playing for the Prince and apparently does so quite happily.

In earlier times, at the beginning of this century, for example, husbands were obliged to believe it was a privilege if the King or Prince of Wales showed interest in their wives. Others considered it their duty to the Royal Family to stand aside while the Prince, whoever he was, courted their wives or even engaged in open, passionate affairs with them. We can only speculate how late into the twentieth century these attitudes endured.

In May 1991 Charles went on a week-long solo painting holiday to Tuscany, at a hideaway villa near Florence. At the same time Camilla flew out to Italy, leaving Brigadier Andrew Parker Bowles, then director of the Royal Army Veterinary Corps, alone in Britain. Camilla spent several days at a villa just thirty minutes' drive from where Charles was staying.

Camilla is also a frequent guest at Balmoral, sometimes with her husband and sometimes without him. Despite being ten years his senior, Andrew has been close friends with Charles for more than twenty years. They used to play polo together. Camilla and Andrew have been married for nineteen years and have two children. Camilla fits in wonderfully with the life at Balmoral, whether it is shooting, riding, stalking, fishing, or sitting over dinner chatting. She is, of course, the exact opposite of Diana, who frankly cannot stand the place or its life-style.

There are other women whom Charles sees and who have his trust, but none can compare to Camilla. Some are old flames who are now "just good friends."

Penny Romsey, thirty-six, happily married to Lord Romsey, Charles's cousin, was once tipped as a bride for the Prince. They dated for some months in the seventies, but nothing came of the romance. In the summer of 1990, Charles went on holiday with Penny to Majorca, and they stayed together at the secluded villa of millionaire Felipe Villalonga. Lord Romsey visited Majorca for a day, and Penny flew back home when Diana and the young Princes arrived for their summer holiday with Charles. Charles and the Romseys often socialize together, but there is no suggestion that Charles and Penny are anything except good friends.

Then there is Lady Dale Tryon, whom Charles calls "Kanga." Since Charles and Diana separated, Charles has seen more of Kanga. She has always adored him, and with her bubbly sense of humor, she helps him relax. They have always gotten on well, sparking off each other's sense of humor with their own private jokes. They also share a passionate interest in country sports. Kanga is renowned for her amazing energy. An Australian by birth, she loves hunting, shooting, and fishing. She has four children and runs her own fashion shop in Beauchamp Place, near Harrods. For a while, after Diana became engaged to Charles, Kanga was banned from the royal circle when Diana took a distinct dislike to the "pushy Aussie." But when Diana decided she wanted her independence, Charles invited Kanga back into the circle. He and Kanga are still close friends.

Charles also sees other women privately. Another country sports enthusiast is Lady Sarah Keswick, forty-five, who sometimes joins Charles out hunting or fishing or just taking a ride in the country.

Candida Lycett-Green, the daughter of the late poet laureate Sir John Betjeman, shares Charles's passion for good architecture. Charles will occasionally see Candida for lunch or supper, where they spend much of their time criticizing modern architecture in Britain. Their views often dovetail. It is partly due to Candida's influence that Charles has been passionately leading a crusade for better architectural design in Britain, a campaign which has won the wholehearted support of the British people.

. . .

Today Charles is no longer the confident, positive man he was when he married Diana in 1981. To some degree Diana has emasculated the Prince of Wales, which has added pain to his recent realization that he will probably not take over the reins of the monarchy for another twenty years or more, a dauntingly long wait for the job for which he has been groomed since birth.

Conversely, Diana now rules her home, her family, the staff at Kensington Palace, and, perhaps more important, her own destiny. She has decided to lead her own life, irrespective of the wishes or the demands of Prince Charles, the rest of the Royal Family, or even the Queen. Diana basically does whatever she wishes when she wishes. She has become a liberated woman, in all sense of the phrase, and has managed to achieve this from an initial position of being trapped and cut off from the real world in the ivory tower of the monarchy.

But Diana is maturing. She now tries not to embarrass the Royal Family openly in any way. She attempts to keep her private relationships secret, which is difficult, given mobile phones and dedicated paparazzi.

Diana is becoming ever more independent. She is even prepared to ignore royal protocol and tradition. Through much of 1991 Diana made it plain that she wanted to buy an open-topped Mercedes-Benz sports car, which she confessed she had always dreamed of owning since she was a teenager. Several were lent to her for her own private use by Mercedes dealers who, of course, realized the worldwide public relations clout it would give the German auto-maker, especially if the Princess of Wales preferred it to the British open-top Jaguar she owned.

Her advisers and Prince Charles told Diana in no uncertain terms that to buy a German Mercedes to replace a British Jaguar would be an enormous blunder, insulting Britain, the British motor industry, and British auto-workers. No member of the Royal Family drives a foreign car. The Royal Family has always made a point of supporting British industry by buying British cars. Prince Charles drives a Bentley Turbo and an Aston-Martin. He would never dream of buying or owning a German or Japanese or other foreign vehicle.

In February 1992, Diana defiantly ignored all advice and got her Mercedes, entering a three-year leasing agreement to pay $2,500 a month for a sleek, metallic red, open-topped Mercedes-Benz 500SL. This top-of-the-range model, bristling with high technology, is powered by a 5-litre, V-8 engine, capable of 150 mph, and valued at around $150,000. Adding insult to injury, Diana disposed of her three-year-old Jaguar and announced she would use her Mercedes only as her "fun car," and never for official engagements.

In Britain, many people consider cars status symbols, and for most car workers, the car is the biggest single investment in their lives. Diana's rash decision did not go down well. Angry MPs accused the Princess of lacking patriotism and said she was "spitting in the face of British workers."

The pro-monarchy tabloid, the *Daily Express*, commented: "We understand Princess Diana's longings. What we find more difficult to understand is her apparent belief that she can gratify them without considering their obvious public impact."

Yet despite all revelations, she still has the support of the nation, who will hear nothing against "lovely Di." After all, she has brought a great blast of fresh air, and undoubted glamour and glitz, to the dowdy British monarchy.

The marriage has turned to tragedy. In hindsight Charles and Diana didn't really stand a chance together. Prince Charles was a highly intelligent, dedicated, rather serious university-educated man who liked opera, classical music, and intellectual conversation with rather conservative people. Diana, a high school dropout from a broken home, loved pop music, dancing the night away, and frivolous fun with young friends.

One British ambassador, who knew them when they first dated, confessed: "It is sad, but it was all wrong from the very beginning. To Diana, Charles was a fantasy figure with whom she was besotted; to Charles, Diana was the young bride who would become the perfect princess, always at his side and willing to fall in with his wishes and his life-style."

Both were totally, inalterably wrong. And the life story of the women they still call "Lady Di" gives ample explanation of what actually happened.

2

In the Beginning:
A Rocky, Upper-Class Start

Diana Frances Spencer was born on Saturday, July 1, 1961, when Prince Charles was nearly thirteen years old. The Spencer family considered the birth of Diana to be of little consequence. A daughter and the fourth child of the marriage, her arrival merited only a nine-word announcement in Britain's establishment newspaper, *The Times*:

"Viscountess Althorp gave birth to a daughter on Saturday."

All such announcements are paid per line by the families, and a brief statement to the world indicates a lack of enthusiasm for the newborn baby. The girl, born to be a Lady but destined to become a Queen, was the fourth child of Viscount Johnny Althorp, whose father was Earl Spencer, and Frances Roche, the daughter of the fourth Baron Fermoy and close friend of King George VI.

Writers have often argued that the similar backgrounds of Charles and Diana would lead them to a mutual need and dependence. Each experienced childhood loneliness, and each needed something the other offered: reliability and a sense of security. At any rate, that's how the theory goes. Yet the more Diana's early life is scrutinized and compared with Prince Charles's, the fewer similarities are revealed in their upbringings.

Another myth should be dispelled as well: that Diana, born on the Queen's Sandringham estate, was simply "the girl next door" and somehow a regular playmate of the young royals. This is not true. Though the Spencer family is one of Britain's oldest aristocratic clans, they had never been close to royal blood in a direct line. Rather, they were on the periphery as friends, acquaintances, and loyal courtiers.

Their eldest child was Sarah, born in 1955, with whom Charles was to have an ongoing love affair for months before becoming involved with Diana; Jane, born in 1957, was their second daughter; and their third, John, born in 1960, survived only ten hours. It was not until 1964—three years after Diana entered their life—that the son they had always wanted—ironically, they christened him Charles—arrived.

Diana was born at home, in the lovely ten-bedroom Victorian country home, Park House, on the Sandringham estate next door to the Royal Family's house in a beautiful, open part of Norfolk. The Spencers were so unprepared they hadn't even chosen a girl's name. But to infant Diana, all was happiness. She accepted Joy Hearn, the midwife, and then her nanny, as surrogate mothers. She slept in a cot in Joy Hearn's room for the first month of her life. "I don't remember Diana ever waking me at night," said Joy when she talked of baby Diana twenty-five years later. "She was breast-fed from the very beginning, and I think that helped her be a perfectly happy and contented baby."

Diana's childhood years were happy. She slavishly followed in the footsteps of her two older sisters and learned to take the rough-and-tumble of being the youngest of three active girls. They would play around the estate, climbing trees, riding scooters and tricycles. Tea trays were enlisted as improvised, precarious sleds to slide down the stone steps at the front of the house. Most people suspect this carefree but none too gentle start in life is the reason Diana was always thought of as a tomboy.

Anecdotes about Diana's childhood are rare. She was

the third surviving child, the third daughter, and because the Spencers had so much wanted a son, some felt that Diana grew up being ignored. She was certainly not made to feel special, which probably accounts for her strength of character—early in life she discovered she had to care for herself; no one was going to go out of the way to make life easy for her.

It wasn't that her parents ignored Diana; it was just that having another daughter was nothing the Spencers hadn't experienced before. And during those first few years of Diana's life, the marriage of Frances and Johnny was going through a rough time. Frances was bored with life in Norfolk, an area of the United Kingdom not renowned for its social life, particularly for someone like Frances, who had always enjoyed the social whirl of London's rich aristocracy. During those first years, disaster impended for the Spencer children as their parents' marriage was wearing dangerously thin.

Frances and John, like most parents, chronicled Diana's early years in an enormous number of photographs which today would be worth a fortune to any publisher. But the great majority of them are safely locked away in her mother's home. Shortly before Diana's wedding, the house was broken into; Mrs. Shand Kydd (Diana's mother's present name) went straight to the bureau where the family photographs were kept. Amazingly, the thieves had completely overlooked these family valuables, and the collection was untouched.

Frances later said, "Those are private, family pictures, not only of Diana but of all the family, taken when the children were growing up. I have no intention of ever publishing them. Not because any of the photographs are embarrassing but simply that they are our own private property, not for general consumption."

Like her sisters, Diana had Gertrude Allen, then a white-haired lady in her sixties, as her nanny and governess. Miss Allen was a local Norfolk institution, having brought up many young aristocrats, including all the children of Lord and Lady Fermoy. A generation before, "Gert" had taught Diana's mother the rudiments of education in the very same room where Diana began her ill-starred education.

Miss Allen, whom everyone later called by the more affectionate name of "Ally," recalls Diana's early days: "When she was born, her elder sisters treated Diana rather like a doll, but they became tired of that as Diana began to walk and run and join in their games. Diana quite naturally wanted to be part of her elder sisters' fun, and that caused some resentment at first, because the two older girls simply didn't want a child quite younger than they were trying to take part in their games."

But Diana proved herself quite a sport, and she tried to copy everything her elder sisters did, even though she was plainly not old enough. Eventually Sarah and Jane accepted their baby sister, and she would delightedly join in many of their outdoor activities.

But Ally also remembered another side to Diana: "She adored her baby brother Charles and treated him just like a doll, in the same way her sisters had treated her. She would dress him in clothes, undress him and then start again, but he didn't seem to mind too much. She was very kind to him and very sweet."

By the time her brother Charles was born, her father had become an accomplished gentleman farmer. Johnny had always known that one day he would take over Park House and farm the family estate. He had started life as an officer in the Brigade of Guards and had served as an equerry to the Queen. Quitting the army soon after marrying his beloved Frances when she was eighteen, Viscount Althorp had gone to Britain's best agricultural college at Cirencester in Gloucestershire for a year's hard work, learning all aspects of farming an estate. It was after leaving Cirencester that Johnny and Frances moved to Park House, in Norfolk.

Built by King Edward VII to accommodate the overflow of guests to Sandringham, Park House, with its ten bedrooms, had come into the Spencer family through Diana's mother, Frances, whose father had rented the property from King George V. Shortly after Frances married

Johnny, her father died, and the newlyweds took over the lease.

With its big rooms and corridors, overlooking superb royal parkland and hidden from the road by trees and shrubs, Park House was ideal for a large, young family. There were horses and ponies, pet rabbits, hamsters, and gerbils. There was a springer spaniel called Jill and a cat Diana loved and had named Marmalade.

There were six servants, including a full-time cook, and from an early age the children seemed to live on pheasant for lunch. Janet Thompson, Diana's nanny when she was age three to nearly six, revealed that the children never made their beds and that their bedrooms were always in a dreadful mess.

Another nanny, Mary Clarke, commented, "The children were all brought up in a very old-fashioned way, as though they were still living at the turn of the century. Manners were very important, and they were urged to have the best of ideals. Very few friends came to the house; the children were expected to play together."

Johnny bought himself a herd of cattle and was ready to settle into a country life with his young wife. They had planned to spend the rest of their lives there, raising a family, educating them in the best traditions of the British upper class, farming their acres, playing their correct roles, and enjoying a local society life to the full.

Within a year of arriving at Park House, Frances was pregnant, and the young couple were blissful. Life was going absolutely according to plan. They were both content, and even after producing two daughters, they still expected eventually to have a son and heir. But as each pregnancy ended in a daughter, both Frances and Johnny began to feel the increasing pressure but pretended it wasn't there. After the birth and death of their first son, in a matter of just hours, the birth of their next child became of momentous significance.

Determined to produce a son and heir to the Althorp title, Frances became convinced her next baby would be the long-awaited boy. Frances was so keen that everything be perfect for her anticipated son that she arranged for her favorite midwife, Joy Hearn, who had helped deliver Sarah, to fly back to Britain from Canada to where she had emigrated. Frances, Johnny, the entire Althorp family, and even Joy Hearn were surprised that the little baby, born with no complications, was a girl. Indeed, for the young couple, Diana's birth was a deeply disappointing moment.

But Johnny was a good-natured man, and Frances was still only in her twenties, and optimistic. They could and did try again. The joy when Diana's younger brother was born was greatly enhanced because he was so wanted. Of course, Diana knew none of this. She was blissfully ignorant of the pressures her parents had been under at that time. But many believe that because of her position as the fourth child, particularly arriving after the death of the hoped-for son, Diana was never very important in the Spencer family hierarchy. The arrival and survival of baby Charles relieved the pressure on both Johnny and Frances. After four unsuccessful tries, Frances had finally proved herself a "good" wife to the Althorp family. She had done her traditional duty to the family's honor and prestige by producing an heir.

In the 1990s, it may seem that even in sophisticated, free, democratic Britain, too much emphasis is still placed on whether only a son and heir, rather than a daughter, can follow the family tradition. The name is important to Britain's aristocratic families; but this could be carried on by a brother's or a cousin's children if necessary, so the name is seldom lost. But remarkably, although Britain has had a Queen on the throne for forty years, there is still that pernicious, nagging demand in the majority of today's antiquated British aristocratic families that they be headed by a man.

In years gone by, sons had to be produced because of British inheritance laws. Eldest sons inherited everything in order to preserve and consolidate the family's power and wealth and to maintain their position in British society. Younger sons were considered expendable as soon as the heir had produced a son of his own to continue the family lineage. Daughters were used to make "good," judicious marriages that bring two families together, increasing the power, prestige, and wealth of both. But they were not allowed to head a family. If no son was produced, the title passed to another branch of the family.

Remarkably, this practice still continues today, although the aristocratic traditions have been ravaged by taxation and the inexorable march of society. The rich families—who constitute a tiny 5 percent of Britain's 55 million inhabitants—have been indomitable. Even in the Britain of the 1990s, the old families, who held onto much of their wealth through successive left-leaning governments, still account for some 90 percent of entrenched wealth.

The last few decades have produced a number of new millionaires, but the real wealth of the nation—in land, art treasures, property, and stock—is still held by the few. And they are determined it will remain so.

Johnny's newfound confidence after finally producing an heir made him a happy man. He loved his quiet life as a gentleman farmer. He had managers to help him work the farm. He enjoyed being an important person in Norfolk's small society scene. He could relax and be himself. He had never enjoyed London life, except as a young, high-spirited Guards officer. Now, in Norfolk, he had what he had always wanted—a loving family. All the Viscount's children saw a great deal of him. Each night he would play with them in the nursery before bedtime. Their favorite game was "bears," in which the broad-backed Johnny would prowl on hands and knees while the children would leap, screaming, onto his back as he pretended to eat them, as though he were a grizzly. The paternal growls were punctuated by shrieks of laughter from the children, especially Diana.

But unknown to the children, storm clouds were gathering. Their father happily sat on local committees, played cricket with the village team, and worked with the local opera group. Gone were his wild days in London as a sophisticated man-about-town. But gone, too, was the man whom Frances had fallen in love with as a teenager fourteen years his junior.

Frances could not escape her inner, nagging torment. For her, the marriage had become stale and stifling. Restless and unhappy, Diana's mother left more and more of the upbringing of her children to Gertrude Allen, their nanny and governess. Frances wanted more out of life than raising four children in a windswept, remote part of England, miles from the bright lights, with a husband she no longer loved or respected—even if he was heir to an ancient earldom that would eventually make her a countess.

As soon as the two elder girls went to boarding school, Frances began visiting London more frequently. The more time she spent in London, the more her tastes revived for the sophistication of London life. In love at sixteen, married at eighteen, she felt, in the 1960s London, which was abuzz with excitement and sexual openness, she had somehow missed out on growing up, dating, the thrill of being chased. Still only thirty, Frances was a good-looking young woman with a spring in her step. Now she regularly enjoyed parties, dinners, cocktail evenings, the theatre, and ballet—the headiness of the social whirl.

Before many months, Frances fell in love. The man was Peter Shand Kydd, a wallpaper millionaire, a graduate of Edinburgh University, a former Royal Navy officer, and married to a talented artist. He had taken his wife and three young children out to Australia, bought a five-hundred-acre sheep farm, but that venture had failed. He had recently returned to England. Diana's mother took an apartment in fashionable Cadogan Place, and in 1967, in a sensationally frank statement to the British press, she said, "I am living apart from my husband now. It is very unfortunate. I don't know if there will be a reconciliation."

To Johnny Althorp, at the farm in Norfolk, the press announcement came as a thunderbolt. He later said, "How many of those fourteen years were happy? I thought all of them, until the moment we parted. I was wrong. We hadn't fallen apart. We'd drifted apart."

In London, Frances's announcement set the tongues of upper-crust socialites wagging, producing a mountain of speculation. No one could believe this beautiful young woman, with such aristocratic connections, could simply walk away from her family and set up a single life in London. The gossips all believed there had to be more to the statement. Why speak to the press at all? Why openly invite gossip and speculation? What had gone so disastrously wrong with the marriage that she had to escape to London after fourteen apparently happy years?

London was then the center of the Swinging Sixties, as *Time* magazine declared in a cover story on the goings-on in London society, encapsulated by the four lads from Liverpool the world came to know as the Beatles. London was the place to be. Suddenly Londoners and London's visitors believed the time had arrived to enjoy life. For the first time since World War II, Brits had started to believe in themselves again. They had finally come to terms with the loss of empire. Winston Churchill's wartime speeches extolling that falling domain were only memories. The British people had stopped mourning and started living. A similar national upsurge in frivolity had taken place in the 1920s, a few years after the appalling slaughter of World War I.

More important, for the young and those who feared they were losing their youth, the contraceptive pill had arrived. Only those who lived through the sixties as young adults can understand the incredible effect of the pill on social life. Overnight, it seemed, the attitude of women to dating changed. The principal argument against girls sleeping with their boyfriends—the horror and shame of pregnancy—had been eradicated.

The arrival of the pill also coincided with a dramatic downturn in the authority of the Church in Britain. Suddenly, people, particularly young people, stopped attending church on Sundays. They preferred to spend Sunday mornings lazing around, or perhaps in bed, doing what their parents had always said they shouldn't do because it could "ruin" a young girl. Gone was the fear, the shame. Women's magazines began to write openly about women's sexuality, even using the forbidden word *orgasm,* a subject never before discussed, and in most middle-class households, never admitted. Now it was out in the open.

That was the mood Frances Spencer sensed during her forays into London. But back home in Park House, Frances's decision to break from her husband devastated her two eldest daughters, Sarah and Jane. Diana, then six, was hardly aware anything was wrong. To her it was exciting to go to London by train to stay in her mother's apartment and go to school in the strange, busy surroundings of the city. Most weekends she would travel back to Norfolk with her little brother Charles to stay at Park House with her adored father. However, the excitement soon turned to the sorrow and bitterness associated with marital breakup when Diana's mother sued her husband for divorce on the grounds of cruelty.

Unfortunately for Frances Spencer, her lover's wife, Mrs. Shand Kydd, had herself already initiated divorce proceedings, naming Frances as the adulteress. In the divorce action, Peter Shand Kydd lost custody of his three children. In June 1968, Diana's parents' divorce became a prolonged, bitter, and highly publicized scandal. Johnny Althorp was granted a divorce on the grounds of his wife's adultery, and, quite extraordinary in Britain at that time, custody of all the children was given to him.

Lawyers believe one reason the judge harshly deprived Frances of her children was that her own mother not only supported her son-in-law but also told the court she did not believe her child was a suitable mother. Outraged, Lady Fermoy would describe Frances's actions as "monstrous" and "unthinkable." How could her daughter possibly turn her back on her four children, no matter what the circumstances, and go off to London? To her mind, Frances's involvement with a married man with three children of his own was indefensible.

To this day, Frances remains acutely sensitive to the charge that she deserted her four children. She has claimed she was the victim of cruelty in the marriage and insists she was a responsible mother who became caught up in a love affair with a married man. Frances has never forgiven her mother, and ill will between them has not been forgotten.

Johnny took Diana and her brother Charles out of school in London and enrolled them in Silfield School at King's Lynn, seven miles from Sandringham. For the next two years, Diana hardly saw her mother and grew increasingly close to her father as he anxiously sought to fill the vacuum, playing both parental roles as best he could. Almost daily, he took Diana to school and collected her in the afternoon. In turn, Diana assumed the mother's role with her younger brother Charles. She would fussily dress him in the morning and bathe him at night. Diana was investing emotions into becoming a child-mother, trying to fill the gap left by the real mother she barely saw.

Everything seemed to be going wrong in little Diana's private world. Her favorite cat, Marmalade, died, and her governess Ally left Park House.

The turnover of nannies was increasingly rapid. Nannies would be employed but found it difficult to control the three daughters and young Charles. The girls didn't want to take discipline handed out by anyone but their father. Unable to do their jobs properly, the nannies quit.

One nanny who stayed two years recalls Diana's stubborn nature as a girl, a trait that was later to cause great consternation in her married life. Nanny Thompson said: "Diana was simply obstinate. She just would not cooperate. I think she may have seen how her elder sister, Sarah, was behaving and copied her. So I did the only thing I could in the circumstances. I'd send her to her room until I felt she had been punished long enough; then she was allowed out.

"Diana didn't like that. But she didn't seem to mind either. It didn't alter her obstinacy.

"I remember that she didn't like having her long blond hair washed. I would lie her down in the bath, with her head on one arm, and start to wash her hair. That was always a fight. She would sulk and struggle to start with. But, as her nanny, I had to win . . . and in the end, after much struggling, and often a few tears, she would have her hair washed."

As a little girl Diana loved going to parties, partly because she had few friends and wasn't invited to many. Nancy Thompson remembered one at Sandringham: "Wearing a new frock, and having allowed her nanny to wash her golden locks, Diana, then five, and her brother Charles went to the 'big house' next door [Sandringham] for tea with Prince Andrew and Prince Edward. After tea I went to see what was happening. I found Diana and Andrew screaming around the house, playing hide-and-seek with the Queen!"

Ironically, a few years later, when Diana was ten, she refused to go to tea at Sandringham, claiming she had a headache. Apparently, she had found the two Princes too rough to play with. That day she stayed in her bedroom all afternoon, dressing her favorite teddy bear in her little brother's old baby clothes and playing mother. It was a form of psychological therapy that Diana was to carry out twenty years later when first she was a nursery assistant, and then when she had two young children of her own.

Every sadness etched a small but enduring mark on her young psyche. Cumulatively they drove Diana to become less confident of herself, less sure of her emotions.

Fortunately, Diana found some solace in horse riding. As was natural for young aristocratic daughters in Britain and her friends around Sandringham, Diana loved riding, as she did most sports and games. Like Prince Charles, she excelled at personal sports. But unlike him, she was never at home with team activities. She preferred to pit her skills, endurance, and sporting instincts against the elements, rather than against other girls. That was why Diana has always loved swimming and diving, both of which she has always been quite good at.

She grew very fond of her pony, heaping affection on it as she had done with her little brother. She was becoming proficient at riding until just after her tenth birthday, when her courage on horseback was to prove greater than her competence. She was becoming too daring, taking too many risks on the nearby fields and fences.

Although it seemed relatively unimportant at the time, Diana fell quite heavily from her pony and broke her arm. The fracture was quite painful, but more crucial was the fact that it took three months to heal.

She never again wanted to ride ponies. That accident instilled in Diana a fear she found impossible to dispel until Major James Hewitt took her under his wing and somehow relaxed her enough to restore the confidence she had believed was lost forever. Prince Charles had tried everything to encourage her back into the saddle and join him in riding, one of his great passions, but to no avail. She told one of her flatmates: "I even prayed to God to give me the courage to ride again. I desperately wanted to please Charles, to be able to ride with him because I realized it was so important for him, for us. And yet I just couldn't relax. I don't know why. I just couldn't. Sometimes I would cry alone at night about it."

To this day Diana has a fear of horses relating back to that old accident. She simply cannot relax when she climbs into the saddle, and despite all the encouragement she has been given by the Royal Family, including the Queen herself, she still doesn't like to ride. The only person she feels comfortable riding with is Jamie Hewitt.

When she takes an occasional ride, it is usually only with the Queen, who asks her to accompany her on a gentle hack around Sandringham. That childhood spill years ago has helped to divide Charles and Diana. Charles loves horses and riding above all else. The great passion of his life has been polo, a sport which he has played competently, though not brilliantly. Many in the horsey world believe that if Diana had been confident, interested like Charles or Princess Anne, they would have something greatly in common. They might have been closer, been able to talk intelligently about a subject they both loved, perhaps creating a bond which was never there.

Like many upper-crust children, Diana did not go to a local school when the time came to begin her education. Instead, as she did for Diana's elder sisters, Gertrude Allen formed a small school in one of the rooms at Park House. A select group of five or six children from the surrounding district was invited to attend this very private education. It was in this room that Diana learned to read and write. The children painted and drew and played outside; during the summer months they would take their lessons in the grounds of Park House.

This method lasted only a couple of years until, Diana entered Silfield School in Norfolk. She did well and appeared to fit in happily with the other pupils, seeming to come out of her shell and leaving behind some of the trauma of her parents' problems.

Diana has since said that she "adored" her two years at Silfield, evidently the only school she ever truly liked. Formal education and Diana Spencer have never been fast friends. But undoubtedly she found emotional security at Silfield against the background of a shattered home life.

Young Diana's childhood was a different affair from that of the man she was to marry. Periodically, Diana led a more cloistered, isolated, aristocratic childhood than did the Prince of Wales. Both the Queen and Prince Philip wanted Charles to be exposed to as many aspects of ordinary life and experience as possible during his formative years. Regularly he was taken to pantomimes, plays, the circus, to museums and art galleries, as well as to sporting activities that were more typically royal, such as shooting, fishing, stalking, hunting, sailing, or simply tramping through the heather on long country walks. In this way he came into contact with ordinary children and his horizons were naturally extended. He was encouraged to read books and to take an interest in everything outside school which might broaden his general education. Despite his unique position, Charles was given a wealth of experience.

It seems no effort was made to educate Diana in the rounded way a middle-class, let alone an upper-class, girl in Britain at that time would have been introduced to everyday life. Amazingly, what does emerge whenever Diana's background is examined is just how little she experienced, or achieved, during her formative years. There was no real encouragement to become involved with any diversions outside the home, no real encouragement to read books, take piano lessons or engage in other musical activity. She missed out on the companionship of the local Girl Guides troop and, later, the young farmers club.

Brought up in the heart of the country, Diana might have been introduced to such sports as bird watching or fishing, shooting, stalking, or rabbiting. She wasn't. Perhaps this was because Diana had no older brother to lead the way. She had hardly any interests outside the family; even family excursions were rare. The nub was this: Diana had no one to direct her life in the way only a mother can. Inevitably, she found time hung heavily on her hands. Despite visits to friends in their lovely but drafty Norfolk country houses, Diana was often alone with her thoughts. It was not so much a sense of loneliness as of being alone.

"In a way she was a sad little kid," a Norfolk family acquaintance recalls. "Not morose, but lost and certainly deprived. What Diana lacked and so deeply missed was a real family life. She may have been the daughter of an heir to an earldom, but any little girl with an ordinary mother, father, and, if you like, a back-street home in the East End of London, was richer by far."

In 1988, after seven years of marriage and two children, Diana confided to a ten-year-old handicapped boy that she had never been to a zoo or a circus in her life until she took Prince William and Prince Harry in 1987. She also confessed that she had no understanding of sports, not even soccer and cricket. Despite her father's good intentions, he proved inadequate to bringing up his children on his own after Diana's mother left. This paucity of experiences, this gap in her background, this near solitude in much of her early life, was to cause Diana and Prince Charles alarming difficulties in the early years of their turbulent married life.

The divorce of Diana's parents became final in 1969. Within a month Frances had wed Peter Shand Kydd, and the newlyweds, hoping to reconstruct their lives, set up home at Itchenor on the Sussex coast. Once again Diana and her brother Charles were to spend weekends with their mother. But this long, heartrending break has become the one episode about which she has never spoken. Deliberately or unwittingly, Diana has set up a mental block of those years in her relationship with her mother, simply removing them from her memory—a normal enough psychological reaction for a young child in those circumstances. To this day, biographers still try to assess the effect of the parental breakup on Diana. Undoubtedly she lacked the everyday discipline of a normal home and missed the maternal affection which all children need as they grow up.

No one was prepared to correct her when she was naughty; there was no one to turn to for support and love when she most needed succor. There is little doubt that the trauma of those early years has been responsible for some of the tempestuous outbursts in her marriage, which she has been unable, or even unwilling, to control during her blacker adult moments.

Her father tried all that was possible to fill the vacuum. He offered her affection and struggled to act the role of a substitute mother, but with little success. Wrought with a sense of guilt over his broken marriage, Johnny spoiled his daughters as he sought to compensate for the absence of a mother to understand and direct them. Johnny Althorp was a man's man, brought up in the stuffy world of the 1930s, when men of his class would have thought it improper, indeed incomprehensible, that a father should concern himself with the upbringing of a child. In his experience, all those matters were quite alien, to be left to the mother, nanny, or governess. Wretched Johnny Althorp was not even capable of understanding what his responsibility was to his four motherless children.

Johnny did invite his own mother and his wife's mother, Lady Fermoy, to spend some time at Norfolk caring for the children. But these grandmothers were never around long enough to have any lasting impact.

Diana's lonely, motherless life was protracted. She was only six when her mother began spending more time in London than Norfolk. With the bitterness of the approaching divorce, her parents hardly saw each other, and Diana saw very little of her mother—perhaps only one weekend in four. This unsettled, often acrimonious home life is probably equally responsible, along with her deprived, cloistered upbringing, for the tempestuous outbursts that have punctuated Diana's marriage to Prince Charles.

The result was a Diana Spencer who was shy, retiring, with little self-confidence, left to grow up very much on her own. She was a lonely and introspective child, a far cry from the graceful and glamorous young Princess she is today.

Eventually, this prim, diligent little girl earned herself the nickname Duchess at Silfield School. Despite the emotional security she found at Silfield, when she was nine, Diana was sent away to Riddlesworth Hall, the boarding school Sarah and Jane had both attended. The school was only two hours away from Park House and prided itself on being a "home away from home" for its hundred and twenty girls. When she set out, complete with a trunk bearing the legend D. F. SPENCER and accompanied by her pet guinea pig, Peanuts, the awkward little girl must have hoped fervently that it would be more than that for her. Perhaps by sending his daughters to Riddlesworth, Johnny Althorp was trying to give his motherless children a home life. But no school can be a substitute for a happy, family-filled home.

During these school years, Diana was outstanding in no area except her affection for younger children. Years later, Jean Lowe, Diana's former headmistress at Silfield, tactfully described Diana as "extremely average. However, she could read well and her writing was clear. One thing I do remember is that all her pictures and drawings were dedicated to 'Mummy and Daddy.'"

Little was to change. Elizabeth Risdale, the headmistress of Riddlesworth Hall, concurred: "I can't remember Diana awfully well because she was a perfectly ordinary little girl. . . . She was average, but I believe she did try hard. The one thing I do remember is how kind she was to the younger pupils."

When Diana married Charles, Jean Lowe wrote in the 1981 Silfield School magazine: "I remember Diana for her kindness to the smaller members of the community, her general helpfulness, her love of animals and her excellence at swimming and indeed her considerable prowess in general physical activities." The only school prize she won at Silfield was an unnamed one for "trying hard."

In summing up Diana's formative years, one may say they were sheltered, aimless, and often lonely. It would be unusual indeed if she hadn't suffered from an acute sense of rejection, so common to children from broken homes. Those early heartbreaks surely still affect her life and have helped shape her relationship with her husband, causing unforeseen, even momentous, problems in adjustment. After such a rocky start in life, it is not surprising that she drifted purposelessly until well into her teens. What is surprising is that, except for her apparently failed marriage with Charles—a seeming replication of her own mother's impatient tenure with her father—she has managed to put it all behind her.

3

Coming of Age:
The Shy Underachiever

There are no reports of Diana or her sisters running wild, in any sense of the phrase, during their childhood and teenage years. Considering their broken home and boarding-school education, some child psychologists would have predicted that one or more of the Spencer girls would have rebelled during their formative years. Diana's rebellion was to take place, but it came later— some believe after she became Princess of Wales and the curiosity piece of the entire Western world.

Diana's childhood portrait as a shy girl with little self-confidence, given scant encouragement and left on her own to emerge as a lonely, introspective child, is a far cry from the Diana of today: the graceful, glamorous young Princess, mother of two young Princes, married to the heir to the British crown, and whose lovely, radiant smile, animated expressions, and beautiful eyes inspire a million hearts when she appears on the cover of the world's glossy magazines.

But those formative years are the ones which affected Diana. Those early personal heartbreaks are the influences which marriage-guidance experts believe underlie and shape her relationships with Prince Charles and her own children. During those bleak, unhappy years, when the bitterness between her parents was most acute, Diana stayed, for the greater part, with her father, sisters, and brother in Norfolk. Her special, caring relationship with her baby brother seems to have been a valuable release for her pent-up emotions. Her "mothering" helped the young Diana pour out her confused emotions toward some genuine goal. Some believe that if Diana hadn't had young Charles on whom to shower affection, she might well have become even more shy and introverted.

To many parents, sending a girl of nine to boarding school would be considered shameful. But not in Britain, and certainly not in the upper-class circles in which her father lived, especially since her father was struggling to bring up his children on his own, with the added responsibilities of running a farm and a large house. To many around the village of Sandringham, Diana's father had changed dramatically from being the happy, smiling, cheerful aristocrat to a rather distraught, even pathetic figure who was seen walking around the village on his own most days, with his shopping basket, buying groceries. Johnny Althorp was convinced he was doing the right thing because, for the first couple of years at Riddlesworth, Diana would be with her two elder sisters instead of passing her evenings mothering young Charles.

Riddlesworth Hall was a fee-paying school—which, in Britain, is called a public school. Its prospectus boldly declared: "The basis of good education has always been the family . . . every child will have the opportunity to be good at something." The middle- and upper-class parents who sent their daughters there expected them to be educated not only in the basic school curriculum but also to be brought up correctly and politely. That is, the girls were to learn how to walk, speak, and hold themselves correctly, as well as conduct themselves properly in the presence of their elders and betters.

Diana's time at Riddlesworth was also spent caring for Peanuts, her guinea pig. She seemed to live for him, proving a doting "mother": feeding the animal religiously, cleaning his cage daily, and, when at home, playing with him on the kitchen table.

Diana's move to her first boarding school was timely, helping to cushion the next severe shock to her psyche. Like the proverbial bolt, into Diana's young life came someone new, someone totally different from any grown-up she had known before—Raine, whose arrival was to have a profound, lasting effect on her father's life and on Diana's.

The Countess of Dartmouth, as Raine liked to be called, was then forty-five and variously described as dynamic or bossy, forceful or overpowering. She was the wife of Johnny's old friend, Lord Dartmouth, and the daughter of world-renowned Barbara Cartland, the extraordinary one-woman fiction factory who has written some 365 books, mostly romantic novels with happy endings.

(Ironically, Barbara Cartland had a long-lasting, platonic romance with the man who had great effect on Prince Charles, his great-uncle, "Dickie" Mountbatten. In fact, Barbara Cartland's relationship with Mountbatten surprised many people when it became widely known. She adored him, believing Mountbatten the perfect "English" gentleman. Toward the end of his life, Mountbatten, living on his naval pension, was rather hard up, and Barbara Cartland, with the fortune made from her writing, happily subsidized him, buying for him exquisitely tailored suits from Savile Row and hand-lasted shoes. When Prince Charles discovered, after Mountbatten's murder, what had been going on, he was furious that the man he most admired had not turned to him for help in sorting out his financial affairs. The news did nothing to encourage a relationship between Barbara and Prince Charles, but rather the reverse. Charles has said, "I can't stand that woman!")

Raine, Cartland's daughter, was already a formidable public figure, constantly badgering the Greater London Council, appearing on television chat shows, and championing the cause of conservation.

Raine began coming to Park House in the early 1970s,

and before long she had become a regular visitor. To their dismay, the girls discovered that Raine was rapidly taking over the place, running it as if it were her own. Diana's father began to rely on Raine for advice on bringing up his three daughters. He had great difficulty talking to his former wife, and he believed he needed a mother figure for the girls. Unfortunately for Johnny Althorp, he couldn't have picked anyone less suitable for this role.

Johnny must have sensed shortly after Raine met the girls that they would not get on well together. But he thought the animosity would pass, that they would learn to like each other. It was not to be, but Johnny persisted, believing the more they saw of Raine, the better their relationship would be. The more Johnny saw of Raine, the more he became dependent on her, and the more Sarah, Jane, and Diana objected to this forceful woman's trying to take the place of their mother.

Sarah and Jane, now more confident in their spirited mid-teens, took an active dislike to her, behaving rudely whenever she came to visit. At first Diana seemed to be ambivalent, but eventually, influenced by her elder sisters, she turned against Raine as well. Johnny found himself desperately trying to play the peacemaker whenever Raine came to stay. When he finally realized he could not win, he was already deeply involved with Raine, and his daughters were away at boarding school most of the time. The girls had become so offhand and objectionable when Raine appeared that Johnny gave up inviting the new woman in his life to the family home whenever the girls were there.

Then, in 1975, old Earl Spencer died at age eighty-three. He had been the seventh holder of the title, which had been created in 1765 and carried the motto God Defend the Right. Diana's father, Johnny Althorp, took the title, and his children all rose in the British hierarchy. Diana's brother Charles became Viscount Althorp, heir to his father's newly inherited earldom. The daughters all received titles; Diana would officially be known as Lady Diana Spencer until her marriage.

The new earldom also meant another upheaval, another

change in the life of the young Diana, now age fourteen. The family left Park House at Sandringham, the house Diana knew as home, and moved into the ancestral home, the eighty-five-hundred-acre estate of Althorp House* in Northamptonshire, where she knew absolutely no one. She was already a shy, reserved young teenager, except with her sisters, and the loneliness in the middle of the empty countryside of Northamptonshire made her life even more bleak.

She spent some of her holidays visiting her mother at her new homes in London and Sussex. She seems to have enjoyed the visits and being away from the overbearing Raine. Raine was very bossy, dictating to the three girls, treating them as though she were their headmistress. Whenever the three girls were together and Raine's name came up in conversation, they would chant in insolent unison, "Raine, Raine, go away . . ."

At this time, Diana would also leave Riddlesworth Hall, where she had won two awards. The first was the Pets Corner Cup, awarded for her loving care of her pet hamster; the second she won at the end of her first year, the Legatt Cup for helpfulness. She had won nothing, however, for academic or sporting achievements. At fourteen, she did manage to pass her Common Entrance examination to West Heath School, founded in 1865 to train students "to develop their own minds and tastes and realize their duties as citizens."

---

* Sixteen generations of Spencers have made Althorp one of Britain's most consistently-occupied stately homes. The first John Spencer bought the property in 1508, and succeeding members of the family altered the mansion from Elizabethan to Restoration to Georgian styles. During those centuries, the wealth of Althorp relied on a family which had farmed profitably, mixed with royalty and the ruling classes, and had married well.

Three of Diana's seventeenth-century female ancestors are understood to have spent time in the bed of Charles II. Indeed, two hundred years before Sarah and Diana were courted by Prince Charles, two other Spencer girls (daughters of the first Earl Spencer), Henrietta and Georgina, were both romantically involved with the Regent, Prince George. Georgina, who was married at sixteen, was known as the "Empress of Fashion," and her extravagance concerning clothes was legendary.

She was following in the footsteps of her mother and two sisters by attending West Heath, near Sevenoaks in Kent. Both Sarah and Jane had done extremely well there. Sarah had starred in the school's plays, excelled in most school activities, from lacrosse to music, and passed six O levels—O levels (O for Ordinary) being the standard examinations, customarily taken by British schoolchildren in seven to ten subjects upon leaving school at age fifteen or sixteen. Brighter students go on to study for three more years in three specialized subjects for their A level exams (A for Advanced).

Sarah's tenure at West Heath ended, however, in tears and disgrace for the Althorp family. At age sixteen she was expelled for the comparatively minor offense of being caught drinking alcohol. With her forceful personality, Jane managed to shake off the severe embarrassment and went on to do splendidly at West Heath, showing not only academic brilliance but impressive leadership qualities as well. She captained the school lacrosse team—a distinct privilege at a girls' public school—and gained a remarkable eleven passes in her O levels.

Ruth Rudge, headmistress of West Heath, perceptively recalled: "Of course I came to know all three Spencer girls very well, and they were all totally different personalities. Diana was not so brainy as the other two girls, but she did have the most endearing qualities. Diana seemed to love children and had an easy, engaging manner with them. I remember she spent many hours caring for the handicapped children at a center near the school. She was a girl who noticed what needed to be done, then did it willingly and happily.

"But," Ruth Rudge continued, "Diana was no goody-goody. She could be naughty—talking when lights went out, hiding her tuck [snacks], and making other girls giggle at assembly or in class with some timely remarks."

Diana has always remembered being quite naughty at school. She once smeared blue eye shadow on her knees and pretended it was a painful bruise that prevented her doing some sporting activity on a cold winter's day; she remembered pillow fights and romps with the other girls in the dormitory, midnight feasts at the end of term, and even occasional custard pie throwing. When caught, the punishment was running six times around the assembly hall or the lacrosse pitch, or weeding the garden. Diana was to confess later, "I became a great expert at weeding."

When Diana was fifteen, Johnny Althorp proposed to the woman who by then ruled his life. They were married in a quiet civil ceremony in London in July 1976. None of Johnny's daughters attended their father's wedding, nor did they receive an invitation.

The relationship between the girls and their new stepmother, Raine, grew even worse. Undaunted by their hostility, the new Countess Althorp took complete control of the estate, which was sadly in need of attention. A keen conservationist, she was determined to restore the house and its art treasures to their former glory. She also realized that in order to accomplish that, she had to raise some money (by actually selling some of the house's treasures), then run the estate as a proper business. Johnny Althorp rightly credited Raine for the way she took over when he realized he needed a strong personality and enthusiastic, hands-on management to revitalize the place.

The management of Althorp exacerbated the hostility of the girls toward Raine. Raine insisted on making all decisions without consulting the Spencer daughters, who argued that, unlike Raine, they were the rightful heirs. Further, they were no longer children but intelligent young women now. Dismayed, they watched as elegant display cabinets were rapidly emptied of their magnificent porcelain and silver. Together with rare eighteenth-century books and glorious paintings, they went under the auctioneer's hammer. Blank spaces appeared on the walls of the great stately home where once Van Dycks and other art masterpieces had hung. The sale attracted a great deal of interest, and eventually, estimates have it, Raine raised a much-needed $7 million.

Shortly before her marriage, Diana confided how much she had been hurt by the sale of so many of the family treasures. She would neither forget nor forgive her stepmother, she declared. Diana knew the auctions were necessary in order to prevent the sale of everything, including the house itself. At least this way Althorp manor had a good chance of being saved.

But Diana still resented and loathed Raine. She felt her stepmother had undermined the special relationship she and her father had developed during the lonely years after her mother had left the family. Years later, Diana was pleased to discover that Prince Charles shared her assessment of her stepmother. He regarded Countess Spencer as "brash," a devastating indictment in his subtle armory of regal put-downs.

But there was another view of the situation. Death taxes in England were crippling. Without Raine's determined, competent activity, Johnny Althorp would almost certainly have had to sell the family estate. The girls were put off by the very extroverted, enthusiastic efficiency that saved their heritage simply because they had never encountered the likes of it at such close quarters.

Before the arrival of Raine, life had been a quiet, unruffled affair with little fuss or organization. Johnny spent hardly any money on the upkeep of his homes, which slowly deteriorated into gentle decay. His had been the quintessential country life of an upper-class British aristocrat who didn't want his everyday routine interrupted by too much efficiency.

Old Billy, who did odd jobs at Park House over the years, remembers: "Viscount Althorp never wanted any major changes or alterations. I would mend the odd gutter or leaking downpipe; mend the fences or do any work that was needed on the windows and doors. But there was no need for major changes, ever, not that I can remember. It was an easy place, no bother."

That quality changed under Raine's driving enthusiasm. To make Althorp a going concern, she pruned the family budget to a minimum. She fired old retainers and faithful servants who had served the Spencer family for decades. She reduced the number of cleaning ladies who came to the house daily and fired some of the older gardeners and men who did odd jobs around the lovely, decaying old mansion. She cut back on the purchase of good wine for the cellar, and the girls found themselves having to launder and iron their own clothes rather than have someone else do it for them. Nothing she did at Althorp pleased the three sisters.

Raine also molded the life she desired and believed the wife of one of Britain's premier aristocrats should be entitled to. She behaved as if these were the 1920s, when the old aristocratic families enjoyed life with teams of servants at their beck and call. There was no six A.M. country start to Raine's day; many mornings, playing the aristocrat for all it was worth, she stayed in bed until eleven reading *The Times*, attending to her mail. From time to time she'd issue orders for the day to the few staff they still kept. In the evenings, the stylish new mistress of Althorp would dress for dinner in a full-length evening gown and insist that poor Johnny, who wanted only an easy, comfortable life, dress in black tie and dinner jacket, even when the two of them were dining alone.

Diana, Sarah, and Jane invariably wore only jeans and shirts, as did all their friends. Whatever Raine did, the girls seemed provoked to do the opposite.

If the girls could see no good in Raine, their father certainly could. Friends believe that without her love and devotion, Earl Johnny Althorp would have died a youngish man. In 1978, he suffered a devastating stroke. Fortunately, he was a fit fifty-four-year-old and somehow managed to survive no fewer than eight comas. His three daughters were told that their father was on the point of death and, if he survived, would live as a mere vegetable. But to everyone's astonishment, he made a remarkable recovery.

The Earl justly gave the lion's share of credit to his wife. "For four months she sat by my bed, holding my hand, and even shouting at me that I wasn't going to die because she wouldn't let me," he recalls. Indeed, she would not. But for Raine, the Earl insisted, "I would not have lived to see Diana married, let alone be capable of walking up the aisle of St. Paul's Cathedral to give her away to Charles."

Even so, cuddly, kindly, bumbling Johnny—he was known affectionately throughout England as "Di's Dad" —did not permit the mistress of Althorp to dominate all aspects of his life. After twelve years of marriage, he told *Daily Express* writer Jean Rook, "If she tries to creep into my study, I chase her out. I'm always fighting her off. If she starts interfering, I tell her to go away and read her mother's novels."

The plucky Earl added, "I tell her to go into another room and watch television. She is mad about 'Dallas,' 'Dynasty,' and 'Miami Vice.' Raine's wonderful, but you have to slap her down occasionally."

The "wicked stepmother" was no favorite of Diana's. She was able to arrange to spend some of her school holidays with her mother, but for the most part she would be at Althorp, leading a quiet life with her sisters and a few friends in the surrounding homes and villages. Teenage parties, barbecues, and village dances were a rarity for Diana. She seldom attended formal dances or country-house weekends or the social gatherings she would have been invited to if she had lived nearer London, for example, in Surrey or Sussex, or one of the more fashionable parts of the country.

Usually lonely on school holidays, Diana became an inveterate letter-writer—corresponding with school chums she missed during the holidays, remaining in her room at Althorp for hours recounting the latest awful "horror" undertaken by Raine or telling of sunbathing topless on the grounds. None of the letters referred to boys or boyfriends; they weren't yet a part of her life.

Norfolk had been her home for most of her life, and she liked the camaraderie of the local shops and the people, with their distinctive, soft East Anglian accents. To keep out of Raine's way, Diana made friends, or rather acquaintances, with many of the locals. She was always friendly, always gave them a smile and a cheery hello, and was open and genuine.

Her relationship with the people of Sandringham and Althorp was to be a first-class education for the role she would have to play for the rest of her life. A central reason

Diana is so liked—*adored* is not too strong a word—by the people she meets and talks to is the ease everyone feels in her presence. She appears so natural. No matter what their background or education, everyone who meets Diana instinctively experiences a warmth, an understanding that is always commented on. There is not an ounce of stuffiness or arrogance in her approach or attitude. Her ability to chat one-to-one with total strangers she meets on royal visits, and the impression it leaves, is one of the principal reasons behind the popularity she enjoys throughout Britain.

But the village small talk of Norfolk and the friendship of a few quiet people going about their mundane lives could hardly provide an adequate background for the role she was to play in later life. She needed an education.

Hard schoolwork and the terror of exams loomed ever closer. Diana found it increasingly difficult to cope, to concentrate and study at West Heath. She was convinced she was the dunce of the family and would never match, or even approach, the academic records of her two sisters. Neither her sisters nor her teachers could persuade Diana that she was bright, or that if she worked hard and diligently, she could pass the exams ahead. She refused to be encouraged, and today most of her teachers believe she never really tried.

She failed her first set of O levels completely. At first her failure was attributed to exam nerves, although not passing even one is difficult to fathom, since not many teenage girls at Britain's fee-paying schools totally fail all their exams. But somehow Diana managed to do just that. Diana retook them five months later, in December. She flunked them again. All of them.

She had been right in her low opinion of herself. She had proved her family, teachers, and school friends wrong. She was miserable, distraught, a failure.

To this day, no one can explain how Diana managed to fail her basic O levels twice. They're not difficult, and Diana had not been overambitious. In her first set, she tried for six subjects, but in December, she attempted only four, which should have made them much easier.

During the 1970s, most girls in Britain sat for a minimum of six exams, and many for eight. None of her teachers reported that Diana was idle or not concentrating at school. Her reports said she was progressing but would have to "try harder" to be successful at her O levels.

Despite her failure, her father urged Diana to stay on at West Heath. But she was so embarrassed at her failures, especially since both her sisters had done so well, that she simply did not want to face her school friends. Her embarrassment was so severe that to this day she fudges the truth about her educational achievements, or lack of them.

She even fibbed to Stephen Barry, Prince Charles's valet, who had befriended Diana soon after her engagement to Charles. Discussing O levels one day with Diana in Buckingham Palace, he asked her, "How many do you have?" Diana hesitated, then said, "Two."

Barry admitted he had none and added, "Well, don't worry. You've done more with your two than somebody else has done with nine."

Whatever Diana's talents, they were not in the academic sphere. Diana knew this and pleaded with her father, telling him she simply could not sit for exams. Johnny Althorp couldn't believe his little Diana was unintelligent. Time and again, he tried to persuade her to take the exams again. If not at school, perhaps at a London "crammer," where many young people who have flunked studied for a term, or a year, before retesting. Diana would have none of it.

With the help of her sister Sarah, she persuaded her father to let her attend the same Swiss finishing school that Sarah had, at Château d'Oex near Gstaad, the Institut Alpin Videmanette.

Fleeing was Diana's favored way of coping with a major problem. She put it behind her and tried to forget the failure had ever occurred. It was not to be last time she dealt with personal problems by running away. She was now seventeen years of age and seemed unable to face the realities of life. Her life had been so sheltered that she had never been overseas, never been on a ship or an air-

plane, never been on an overseas holiday—a devastating
illustration of the kind of "backwoods," deprived life
young Diana had led.

So it was with some excitement, mingled with some
trepidation, that she set off for Switzerland. But the thrill
of being abroad on her own soon waned. Before long,
Diana was homesick and unhappy. For the first week she
cried herself to sleep each night. Once again, she decided
the way out was to run away. Six weeks later, she returned to London in tears.

Diana told an old school friend from West Heath how
miserable she was, and what a failure she had become.
She felt cut off from her father because of Raine, separated from her mother because of Peter Shand Kydd, and
no longer close to her two sisters because they were so
busy with their own lives and believed that Diana was old
enough to look after herself. She saw little of her brother,
Charles, now at boarding school. It was her own fault she
had left school early, with no qualifications of any kind. It
was her fault she had little ambition and no idea what she
was going to do with her life.

Diana had acquired a few assets during her school
years. She had learned to be an excellent swimmer and a
good diver. During her six-week stay in Switzerland she
had become a competent skier. And while she left West
Heath with no exams passed, she had won an award,
handed to her at the behest of the headmistress: the Miss
Clarence Award, presented only to "outstanding pupils"
for service to the school. At the time, Diana remarked, "It
is one of the most surprising things that ever happened to
me."

It was a reward for her social work outside the school.
As part of their extracurricular work, girls at West Heath
were expected to take an active interest in the local community. Diana would visit an old lady in nearby Sevenoaks every week and sit and chat with her, do whatever
shopping was necessary, make her a cup of tea, tidy up,
and see that the old lady was happy and comfortable. She
also paid a weekly visit to a nearby home for handicapped
children.

The Miss Clarence Award revealed Diana's positive, endearing qualities, which had not shown themselves in scholastic or sporting achievements. It showed that the future Princess had a rare quality of understanding and service—born of a shyness that made her want to help people—which she gave generously to whoever needed it.

It was also at West Heath that Diana's first recorded encounters with the opposite sex had taken place. Every term, West Heath girls would be invited for dances at Tonbridge School, a nearby boys' fee-paying school (what the British call a public school), and some of the girls would pair off with their dancing partners for a walk outside. It was behind the Tonbridge School fives courts that Diana had her first kiss. She was fifteen years old.

A former Tonbridge pupil said, "It all came back to us when, a few years later, we read with astonishment that Diana was dating Prince Charles. It was the same girl that we had danced with, and I know of at least one boy who took her outside for a kissing session. But it was nothing more, definitely not, according to the boy. But he has sworn us to silence."

Back from Switzerland, Diana hadn't the faintest idea what she was going to do. She didn't want to learn basic skills such as shorthand and typing, cooking, or working as a personal assistant. She couldn't pursue academic studies because she hadn't passed the basic exams. Yet she knew she couldn't simply sit around at home in Norfolk, especially with the "awful" Raine in command, nor could she live with her mother and her new husband, where she felt like an intruder.

Instead, she followed her sisters to London, the "Big Smoke," to find work. With no qualifications, she did the one thing she liked: looking after children. Many well-to-do mothers in London employ young women to "nanny," to help bring up their children while they work, socialize, or go shopping. For class-conscious young mothers, Diana was a perfect au pair. She spoke well, dressed like a

"Sloane Ranger,"* and came from an impeccable social background. And she loved children.

The mothers didn't care that Diana had no academic qualifications. Those who knew she was a titled Lady were impressed and hoped some of her breeding might rub off on their youngsters. Diana seemed not to mind that the pay was hardly enough to feed herself, let alone buy clothing.

Diana first worked as a mother's help in Hampshire, then spent several months in and around London odd-jobbing, mainly looking after children while their regular nanny was away. She even worked as a char lady in several London homes when she was short of money. She would dust, polish, and do the laundry, ironing, and vacuum cleaning when necessary, and then baby-sit in the evenings.

Some families knew her background, but Diana preferred anonymity; most never knew she was the daughter of the Earl of Spencer, believing simply that she was a young, well-brought-up girl who needed pocket money.

Of course, Diana was more fortunate than the typical single girl in London. Although at first she stayed at her mother's London flat, then shared other flats with other girls, her mother advised her to buy an apartment. Money had been left to her in trust by her great-grandmother, and Diana eagerly went house hunting. She finally chose a three-bedroom apartment in Coleherne Court, Fulham, West London. It cost about $150,000 in 1978, quite an expensive apartment at that time. The location was good, and the place large enough to invite other girls to share, so sharing was Diana's solution to paying for its upkeep.

Diana loved the idea of sharing—and eventually had four flatmates—because it was a way to meet other young people, especially young men. She was still amazingly

---

* Sloane Rangers are upper-crust young women who live around the Sloane Square, Chelsea, area of London. Sloanes were once assumed to have no ambitions or career goals, and to enjoy young singlehood before snaring some young man from a wealthy background or with his own handsome income.

shy, but being a home-owner gave her a certain cachet, and therefore confidence, with her peers. Diana threw herself into London life. She bought an old "sit-up-and-beg" bicycle (an old-fashioned, 1930s-style bike) with a basket on the handles and began cycling around the busy London streets. She loved it. Bicycling saved her money, and she could avoid the "horrid" bus or tube. The one incongruous note in her London flat was the girls' bicycles cluttering the entrance hall, but no one minded. If left outside, they would disappear overnight; it was one of the penalties of living in central London.

Quickly, Diana learned to enjoy her new life. The girls invited young men for supper. The boys would bring a bottle of "plonk" (cheap wine), while the girls would supply the easy-to-cook spaghetti and bread and cheese. Diana went out on dates, but for her, young men were few and far between.

One of her flatmates said, "Diana was fussy. She liked to go out to dinner parties, the theatre, the cinema, but she never seemed to want a steady boyfriend. She never wanted to get involved. We put it down to her shyness. Of course she probably kissed and cuddled. We all did at that age. But there was never anything more, as far as we knew. And we would have known, I'm sure."

The first girl to move into Diana's apartment was her West Heath friend, Carolyn Pride. Now thirty, the same age as Diana, Carolyn commented, "We were really fluffy-headed Sloanes." At the time she lived with Diana, she was training as a soprano at the Royal College of Music. She is now living in Central London with her husband, brewery heir William Bartholomew, and their young son and daughter.

Carolyn says of that era: "We did have a great time together and we all got on so well. It was fun, with lots of laughter and silliness, but we were young and learning to enjoy life. But there was nothing wild about any of us.

"When news broke that Prince Charles was dating Diana, we sat around discussing it all, of course. One idea was to set up a backing group [backup singers] called Princess Di and the Flatmates. But we were only joking."

Carolyn is still a close friend of Diana's, and they meet occasionally for tea or a drink and a chat. She is godmother to Prince Harry. "It's a godmother Mafia, actually. Diana is godmother to my son Jack, and we all take a great interest in each other's lives and children."

Carolyn has also been support for Diana during the period of growing concern about her relationship with Charles. Carolyn says, "I believe in marriage. I have divorced parents, so I know how difficult it can be. But my husband and I seem to have grown closer over the years. Neither of us feels tied by marriage. It is so important to be close to one another, emotionally. Then, if you are both truly independent, you can handle it when you're apart. You don't have to be belligerent about it. And you can help each other in some way, in important and trivial matters. For example, I iron William's shirts because I want to. I don't feel hard done by doing so."

Another of Diana's flatmates was Anne Hill, two years older than Diana and the oldest of the four girls. She worked as a secretary to London estate agents Savills at the time and took command of the press inquiries when the news broke that Charles was dating Diana. Anne, now married to an Australian landowner and living in New South Wales, recalls those heady days. "They were hectic but great fun. The others, including Diana, always complained that I was the bossy one of the flat, organizing everyone and everything. Diana was always quiet and shy, but she had a wonderful sense of humor. And we have always kept in touch. Now I have been married eight years and we have three children. Life has been very good to me, and I fortunately have a wonderful relationship with my husband. Noel and I have a real family life."

Despite the camaraderie of the Fulham apartment, Diana decided she needed to do more with her life. She was fed up with cleaning other people's houses and looking after their children. She wanted a challenge.

She had always loved dancing, and still does. At school she would always show everyone else how to do the latest craze. Turning up the radio and dancing to pop music made her feel free, perhaps even a touch wild, releasing her emotions. Dancing was the one time when Diana showed no signs of shyness or embarrassment. People have always told her she was a natural: she moved well, was graceful, and looked good on the dance floor. Growing up, she had often thought of becoming a professional dancer, although at five feet, ten inches, she was too tall.

Now Diana was determined to apply for the job of student teacher at the famous Betty Vacani children's dancing school in Knightsbridge. She had to pay $170 a year for the privilege of learning how to teach dance. Despite her confidence, she was told she was not good enough for the demanding Betty Vacani, that other students at the school were more talented. After three months, Diana felt she was out of her depth and would never make a professional dance teacher. Rather than brave it out and try harder, she again took the easy route out of crisis. She quit, too shy to tell the principal, and even Miss Vacani, she was leaving. It was another disappointment, another confirmation that she was a failure at seventeen. And it hurt.

After a few days' absence, one of the teachers phoned Diana at her apartment. She said she couldn't attend anymore because she had hurt her foot, but the very next day she flew to Switzerland for a skiing holiday. Though she never returned to Betty Vacani's academy, her passion for dancing was to flare spectacularly again and again in her life.

Though miserable about her latest failure, Diana was determined to be a success at something—anything. Besides dancing, the other skill which people praised her for concerned her warm and caring way with children. Why not capitalize on that? She didn't want to be a nanny again, but she knew she wanted to do something involving very young people.

Finally, she found a permanent position to her liking— as a helper at the Young England Kindergarten in St. George's Square, Pimlico. The children were small, and Diana was responsible for groups of five youngsters. She loved the work, and the children, in turn, seemed to adore her, responding to her natural, open approach.

At last Diana was happy and relaxed. She adored single life in London. Flatmates came and went, typical of young women in London. Without any qualifications, they somehow made a living, enjoyed parties, went to dinner and makeshift suppers, the wine bars, sometimes attending the theatre, concerts, dances, all in the company of affluent young men. Diana went out socially, but never seriously with anyone. A mild flirtation, a good-night kiss, holding hands in the cinema, and a few romantic dinners, but no love affair.

Until Prince Charles Philip Arthur George of the House of Windsor and heir to the British throne.

4

—❯❯❯≪≪—

A Prince Grows Up

Charles's arrival in the world received a totally different reception than Diana's. The official announcement of Charles's birth on Sunday, November 14, 1948, was met with adoration and marked by celebrations held throughout Britain and its dominions around the world.

That night would be remembered in pubs and clubs throughout the land. The much-awaited birth of the heir to the throne gave the nation a feeling of relief. Perhaps the horrors and misery of the grueling war years were finally over.

Everyone, it seemed, from the rich to the poor, wanted to celebrate the birth of Prince Charles. Presents began to arrive from all over the world. From the United States, where Americans had read of Britain's poverty after six years of war, a staggering one-and-a-half tons of diapers were donated, all apparently destined for the baby Charles. Diplomatically, his mother, then Princess Elizabeth, decreed that no presents could be accepted by the Royal Family; everything, including the diapers, was distributed to expectant mothers by a special operations room set up to collect and dispatch the hundreds of gifts.

Lying in his grand, four-poster cradle in Buckingham Palace was a prelude to life ahead. He was always to be in the limelight, surrounded by privilege, grandeur, and servants. His early years were not spent with his mother and father; instead he was tended day and night by two royal nannies, two nursery maids, and a nursery footman to handle the heavy work.

His mother saw him only twice a day. He was carried to her after breakfast for thirty minutes, and then for another thirty minutes just before his bedtime. In those early years, weeks would pass without Charles seeing his father, who was then an officer in the Royal Navy. Christmas was often spent with his grandparents, King George VI and Queen Elizabeth, now the Queen Mother.

Charles received his early lessons and discipline from a Scottish tutor, Miss Catherine Peebles, whom he called Mispy. Even at the age of four, Charles showed signs of being rather serious, a little shy, and not at all boisterous and aggressive, like his younger sister Anne.

Charles was nine when he was sent to his first boarding school, Cheam, one of Britain's oldest preparatory academies. School proved a shock. He had to share a dormitory with nine other boys, care for his own clothes, clean his shoes, make his own bed, and serve at table. The other boys were suspicious of him. Charles felt miserable and alone for the first three terms. It was a problem which was to dog him throughout his school and university career, one which he never satisfactorily solved.

At thirteen, Charles left Cheam for Gordonstoun, his father's old school, in Scotland. Unique among British public schools, it was to leave a deep impression on the young Prince. Gordonstoun came into existence in part because of Prince Max of Baden, the last chancellor of Imperial Germany, who was angered by the defeat of Germany in World War I. The German Prince's ideals were taken up by Dr. Kurt Hahn, an educational philosopher. He founded Gordonstoun, placing emphasis on stamina and leadership, principles which Prince Max believed were responsible for Britain's victory in World War I.

The school has frequently been described as a remote Spartan outpost with a Boy Scout approach across an assault course toward eventual manhood; the rigors include cold showers twice a day and a morning run in T-shirt and shorts in sun, rain, or snow. The school motto, *Plus est en vous,* "There is more in you," encourages the boys to compete not against one another but against themselves, to discover their own inner strengths and improve their own best performances. It is a philosophy Charles has never forgotten, and he tries to instill the same in his sons.

Charles worked hard at school and left Gordonstoun with six O levels and two A levels, in history and French. Although at first he had been unhappy there, he enjoyed his last two years and believes the school gave him the strength of character to face his future responsibilities.

In January 1966, at seventeen, Charles went off to Australia, to Timbertop, an annex of the prestigious Melbourne school, the Geelong Church of England Grammar School, for two terms as a prefect. He was accompanied by his father's former equerry, David Checketts, a former RAF officer. Upon returning to Britain, Checketts commented, "I took out to Australia a boy. I came back with a man."

Then it was off to three years at Cambridge, studying as an ordinary student, living in college, and with no special privileges. Against the advice of his tutors, who believed him capable of a first-class honors degree, Charles opted for a broad education, choosing anthropology and archaeology in his first year, then history in his final two. He chose the generalist route, instead of concentrating to earn a better degree, because he believed that as a future King of England, it was his duty to Crown and country.

Charles's attitude toward learning is the exact opposite of Diana's. She didn't want to gain knowledge, to study, or to learn anything. Charles, with his natural appetite, even hunger, for learning, went to Cambridge to educate himself as broadly as possible. His complete inability to understand Diana's attitude became a further stumbling block to a successful marriage.

Charles left Cambridge with a B.A. honors degree in

Class II, division II, called a 2.2 in university parlance—a rather ordinary degree. His tutors believe that if he had not been subjected to royal disruptions (for example, taking a three-month break to learn Welsh at Aberystwyth), he would have earned a better degree.

Happy that he had taken the advice of his great-uncle Dickie Mountbatten to attend Cambridge, he accepted Mountbatten's advice again, going on to the RAF flying school at Cranwell in 1971, to train as a pilot. Charles loved flying for the same reason he loved other individual sports, like riding, shooting, fishing, and stalking—it was Charles pitting himself against some*thing*, not some*one*. (Polo he considered a competition with the horse as much as a match against the other team.)

After flying at more than a thousand miles per hour in a Phantom jet (which made him a member of the Ten Ton Club), Charles was determined to do the whole flight course. And that included a parachute jump. No other member of the Royal Family had ever parachuted, let alone the heir to the throne.

Doing so nearly ended in tragedy. As he jumped from an RAF Andover over Dorset, he fell into the plane's slipstream. As he hurtled toward the ground, his legs became entangled in the parachute rigging above his head. Remaining cool, Charles managed to extricate himself. Experts later remarked that if he had panicked, he probably would have been killed.

Afterward, a half-smiling, trembling Charles said, "They didn't tell me anything about this. I was looking up at my feet and realized it was all wrong. I was in a U shape. So I told myself to free my legs, and quickly. So I did." But the danger had been very real, and he knew it. Charles has never since spoken about the incident.

Six months later, in September 1971, Charles moved on again, this time to the Royal Naval College at Dartmouth, joining as a lowly acting sublieutenant. He was now following in the footsteps of his father, his grandfather King George VI, his great-grandfather King George V, and, of course, Lord Mountbatten.

Within six weeks Charles had completed and passed

out from Dartmouth in a course that normally takes twelve weeks. Days before his twenty-third birthday in November, he joined his first ship, the guided-missile destroyer HMS *Norfolk*. Charles hated his nine-month stint aboard *Norfolk* because he was convinced the ship's officers—all high-flyers and many the sons of aristocracy—had been especially selected by the Admiralty. He found them starchy, formal, and creepy. They acted falsely, behaving as they thought they ought to behave in the presence of the heir to the throne. It made him sick.

As a result, Charles spent far more time than an officer usually would with the petty officers and ratings. Here he met Chief Petty Officer Michael Colborne, who would later work with Charles in an official capacity as comptroller of his office. They discovered an empathy from the start: Charles admired Colborne's warm frankness, his honesty, and Colborne admired Charles's sensitivity and concern for those around him. It became a friendship that would last.

Charles later asked Colborne to act as an "unofficial uncle" to Diana, someone older who could advise and help her over the thousand and one different things that she would have to know about on joining the Royal Family and living the life of a royal. Diana became very fond of Colborne and relied on him to tell her the proper things to do. He suggested what newspapers and news items she should read, what she should say to people and what not to say, how to behave in public, and what to wear and not wear on certain occasions.

While on the *Norfolk*, Charles was given his one and only introduction to the seamy side of life. When *Norfolk* dropped anchor at Toulon, in the south of France, all the officers' wives were flown out at the expense of the Royal Navy to join their husbands at the Officers' Club in Toulon. Charles became deeply angry that only officers' wives were brought to the French port and argued that everyone on board should be allowed the same privilege; and if that was too expensive, then no wives should be allowed to join their husbands.

Charles heard that the petty officers and ratings were

going out on the town one night, so instead of staying with the officers, he joined them. They went drinking in low dives, toured the red-light district, saw the girls sitting half-naked in the brothel windows, watched the prostitutes in the cafés and streets plying their trade. He stayed at one café and watched for thirty minutes as a couple of naked strippers danced on the tables.

Charles exclaimed, "Now I've seen everything. I had read about this sort of thing but never really believed it went on. This is unbelievable. It's like a film set. And the girls, they're showing absolutely everything. I'm amazed." So he put his hand in his pocket and bought all the ratings drinks to celebrate his baptism. He also won their admiration.

After complaining to Lord Mountbatten, who as a former Sea Lord, had enormous influence in the Admiralty, Charles was transferred to a small frigate, HMS *Minerva,* a normal, ordinary ship with officers and crew who had no pretensions. He enjoyed that tour immensely, showing the flag around the world. A year later, he was transferred to another Leander frigate, HMS *Jupiter*.

For four months he went on a helicopter pilot's course aboard the aircraft carrier *Hermes*. In the autumn of 1975, he achieved his ambition—he was given the captaincy of his own ship, HMS *Bronington,* one of the smallest Royal Navy vessels afloat, just 193 feet in length and only 360 tons, with just four officers and thirty-three men. It was an old, wooden-hulled coastal minesweeper named after a tiny Welsh village. But for ten blissful months, Lieutenant Commander HRH The Prince of Wales and his young crew, whose average age was only nineteen, patrolled the harsh, bitterly cold North Sea, searching for old World War II mines and blowing them up.

Charles would have liked to continue his naval career and make a life's work of it, like Mountbatten, but he knew that was not possible. He had a duty to the nation and to his mother to remove some of the burden from her shoulders and carry out his share of royal engagements. He was twenty-eight years old, and it was time to start his real work.

He was happy being a bachelor prince. He enjoyed being a man's man, being in effect "Action Man," a nickname which he hated. But that was Charles's life: playing polo, skiing, hunting, shooting, fishing, sailing, piloting planes and helicopters. He didn't want to settle down and worry about a wife and children.

For the next three years the bachelor Prince thoroughly enjoyed taking on a massive workload of royal engagements. He worked hard and played hard, and the British tabloid press had tremendous sport trying to keep up with his string of lovely girlfriends, some just dates, while others, with whom he was more discreet, became lovers.

It is difficult to overemphasize the role Mountbatten played in Charles's life. To all intents and purposes, he had taken the role of surrogate father as well as adviser on every step in his career. And the Queen seemed to rely more on Mountbatten for advice, particularly in reference to her son Charles, than she did on her own husband, Prince Philip.

At every turn, the young Prince had sought out Mountbatten's counsel. When on leave from the navy, Charles would nearly always visit Uncle Dickie at his home at Broadlands, in Hampshire. They would sit and chat or go for a walk together. Mountbatten loved and cherished the relationship as much as Charles. They saw eye to eye on most matters, and Charles found that Broadlands became a much-needed home to him.

Prince Charles had never really enjoyed a home life, in the ordinary sense of the phrase, so he always yearned for one. He had always been distant from his parents, his mother because he had been brought up to be in awe of her, his father because Prince Philip believed that children should be taught to fend for themselves, in all matters, from a very early age.

All of this, of course, was to have a profound effect on Charles's marriage. No matter how much Diana tried to make a home for her children—and Charles—the more Charles seemed unable to cope with the mundane side of family life. Undeniably, one of the main reasons their marriage failed was their essential incompatibility—they were unable to develop a true friendship between them. But also Charles had never experienced a home life and simply didn't know, didn't realize, that couples have to work hard to make marriages succeed.

Also, almost everything had always been done for him. And the older he became, the more ordinary things were done for him. He never had to cook or even make a cup of coffee, never make a bed or wash clothes, never iron a shirt or clean the car or mow the lawn. And after the initial thrill of becoming a father, Charles turned over the care and upbringing of William and Harry to Diana and nannies. There was nothing Diana could use that would help her build a future for the two of them. Charles had no ambitions for himself because he was waiting in the wings—trying to be patient—to be King.

To Charles, friendships were terribly important. His greatest friend was Mountbatten, but there were many others. There was his first equerry, David Checketts; at Cambridge there was Lord Butler, the former Tory Home Secretary; philosopher Sir Laurens van der Post; palace comptroller Michael Colborne; his Highgrove horticulturist; and others.

And in a remarkable way, Charles often became good friends with many of the women who entered his life, and not just with those girlfriends with whom he went to bed. He wanted the same relationship with Diana that he had found with Camilla Parker Bowles; he hoped that he could mold Diana to be a friend like Camilla. But that was simply not possible. For Diana and Charles had so little in common. Diana was a product of the 1970s, when TV and Walkmans, fast food and loud music had become the norm for British teenagers. And Charles was deeply rooted in the old, traditional ways, and he couldn't change, didn't want to change. Some courtiers have suggested that the real gulf between Charles and Diana was not thirteen years but thirty.

Mountbatten's assassination in August 1979 was a terrible personal tragedy for Charles. Mountbatten was on holiday with his family at his home in Ireland, at Warren Point in County Down. He loved having young people around him. At seventy-nine, despite occasional lapses of memory, Mountbatten remained energetic and spritely, full of schemes and ideas for the future. That day, the Earl planned to sail gently in *Shadow V*, the family's small, thirty-foot boat, and check their lobster pots. He was accompanied by his daughter Patricia and her film producer husband John (Lord and Lady Brabourne) and their twin fourteen-year-old sons, Nicholas and Timothy, as well as John's mother, the Dowager Lady Brabourne. A young local boy, Paul Maxwell, went along to help.

As the tiny vessel cleared the harbor of Mullaghmore and slowed to approach the first of the lobster pots, it exploded beneath Mountbatten's feet from a bomb the Irish Republican Army had planted. The boat disintegrated. Paul Maxwell and Nicholas were killed outright. The Dowager Lady Brabourne, aged eighty-two, was fatally injured. The only survivors were John and Patricia Brabourne, who suffered fractured legs, and Timothy, who was severely injured.

Lord Mountbatten was found floating face down amid the bobbing anoraks, fishing lines, and plimsolls, his limbs remarkably unscathed. He had been killed instantly by the blast. Before the day was out, the Provisional IRA was boasting of its responsibility for the "execution" of the old statesman and warrior.

Prince Charles was in Iceland at the time, enjoying a quiet fishing holiday with his friends Lord and Lady Tryon. Charles, numbed with shock and grief, went for a solitary walk. Dale Tryon found him sitting by the side of a beautiful fjord, sobbing uncontrollably. He had never before felt such a sense of loss.

Back in Britain, Charles was distraught. During those first few days, he would break down and cry, unable to contain his grief. His mood swung between rage and despair. In one uncharacteristic outburst, Charles said, "I'm going to raise an army to go and get those murdering bastards." But that was a moment's aberration.

He saw Prime Minister Margaret Thatcher; he wrote letters to all members of Mountbatten's family; he checked to make sure that everything was being done for those who survived the bombing.

In a letter to John Barratt, for many years Mountbatten's private secretary, Charles poured out his feelings for his uncle: "I was thinking to myself how incredibly fortunate I am to have been so close to Uncle Dickie in the past ten years or so. I have learnt so much from him."

At his funeral service, Charles delivered a moving and unusual eulogy. "Without the heroic efforts of people like Lord Mountbatten, this country, and many others like it, might even now be under the sway of some foreign power, devoid of the kind of the liberty we take so easily for granted in this day and age. Perhaps the manner of his passing will awaken us—or is it too much to hope for?—to the vulnerability of civilized democracies from the kind of subhuman extremism that blows people up when it feels like it."

Besides being a personal loss, Mountbatten's assassination also made Charles realize how vulnerable the English monarchy was. His life could be snuffed out as easily and he'd leave behind no heir. Now he realized he had a duty to find a suitable wife and produce children for the Crown.

Charles felt dispirited, desolate, and alone. There was only one person he could turn to, only one who he knew would understand and give him the comfort and emotional security he craved for: his old flame, his close friend, Camilla Parker Bowles. During those next six months, Charles sorted out his life and decided his future, with Camilla's help.

5

———————— ✦>>>>⚜<<<<✦ ————————

The Women Who Would Never Be Queen

From the time the Prince of Wales first went up to Cambridge University as a freshman, in October 1967, until the official announcement of his engagement to Lady Diana Spencer, in February 1981, Charles's name had been linked with any number of prospective brides.

Some of the young women were suitable for the Crown, but many were not. His dinners and outings to the theatre with attractive, nubile women were a source of considerable interest, not only to the media but also to the public at large. Britons love gossip, particularly about the royals; they cannot read enough about the glamour and excitement of royal goings-on.

The public had been starved of any royal romances to spice and titillate their imaginations since the ill-fated affair between Charles's aunt, Princess Margaret, and the dashing Royal Air Force officer, Group Captain Peter Townsend, in the 1950s. That love match had ended in heartbreak for both parties when Margaret was persuaded that it was inconceivable, in those prim postwar days, that a member of the Royal Family should marry a divorced man. The Prince of Wales's coming of age would, the public hoped, provide some sorely-missed excitement and romance on the royal scene. And they were not to be disappointed.

Lucia Santa Cruz, the daughter of the former Chilean ambassador to London, was the Prince's first girlfriend, a beautiful, statuesque blonde who, at the time, worked as a research assistant to Lord Butler while Charles was at Cambridge. Lucia was four years older than the Prince, but this didn't inhibit their outings to the theatre or to dinner in Cambridge.

But despite the publicity, which made him seem like a busy suitor, Charles was wary of becoming involved in a "meaningful" relationship throughout his three years at Cambridge. In truth, he was still a serious, rather diffident young man who was embarrassed in the presence of girls. He had been brought up to regard members of the opposite sex with deep respect; his own mother was the most important person in his household, and although his father was a strong character, he generally deferred to his wife and always discussed matters with her respectfully. Charles's father, Prince Philip, never forgot that he had been a penniless young naval officer who had married the heir to the crown.

Charles, too, showed great respect for his mother. Perhaps this special relationship between a dutiful son and an all-powerful mother had made him shy, hesitant, and awkward with girls. He had also been educated at exclusively male schools, and although he had learned to take the rough-and-tumble of everyday life with members of his own sex at Gordonstoun, he had never been taught how to respond to girls. In fact, he had scarcely ever mixed with them at all. They were an enigma to him, and it was a long time before he could relax in female company.

During his years at Cambridge, Charles's relationship with Lucia was plainly that of a young man who admired a striking, good-looking older woman with a mind of her own. She gave him self-confidence as he slowly learned from her the skills and intricacies of courtship. But she was an odd choice for Charles. Not only was she foreign, dazzling, exotic, and Roman Catholic, she also had political views far to the right of Charles's own burgeoning liberal ideas. Once the Prince became more self-assured, due to her tutelage, his attachment lessened, and he eventually began meeting other women to whom he was more attracted.

Uncle Dickie had offered Charles the following advice while at Cambridge: "I believe in a case like yours, a man should sow his wild oats and have as many affairs as he can before settling down." But Charles was never a natural womanizer. Indeed, many of the girls he openly dated, and whom the press made a fuss over, were never more than friends.

In 1972 Charles met Lady Jane Wellesley, daughter of the Duke of Wellington, and the first intense relationship of his life. Their romance continued intermittently for two years, and many socially upper-class Englishwomen who like to believe they "know" what is acceptable in royal circles believe that Lady Jane would have made the ideal future Queen. She had the right upbringing, the right background, and, with a landed Duke for a father, she also had the perfect pedigree.

Jane Wellesley was vivacious, pretty, and intelligent and possessed a great sense of humor. For a while it appeared that Charles was very attached to her, perhaps truly in love. They saw each other regularly when he wasn't at sea or on a flying course. He would often call around to see her at her modest, three-bedroom, terraced house in Fulham, her sit-up-and-beg bicycle parked outside, signaling that she was at home. They would sit around the kitchen table and chat, eating toast and drinking mugs of tea, or watch her old-fashioned black-and-white television together. The contrast of her understated life with the grandeur and formality of the palace was striking, and Charles adored it.

It was 1973, Charles was twenty-five, and there was mounting pressure on the couple to marry. But although he was fond of Lady Jane, Charles simply did not feel the time had come for him to settle down. Finally, the friendship grew stale.

For the unstuffy Duke's daughter, the pompous obligation to address her friend as sir had done nothing to perpetuate the romance. Many young women Charles dated simply couldn't stand the custom. Jane thought the straitlaced protocol was absurd. She later complained to a girlfriend, "I feel an absolute fool after we have been amorous and close and affectionate, that he should happily call me Jane in those lovely tender moments, and I had to call him darling or whatever, but never Charles. And when he left, whenever that was, I would always have to say sir. It really annoyed me."

One girl who couldn't and wouldn't bear such nonsense was Laura Jo Watkins. Her father, Admiral James D. Watkins, was a military engineer who helped design President Reagan's Star Wars missile defense system and would go on to become President Bush's first Energy Secretary.

The admiral's daughter met the sailor Prince when his ship berthed in San Diego, California. She was the quintessential all-American girl: a beautiful, blue-eyed, long-legged blonde whose frankness enchanted Charles. Her looks were more than matched by her attractive personality. The couple swiftly discovered that they got on rather well. Indeed, Charles became more attached to her than has been realized. She was the perfect-looking woman for him, and he loved her infectious, spontaneous sense of fun, as well as her overt sexuality—a blessing for the shy Prince.

Laura Jo knew she could never become Queen of England, but she was determined to enjoy her fling with the future King. Sometimes, when she was bored with addressing him as sir, she would call him Prince, deliberately elongating the word to sound very American, making it plain that she was teasing him.

A year later, Laura Jo turned up in London as the guest of the American ambassador, Walter Annenberg. While she remained in the capital, she spent a great deal of time with Charles. She would be delivered by chauffeur-driven car to the side door of Buckingham Palace, then be shown to the Prince's quarters, where a cold supper would have been prepared with a bottle of wine and a decanter of port. Astonishingly, almost no one knew of the relationship.

But after she returned to America, the Prince and Laura Jo met only once more, when they spent a couple of days together the following year in the States. Later, Laura Jo, who has never lost contact with the Prince, described Charles as "a great guy." He liked that.

Charles is attracted to tall striking blondes. He enjoyed the effect on those around him when he appeared with yet another glamorous, but never tarty, long-legged blonde. There was a naïveté about this need to be seen by the press and public with beautiful young women, most of whom knew Charles would never marry them.

The world's most eligible bachelor seemed finally to have lost his innocence and unworldliness. He would date girls openly, taking them to restaurants, the theatre, opera, or ballet, and often he would invite them to watch him indulge his greatest passion, polo. In fact, he would frequently parade his latest girlfriend to the media and the public at a polo match.

Suddenly, the interest in the woman would become avid, almost prurient. It didn't matter whether she was a friend, an acquaintance, or even a virtual stranger staying at Windsor as a guest of the Royal Family. The heir to the throne was growing older and more marriageable. The world's appetite for accounts of his love life seemed insatiable. Whenever the press saw him with an attractive female, they put two and two together and invariably got five.

In 1972, Charles met a woman who was to become not only very special to him, but perhaps the most important woman in his mature life. Her name was Camilla Shand. They were about the same age, he being twenty-three and she twenty-two. Their involvement was like no other he had yet experienced. At first he wasn't physically attracted to her. After all, she didn't conform to his rather stereotyped image of the perfect woman. Camilla was no long-legged blonde. She was dark, animated, and very bright.

She had a quick mind and, more important, she understood Charles. She knew what made him smile or laugh, and she encouraged him to open his mind to her and talk without constraint.

Whenever they met, they simply spent the evening together locked in lively discussion, chatting as if they had known each other for years. He was not obliged to be rigid or formal, for she was not a girlfriend. Rather, she was a real *friend*, a companion with whom he could relax and be himself. And for Charles, that was rare indeed.

Camilla Shand is the daughter of Major Bruce Middleton Hope Shand MC* and Mrs. Rosalind Maud Shand, as well as the niece of British building chief Lord Ashcombe, whose ancestors were responsible for building half of Belgravia, the most fashionable part of London's West End. She is also the niece of Sir Geoffrey Howe, Britain's former Foreign Secretary and, earlier, Chancellor of the Exchequer in Mrs. Thatcher's government. But her most interesting family connection came from her mother's side: Camilla is the great-granddaughter of the celebrated Edwardian, Mrs. George Keppel, the mistress of Edward VII.

Camilla's grandmother, Sonia Rosemary Cubitt, recalled playing with Edward VII, then an old man. She used to call him Kingy, and remembered sliding pieces of buttered bread up and down his trouser leg, a game he actually encouraged.

Camilla had been a debutante at eighteen and moved in smart society circles. She was in her early twenties when she first met Charles, and she was dating an officer in the Household Cavalry, Captain Andrew Parker Bowles, a polo-playing friend of Charles ten years her senior.

The more Charles saw of Camilla, the more intrigued he became. He realized that she was indeed a real woman, the likes of which he had never known before. He enjoyed being with her, doing the normal things young people do—talking and joking, having fun—still a

---

* Military Cross, a highly prestigious award for bravery given to officers in the British forces.

novelty for the Prince. Best of all, there was all-important chemistry between them.

He invited her to Buckingham Palace for dinner, as he had other girls, but this was different. Dinner that night was an utterly relaxing and totally enjoyable experience. There was never an awkward silence, never an embarrassing moment that they couldn't both instantly laugh off. The Prince was smitten. It is not known whether Camilla and Charles became lovers in those early months, but whenever they were seen together, an exhilarating, animated intensity existed between them. They were acting, in short, like a couple in love.

Camilla adored being the subject of a great deal of attention from the heir to the throne. They had fun together, and she knew they had become sexually attracted to each other, but she had no idea whether Charles would translate his affection into marriage. He had already explained that he would have to remain at sea for some years and that he didn't intend to marry straight away. First he had to settle down into civilian life and take more of the burden of royalty off his mother's shoulders. He told Camilla all this, but he failed to mention that he was in love with her and wanted her to be his wife—and the next Queen of England.

Charles still hadn't learned the communications skills needed in love and courtship. He hadn't yet grasped that being in love required more than just a demonstration of feeling when he was with the woman he desired. Relationships needed nurturing, and thoughts and intentions had to be spelled out. Unaware that he had to express his love, Charles stayed away at sea, occasionally writing open, friendly, and amusing letters to Camilla that were largely devoid of passion or feeling.

Camilla was still being wooed by her cavalry officer, who had just been promoted to Major. She enjoyed life in London with Andrew Parker Bowles's fellow officers and their wives and girlfriends. She knew she could look forward to a full, happy life as the wife of an officer in the elite Brigade of Guards. Her family was affluent, so she would never want for money.

In February 1973, Charles and Camilla exchanged a tearful farewell in his rooms at Buckingham Palace. The Prince was about to go to sea for six months on HMS *Minerva*. Though he wanted to tell Camilla to wait for him, he couldn't ask her. He simply didn't know what to do: suggest that she wait in the hope that one day they might wed, or let life take its course.

Charles sailed from Portsmouth feeling a deep sense of loss. One month later, the engagement of Camilla Shand with Major Andrew Parker Bowles of the Blues and Royals* was announced in *The Times*.

On HMS *Minerva*, Charles continued to write to Camilla, but she had other things on her mind, namely, her imminent marriage. The glittering society wedding took place on July 4, 1973, in the Guards Chapel, just two hundred yards from Buckingham Palace where, five months earlier, she had kissed a sad farewell to Charles in his suite of rooms.

The wedding of Camilla to his good friend Andrew cast a shadow over Charles's life. In the months immediately before and after Camilla's wedding, Charles confided in his brother officers on *Minerva* that he was "very fond" of a young woman, but he never revealed her name. Certainly he wouldn't have confessed that she was not only married, but the wife of a fellow officer and friend. But he still carried a torch.

Prince Charles tried to forget Camilla. He was determined to forgo seeing her. His upbringing and sense of fair play forced him to reject her because she was the wife of another man. But the bond between them was too strong.

They kept meeting by chance at social functions in London or weekend house parties in the country. Inevitably, they would spend much of the time in conversation with each other, seemingly oblivious to all around them. It was clear to everyone that they enjoyed laughing to-

---

* The Blues and Royals are part of the Household Cavalry, which is the sovereign's elite escort, and which is itself part of the Brigade of Guards, the senior regiment in the British Army.

gether and being in each other's company. Their friendship deepened.

In 1975, Camilla and her husband had their first child, a son named Thomas. Charles was thrilled to be asked to stand godfather and attended the christening. To this day he sends the boy an annual birthday present inscribed "With love from your godfather, Charles."

Shortly after their wedding, Andrew and Camilla moved into Bolehyde Manor, a beautiful seventeenth-century manor house in Wiltshire bought for them by their families. The house, reputed to be haunted, has a hundred acres of pastureland and another fifty acres of woodland. The Prince would visit from time to time; it was here that Charles and Camilla would wander for hours with the dogs in the solitude of the woods. On these occasions, Charles would dismiss his ever-present bodyguard and suggest he return at the end of the day so the couple could be alone together. The depths of their regard for each other, which continued until a few weeks before he began seeing Diana, was the best-kept secret of Charles's entire life.

Very few people knew of the relationship between Charles and Camilla. The press certainly did not know until many years later. Naturally, Charles told Uncle Dickie, who advised him to keep it low-key, imploring him not to bring it out into the open. But Mountbatten did not urge him to give up Camilla, but only cautioned him to be discreet.

Both Charles and Mountbatten had long been fascinated by the trauma of nearly forty years before, when the Prince's great-uncle, Edward VIII, had given up the British throne for the love of an American divorcée, Wallis Simpson. Mountbatten undoubtedly saw parallels between Charles and the love-struck Edward.

If, during those years, Charles ever considered asking Camilla to divorce her husband and marry him after a respectable lapse of time, one thing would have stopped him—the one trait he possesses in abundance that the Duke of Windsor did not: a sense of duty. He wanted Camilla, and he realized that he was going to find it very difficult, if not impossible, to meet another woman like her. But there was no question of his giving up the throne for her. Reared with a remarkable sense of duty and loyalty to his mother, to the Crown, and to the traditions of monarchy, even contemplating such a possibility would have been insupportable.

To be sure, many similarities appeared between the lives of the young Edward and Prince Charles. They both loved freedom and adventure, both shared a passion for polo and riding, and both cared deeply about the lives of their subjects. In fact, the reason Edward VIII was so popular when he came to the throne upon the death of his father, George V, was the reputation he enjoyed as a ruler who cared about the millions of wretched, jobless people at the bottom of the heap. This was the hungry thirties. The new King, everyone hoped, would be their savior. A new, better era would begin.

But, unlike Edward, who enjoyed a riotous social life before he met Wallis, Charles has never been a social butterfly. While Edward's concern for the underprivileged could sometimes appear superficial, Charles's is absolutely sincere. Edward paid lip service to helping the poor, but Charles, with his Prince's Trust, has been responsible for many community projects in deprived areas. He is a much more serious, thoughtful man than his rather weak forebear.

Edward was known to attend four parties a night and was a devotee of the fashionable nightclubs. Prince Charles, on the other hand, has hardly ever been seen inside a nightclub. He says he could not bear the thought of being seen dancing in some rowdy night spot, no matter how fashionable. He is a much more private person who has no need for ostentatious demonstrations.

Edward maintained that marriage to Wallis was an "indispensable condition for his continued existence." Charles could never be that thick.

From 1972, when they first met, until the spring of 1980, Charles and Camilla saw a great deal of each other, sometimes at country house parties or at dinner in Charles's apartment at Buckingham Palace. Camilla would arrive and leave by the back door so as to arouse as little suspicion as possible. They also met privately, and quite secretly. Charles's relationship with Camilla continued intermittently. Many times he tried to cool their involvement by dating other women, but it was hard to find anyone else with whom he could share such empathy.

The only other woman with whom Charles enjoyed a comparable friendship was Australian-born Dale Tryon, who began her working life as a reporter on a Melbourne newspaper. She met the Prince when she married his friend, City banker Lord Anthony Tryon, the son of the Queen's former treasurer. Like Camilla, she is a mature, worldly woman who can offer both advice and much-needed emotional support.

The Prince was soon captivated by her lively, bubbling personality. She, too, seemed captivated by him when she tagged along on fishing trips to the Tryons' fishing lodge in Iceland, even if she was the only woman present.

In 1977, Charles, then in his late twenties, visited Australia. Dale flew out alone to her native land, attached herself to the royal party, and assumed the role of unofficial hostess—somewhat to the surprise and dismay of Charles's official aides, who reported that she tended to overdress on occasion. Dale even invited Charles to a party at her parents' house, which, by all accounts, the Prince enjoyed enormously. The momentary absence and then reappearance of a slightly disheveled Prince, with lipstick traces on his face, caused his staff moments of severe anxiety.

Charles obviously enjoyed being with Dale. She paid him the compliment of inviting him to be godfather to her son, also named Charles, born in 1976, an honor the Prince takes very seriously. Indeed, shortly after moving to Highgrove, he gave a party especially for young Charles and his twenty other godchildren.

Dale Tryon and Charles remained close friends until Charles's marriage. Soon after the wedding, Diana made it clear that Kanga was not welcome at Highgrove, a situation that remained unchanged until 1985, when, surprisingly, she extended an olive branch. Dale had founded a smart Knightsbridge dress business in 1981, and relations with Diana improved to such an extent that the Princess began wearing Dale's clothes at important public occasions such as the Live Aid charity concert at Wembley.

As a result of the women's reconciliation, Charles's friendship with Dale Tryon rekindled. When his marriage to Diana was rumored to be in difficulty, Dale accompanied him on a fishing trip to Scotland, which caused much speculation. As it always had been in the past, her public role was adviser, confidante, and good friend. And Dale has never concealed the fact that she finds Charles "handsome, attractive, and sexy."

If Camilla and Dale were Charles's closest female friends, there was no shortage of other young women over the years whose names were linked with his romantically. The array of aristocratic and eligible women he was seen with is impressive. There was Lady Victoria Percy, daughter of the Duke of Northumberland, and her sister, Lady Caroline Percy; Lady Leonora Grosvenor, daughter of the vastly wealthy fifth Duke of Westminster, and her sister, Lady Jane Grosvenor; Lady Camilla Fane, daughter of the Queen's closest friend, the Earl of Westmoreland; Bettina Lindsay, daughter of Conservative politician Lord Balniel; Lady Henrietta Fitzroy, daughter of the Duke of Grafton; Georgina Russell, daughter of the diplomat Sir John Russell; Lady Charlotte Manners, daughter of the Duke of Rutland; and many more whom Charles took out to dinner, to parties, to weekend country parties. But only those who truly interested Charles were invited for the famous weekends in blustery, rain-swept Scotland to check out whether they had the stomach for the sort of life he loved.

Charles also pursued intense relationships with girls who were deemed unsuitable candidates for marriage to a future King. For example, he was more than fond of Davina

Sheffield, the beautiful, blond daughter of an army officer, whose easygoing, open nature and sense of adventure struck a chord with the Prince. They met often during 1974 and 1975, when he was on leave from the navy. She was a guest at Windsor Castle and Balmoral, an honor bestowed only on the most favored.

Davina went to Vietnam in 1975, toward the end of the war, to work in a Saigon orphanage for a few weeks, but returned home to devastating personal tragedy: her mother had been murdered by robbers who broke into her mother's Oxfordshire home. Davina turned to Charles for emotional support, and they started dating again in 1976. Their happiness was short-lived. Britain's tabloid press, sniffing a serious romance, began to investigate her background. They didn't take long to learn she had lived with a young man in his rose-covered country cottage for six months and, to their delight, he talked openly about their life together. Then, even more joyfully, they discovered that after bathing in Devon one summer's day, she had been discovered naked in the men's changing room. For any serious girlfriend of the Prince to have a "past" was inconceivable. The sensationalist newspaper stories destroyed the relationship.

Another girl whose past returned to haunt her was Fiona Watson, daughter of Yorkshire landowner Lord Manton. The Prince dated her until it emerged that she had committed the apparently unpardonable sin of displaying her impressive 38-23-35 statistics in full color as a *Penthouse* centerfold!

Mystery surrounds one girl with whom Charles apparently became deeply entangled in a turbulent affair when he was twenty-nine. She was Anna Wallace, daughter of a wealthy landowner with homes and estates in England and Scotland. Charles's friends believe he actually fell in love with her; some even believe he asked her to marry him, although this has never been verified and, in retrospect, appears unlikely.

Anna Wallace was twenty-three when she met the Prince out hunting. She loved the sport so that she was nicknamed Whiplash, because of her treatment of her horses in her desire to gallop faster than the rest of the field. She was also called Thunderthighs, the origin of which is less clear. Anna disliked both names.

She typified the sort of young woman to whom Charles was attracted, the sort of tall, good-looking blonde who couldn't fail to turn heads. She was a strong, independent young woman who detested the cloak-and-dagger life she had to lead when dating Charles. The ritual of addressing him as sir was anathema to her. A popular girl who had enjoyed romances with a string of successful men—including a banker, a stockbroker, and a property developer—she had always behaved with complete propriety. Nevertheless, those in the know calculate that Charles was unlikely to consider her as a future Princess of Wales and eventual Queen.

The Prince was clearly captivated by her. A mutual friend says of their romance: "Charles was passionate about Anna, and jealous, too. He clearly wanted her sexually, and often, it seemed, he felt more for her than she did for him. That might explain why he found her so exciting and such a challenge." To some of Charles's friends, however, she was a snob and behaved like one.

Their affair ended dramatically at a dinner dance at Windsor Castle in honor of the Queen Mother's birthday in 1978. At the end of the party, Anna had a very public row with Charles. Furious because she felt the Prince had been ignoring her, she lashed out, "Don't ever dare do that to me again!" Her voice growing ever louder, she carried on: "I have never been treated this way; I am not used to being ignored; and nobody, not even you, behaves that way to me."

In full view of the embarrassed onlookers, the Prince tried to calm her down. He had to dance with many people, he explained. Anna was not mollified. She strode off into the night, doubtless leaving Charles to reflect that she would have made a singularly inadequate Princess of Wales. To no one's surprise, except perhaps Charles's, a few months later Anna's engagement to wealthy farmer Johnny Hesketh was announced.

Perhaps the women who behaved most naturally with

him were those who knew they had no chance of becoming Queen, that is, those whom the press quaintly calls "commoners," girls from ordinary, nonaristocratic families. These girls had nothing to gain by being sycophantic. He had a wonderfully happy, and completely secret, affair with one such girl—a blond Welsh girl we'll call Jennifer Smith (not her real name) whom Charles met while on a naval exercise flying helicopters in Canada in 1975. She worked at a switchboard in a large office, and was almost certainly one of Charles's secret lovers. Although some members of his staff frowned on the relationship, Charles loved the secrecy and excitement of the illicit affair with a nonaristocrat, a truly foreign experience for him.

Jennifer would arrive at night at Charles's hotel in Canada. To allay suspicions, in company with one of Charles's closest officials, she would be ushered in through the lobby holding a bundle of important papers as though she were part of his secretarial staff. She would be taken to Charles's suite to dine with him. In the morning, one of his equerries would be dispatched to Jennifer's room to rumple the bedclothes and bath towels to make it appear she had spent the night in the room booked for her. Whenever she returned to Britain, she would phone Charles and they would meet for an occasional evening together.

A polo friend of Prince Charles pointed out that Charles's attitude toward women was remarkable. He said, "In Charles's unique position he could have any woman. For ten years he was undoubtedly the greatest catch in the world, even if it was only for one night or a wild fling. There must have been lots of women who would have wanted an affair with Charles simply because he was the Prince of Wales, a future King, and quite a good-looking chap as well.

"And yet Charles never used women. I can never recall a woman whom he laid, just for the hell of it or because she had thrown herself at him. He wasn't like that. Sometimes when we were talking at polo, his eye would catch a pretty girl, and he would look and we would smile in a knowing way to each other. But he wouldn't go after the

girl, even when they gave him the eye. He was always a
gentleman, always played it correctly. He never wanted to
take advantage of the fact that he was the Prince of Wales
and use his position.

"And more than that. If you examine the girlfriends he
has had in his life, a remarkable number of them are still
his friends. Now, for any man, it is very unusual to remain
close friends with old lovers. But he did. And he still
values their friendship today."

Charles became seriously attached to two other women
besides Camilla and Dale. One was Diana's eldest sister,
Sarah. Lady Sarah Spencer and Charles went out together
on and off for nearly a year. They were often seen together at polo, the theatre, and at weekend country house
parties.

The other involvement was Amanda Knatchbull, the
granddaughter of Lord Mountbatten, and the second
daughter of Lord and Lady Brabourne.

Mountbatten's greatest wish was to match Charles and
Amanda, and he certainly encouraged the affair. He even
wrote Charles, suggesting how to woo Amanda—wining
and dining her, giving her little presents, making a fuss
over her.

In his memoirs, *With the Greatest Respect,* Mountbatten's secretary and confidant, John Barratt, claims Charles
proposed marriage to Amanda when the two of them were
on holiday together at Eleuthera, in the Bahamas, where
the Brabournes had a holiday house. When Charles returned home, he allegedly confided in Uncle Dickie that
Amanda had laughed and said, "What a funny idea." She
had explained that she had her own life, she was planning
to go to university, she was too young. She was twenty,
nine years younger than Charles. It would be sensible to
give themselves time to see how things worked out. After
this, the relationship seemed to cool.

Amanda and Charles had seen much of each other as
children and got along well. Like the Prince, she had

Diana Frances Spencer at eight weeks old being christened at Sandringham Church, August 1961. She is being held by her mother, Frances Roche, the daughter of the fourth Baron Fermoy and close friend of King George VI, while her father, Viscount Johnny Spencer Althorp, looks on.

Diana, the pretty blond baby who would become the Princess of Wales.

Diana with her brother, Charles, whom she mothered in her own mother's absence.

A family portrait, which includes (in front, left to right) eight-year-old Di, her younger brother Charles, her older sister Sarah, and her other sister Jane. Behind Diana, on her right, is her grandfather, Earl Spencer.

During the winter season, January 1977 to Easter, 1978, seventeen-year-old Diana Spencer (far right) attended the Institut Alpin Videmanette in the Swiss Alps. She lived with the other girls in the "cuckoo clock" style wooden chalets. Her chalet mates were the daughters of wealthy international businessmen, members of parliament, and European gentry.

The Spencer family home at Althorp, where Diana grew up.

A typical room at Althorp House, where Reubens paintings adorn the walls.

Diana's mother, Frances, miserable in her marriage to Diana's father, fell in love with a married man, Peter Shand Kydd, a wallpaper millionaire and the father of three children. In the resulting scandal, both divorced their respective mates and married. Frances is seen here at the time of her divorce. The divorce devastated her children. Frances's own mother, Lady Fermoy, described her daughter's actions as "monstrous" and "unthinkable."

Diana, who had no academic qualifications, went to London, where she became the perfect au pair for class-conscious mothers. Many well-to-do mothers would employ young women to help bring up their children. Here Lady Diana, who loves children, holds on to two youngsters at nursery school.

Lady Diana, seen before her engagement to Prince Charles, as she steps into her car outside her London flat and heads for work at a London kindergarten school. (Photographers International).

The handsome Prince Charles, nearly thirteen years Diana's senior, prepares to play polo. (Photo taken 1986.)

The happy early days. Charles and Diana leaving St. Paul's Cathedral after a wedding rehearsal in 1981.

been a student at Gordonstoun, and then read anthropology at Kent University. They had a great deal in common.

John Barratt claims the romance between the young couple was serious. He recalls: "One day in Mountbatten's bedroom at Broadlands, I asked him if there was something going on between Amanda and Charles. He went bright red and said, 'Oh God, I knew you'd stumble on to it.' But he stressed that it was a secret within the family, and that he did not want anyone to know about it. Yes, he said, the Prince of Wales was quite taken with Amanda, but things would have to proceed slowly and carefully if they were to result in a marriage."

But it was not to be. Charles also felt Amanda was unsophisticated and even suggested that she didn't dress well. Mountbatten responded by arranging a five-thousand-dollar dress fund for Amanda and invited Sacha, Duchess of Abercorn, who was renowned for her taste, to take Amanda in hand and dress her so that Charles would find her attractive. Amanda was a striking, but not beautiful, young woman, and just before Mountbatten's murder, she had matured into a quite stunning-looking girl. She went with Charles for a weekend to Balmoral in the summer of 1979, but within weeks Mountbatten was dead.

John Barratt commented, "They really did like each other, but I think the magic ingredient of love was missing from their relationship. Perhaps Lord Mountbatten was right, and they would have grown to love each other. I certainly feel that Prince Charles would have more of a soul mate in Amanda than he later did in Diana. Amanda is interested in the arts and environmental issues."

Amanda herself has confessed, "I regarded Charles as I would a brother and was very fond of him." But there was no love match.

Earl Mountbatten had previously tried to marry off Charles to Princess Caroline of Monaco, the daughter of the late Princess Grace and Prince Rainier. In his book, John Barratt wrote: "When Mountbatten and Charles went to Monaco, Princess Grace was so worried about Mountbatten's reputation as a matchmaker that she warned him off trying to pair Charles up with Princess

Caroline, who was, she told him, 'a good Catholic girl.' I sat opposite Charles and Caroline at dinner, and knew instantly that Princess Grace had nothing to worry about: they both looked bored to tears all evening, and Prince Charles commented to us afterward that Caroline 'had more makeup on than heaven knows what.' "

Until his assassination in 1979, Mountbatten's country home, Broadlands, was an open house for Charles. There he could escape for a quiet, romantic weekend safe from the prying eyes of the press corps or from the knowledge of everyone at Buckingham Palace.

John Barratt revealed that Charles spent weekends at Broadlands with Georgina Russell, Jane Wellesley, Lucia Santa Cruz, and Camilla Shand; that Mountbatten once gave Charles a mild lecture on the need—for the sake of the Royal Family as well as for the reputations of the girls he dated—for discretion.

It was ironic that for a full twelve months or more, Charles should have been involved with Lady Sarah Spencer. Red-haired Sarah, then twenty-five, was the dynamic rebel of the three Spencer girls. It was Sarah who was expelled from school for drinking alcohol, with the result that she never again touched another drop. And Sarah was always the Spencer girl renowned for enjoying herself—partying, dancing, skiing. Charles had known her slightly, having met her at Sandringham when she was a teenager.

When Charles and Sarah began dating in 1977, the world came to believe that he had finally found his future Queen. Charles would often call round to her house off the King's Road, Chelsea, dropping in for a cup of tea, an evening snack, or a chat. To many, this was the *real* romance that everyone wanted for the world's most eligible bachelor. Tongues wagged when he took Sarah to Klosters, where they shared a chalet with other people, for a ten-day skiing holiday in February 1978. Charles was certainly smitten by Sarah, believing himself in love with her for months. They were seen together a great deal during those twelve months.

A strong, some might say headstrong, young woman—which appealed greatly to Charles—Sarah was always in control of the situation. Charles wooed her as though they were already engaged, sending her flowers, arranging intimate, champagne-and-candlelight dinners, and treating her with respect and deference. Sarah liked being Charles's escort, enjoyed his company, and made him laugh.

Charles thought he had found his future Queen in Sarah, but he wasn't entirely sure, particularly when she began to boss him about, taking command of situations. Though in her own way she loved him dearly, Sarah was never *in love* with Charles. She wanted a passionate love affair with the man she married and knew in her heart that, however flattering it would be to marry the Prince of Wales and become a member of the Royal Family, she was not prepared to make that commitment if she didn't love the man. And she didn't.

The relationship came to a rather sudden end after their Klosters holiday. She commented to the press, "If he asked me to marry him, I would turn him down. I'm not in love with him. I wouldn't marry anyone I didn't love, whether he was the dustman or the King of England!" And later she commented, "Charles is a romantic who falls in love easily."

Within a year, Sarah, who was ready for love, met a former Coldstream Guards officer, Neil McCorquodale, the son of a wealthy farming family from Leicestershire. Ironically, Neil is the cousin of Raine, the stepmother whom the Spencer girls could not abide. Sarah and Neil were married in 1980.

Within six months after his breakup with Sarah, Charles had turned his attention, among other girls, to her younger sister, the much quieter, shy, gentle Diana, the baby of the Spencer family. Sarah was thrilled when Diana told her that Charles had asked her out. But Sarah

warned her sister that Charles was really an incurable
romantic and she ought to watch out. Diana evidently did
not listen.

Within months after his breakup with Sarah, Mountbatten
was killed. That tragic death changed Charles's life dramatically. It left a great void in his confidence and also led
to his marrying the girl he did, in accord with his uncle's
advice—Diana Spencer.

Millions of television viewers witnessed Charles fighting back tears as he read the lesson at Mountbatten's funeral service at Westminster Abbey. At the grave in
Hampshire, Charles lay a wreath inscribed "To HGF from
HGS" (honorary grandfather from honorary grandson).
Since his death, no one has been able to fill the role that
he played for Charles.

Desolated, miserable, the grieving Charles inevitably
turned to the only person in his life he felt he could trust,
Camilla, and she became the steadying support he so obviously needed. The love between them during those next
six months was deeper than they had known before. Once
again, Charles realized that here was the woman he
should have married. She had the strength he needed and
the warmth he yearned for. He wanted her desperately.

Andrew Parker Bowles was posted to Rhodesia to accompany Lord Soames, who had been appointed to pre-
side over the elections which were to bring democracy to
Rhodesia, one of the last British colonies in Africa. Society
gossips speculated that he was appointed to Salisbury*
because Charles needed the emotional support of his
wife. Whether or not Andrew recognized the depth of
affection between his wife and Charles is open to debate,
but in fact he was gone from London from October 1979
to May 1980.

During those six months, Charles and Camilla spent a

---

* Salisbury was the capital of Rhodesia. In 1980, when the country
gained independence, the country was renamed Zimbabwe and the capital is now called Harare.

great deal of time together. The Prince had never known such trauma and had difficulty coping. He gained great strength from her as she tried to advise him the way Mountbatten might have.

Finally, Camilla persuaded Charles that he would have to sacrifice his special relationship with her and marry.

Over the years, Uncle Dickie had told the Prince to marry a trainable young innocent who could be molded to suit the job of being the Princess of Wales. Lady Diana Spencer fit the prescription perfectly.

Or so it seemed.

6

---※≫≪≪≪---

The Courtship: The Secret Arrangement

As Charles read in the popular newspapers that it was time for him to settle down, he was being subjected to parental pressure. His father, the Duke of Edinburgh, advised him: "It's about time you got your finger out and got married. You don't want to miss the boat." More significantly, his mother, the Queen, made him understand that he had to come to terms with marriage.

Coincidence, more than anything else, led to Charles's meeting Diana just after he finally renounced for good the fantasy of marrying Camilla and became determined to find a suitable young woman who could be shaped into a good wife and future Queen.

Charles was desperately worried about making a mistake. For the Prince of Wales and future head of the Church of England, marriage had to be forever. Divorce was impossible, no matter how dire the circumstances. It was a lifetime commitment, and he had to get it right the first time.

His worries were compounded by newspaper reports of marriage breakdowns and divorces among his friends. After the Divorce Act of 1969 had relaxed Britain's stringent requirements, the rate of divorce accelerated sharply. In the 1980s, one in three British marriages ended in divorce court. Charles also knew that some of his friends had fallen desperately in love and then parted when their love died. This was not an alternative for him. He was tormented about whether he should look for a love match or try an arranged marriage with a suitable, willing candidate.

In the end, fate intervened. One day Charles became aware that the shy young sister of a former girlfriend had turned into a tall, pretty teenager—and he was attracted to her.

They didn't exactly meet by accident. They had met occasionally at Sandringham, when the two older Spencer girls were more interesting, and Charles had hardly taken the slightest notice of Diana. Charles met Diana again in January 1979, when the Queen invited her and her sister Sarah to a house party. Charles and the other young men would be shooting, but there was always dinner and the evenings. The invitation was not surprising. In 1978, sister Jane had married Robert Fellowes, a member of the Queen's personal permanent staff. Robert, of course, knew that the affair between Charles and Sarah was over, but both Spencer girls were eligible young ladies, and other young men were to be at Sandringham that weekend.

Diana was eighteen-and-a-half, young for her age, innocent and shy. She danced with Charles that Saturday night, and he found her charming, happy, and a sparkle in his doom-laden world. A week later he phoned to invite her to a private dinner at Buckingham Palace. Heart thumping, Diana accepted. But the affair did not start there. Charles was still seeing Camilla, as a friend, and occasionally escorting other girls to the theatre, ballet, opera. But every so often he would phone Diana to go out. And when he was with her, he began to relax.

Apart from Diana's unspoiled good looks, her easygoing temperament and her natural, friendly demeanor appealed greatly to Charles. She was completely without artifice: she laughed when she was amused, she put on no false air of sophistication, and she was open and honest. He believed that he had perhaps found a girl of whom Mountbatten might have approved. All he had to do was win her heart and then coach her in the role she would have to play for the rest of her life—a member of the Royal Family, his wife, and, one day, the Queen of England. Back then, Charles probably didn't realize how formidable was the task.

But first he had to be sure Diana would make the grade and pass the trials necessary to enter the royal circle. All of Charles's serious girlfriends who visited Balmoral were subjected to the "Craigowan Test," which involved sitting around quietly all day reading in the house or, worse, actually accompanying the royal party on the inhospitable Scottish moors, where they were expected to stalk or walk or help with the guns.

Sometimes they would have to sit for hours, frequently bored witless, on the banks of the river while the wader-clad Charles fished, often completely oblivious to whoever sat on the bank behind him. Charles has always loved the peace and solitude of Balmoral and enjoyed fishing or shooting, often with only his own thoughts for company. Since this was so important a part of his life, he believed girlfriends had not only to accept it but also to enjoy it. At Balmoral, any potential wife could not be a person in her own right, but merely a silent, supportive, decorative appendage. The test was important for any prospective, long-term girlfriend; if she failed that early hurdle, there was really no point to continuing the relationship.

With some trepidation, Charles took Diana to Balmoral in September, just a few weeks after he had first kissed her, aboard the royal yacht *Britannia* at Cowes. Diana was not an outdoor, horsey girl, but he hoped she would enjoy life at Balmoral because she had grown up in the country with a similar social background.

Nineteen-year-old Diana took her needlepoint and two Mills and Boon books—escapist romantic fiction in the style of her step-grandmother, Barbara Cartland—which were popular with many girls of her age. Diana was addicted to them.

Each day Charles and his friends went out shooting, and each day Diana, along with the other married and unmarried young women in the party, dutifully trooped across the moors to join them for a picnic lunch. At dinner she wasn't seated next to Charles, and every evening the Prince danced with every woman in the room as well as with her, as a gentleman should. It wasn't the sort of romantic idyll so lavishly described in Mills and Boon books.

Three weeks later, Diana was once again invited to Scotland, this time to a smaller and more intimate gathering at Birkhall, the Scottish home of the Queen Mother. The canny staff, with their servants' intuition for seizing on the smallest clues, quickly began to speculate that perhaps, at last, Lady Diana was "the one"—the girlfriend destined to become Princess of Wales.

Shortly after their weekend at Birkhall, Charles took Diana to see Highgrove, the country home in Gloucestershire that Charles had purchased earlier that year for £800,000. At the time, it was only half furnished, still undergoing renovations. The house had only three bedrooms completed, but Charles didn't seem to mind the mess. Indeed, for a fastidiously organized soul, he appeared to enjoy the informality of the place after his years in the stiff, orderly atmosphere of Buckingham Palace. And although he appeared to have very little idea of how to decorate and furnish the place, he enjoyed the thought of finally having a home to call his own.

During the autumn of 1980, Diana often visited Highgrove on weekends, but she never stayed the night. Charles would return to Highgrove from an official duty or function at around four P.M., and they would take tea together. Later they would walk around the grounds before a simple supper, like an omelette and salad. Then, at about nine-thirty, he would drive her back to London.

Charles also took Diana to meet Camilla Parker Bowles, to get Camilla's opinion of the girl he was seriously considering marrying. He trusted that Camilla would instinctively know not only whether Diana would make him a good wife, but also if she would make a good Queen.

Camilla encouraged Charles's courtship of Diana. (What he would have done if Camilla or anyone else had disapproved of Diana is anybody's guess.) In fact, it was in the inauspicious surroundings of the Parker Bowles cabbage patch that Charles first discussed with Diana the possibility of marriage.

During those autumn months, Charles saw more and more of Diana, and the newspapers began to believe that she was indeed to be his bride. Time and time again, of course, the press had incorrectly speculated that the Prince was about to announce his engagement to any number of girls. But this time, Diana seemed to be the chosen one. Thus began an elaborate game of cat and mouse, as Charles tried to outwit the rat pack, the nickname given to the reporters and photographers who made their living trailing the Royal Family. By now, they had begun to follow Diana's every move.

Stephen Barry, Charles's valet for twelve years, was closely involved in the intricate arrangements the Prince made to ensure that their meetings remained, as far as possible, secret from the press. In his book, *Royal Service*, Barry describes how he used to wait at Buckingham Palace for Diana's phone calls. When he picked up the phone, she would say simply, "It's Diana," give the address where she could be found, and he would drive over to collect her.

Diana would usually take a taxi from her apartment in Coleherne Court, in the Earl's Court or Fulham area of West London, to her mother's, sister's, or a friend's apartment. Once reporters were satisfied they had seen her enter her ostensible destination, Barry would arrive to drive her to Buckingham Palace for the evening and later, discreetly, return her to her own flat. Most times it worked well, so that many of her meetings with Charles went unrecorded.

Considering that she was literally under siege, Diana managed to cultivate a remarkable relationship with members of the royal press corps. She talked to them, took them into her confidence, even joked with them. The cynical rat pack not only began to trust the shy young girl but were actually won over by her natural charm. Soon newspapers began positively to fawn over her. She was packaged and presented in a way that guaranteed her a place in the hearts of the general public. Was she not living proof that fairy tales can come true—an "ordinary" girl who made a Prince fall in love with her and was destined to live happily ever after in the palace?

The magic ingredient which the world wanted to believe and which the media hyped out of all proportion was Diana's common touch. *Common* in this case meaning she had not been brought up as an aristocrat but as a normal member of Britain's upper-middle class. She had shopped in the January sales and traveled by bus and tube. She had queued at the local supermarket, done her own laundry and cleaning, had even worked as a char. The public was led to believe that the Prince's eye could have fallen just as easily on any pretty girl.

Of course, this was nonsense. Diana might have enjoyed an "ordinary," down-to-earth life-style, but her pedigree was faultless. As previously noted, she comes from a long-established aristocratic family and is, in fact, very distantly related to her husband through Henry VII, James I, Charles II, and James II. As far as breeding goes, she could hardly be more suitable. But the fairy-tale-loving public lapped up the media creation.

One media story, however, enraged not only Charles and members of the Royal Family, but also Diana and her family, because it was gratuitously demeaning, with no basis in truth whatsoever. The tabloids were always nosing around for stories on the Prince's girlfriends. In September 1980, six months before their official engagement, and even before the public realized that Diana was the chosen bride, the *Sunday Mirror*—a mass-circulation tabloid newspaper—ran a front-page exclusive claiming that Diana had been driven to the royal train when it was in a siding overnight in Wiltshire and that she had spent the night with Charles.

Until recently, Buckingham Palace often rented trains

for royals who had to attend an early-morning function far
from home. The Prince, usually accompanied by his valet,
his secretary, and his bodyguard, would catch the train in
London the day before and stop in a siding near his destination so everyone could get a good night's sleep before
the official appointment. Local police were alerted so they
could guard the train. Charles could not possibly smuggle
Diana, or any other girl, on board his train without many
people knowing.

To this day, no one who was aboard the train that night
or who guarded the train has ever suggested that Diana
was present for a moment. The story was false; the incident simply never happened. Virtually everyone con-
nected with that story now admits there was no truth in it.

What angered the Palace and the Queen was that the
Sunday Mirror editor, Robert Edwards, a reputable, well-
respected, experienced newspaperman, refused to withdraw the story or acknowledge that the incident hadn't
taken place. He prominently reported the Prince of
Wales's personal, unequivocal denial, but would make no
concessions on behalf of the newspaper. Edwards argued
—rather disingenuously, some thought—that, after all,
the Queen's press office had deceived him years before
when they denied that Princess Anne would become engaged to Mark Phillips shortly before the engagement was
officially announced, a ploy guaranteed to infuriate editors
hungry for exclusives.

What outraged Charles, of course, was the sullying of
Diana's reputation, which, until the *Sunday Mirror* story,
had been so chaste that no newspaper had even managed
to find a serious boyfriend in her past. But now the world
was intended to believe that Diana secretly boarded a
train at two A.M., spent the night with the Prince, and stole
back to London before dawn. There was little doubt what
that story meant, observed one commentator dryly.

At the time, no one realized that Charles was so acutely
enraged because he was probably already planning to
marry Diana. It was fine for *him* to be seen as a philan-
derer, but his potential wife needed an immaculate reputation of unquestioned chastity. Certainly she could not

appear to be a young adventurer willing to risk her name for a night of passion on a royal train in a country siding.

Relations between the press and the Palace were always wary at best. The Palace wanted Prince Charles to be allowed to conduct his romances in private; the press wanted to sell papers. No member of the Royal Family has friends in the media, no matter what reporters or commentators try to suggest. What is extraordinary is how well Diana dealt with the press. She understood that they were simply doing their job, an attitude that tended to disarm them. But she also confided to one of her flatmates, "I am terrified of them. Everywhere I turn they are there, poking their cameras at me, asking me questions, following me whenever I step outside. I don't know how I'm going to cope."

The romance flourished. After reporters discovered that Diana had celebrated Charles's thirty-second birthday with him privately at a small house on the Sandringham estate, the world decided that she was the girl he was going to marry.

Diana was now besieged by unruly mobs of photographers every time she set foot outside. At New Year's, when the Royal Family invited her to Sandringham, the reporters and photographers were so intrusive, she had to spend most of the time indoors.

The public embraced Diana wholeheartedly, even before an official announcement was made. The only misgivings voiced were that Diana was very young—only nineteen, and totally inexperienced in the ways of the world—and her lack of scholastic ability, which worried those who thought Charles needed a wife with more intellectual interests.

Diana must have been relieved when Prince Charles finally proposed to her in late January, during a quiet weekend at Highgrove. She was smuggled down the narrow country lanes and into the Gloucestershire house through one of the farm entrances, outwitting the watching, waiting newspapermen. Stephen Barry brought down a picnic for the couple because Highgrove was still so full of workmen that using the kitchen was impossible.

Over a bottle of champagne, Charles asked Diana to marry him, and then he urged her to "think about it before giving an answer."

He always advised people to mull over important decisions. Marriage to the heir to the throne might sound irresistible, but he wanted her to know it was not an easy position. It could be grueling, living perpetually in the public eye. She would never be able to hide herself in a crowd, nor eat privately in a restaurant, nor go shopping alone. He knew she was already familiar with a few of the problems that lay ahead, but they were nothing compared to what would follow. She would never again be free to do as she liked.

Diana had no doubts. She was ecstatic, despite having to keep the engagement a secret for three weeks until the Queen made the official announcement.

Her sister Sarah did not need to be told of the engagement. "I saw Diana in her flat," Sarah recalls, "and I guessed when I saw her face. She was totally radiant, bouncing and bubbly. I said, 'You're engaged,' and she said yes. I was so happy, so thrilled for her, for it was the first time in her life that Diana had felt really secure."

In truth, the Prince was taken aback by the speed and certainty with which Diana accepted his proposal. One friend said later that if their roles had been reversed, Charles would have taken weeks to make up his mind. He still wanted her to take time to consider the enormous implications of such a decision and suggested she go to Australia for a three-week holiday with her mother.

Once Diana set off, the Prince of Wales's office at Buckingham Palace started planning the yet-unannounced July wedding, drawing up the guest list and working out the monumental catering arrangements. Everything was done under conditions of great secrecy, and, extraordinarily, there were no leaks.

Diana was unwavering. She'd made up her mind and nothing would make her change it.

When she returned from Australia, Charles, always the

romantic, arranged to greet her with a huge surprise bouquet to be delivered to her apartment. What followed was near farce. An aide was hastily commanded to organize the flowers. A discreet florist was commissioned to assemble a magnificent bouquet and deliver it to Diana's address. But the florist could not get into Coleherne Court. There was no sign of a caretaker and no response from Diana's bell. In near panic, he reported back to Buckingham Palace that he couldn't make the delivery.

A royal aide nervously assessed the situation. A jet-lagged Diana was probably deeply asleep after her journey halfway around the world and couldn't hear the doorbell. But the only way to get the florist in was to telephone her.

With some trepidation, the aide dialed and eventually woke Diana. With profuse apologies for disturbing her, he explained the difficulty. At once Diana considerately brushed aside the apologies and arranged for the caretaker to open the main door and receive her Prince's homecoming bouquet, which was spectacular but no longer a surprise.

A special, romantic weekend was planned by the Prince before the engagement was to be made public. When the Princess-to-be had been home from Australia for three days, Charles invited her to Highgrove. He intended a tranquil, relaxed Friday to start what *he* knew would be Diana's last weekend as a private citizen. He especially wanted his fiancée to see him riding his favorite hunter-chaser, an eleven-year-old called Allibar. Before dawn, the couple drove fifty miles into the Berkshire countryside to trainer Nick Gaselee's stables in Lambourn.

The Prince took the £15,000 racehorse for a brisk seven-mile workout before slowing to a comfortable walk. Suddenly, as Charles headed back in the crisp morning air to a rendezvous with Diana on the Berkshire downs, he realized something was wrong. He dismounted and moments later, the handsome gelding rolled over and, its head cradled in Charles's arms, died. Allibar had suffered a heart attack.

In tears herself, Diana sought to comfort her shocked,

inconsolable fiancé. Later, when Charles returned to Highgrove, white-faced and silent, the staff immediately knew there had been a mishap. For a while he remained alone. Then, remembering the demands of duty, he prepared to leave for a commitment in the West Country. "Please, please take care of Lady Di while I am away," he urged his staff. "Look after her until I can get back."

Four days later, on February 24, 1981, came the formal announcement of the couple's engagement, done with some theatricality. The news was first told to the Prince's staff. Then, at the opening of a routine investiture (when honors are awarded by the sovereign) at Buckingham Palace, the Lord Chamberlain, Lord Maclean, stepped forward and declared that Her Majesty had commanded him to read an announcement:

"It is with the greatest pleasure that Her Majesty, the Queen, and the Duke of Edinburgh, announce the betrothal of their beloved son, the Prince of Wales, to Lady Diana, daughter of the Earl Spencer and the Honourable Mrs. Shand Kydd."

As those waiting for their honors beamed in approval, the Prince and his fiancée went into the gardens for the official engagement photographs to be taken and to show off Diana's engagement ring.

Diana was never told of the embarrassment suffered by Charles and the Queen over the ring. Garrard, as the crown jewelers, were automatically invited to present a selection of rings to Diana and Charles. A tray was brought to Buckingham Palace, and the couple decided on a beautiful sapphire surrounded by diamonds. The ring was then submitted for approval to the Queen, who asked who the designer was. Only then did it transpire that the ring was an ordinary Garrard catalogue ring which anyone in the world with £24,000 could order; it had not been especially designed in consultation with Charles and Diana, as the Queen had expected.

Charles's private secretary, Edward Adeane, summoned Garrard's jeweler, Mr. Summers, to the palace and gave full vent to his fury. Obviously, he was transmitting the anger of the Queen, who would have preferred to give

Diana one of her own antique rings, which would have been more appropriate than one from a catalogue. But it was too late to change; Diana needed a ring to show the world at the official engagement announcement. The following day Diana was photographed proudly showing off the sapphire-and-diamond ring as she and Charles posed for pictures on the grounds of Buckingham Palace. Diana didn't know about the fuss and probably wouldn't have cared. It was the ring she had wanted and she was happy.

As soon as the betrothal was announced, Diana immediately moved into Clarence House, protected from the media by the Queen Mother and her staff, which included Ruth, Lady Fermoy, her closest friend and lady-in-waiting, who was also Diana's grandmother. Ostensibly, the Queen Mother and Lady Fermoy were to instruct and advise Diana on protocol, behavior, and dress, as well as to prepare her for the role to which she had committed herself for life. And indeed they did—briefly.

For unknown to all but the family and trusted members of the staff, two days later Diana moved into Buckingham Palace itself.

The Prince of Wales is expected to marry a virgin, which Diana was when they met, and no one moves into Buckingham Palace without the Queen's personal knowledge and consent. What was remarkable was that not only did the Queen give her blessing to this arrangement, but that Diana was not secreted some distance away from Charles's suite of rooms. Instead, she was provided with a bedroom, sitting room, and bathroom on the same floor, in between his and Princess Anne's apartments. Astonishingly, the press failed to discover this arrangement, and for four happy months Charles and his fiancée were left alone, without interference or interruption. When the Prince was in London, they would spend all their time together.

The Prince still had to carry out his official duties, but as Diana had none yet, she was free to come and go as she pleased. When she was alone, she would often go visit her mother, who had rented an apartment nearby, or meet her girlfriends for lunch. Sometimes she would spend the lunch hour talking to the Prince's closest staff in the staff office at Buckingham Palace, quizzing them about Palace life and protocol. For the rest of the day she'd be happily ensconced at the palace, watching television, embroidering, or listening to her favorite music—usually Dire Straits—on her Sony Walkman. In the evenings she was alone with Charles. It was an ideal, if unreal, existence, that bore no resemblance to her life at court in the time to come.

Diana started to become noticeably less shy, and she was learning to cope with the near intolerable media attention that followed wherever she went and the curiosity of a public eager to catch even a momentary glimpse of her. She grew more confident about her behavior, her dress, and even her relationship with Charles. She was developing into a poised, self-assured bride and future Princess.

The only blemish in those months of happiness was being separated from Charles. A year earlier he had scheduled official visits to Australia and the United States. She, of course, could not accompany him, but they talked every night during long telephone conversations.

While he was gone, the bride-to-be spent a good deal of time with the Emanuels, the young husband-and-wife designer team who would soon be the most fashionable dress designers in the country, finalizing the details of the most important dress she would ever wear. She spent time rehearsing her walk up the aisle by marching around the palace ballroom with a makeshift train of two bed sheets tied together, so as not to stumble in front of the world's television cameras.

The couple were inundated with invitations, but royal calendars are planned six months in advance and virtually nothing is ever changed. Their mailbag was now crammed with an astonishing twenty-five thousand letters a week, and a team of people had to be brought in to cope with them. Diana enthusiastically read all the congratulatory telegrams which poured in, every one of which received a reply from the Prince's office; she was fascinated watching the replies being drafted.

During the next six months, living at Buck House, as the palace is often called, Diana underwent a remarkable transformation. Her "Shy Di" image, complete with photographs of her holding little children in a London play school, dissolved as she emerged a slim, attractive, well-poised, smiling personality. She had been groomed and polished from a slightly awkward, natural girl into a perfect Princess.

Much of the metamorphosis was undoubtedly due to Diana's own determination to be worthy of her Prince. But she also owed a lot to her sister Jane, who had worked as an editorial assistant on *Vogue* magazine in London. Jane still knew many people on the staff whom she could trust to be utterly discreet.

During those months in the palace, Diana would regularly visit the *Vogue* offices—often twice a week—for talks and consultations. They covered not only fashion but also makeup, hairdressing, and deportment. *Vogue* fashion editor Grace Coddington, a former model, taught Diana how to walk and sit and face cameras with confidence.

One of Diana's favorite London fashion designers, Bruce Oldfield, later explained how he received the royal seal of approval. "It happened just before the royal wedding, after the engagement had been announced. *Vogue* magazine were asked to pull a lot of designers' clothes together so that the Princess, Lady Diana as she was then, wouldn't have to go running round the shops, fighting off the paparazzi. She went up to the editor's office and chose some things, and one of them happened to be mine."

Each day Diana would eagerly read everything that was written about her in all the newspapers and most of the magazines as well. She was fascinated with her new fame and pleased with what she read. It seemed the press, which generally reflected public feeling, was happy for her. Her confidence blossomed.

After a month at Buckingham Palace, she decided she wanted to meet everyone who worked in the austere edifice that was now her home. Usually, if she wanted anything, such as a meal, a cup of tea, or a dress pressed, she would pick up a telephone. Her every wish would be carried out automatically. But that wasn't the sort of life Diana was used to, so she wanted to see who had been doing her bidding.

She met the telephone operators and the maids, the cooks and the kitchen staff, the porters and the cleaners. No member of the Royal Family had ever taken the trouble to meet and talk to the staff on equal terms before. Naturally, Diana's action won her the eternal devotion of those who worked at Buckingham Palace.

Elsewhere, in another palace two miles away, brisk preparations were in hand to accommodate a new mistress. The year before, Charles, deciding it was time to get out from under his parents' roof, had chosen to live in Kensington Palace—KP in royal shorthand, also nicknamed Coronet Street, a play on the title of the British soap, "Coronation Street," set in the working-class back streets of Manchester.

Charles was offered apartments nine and ten. After touring them, he had some reservations. Historical, red-brick Kensington Palace does not compare with the grandeur of Buckingham Palace. With doubt in his voice, he asked his aides what they thought about his potential new home. "Frankly," said one man known for directness, "I think it's rubbish."

"Why, what's wrong with it?"

"Well, for a start, you like light and air and sunshine. The place will only get the sun very early in the mornings and maybe late evenings, in midsummer. The ceilings are low, which you hate. And, if you open the windows, you are going to get a great deal of noise."

Aside from that, the Prince was reminded, at Kensington Palace he would be surrounded by the rest of his family. In the other KP apartments lived Prince and Princess Michael of Kent and their children, the Queen's divorced sister, Princess Margaret, and other assorted lesser royals and senior servants.

It was less than ideal for the Prince of Wales. Nevertheless, the Queen prevailed in the end. She was determined that Charles, still single but heading for his thirty-second birthday, have his own household. "You are the Duke of Cornwall," she observed pointedly from time to time, implying that if he didn't like Kensington Palace he should find his own place and set himself up independently, using the income of over £1 million a year from that duchy, if necessary.

So far as a London residence was concerned, Kensington Palace seemed to Charles to be the best, indeed, the only option. Reluctantly, he took it on.

One aggravating task lay ahead: furnishing the Prince's new apartment. "It sounds unbelievable," recalls one staff member, "but the Prince had to fight for furniture. There were storerooms after storerooms at Buckingham Palace and at Windsor Castle, bursting with the most magnificent pieces of unused, long-forgotten antique furniture. The family have no idea what treasures lay undisturbed, for decades, even centuries. Yet when it came to acquiring a few pieces for the Prince at Kensington Palace, you'd have thought he wanted to raid the Tower of London and seize the Crown Jewels themselves."

It was extraordinary, for the Queen is indisputably the richest woman in the world. Quite apart from castles and palaces, she owns probably the finest art collection on earth, bursting with Old Masters, as well as an unrivaled hoard of jewels and estates valued at over £1.2 billion. All told, she is reckoned to be worth around £5 billion, or $8.5 billion, although many of the treasures and the lands are passed from sovereign to sovereign. Nor is Prince Charles in any danger of finding himself on the breadline. An authoritative 1989 survey by the *Sunday Times* calculated *his* fortune at around £200 million, placing him a joint twenty-ninth in a table of most monied Britons.

"Despite vast wealth, generosity, especially to each other, is one of the family's least conspicuous traits," the staff member added.

.   .   .

For Prince Charles, the six months before his wedding
were wonderfully happy. Diana was close at hand and a
joy to be with. Everyone who knew Charles well reported
that he had blossomed into a new man, full of good humor
and confidence, brimming with a joie de vivre they hadn't
seen in him for years. He seemed to have suddenly become very young again. His fears of making the wrong
marriage had evaporated; Diana was indisputably the
woman for him. He was so happy when he was with Diana that he knew he had been right to wait all those years
and right in having rejected all his other women.

Whenever they were apart, whether for a day or a
week, they would throw their arms around each other
when they were reunited, a spontaneous act of love and
companionship. Those at the palace who had known
Charles for years said he had never acted so naturally and
unaffectedly before. His happiness was infectious, and his
staff rejoiced for him. Life for the couple seemed blessed.

Stephen Barry described Diana and Charles in those
first few months of bliss: "Diana seemed bowled over by
Charles. She worshipped the ground he walked on. She
was constantly kissing and touching him, telling him how
much she loved him. Whenever he went out on a royal
engagement, or just to look through papers, she said
good-bye to him as though he were going away for a year.
And she could not wait for his return. She would keep
asking me when he was coming back and was nervous
until he returned. Then she would rush up, throw her
arms around him, and hug and kiss him.

"I had never seen anyone be like this with Charles
before. But he seemed to like it. He would respond to her
affection and kiss her, but not as enthusiastically and fervently as she wanted. At times I was rather embarrassed
for the Prince because Diana was over him like a rash."

As the wedding day approached, Diana seemed to be enjoying the attention and the privileged life into which she

had been catapulted. Only months earlier she had been able to walk around London and no one would notice the tall, pretty girl as she went about her life. There was nothing to distinguish her from thousands of others: she wasn't gregarious, didn't drink much, went to a few parties and charity balls, wasn't seen around with the sort of loud-mouthed, hard-drinking upper-class chaps favored by her contemporaries. She favored a quiet life. Now it had all changed dramatically.

The first attack of nerves came at a polo match. She was watching Charles play at the army polo club at Tidworth in Wiltshire and was nervously toying with a small bouquet a little girl had given her. When photographers began closing in, Diana suddenly turned and fled in tears. A white-faced Charles rushed over, put his arms around her, and began guiding her to his car. The crowds were so dense that military police had to clear the way. "The occasion was just too much for her," Charles said, referring to the throngs of people who stood staring at his young fiancée, discussing her as though she weren't there.

Later, Diana told her sister Sarah that she believed her nerves were getting the better of her, not only because of the apprehension she felt about the wedding—after all, *millions* of people would be watching her—but also because she had been desperately trying to lose weight, to take off those pounds which gave her a somewhat chubby, less than fashionable figure. She had shed over fourteen pounds during the previous six months.

Diana's prewedding nerves surfaced at least once again, but that was kept a well-guarded secret. The episode was revealed by one of Diana's relatives about whom the family has always kept a rather discreet silence—Reinhold Bartz.

Bartz was a penniless German who married Diana's first cousin, Alexandra Berry, while he was working in a London pub and she was employed in a factory stuffing feathers into pillows. He had led a bizarre life, drifting around Australia and Europe. Later, after he and Alex had married, she told him she was Princess Diana's cousin; as children the two girls had played together. He was astonished, and skeptical. "At first I didn't believe her, but after I met Lady Fermoy and other members of the Spencer family, I realized it was all true."

Diana, according to Bartz, seriously thought of calling off her wedding shortly before the big day. "It was just a few days before the wedding. Diana was attending a cocktail party at the palace, and my mother-in-law was there as well as other members of the Spencer family. Fortunately, Diana's other sister, Lady Jane Fellowes, who is married to the Queen's deputy private secretary, was also present. Apparently, Diana suddenly fled from the room in tears. She just cracked under the strain."

Jane followed Diana and tried to comfort her inconsolable sister. She took her back to her apartment, where Diana collapsed on the bed in a flood of tears. For twenty-four hours, the wedding hung in the balance. Jane kept everyone away and stayed with Diana, comforting her and nursing her, quietly instilling confidence back into her. Diana had, in effect, suffered a minor breakdown.

Charles was on the phone throughout those crucial hours, keeping the Queen informed in case it should be necessary to postpone or cancel the wedding. The Queen, however, was determined that the wedding go ahead as planned. She told her senior advisers to take no notice of any rumors about Lady Diana's condition. Charles, of course, was far more worried than his mother, especially as both Jane and the Queen had told him not to see Diana until the trauma had passed.

To this day, Charles believes that Diana was simply suffering from prewedding nerves, a common affliction. The attack was understandable, given a ceremony of great splendor before assembled royalty, television cameras, and hundreds of thousands of spectators, and given that the bride was an inexperienced, unsophisticated nineteen-year-old.

Charles never realized how close Diana had come to calling off the wedding. She has since confessed to her sister that if she hadn't been marrying Prince Charles, and if she hadn't felt an awesome sense of responsibility to the whole nation, she would never have gone through with it. When faced with trouble, her instinct had always been to turn and run. But this time she couldn't. Instead, she had to face up to life. She had begun to grow up, at last.

7

The Wedding of the Century

As the first gray light dawned in London on Wednesday, July 29, 1981, a remarkable sight appeared. The city streets, usually bare and lifeless at such an inhospitable hour, were thronged with tens of thousands of happy, noisy people. An excited buzz of conversation, punctuated by an occasional snatch of singing, could be heard. Though it was early, few had slept. They were too excited to rest for long, and besides, they didn't want to miss a second of the day of the historic marriage of a Crown Prince, the day on which His Royal Highness The Prince of Wales was to marry Lady Diana Spencer.

People had started arriving three days before in order to get a good view of the pageantry and splendor reserved for exceptional royal occasions. For those camped along the bridal route, it was a once-in-a-lifetime chance to see the entire Royal Family at close quarters and to witness a spectacle of unsurpassable grandeur.

The Prince of Wales and his bride had captured the imagination of the nation—indeed, the world—in unprecedented fashion. Never before had such notice been taken of a royal wedding. Dozens of television cameras and a complex assortment of broadcast units were poised along the route from Buckingham Palace to St. Paul's to transmit the royal nuptials via satellite to the millions around the world who waited patiently to see the fairy-tale lovers. Yet more cameras were waiting inside the cathedral to broadcast the ceremony itself. Never before had such a private romance become so wholehearted a public love affair.

A century earlier, Walter Bagehot, the renowned Victorian authority on the British Constitution, wrote, "There is nothing the English enjoy quite so much as a royal wedding." Rarely had his words been so spectacularly endorsed. On that sun-filled July day, the whole nation seemed to overflow with good will.

Since Charles and Diana's engagement five months before, the intensity of their relationship had been plain for all to see. They clearly adored each other. Their exchange of intimate glances illustrated their obvious happiness and love. The openness of such love did much to capture the imagination of the country, unused to any public display of emotion from its rather serious Prince of Wales.

Those close to Charles had worried for some years that he was becoming a lonely bachelor, frankly carrying out his royal duties with little or no enthusiasm and coming alive only during a dangerous or challenging pastime like playing polo or piloting a helicopter. He seemed to be searching for some sort of fulfillment in life, and failing to find it.

Falling in love changed all that. Diana's youthfulness and sense of fun were infectious. Suddenly, Charles was full of a sparky, boyish enthusiasm that had been absent for years. At last his life seemed to have some purpose. Now he was utterly content and brimming over with happiness.

The Royal Family could see the beneficial effect Diana had on him. All of them were delighted when he expressed his wish to marry her, none more so than the Queen Mother. She believed the gentle, self-effacing quality she saw in Diana, combined with her naturally friendly nature, made her an ideal royal wife. In time, these attributes would enable her to be shaped into a much-loved Princess and later a Queen.

The Queen was also happy for Charles. She tried to encourage Diana to relax in the unaccustomed spotlight, assuring her that she would soon secure her niche in Britain's first family. Most girls have trouble establishing a good relationship with their mothers-in-law. It is even more difficult when your mother-in-law is a reigning monarch, as Diana soon learned.

She had better luck with the Duke of Edinburgh, who was pleased that his eldest son had found a woman that he, too, could admire. Heartily, Prince Philip remarked, "I was worried that Charles had missed the boat. But this Diana is a cracking good-looking girl." Philip had always feared that Charles would, in the end, marry a "bluestocking"—a serious-minded woman interested only in the cerebral and cultural pursuits Charles favored. Such a daughter-in-law would be anathema to him. With Diana, Philip was impressed and relieved.

Charles's younger brothers, Andrew and Edward, found Diana attractive and good fun. Both were surprised and delighted that their serious elder brother had chosen a bride who was fun and not a little irreverent. As Charles and Diana grew closer, for example, she abandoned the obligatory sir and, becoming bolder, teased him that he was old before his time, balding and "square."

It was important to the monarchy that the heir to the throne had finally found a wife and would, in time, produce the next heir. And the nation was happy that the Prince of Wales, of whom they were genuinely fond, had found a bride who so clearly had won his heart.

During their engagement, the couple were inseparable whenever the Prince was not working or on a foreign tour. They walked through the gardens or sat in the Prince's suite in Buckingham Palace, holding hands and planning their future together. Charles introduced Diana to all his relatives and friends, and she enchanted everyone she met. Many, of course, commented on her shyness; they interpreted it as an endearing indication that she would make Charles a dutiful wife—that is, one prepared to tolerate his deficiencies, understand his work and his special position, and to be a loyal, supportive partner.

A few of his friends who harbored reservations kept them quiet. How could they tell the Prince of Wales they were concerned that the two had little in common and their temperaments seemed incompatible? However, the more the doubters saw the couple together, the more they came to believe that this couple were truly in love and not afraid to show it. Surely, they hoped, such a love could transcend any differences.

As July 29, the royal wedding day, approached, presents began to arrive from the people of Britain by every post—a total of three thousand before the end of June. Every morning Diana would go to the Wedding Present Centre, especially set up in Buckingham Palace's private cinema, to view the latest arrivals. These were happy, exciting days for her, and she struck up a warm relationship with the palace staff.

The wedding was meticulously planned. There were endless meetings between Edward Adeane, Charles's private secretary, officials from the Lord Chamberlain's office, the Keeper of the Privy Purse, and the Master of the Household, who were working around the clock in preparation.

The Prince did not simply leave the arrangements to his staff. Few are aware of just how personally involved Charles was. The Lord Chamberlain traditionally organizes such rituals, but Charles demanded that he be informed of everything so that he could approve every detail. Charles even agreed to provide the commentary for a BBC television prewedding program.

Charles was determined to be married in St. Paul's Cathedral,* even though Westminster Abbey was the tradi-

---

* St. Paul's is a stunning building that cannot fail to stir all who enter it, whatever their religious convictions. The present cathedral is the third to be built on its site. The first, built in 604, was destroyed by fire in 1087; the second was built in the eleventh century with a spire of an astonishing 489 feet, but this too burned down, in 1561. The site remained a ruin until after the devastating Great Fire of 1666, when the St. Paul's of today was built as a statement of London's faith and self-confi-

tional setting for royal weddings. He loved the beautiful old cathedral, and since it was considerably larger than Westminster, more guests could be accommodated.

The Lord Chamberlain, Lord Maclean, was distinctly uneasy about the choice of St. Paul's. It is much farther away from Buckingham Palace than Westminster, and the route is exposed, making security from a terrorist attack impossible to guarantee. He was mindful that in the past ten years, over two thousand people had been killed in the Irish troubles; the wedding might seem to the IRA an ideal opportunity for an assassination. The cost of policing the route would be prohibitive. Further, the Lord Chamberlain worried that not enough police and members of the armed forces would be available to line the route. But when he voiced his doubts, Charles replied simply, "Well, stand them further apart."

For security reasons, it was suggested that the Royal Family forgo the open carriages normally used on such occasions and use Rolls-Royces instead. The Queen would have none of it. At the time, nearly three million people were unemployed in Britain, the economy was in the doldrums, and not three weeks before there had been serious rioting in Liverpool, Manchester, and London. The IRA was active. A deranged man had fired blanks at the Queen during the Trooping of the Colors the previous month, and both the Pope and President Reagan had recently been attacked. But the Royal Family were united in their determination not to let fear of assassination spoil the greatest day in the life of the Prince of Wales.

---

dence. Three hundred years later it miraculously survived the Blitz of World War II, while all the surrounding buildings were totally destroyed.

Designed by Sir Christopher Wren, the cathedral is a tribute to his inventiveness. Its famous dome remains supreme even among the skyscrapers that threaten to dominate London's skyline. After presenting daringly modern designs, Wren was forced by the Church authorities to return to the basic plan of a Gothic cathedral with a nave, aisles, a crossing, transepts and a chancel, forming a Latin cross. He was given a freer hand in the interior, and he allowed for a great deal of natural light to enter the building from windows of the nave. It is, in fact, the perfect cathedral for an exceptional wedding.

Prince Charles then set about planning the music, which was, he emphasized, his number-one priority. He had heard the opera singer Kiri Te Kanawa and, when he had met her on one of his official visits to New Zealand, had been enchanted by her attractive personality. He particularly hoped she would sing at his wedding because he wanted everything to be exactly right—which meant his favorite music should be played and sung by people he admired and liked. Te Kanawa was an excellent choice; her exquisite rendering of "Let the Bright Seraphim" was one of the most beautiful elements of the service.

Charles also selected the musical works for the choir and diligently studied the plan and all the timings for the ceremony. He was precise and fussy, knowing exactly and intuitively what would be best. This, after all, was what he had been trained for during much of his life: to produce royal spectacle. Diana probably had less say in the ceremony than the average bride, although her favorite hymn —"I Vow to Thee My Country"—was included.

Diana also had little say in the guest list. The Queen and the Royal Family made most of the decisions about whom to invite, but Diana and Earl Spencer were allowed to make suggestions.

The only real problem was whether to invite Diana's stepmother's mother, Barbara Cartland. The Royal Family, of course, are absolute sticklers for doing everything correctly and certainly did not want to appear vindictive or high-handed by not extending invitations that were proper and expected according to society's unwritten rules. The courtiers also recognized that Barbara Cartland had an extraordinary following of loyal readers whom the Palace would not wish to upset without good reason. On the other hand, the rules about a stepmother's mother are not as traditional or clear as rules about blood relatives. In the end, Charles allowed Diana to decide. Diana was adamant: no Barbara Cartland.

Earl Spencer noted one benefit to having the Royal Family take over all the arrangements. As he often joked, he did not pay a penny toward the cost of his daughter's wedding.

During the prewedding period, Diana truly won over the British public, an admiring but normally cynical body as far as royalty is concerned. Diana, they agreed, looked gorgeous, and it was obvious she had no airs. She even agreed to attend the end-of-term party at the Young England Kindergarten, where she had once worked. Always most comfortable among young children, she looked radiantly happy as they clambered boisterously over her. Afterward she commented, "I ended up battered and bruised. I had so many children crawling on top of me. I've got more bruises on my bottom where they pinched and clung to me than you would think possible!"

At a Buckingham Palace garden party for two thousand disabled people, just days before the wedding, the heavens opened and rained torrents. Diana, dressed in a stunning red-and-white outfit with a red boater, was soon drenched. She refused to take cover until she had said hello to everyone.

The public, accustomed to royals who behaved as though they lived in a different world, had at last found someone with whom they could identify, someone who put people before protocol.

The celebrations began in earnest the night before the wedding. A stupendous fireworks display burst over Hyde Park, and a chain of a hundred and one beacons was lit on hills throughout England, Scotland, and Wales. Prince Charles set off the chain by lighting the first bonfire at 10:08 (it was scheduled for 10:00), and the displays began.

The whole of London seemed to be packed into the royal park. The massed bands of the Household Brigade of Guards played for two hours, together with the Morriston Orpheus Choir and the Choir of the Welsh Guards, and to round off the fantastic night, the Royal Horse Artillery fired salvos.

For hundreds of thousands of people who turned up in Hyde Park it was a night to remember. An estimated twelve thousand rockets were fired into the sky, and over two tons of explosives went off. The finale consisted of an exploding replica of Buckingham Palace, with huge sparkling likenesses of Charles and Diana filling the night sky. Nothing on such a grand scale had been seen since the spectacular pyrotechnics ordered by King George II, in 1749, to mark the Peace of Aix-la-Chapelle, and for which Handel wrote his *Music for the Royal Fireworks*.

Drinking, dancing, and partying carried on throughout the night. Such a sense of unity and national pride hadn't been experienced since the Coronation of Queen Elizabeth II in 1953. At last, in the face of the country's economic decline and grave employment problems, the people felt they had something to be proud of.

By dawn, July 29, there was hardly an inch of space to spare within a hundred yards of St. Paul's. By nine o'clock, when the first invited guests began to arrive, over a million people were crammed onto the sidewalks lining the route, complete with camping stoves, food, drinks for the children, and more than a few bottles of champagne to toast the happy couple.

Anyone who had feared a typically English rainy summer's day was happily proved wrong. From the moment the sun rose above the gray London streets, the day was radiant. A gentle breeze rippled through the trees in the royal parks and took the edge off the heat. The weather was perfect.

Diana awoke before six-thirty that morning—in her excitement she had hardly slept at all—and was taking a long bath at the Queen Mother's London home, Clarence House, where she had returned the previous day. She listened to the early-morning prewedding radio shows and peeped from behind curtains to see the thousands of people lining the Mall. For a moment, she was transfixed. It was awesome, she confided later to a girlfriend, to realize that *she*—who had been a mere teenager only twenty-eight days before—was the center of it all.

As soon as the television broadcasts started, Diana

turned on the TV and switched from one channel to another, watching everything she could while consuming an enormous breakfast of orange juice, grapefruit, bacon and eggs, and toast and marmalade.

The first person in a procession of many to arrive at Clarence House was Kevin Shanley, Diana's hairdresser, who had brought with him three hair dryers ("just in case"), ten combs, and ten hairbrushes. He washed and blow-dried her hair, then styled it into the natural, informal style she preferred. When he finished, makeup artist Barbara Daly went to work, instructed by Diana to make her look as natural as possible; Charles disliked heavily made-up women. The makeup took forty-five minutes. The Emanuels arrived with the best-kept secret of all—the dress. Diana retired to her room with her sister Jane, who had come to help her dress. Together they watched the excited throngs lining the wedding route on the television set in the room. Diana was happy, wanting to get on with dressing and to get to the church.

But once she put on her magnificent gown and saw herself in the full-length mirror, she burst into tears. Jane ran to help her mop the tearstains and comfort her. Diana was uncontrollable. The other women in the room—maids, dressers, a lady-in-waiting, and a flower arranger—left so the sisters could be alone while Diana strove to master her emotions for the ordeal ahead. Half-sobbing, Diana told Jane, "All I want to do is marry Charles. I can't face all this . . . look at everyone . . . I can't go through with it."

But somehow she did.

Barbara Daly returned to repair the damage to the makeup, which was light, so the revisions took only a matter of minutes. However, Diana's eyes had to be bathed and redone.

Everyone agreed that the Emanuels' dress was a sensation: an elaborate, flowing creation of ivory silk paper taffeta, hand-embroidered with tiny mother-of-pearl sequins, with lace-flounced sleeves, and a stunning, twenty-five-foot-long train, trimmed and edged with precious old lace. The huge crinoline skirt was puffed with one hundred yards of netting so that it billowed majestically. Forty-four yards of silk had been dyed ivory to suit Diana's complexion and to prevent its appearing a glaring white blob under the television lights. Diana's little bow, which had become her trademark in those early days, rested below the ruffled neckline on the boned bodice.

How deep the V of the neckline should go had been the subject of fierce debate. Diana had wanted a deep décolletage to reveal some flesh. The powers at Buckingham Palace decreed that since she was marrying the future head of the Church of England, her dress had to be particularly demure. As far as the world knew, Diana was one of the world's few surviving twenty-year-old virgins. In the end, there was compromise: Diana persuaded the Emanuels to give her a deep V, but a froth of ruffles was added to temper the effect.

When Diana was finally dressed, David Emanuel sewed a last stitch in it, an age-old custom meant to bring luck. Clad in such a dress and wearing the Spencer diamond tiara and her mother's diamond earrings, Diana looked every inch a fairy princess. Inside, she was trembling like a leaf.

Slowly and nervously, she walked downstairs while a dozen people carried the train behind her and helped her into the glass coach that was to take her and her father to St. Paul's.

Prince Charles, too, had been wide awake that morning when Stephen Barry went to call him at seven A.M. When Stephen turned on the radio, Charles listened to the pre-wedding program while he shaved, bathed, and dressed in a casual shirt and brown cords. He calmly ate a breakfast of grapefruit, fruit juice, and a boiled egg with toast. After all, all his life he had been prepared to cope with grand occasions, and this was no exception. After breakfast, Stephen began dressing the Prince in his naval uniform.

Charles wore the full dress uniform of a commander of Her Majesty's Royal Navy, together with a splendid blue sash that designated him a member of the ancient order of the Knights of the Garter. He looked magnificent. Fifteen minutes later, when he walked down the main stairs to the Grand Entrance of the palace—which cannot be seen from the Mall—all the members of the staff who were not going to St. Paul's stood at the bottom of the stairs and clapped. As he walked outside, the Prince shook hands with as many people as he could. "Thank you, thank you," he said warmly to each, before climbing into the coach with his brother Andrew for the journey to St. Paul's.

Andrew and their younger brother Edward would serve as Charles's "supporters," since he was not having a best man. Prince Andrew, as principal supporter, was responsible for the best man's traditional tasks, such as care of the wedding ring. The ring, which had been delivered to Buckingham Palace earlier that week, was made from the same piece of 22-carat Welsh gold as the wedding rings of the Queen, Queen Mother, Princess Margaret, and Princess Anne.

Inside the cathedral, the guests waited expectantly. Never before had such a distinguished collection of people been gathered together. Present were not only the entire British Royal Family and Diana's family, but also most of the crowned heads of Europe, monarchs from Africa, the Middle East, and Asia, 160 foreign presidents, prime ministers with their wives or husbands, politicians, civil servants, royal staff members, Diana's flatmates—who had front-row seats—and even the odd film star. Diana's divorced parents sat side by side in the front row, with their respective partners situated a discreet distance away.

Mrs. Nancy Reagan represented the President of the United States, who hadn't yet fully recovered from an assassination attempt four months earlier. Royal-wedding fever, in fact, seemed to have swept through the United States nearly as enthusiastically as it had in Britain. As ABC commentator Peter Jennings explained, "It's the last of the great royal spectacles. It's got color, sweep, music, occasion, and it's a great romantic story. It captures the imagination."

. . .

A thirty-minute peal of the giant bells known as Great Tom and Great Paul, accompanied by the twelve big bells in the northwest tower, heralded the event. As Diana stepped from her carriage, a barely audible sigh of admiration rippled through the onlookers.

As she marched up the red-carpeted steps of St. Paul's, Lady Sarah Armstrong-Jones and colleagues fought to control the river of ivory material flowing behind her. Inside the cathedral, David and Elizabeth Emanuel took over, adjusting her dress, her veil, her train, to be sure everything looked perfect for the grand entrance.

Diana had been given precisely three-and-a-half minutes to walk with her father, towing her train, up the long aisle of St. Paul's. The Lord Chamberlain and his staff pride themselves on clockwork efficiency and believe that strict timing is essential to achieve that.

Neither father nor daughter smiled as she approached Charles, while the congregation turned to watch the nervous bride. Diana appeared to be concentrating on making it to the altar ahead. She was most conscious of the need to support her father down the aisle, for there was serious doubt, at one point, that Earl Spencer, still suffering the effects of his stroke, was physically capable of giving the bride away. He went privately to St. Paul's a number of times to practice walking the distance and be sure he could manage it.

Afterward he said, "I was determined to walk Diana down the aisle, if it killed me. It was my duty, and I was not going to forgo it, if at all possible. But I must confess that far from me supporting Diana that day, she supported me. She was wonderful."

Diana heard the Archbishop of Canterbury tell the world:

"Here is the stuff of which fairy tales are made: the Prince and Princess on their wedding day. But fairy tales usually end at this point with the simple phrase 'They lived happily ever after.' This may be because fairy tales regard marriage as an anticlimax after the romance of courtship. This is not the Christian view. Our faith sees the wedding day not as the place of arrival but the place where the adventure really begins. Those who are married live happily ever after the wedding day if they persevere in the real adventure, which is the royal task of creating each other and creating a more loving world."

The Archbishop led the couple through the marriage ceremony. Apart from an endearingly nervous slip when she muddled Charles's names—thereby nearly marrying the Duke of Edinburgh!—the ceremony was faultless. Diana, in common with most modern brides but unlike previous royal brides, had opted to leave out the promise "to obey" her husband. Everyone in the cathedral noticed the wording "to love, honor, and cherish." Soon they would discover the reality of that oath.

As she took her wedding vows, Diana bade a final goodbye to the freedom she had known all her life—the freedom to do anything she wanted on the spur of the moment, to walk down a street alone, visit friends, go for a drive or to the cinema, have a private lunch in public or pop into a pub for a drink and a chat with a friend. Today, she was not simply marrying a man, but was embracing a job and all that it involved for the future. She had married a man for whom duty had and would always come first. And she, too, would soon discover that she had to feel as much commitment to the job, if not more, than to the man she was marrying.

At the end of the service, Diana looked relieved but still nervous as she and Charles walked up the aisle and out into the open air. A faint smile swept across her face when Charles spoke quietly to her, reassuring her, urging her to relax. The ordeal was over. They were married at last.

Out on the cathedral steps, the television cameras closed in on the couple. The world could clearly see Charles say to her, "Wave now." The Princess obeyed instinctively. Up went her slender arm, the gold band glinting in the sun. The crowd roared their appreciation.

As the couple drove back to Buckingham Palace in an open landau, the crowds radiated tremendous warmth and good will. The moment more favored by television than any other was the gathering of the entire Royal Family on the balcony of Buckingham Palace. Thousands below waved flags, sang, and shouted, "We want Di! We want Charlie!" Charles said, "Well, how about a kiss?" Diana turned to him and said, "Whyever not?" So, completely spontaneously, they kissed, on the lips, quickly. A thunderous cheer went up. It was exactly what the people wanted, a sign of real affection from the royal couple.

The day had been a complete triumph. Everything had run with split-second precision and efficiency. Britain is, of course, perhaps more practiced than most other nations at organizing such spectacles, but when it was finally over, a mighty sigh of relief could be heard throughout the palace. Most of the staff had been working virtually day and night for weeks to ensure the wedding's success.

At the end of the day, after her son and his new wife had left for their honeymoon, the Queen went for a walk in the Buckingham Palace gardens. Suddenly she noticed a figure lying on a bench in the garden. Surprised, she asked a nearby policeman, "Who's that?"

"I don't know, Your Majesty," he replied.

Another policeman, dispatched to investigate, reported in some astonishment, "It's Sir John Miller."

Sir John, an amiable military figure, was the Crown Equerry at Buckingham Palace and one of the main organizers of the event. Exalted but weary, he had just returned from Waterloo Station, where he had seen off the Prince and Princess, and received a parting thank-you kiss from Diana. He had worked virtually nonstop for weeks to make the day perfect. Now it was over. He was so exhausted when he got back to the palace that he had fallen asleep almost as soon as he sat down. The Queen let him sleep.

The Prince and Princess spent their wedding night at Broadlands, Lord Mountbatten's home, in the beautiful Hampshire countryside. Since his murder, it had been the home of his grandson, and Charles's friend, Lord Romsey.

The Queen and Prince Philip had also spent the first night of their honeymoon at Broadlands, and it was a poignant choice for Charles. It had been more of a home for him than his own while Mountbatten was alive.

The couple spent their honeymoon aboard the royal yacht *Britannia,* sailing in the Mediterranean. Stephen Barry, in his book *Royal Service,* described it: "They were an enchanted fourteen days. For the first time in years I didn't have to call Charles in the mornings. He slept as long as he wanted and we merely had to send in a cold breakfast when he rang.

"He and the Princess spent most of their evenings alone on the royal deck and we never knew at what time they went to bed," Barry recalled. "Their quarters were very simple but comfortable and charming. Everything on the royal deck is white with red upholstery and gray carpets. They spent most of the time during the day alone on the veranda of the royal deck and took their meals in the sitting room nearby.

"Most days, as we steamed along the North African coast we would try to find a deserted beach where the couple could be alone. First, a small boat would go out to make sure the beach was deserted, that there were no pressmen about. Then another boat would take the couple ashore and most days they would picnic on the beach. The Prince loves to sunbathe and the Princess loves to swim, so they were both content. The Princess spent a lot of time snapping away, mostly views and pictures of Charles."

Later, Barry commented: "Diana was wonderfully happy on her honeymoon. She was in the seventh heaven. She spent the entire time with Charles. She didn't even want to be separated from him for a moment. She never seemed to stop kissing him; there was a look of absolute adoration in her eyes the entire time. I don't think I ever saw her so happy ever again. Not that degree of radiance. She was blissfully happy.

"And Charles too seemed to be enjoying himself. But he was more sober, more relaxed about the whole honeymoon. He didn't appear so ecstatic, but then I would never have imagined he would behave in the way Diana did."

At one moment on board the *Britannia,* Diana turned to Charles at table and asked, "It will be always like this, won't it?"

"Yes, of course. Of course, it will," Charles answered as he kissed her.

Although most of the time the couple were alone, Charles and Diana joined in with all the crew, officers, and staff whenever there were parties on board and barbecues ashore. Diana tried to make the honeymoon fun for everyone.

When they returned to Britain, they looked radiantly happy. During those first few weeks, everyone who saw them together commented on the tenderness they showed to each other and the obvious love between them.

Three months later, Prince Charles spelled out his feelings about his wedding day when he made a speech in the City of London's ancient Guildhall: "We still cannot get over what happened that day. Neither of us can get over the atmosphere. It was electric, I felt, and so did my wife.

"I remember several occasions that were similar, with large crowds: the Coronation and the Jubilee, and various major national occasions. All of them were very special in their own way, but our wedding was quite extraordinary as far as we were concerned. It made us both extraordinarily proud to be British."

8

---※≫≫≪≪---

Royal Reality Overwhelms the Young Princess

To avoid unwanted media attention, the honeymoon had been planned with the care and secrecy of a military operation by Edward Adeane, Charles's private secretary, with the help of senior Royal Navy officers. While Charles and Diana visited coastal towns and villages, and even went ashore to have lunch or supper with friends, the press flew from one Greek island to another on the slightest rumor, hoping for a sighting. One newspaper even hired a Lear jet, but to no avail.

Within days of returning to England, the royal couple held an informal press conference on the understanding that, afterward, the press would leave them alone. Everyone at this press conference reported that the couple were "simply in love," unable to take their eyes or their hands off each other. Diana described the honeymoon as "fabulous" and said she "could highly recommend marriage." She added, with a great smile, "It's a marvelous life."

The photographs released to the press—taken during and after the honeymoon—showed a bride and bridegroom very much in love and enjoying life together. When they came back from their honeymoon, they immediately joined the rest of the Royal Family at Balmoral. Diana rapidly came down to earth when she realized that life wasn't always going to be like those lazy, sun-filled days she had enjoyed with her new husband on the royal yacht. For one thing, she no longer had her husband to herself. There were no opportunities for intimate moments or demonstrations of affection. Suddenly, her husband was public property, and she discovered that the most important person in his life did not seem to be his wife, but his mother.

An inkling of what was in store for her came on the first night at Balmoral, as she and Charles dressed for dinner, their first formal meal with the rest of the family. As usual, a number of distinguished guests were staying with the Queen and Prince Philip. First, Diana discovered, she could no longer take as much time as she wanted to dress and make up. She now had to conform to the rigid discipline of a royal household.

The couple were expected downstairs for predinner drinks at precisely seven-thirty, and of course Charles was ready and waiting at seven-twenty-five. He had been brought up to know the routine, which in effect set a strict rule that under no circumstances did you keep the Queen waiting.

Charles adored his mother and accepted without question the somewhat rigid life-style at Balmoral. It was her husband's utter devotion and acquiescence to the Queen, her mother-in-law, that first started to infuriate Diana. She felt that Charles would always side with his mother in any discussion, let alone an argument. No matter what views she expounded, even if he thought differently in private, he automatically agreed with his mother. Diana told friends that when Charles was with his mother, he became a different person. Once, after Charles had told her she looked ravishing in a plunging neckline, the Queen gently mentioned at dinner that the dress was a little revealing for a member of the Royal Family. Far from challenging his mother, Charles nodded his agreement with her opinion. Diana had spent most of her life getting her own way, managing to persuade her father on many decisions. She didn't like this one bit.

In the five months before the wedding, when she had stayed at Buckingham Palace, Diana had been treated as though she wasn't really staying there at all. She had been left largely to her own devices and, surprisingly, had only been invited for tea a couple of times with the Queen and to a few informal dinners in the Queen's private apartment. There had been no formal dinners for her to attend, no gradual process of training. Now she was being thrown in the deep end at Balmoral, and it was a shock for a girl barely out of her teens.

Suddenly, the reality of her life for the rest of her days hit her—hard. Diana, who had never practiced discipline before, was now expected to stand and talk to whoever happened to be staying for the weekend, be it a Prime Minster, bishop, professor, businessman, or another royal, for exactly thirty minutes. She would be offered one drink, sometimes two, but no more.

Diana would usually take a soft drink, but on occasion she would drink a dry sherry or perhaps champagne, if it was being served. The royal ritual never changed. The butler would ask, "May I get Ma'am a drink?" He would get what she asked for and bow slightly as he presented it. It was so very different from her flat in Earl's Court and the bottles of cheap red and white plonk that she used to enjoy with her friends. In twelve short months, her life had turned upside down.

Diana was an unsophisticated young woman, not naturally gregarious. She didn't feel up to the challenge of making polite conversation with whoever happened to be around. She was happy taking part in small talk with her girl-friends on such froth as the latest pop group, hairstyle, or fashion or exchanging gossip with old school chums. But Balmoral and the Queen's dinners were heavy-duty. She hated it, found it boring, and was hopeless at it. Her sunny, happy honeymoon became a dim memory. The joy of her life with Charles evaporated almost overnight as she watched him, totally at ease, knowledgeably chatting with everybody he met about things of which she knew nothing and cared even less.

On the stroke of eight, when dinner was announced, Diana had to take Charles's hand and walk to the table with a dignified manner. Like all the other guests, she was obliged to remain standing for a moment until the Queen was seated. Usually she would not be allowed to sit next to Charles. Often she would be seated between two men with whom she had nothing in common and whom she considered far too old or intellectual to engage in conversation which wouldn't bore her or them.

From her early teens, Diana had had a knack of talking easily with ordinary people, but the Queen and her guests were a very different matter. She had observed how Charles regarded his mother with total respect and esteem, and she was genuinely frightened of looking or sounding foolish before her. Because of her complete lack of educational achievements, Diana felt unable to carry on conversations with those whom she believed intellectually superior to her and, consequently, would fall apart on such occasions, remaining silent rather than risking making a fool of herself.

Shortly after her marriage, Diana confessed to a friend, "All I can talk about with them is the bloody weather!" She also told Charles's equerries, "I am absolutely petrified of the Queen. I shake all over when I'm in her presence. I can't look her in the eye, and just go to pieces whenever she comes into the room. She tries to be nice and put me at my ease, but I am so embarrassed when I'm with her.

"Charles tries to help me by cracking a joke, but I look at the floor and blush madly. I can hardly raise a faint smile."

In those early days at Balmoral, and even the following year, Diana would sit at the table and say absolutely nothing throughout the meal. There would be witty, sophisticated talk, in-jokes which only the Royal Family understood, innuendo and suggestion, all of which went over her head. She wrote to one of her flatmates: "I feel totally out of place here. I sometimes wonder what on earth I've got myself into. I feel so small, so lonely, so out of my depth."

Dinner was a *very* unhurried affair. It didn't matter whether Diana was hungry or on one of her strict diets; she was not allowed to leave the table until the Queen had decided that dinner had ended and it was time to repair to the drawing room. Sometimes dinner would take one hour, sometimes two, depending on the guests and the conversation—and the whim of the Queen. Charles, of course, was accustomed to it, but Diana was used to having a quick meal and running off to whatever she wanted afterward. This rigid adherence to stuffy protocol stifled and bored her.

But what horrified Diana most of all and really started discord in the early days of the marriage was the realization that this ordeal was not just a one-time affair. This ritual would take place every single night they were at Balmoral or Windsor Castle with the Queen. This was going to be her life for the rest of her days. Despite the reassuring and patient counseling she had received before the wedding from experts like Charles's office boss, former naval Chief Petty Officer Michael Colborne, and the Prince's private secretary, the lawyer-courtier Edward Adeane, Diana hadn't grasped that it was all going to be so excruciatingly *formal*. The efficient, pedantic Adeane had irritably recognized that challenges lay ahead when he found that his Princess-in-training didn't know the capital of Australia!

September 1981 was a bad month for Diana. She simply couldn't settle down to her new life as a member of the Royal Family. She was confused and unhappy; she spent most of her time walking around the estate on her own, her eyes filled with tears, not knowing what she was doing or whether she would ever fit into this strange existence.

When she was alone with Charles at night, she would try to explain how she felt. She begged him to take her home to Highgrove or London. She longed for the comforting familiarity of London and her friends; she wanted to browse round the smart Knightsbridge shops and see and talk to people she could relate to.

The highly disciplined Charles wouldn't countenance the idea, knowing it would upset his mother. The longer the couple stayed at Balmoral that autumn, the more lonely, upset, and depressed Diana became.

Diana was bored as well. It rained almost incessantly during her first stay at Balmoral, which lasted eight weeks. There was little to do other than walk, and there was no one her age to talk to. Her mother-in-law would extol these same qualities on BBC's two-hour television extravaganza on a year in the life of the Queen. Called "Elizabeth R," it celebrated the Queen's forty years on the throne. The Queen mentioned proudly, "It's rather like hibernating when you come and stay at Balmoral. It's lovely here. You can walk for miles without meeting another person."

Diana tried to make friends with the staff at Balmoral. She didn't want to go out with the other royals every day, standing around cold and wet while the men were shooting. Instead, she tried to cheer herself up by wandering repeatedly into the kitchens.

According to a royal maid, "Diana came in smiling and being friendly and introduced herself. Everyone was taken aback. It is very, very unusual for a member of the Royal Family to come into the kitchens, except on special occasions when the Queen decides she wants to look around, inspect, show a little interest.

"But this was totally different. Diana came in and began to chat to everyone who was there as though she was a friend of ours. But she isn't one of us. She's one of them.

"She began to pop down to the kitchens frequently, chatting to one of the young footmen or a maid and being really friendly to all of us. No royal had behaved like this before. And we didn't know how to take it."

The senior staff below objected to the Princess of Wales venturing into their turf. They did not approve of what they called "Scandinavian practices," whereby the royals are friendly with their employees. There always has been, and still exists in the 1990s, the most strict relationship between the royals and those who work for them. Below stairs these include all kitchen staff, household maids, servants, footmen, drivers, grooms, and gardeners. Their relationship is never allowed to be more than that of master and servant. The gap between the below-stairs staff and Royal Family is even greater than between the royals and those who work closely with them above stairs, that is, the personal staff of the Royal Family, such as private secretaries, office staff, and ladies-in-waiting. This sense of hierarchy is mirrored among the servants. Below stairs there is a further strict caste system; those in senior positions are treated with great respect and trepidation by junior servants.

The royals, however, are most polite to their staff, no matter how lowly their position. They always end their orders with the polite words "if you don't mind." In reply, the servant will usually bow and say, "Yes, Ma'am," or "Yes, Sir," and retire.

One day, after Diana had visited her "new friends" in the kitchen yet again, the Yeoman of the Glass and China, a responsible position, approached her as she walked through the door to greet everyone with the cheery hello. Pointing at the door, the Yeoman told her politely but bluntly, "Through there, Ma'am, is your side of the house; through here is our side of the house."

Diana was taken aback, unsure how to respond. The Yeoman stood still, without another word, effectively barring her way into the kitchen. The Princess had no recourse. She blushed madly and disappeared, never to return downstairs.

At her parents' homes, Diana had always chatted with the staff, and no one had ever objected. Now, with this avenue of friendship closed to her, she felt even more lonely and unhappy. She had yet another reason to hate the royal country retreats.

        ·   ·   ·

On several occasions during the early days of marriage, Diana lost her composure. One minute she would burst into tears for no apparent reason, the next she would become frustrated, angry, and resentful, often in front of others. Charles, brought up to avoid public displays, was embarrassed and unhappy at these emotional outbursts.

Charles had no idea what to do. He needed to talk to people he trusted about his wife's peculiar behavior. He had some of his closest friends, including Lord Romsey and his wife, who are also friends of Diana's, come to Scotland to cheer her up. Lord Romsey went out stalking with the Prince, and Lady Romsey was commissioned to go out for walks with the Princess. Other friends of Charles who knew the couple well were also summoned to Scotland to sort things out. By this time, Diana was spending whole mornings shouting and sobbing at whoever would listen.

Sometimes she would turn in desperation to Stephen Barry, Charles's valet. "I don't know what to do, I feel so unhappy here," she sobbed to him one morning. "Charles doesn't understand me. He would prefer to be out shooting or stalking or riding or chatting to his mother rather than be with me. Can't he understand that I need him to look after me? I feel he's abandoned me. He just leaves me here all day. I hate it."

The more unhappy and irritable Diana became, the more concerned Charles grew, until he finally began to worry that her problems might prove insurmountable.

One early attempt to draw his new wife into his traditional circle of pals had already misfired. Not long after their honeymoon, the Prince had arranged a dinner party at Kensington Palace for his closest polo chums—among them the Canadian stores billionaire Galen Weston and the Hipwood brothers, brilliant polo players, and their wives. Young, rich, and boisterous, he calculated, the players and all their wives and girlfriends would enchant Diana and, in return, would delight in her. He figured wrong. On the whole, Diana found his friends coarse, juvenile, and stupid. At twenty, she might be neither an intellectual nor yet very grown up, but in her opinion her husband's polo pals were, for the most part, just down-right childish.

The Prince consulted a select handful of his older, more mature friends—those he felt he could entrust with this unexpected problem of a moody, volatile young wife. Such behavior was entirely new to the Royal Family. His friends tried to reassure him that Diana simply needed time to settle down; eventually she would learn to accept the discipline and protocol that, at the moment, terrified and bored her. Everything would be all right in the end, they told him.

Mountbatten had emphasized that Charles's wife, who-ever she was, would need to learn all that was required of her and adjust to living the disciplined life all members of the Royal Family must lead. And Charles knew that when she became Queen, his wife would need to be even more disciplined, more controlled, and more gracious than most other royals. Again and again Diana would angrily de-mand to be allowed to leave Balmoral and fly down to London to do some shopping or spend the weekend with her friends. The more she complained, the more he put his foot down, adamantly insisting that she stay, perhaps believing that her training had to begin immediately. It must have crossed his mind more than a few times at Balmoral that he had made the wrong choice of wife.

Diana wasn't thinking about how she was expected to behave or what protocol demanded. She perceived that she was shut up in a damp, cold Victorian castle with people who couldn't understand or care how she felt and were forcing her to behave in ways they thought fit. She was relieved when the Balmoral holiday finally came to an end. Now she fervently hoped that she and Charles could settle down to a happy married life together beyond the all-pervading influence of the Queen.

Back at Kensington Palace, Diana tried, as do most newly-wed girls, to organize her life so as to spend as much time as possible with her husband. She attempted to make op-portunities for them to be alone, without the constant stream of secretaries, equerries, valets, and servants who always seemed to need to discuss urgent matters with the Prince of Wales, interrupting whatever the couple were doing. She began to feel that Charles was the chairman of some large company and that she was simply his social secretary.

It seemed everyone else had more of a claim to his attention than she did. She became jealous of the hours Charles spent discussing whatever it was with his secretaries and officials. The more he continued to do so, the angrier she became. The people around Charles, who had spent years tending to his every need, began to feel her animosity toward them. It was a difficult situation for them as well.

To Charles, of course, a life almost entirely devoid of privacy was quite normal. He thought nothing of going away for two or three nights, returning home for a couple of nights, and then going off again to a distant part of the country to make another speech, open another factory, or attend another meeting. Apart from his public engagements, he spent at least one day a week running the affairs of the Duchy of Cornwall. It had never occurred to him that things would be any different after he was married.

But Diana proved to be considerably more headstrong and opinionated than either Charles or the Royal Family expected. She had very definite ideas of how she wanted their married life to be, and that included spending time *alone* with Charles, not sharing him with assorted flunkies or seeing him only at dinner, or worse, only minutes before bedtime.

She began to complain and refuse to cooperate when engagements were planned for her and Charles. She would go through her diary with a lady-in-waiting and object to what had been arranged for the following day. Forthrightly, she would tell Charles she wasn't going to do it.

To say that Charles was shocked is an understatement. The idea that a member of the Royal Family should refuse to carry out any official duties had never entered his mind; it was unthinkable. But Diana obstinately refused to give way. She was going to do what *she* wanted.

In a rage one day, Diana decided she had had enough and was going out shopping, *alone*. She jumped into her car, parked in the courtyard at Buckingham Palace, and was adjusting her seat belt when there came a tap on the window. It was Paul Officer, one of the policemen from the Royal Protection Squad. He opened the door and climbed in beside her.

"I don't need you, thank you. I'm going out on my own," she said.

"I'm sorry, Ma'am. That's not possible," he replied. "I'm sorry, but we're part of your life now. We have to accompany you. You know that."

A furious Diana got out of the car, slammed the door, and ran back inside. The staff at Buck House began to refer to her as "The Princess in the Tower."

In November 1981, only four months after their wedding, Charles began to realize communication had completely broken down between them. Diana, seemingly so docile before the wedding, didn't seem likely to change. He didn't want to tell his mother, because he knew she would suggest it was up to him to put his house in order and not tolerate any more nonsense from his wife. Charles was sensitive enough to realize that because Diana was floundering in a difficult, alien world, treating her aggressively would probably make her worse.

Stephen Barry recalled: "On one occasion Diana was due to escort Charles to an official dinner, and she just did not want to go. Charles was getting dressed at the time into white tie and tails, and Diana came into the room, still in her day clothes.

" 'I'm not coming,' she said, 'I can't face it. You'll have to go on your own.'

"Charles said, 'You can't do that. We have accepted. We have to go.'

"But Diana just stood there. I looked across to her. She was standing there, crying, the tears rolling down her face. I felt terribly, terribly sorry for her. Charles went over to her as I quietly left the room. That night, though, she didn't go out. Charles went on his own. Before he left, he said quietly to me, 'Look after her. I don't think she's feeling very well.'

"I knew what was the matter. She was unhappy and depressed."

Part of the reason was that Diana had not yet found the confidence to deal with people she had to meet. She didn't mind talking quietly to people, one to one, but she could not face talking to crowds of strangers; she didn't know what to say—she felt awkward and embarrassed.

She confessed all this to Oliver Everett, one of Charles's polo pals who had been one of his secretaries, was seventeen years older than Diana, and knew the royal ropes. Diana began to depend on him for everything, doing nothing before she had spoken to him. She begged Charles to allow Everett, a confident, helpful, kindly man, to become her secretary. Seeing that Everett seemed to be the only person able to manage his volatile wife, Charles readily agreed.

Diana was delighted. For the next two years, until 1983, Everett became her constant companion and confidant, educating her in the ways of being a royal, teaching her how to cope, and above all, giving her the confidence she needed to handle the situation and her life.

When Diana became pregnant in the autumn of 1981, Charles knew he had to find a way to placate her fiery moods and temper. He had hoped the pregnancy and the thought of becoming a mother might calm Diana and make her happy, but it seemed to have a reverse effect.

Stephen Barry reported what occurred one day in December: "Diana came into his study and said she wasn't feeling very well. She asked Charles to stay at home with her. She explained she needed him because she was feeling awful. Charles suggested she lie down and he would ask the doctor to come by and see her. She said she didn't need the doctor, she just needed him, his company.

"Charles talked to her quietly, telling her he had to go out due to an official engagement. It was his duty. The word seemed to light a spark in Diana. 'Duty, duty! That's all you think about is your bloody duty,' she screamed at him. 'Well, it's about time you started thinking about me. I'm your bloody wife.' She ran from the room, slamming the door behind her.

"Charles looked down at the ground, shaking his head, as I busied myself with helping him prepare. He said nothing, but he looked very serious."

So Charles began to take a new, softer line with his wife. He tried to give way to her demands, even those he had previously turned down. Everything she wanted she got. Because he was becoming more considerate toward her, Diana began to feel her campaign for the right to see her husband more frequently and to have some say over her own life was beginning to work.

Edward Adeane, Charles's private secretary, bore the brunt of Diana's distress. She told him point-blank that she wanted to see more of Charles and that Adeane had to stop butting in whenever they were alone. As a result, all the official papers that Adeane would bring for the Prince were not being read or signed; the boxes they came in weren't even being opened. Adeane rapidly lost patience as Diana kept Charles away from his official work more and more and the work piled up.

Matters became worse and the relationship more strained. Whenever Adeane complained to the Prince, he would be told that, for the time being, it was the only way Charles could keep the Princess happy and life at home on an even keel. Charles also warned Adeane that this new, softer approach might have to last for the whole of her pregnancy.

Adeane took his complaints straight to the attention of the Queen. Diana soon found herself being "advised," in no uncertain terms, by one of the Queen's ladies-in-waiting, Lady Susan Hussey, that she had better accept the life she had married into because no matter what she did or how much she complained or demanded, nothing would ever change. The Royal Family had their own rules of duty and behavior, and no twenty-year-old upstart would alter it, even if she was the Princess of Wales.

Everyone would probably have been better served if the Queen herself had taken Diana to one side and striven for a closer, maternal relationship with the young, inexperienced Princess, gently pointing out that she simply could not carry on as she was doing and reassuring her that it would all work out in the end. But that is not the way the Queen works. Any messages she wishes to impart to other members of The Firm are passed through one of her efficient and most loyal ladies-in-waiting.

As one of Charles's secretaries commented: "The telephone goes and a very sweet, utterly refined upper-class female voice will suggest something in a most gentle, delicate manner. You know of course that the lady imparting the message is one of the Queen's ladies-in-waiting, and you understand fully that this suggestion is an order from on high which must be obeyed. But one has to admit that it's done awfully well."

Word was beginning to leak out that the couple's marriage was not going well. Editors ordered all royal photographers and reporters to keep a close eye on the young Princess of Wales and to photograph her every move. Relentlessly the pack stalked Diana, even trailing her in a car when she left the palace to visit friends or go shopping or have tea. Wherever she went, newspeople followed her and cross-examined any staff who helped her in any way. Shopping—one of her favorite occupations—became such an ordeal that managers of Diana's favorite store, Harvey Nichols in Knightsbridge, arranged for her to shop in the early morning, before the store officially opened at nine A.M.

Prince Charles decided to have a quiet word with his mother. He explained that while nothing was intrinsically wrong with the marriage, Diana was upset and unhappy with her new life. Her state of mind wasn't being helped by the constant harassment of the press. He didn't need to point out to the Queen that pregnancy aggravated everything. He was genuinely concerned that Diana's moods might have a deleterious effect on the unborn child. He believed that if she were given more peace and more room to breathe, she would have a chance to pull herself together and settle down to life as a royal wife. It was only a hope, but Charles thought it worth a try. The Queen agreed.

Despite a barely disguised antipathy to the media, the Palace decided they had little choice but to seek the aid of the press and television. The Queen's Press Secretary, Michael Shea, an urbane former diplomat and a crime-thriller writer in his private life, formulated a plan with the Queen.

On a Tuesday, eighteen days before Christmas and four-and-a-half months after the wedding, the editors of national newspapers, television, and radio were invited to Buckingham Palace to discuss with Shea how to balance the very real public interest in the Royal Family—and in particular the Princess of Wales—with their need for privacy. It was the first meeting of its kind in twenty-five years.* No demands were made, no orders issued. But after painting a picture of an immature Princess in turmoil, Michael Shea suddenly told the gathering, "Now, you are about to meet the most anxious mother-in-law in the land," and the media executives were ushered into the presence of the Queen.

She chatted informally with them. The Princess, the newspeople were told, felt totally beleaguered. There was concern, too, about the effects that relentless hounding might have on the young mother-to-be, who had not been subjected to the continuous public exposure since early childhood, unlike other members of the Royal Family. She was finding it very difficult to cope, and the people who loved her and cared for her were anxious.

The Queen also feared the long-term effects such unprecedented and zealous press harassment would have on Diana, and she was worried that if the press didn't cool things down, Diana's anxieties about the media might

---

* In 1956, when Charles was eight, he became the first heir to the throne to attend an ordinary school. The anxious Queen invited the media for a discussion because she feared they might be too obtrusive in their efforts to report on and photograph the young Prince at school. On that occasion, most newspaper editors readily acquiesced to her request to leave him alone after initial photographs.

continue in the future, when she would be playing a more important role in the life of the country.

The subject of photographers pursuing Diana in the village high street at Tetbury, near Highgrove, was raised. The off-duty Princess, it appeared, could not even step out for a packet of wine gums—small, nonalcoholic fruity sucking candies—without coming face to face with a lens or two. Barry Askew, the recently appointed editor of Britain's largest-selling Sunday tabloid, the *News of the World*, had a question. "Would it not be possible," he inquired deferentially, and with a certain devastating logic, "for the Princess to send a servant out to buy her wine gums?"

"That, if I may say so, is quite the most pompous suggestion I have ever heard," the monarch responded majestically.

The press used to observe a voluntary code of conduct that left the Royal Family in peace while they were on holiday. But all that had been abandoned in the scramble to get exclusive pictures of the young Princess.

It was hoped, said Michael Shea, that this tradition might be resumed when the Royal Family went to Sandringham, and that the editors would consider the private life of the Princess *private*, and *not* use material from freelance or foreign photographers that invaded her privacy.

For a while after this meeting, the British newspapers did leave the Princess alone, but she had become such a hot property—magazine editors at this time reported that a cover of Diana in color boosted sales by a remarkable 10 percent—that it wasn't long before they once again had their prying lenses trained on her as soon as she set foot outside the gates of Kensington Palace.

The couple's marital problems worsened, as so many problems do, at Christmas. The family gathered en masse at Windsor Castle and then went on to Sandringham, the Norfolk house close to the home where Diana had been raised. She should have been happy being on home territory, but this time she had something else to make her angry: game shooting.

Most members of the Royal Family, particularly the

Duke of Edinburgh and Prince Charles, are keen shots. It is very much a "royal" sport. It is enjoyed by most of Charles's friends, and is taken with the utmost seriousness by those who participate. Being a good shot is a virtual necessity among most of the English aristocracy; regular holidays are planned around the shooting seasons. Rearing game birds to shoot is a peculiarly British upper-class pastime which leaves most of the rest of the people unmoved. Those who do not shoot consider it a slaughter of beautiful birds.

The growing controversy about blood sports in the United Kingdom has had no impact whatsoever on the Royal Family. Charles, who used to shoot frequently with Lord Mountbatten, loves what he fervently believes is a sport and is proud that he is a good shot. But although Diana was raised in the English countryside, where those who love shooting regard those who disagree as practically subversive, she passionately felt that rearing game birds for the purpose of killing them was brutalizing and disgusting. She accompanied Charles and his guests on one shoot and was visibly upset by what she witnessed. She tried to persuade Charles not to kill birds—in vain. She never went on another shoot with him.

During that New Year's holiday at Sandringham, shooting became a great bone of contention between the couple. Every day, as Charles was about to go out, he and his wife would argue violently. She would usually begin by asking him not to go. Then she would plead. Finally she would shout obscenities at him, describing in no uncertain terms what she thought of a man who could coldbloodedly kill harmless pheasant, partridge, and grouse.

Charles was utterly dumbfounded that his wife could hold views so opposite to his. She had certainly never propounded such ideas when they were engaged and had been living close together for over four months. He was appalled by her behavior. Worst of all, she was becoming an embarrassment.

One morning at Sandringham, the Queen was accompanying her son and husband, while they went out shooting, to watch the gun dogs at work. Charles asked Diana to go with them. She refused. He then tried persuasion, then pleading. Instead of yielding, Diana begged him to stay home with her, but Charles had already agreed to go. Staying with his wife was impossible.

As he left the house to join his parents, who were already waiting outside, an overwrought Diana rushed to a window and screamed at Charles: "You fucking bastard. There you go, leaving me alone again. Go if you want, you shit, you bastard!" The Queen and Prince Philip heard every word.

Hunting was another bête noire of Diana's. She believes it cruel and feels man has no right whatsoever to hunt the fox. She thinks that people who want to practice the art of hunting and riding over fences and open ditches should only "drag-hunt," in which a horseman drags the carcass of a dead fox across the countryside for hounds and huntsmen to follow. She is also adamantly opposed to hunting deer.

To Charles, these attitudes were near heresy. The Royal Family is very keen on horses and riding. Although she is in her sixties, the Queen still enjoys a quiet ride around Sandringham or Windsor Park. Princess Anne is a skilled National Hunt rider, and Charles's favorite sport is polo. It was inevitable that he should follow the aristocracy's custom of riding to hounds, which he considers a wonderful sport because it pits the skill of the rider against a horse, which neither knows nor cares whether the rider is a prince or a pauper (although it has been pointed out that precious few of the latter are seen on the hunting fields of England).

Charles decided that if Diana could learn to ride again, this might help narrow the chasm between their attitudes toward country life and the hunt. Because she was conscious that she complained a great deal, Diana decided to make the effort. She tried hard but was obviously apprehensive whenever she went for a lesson. Charles tried walking around Sandringham with her on a leading rein, but she simply could not overcome her fear. Further, she felt that even if she had lessons for a year or more, she would never be able to keep up with Charles, especially on the hunting field, which demands a fairly high standard of skill. She took the easy way out. She stopped riding.

Charles did finally persuade Diana to *walk* her horse to hounds. Unfortunately, the stark reality of chasing a fox round the countryside until it was half dead from exhaustion and then watching it being torn to pieces by a pack of hounds hit her viscerally. All her anti-blood-sport feelings rushed to the surface. She was determined she would never go hunting again and would do all in her power to dissuade Charles from doing so as well. This provoked still more bitter arguments, which further undermined their already shaky relationship. They had been married barely six months, and their marriage was rapidly coming apart.

Charles was at his wits' end. He knew that no matter what happened he could *never* divorce Diana, under *any* circumstances. Neither the Queen nor he himself would even consider it. If necessary—and Charles was simply preparing a worst-case scenario, since the marriage was still young—the only option available was to lead separate lives while appearing to the outside world to be still married.

The Queen realized that Diana had a daunting task ahead of her. After all, the great majority of men and women who have married into the present Royal Family have never really accepted the discipline of the system and become out-and-out royals, as she would have liked, but have instead led their own private lives. Princess Anne's husband, Captain Mark Phillips, never wanted to be an on-duty royal who undertook official duties. He opted out of the system and made himself a career as a horseman and gentleman farmer, spurning the distinction of a title from the Queen—despite her urging—that would ensure that her grandchildren would not be commoners.

The aristocratic Sir Angus Ogilvy, the husband of Princess Alexandra, a cousin of the Queen's, decided to keep his job in the City of London as a director of various companies rather than join The Firm. He is hardly ever seen at his wife's side when she is on official royal duties.

Princess Margaret's former husband, Lord Snowden, started off by escorting his wife to all her official functions, always walking a few steps behind her, seemingly at loose ends. But when the marriage ended in divorce, Lord Snowden returned to being a full-time photographer.

In contrast, Princess Michael of Kent, whose divorce and Catholicism made her a very controversial bride indeed for Prince Michael, who is another cousin of the Queen's, took to her royal duties with such enthusiasm, that early on in her marriage it was said "she was more royal than the royals," and she was sometimes described as "pushy." After receiving a great deal of unwanted publicity about her friendship with an American millionaire, Princess Michael virtually retired from official duties.

But these are the "minor" royals, on the fringe of the inner circle and therefore more or less at liberty to do as they please—within reason. The Princess of Wales does not have that alternative. She knew when she accepted Charles's proposal that she would necessarily become a full-fledged member of the Royal Family and abide by all the rules of behavior that were expected of her. She cannot opt out of her royal duties and return to her job at the Young England Kindergarten. Because she is Charles's wife and the country's future Queen, her career is to be the Princess of Wales, and she must play an integral part in Charles's public life and be seen to be taking on royal duties and engagements. Furthermore, she at least has to seem to be enjoying them.

As the months dragged on, Charles became more concerned about Diana's apparent inability to come to terms with the life she must lead. The poise apparent on her wedding day was gone. She had once again turned shy whenever she was in the company of anyone but Charles. When they were alone, she would beg him to stay and look after her and not spend so much time on his official duties.

Many who had worked alongside Prince Charles for

some time were pessimistic. The pair were simply too different in age, interests, and temperament to develop a mature, congenial relationship. The more his friends saw the couple together, the more they thought Charles had concluded he had made a dreadful mistake.

Within months of their wedding day, Charles realized that what he had feared, what he had discussed endlessly with Earl Mountbatten and his closest aides, had occurred. The warmth and love that he and Diana had shared during the happy months before the wedding and throughout their honeymoon were gone.

And there was a lifetime ahead.

9

❯❯❯❮❮❮

A Dogged Di Confronts the Prince and Gets Away With It

Before she married Charles, Prince of Wales, Lady Diana Spencer was pictured by the media as a naïve, rather placid young kindergarten teacher who had captured the heart of the heir to the throne, an erroneous idea—in fact, a myth—embraced even by some of Charles's staff.

Underestimating Diana was a fatal career error. Before long, nearly forty employees, from Charles's closest senior aides to his menial household staff, quit or were fired. With one exception, it now appears, they all had to leave their posts either because Diana wanted to be rid of them or they found it impossible to work under her command. The kindergarten aide proved not so simple or pliable after all.

Friends of Prince Charles maintain, probably accurately, that Diana was determined to replace all the key staff members she inherited when she married. They were essentially Charles's people, and she wanted her own retinue who would be faithful, above all, to her personally.

As Diana saw it, most of her husband's loyal staff tended to treat her as a young, inexperienced interloper who didn't know how to handle employees or behave in the best traditions of the Royal Family. At the time, of course, that was quite true.

Perhaps the most important member of the Prince's staff is the private secretary, because of the influence he can have not only on Charles himself, but also on his friends and acquaintances, his life-style, the functions he attends, and, as it turned out, the Prince's new wife. Charles selected an old friend, the Honorable Edward Adeane, for this position.

Adeane had been virtually destined for royal service. His great-grandfather, Lord Stamfordham, had been private secretary first to Queen Victoria, then to the Prince of Wales in the early years of this century. The family was steeped in the tradition of royal service. Edward himself had been a page boy to the Queen, and his father, Lord Michael Adeane, had been first equerry and then principal private secretary to Charles's mother, the Queen.

The son, Edward Adeane, was a brilliant barrister, nine years older than the Prince, but appearing to be even older. Unmarried, dapper, and with an impeccable educational background of Eton and Cambridge and having an old-fashioned air, he was a perfect royal courtier.

Adeane neither hunted nor played polo, but he did share the Prince's enthusiasm for shooting and fishing. Edward would often return from country weekends with a brace of pheasants or a fresh salmon. His life was one of wealth and privilege. He lived at Albany, the select block of apartments off Piccadilly where only the rich and famous reside, and he belonged to the exclusive Brooks Club.

Edward Adeane was a shrewd adviser and counselor whose job, he thought, was to make sure the Prince of Wales, and even the Princess of Wales, carried out their duties in the proper royal manner. He never wavered in his conviction that the dignity of the Crown should be preserved and put first at all times.

Although he had a lucrative practice as a libel lawyer, Adeane unhesitatingly gave it up to continue the family tradition of service to the Royal Family. Edward confidently expected that for the rest of his working life he would serve Charles as Prince of Wales and later as King.

He was wrong. Within a few years Diana had maneuvered Charles's trusted friend and adviser right out of a job and thrown his family tradition into a dustbin.

Adeane was more conservative than Charles. He had considerable reservations about many of Charles's ideas, and though the two men admired each other, they often disagreed. Adeane wanted Charles to carry out the traditional role of the heir apparent and not use his position and power to promote interests like the Prince's Trust for underprivileged youngsters or to make controversial statements on modern British architecture. He preferred that Charles maintain a lower profile and not challenge the establishment.

Still, Charles and Edward had a good working relationship. Charles respected his friend's intellect, though he thought him out of touch with modern life.

Adeane's relationship with Princess Diana began poorly. He was incensed by Diana's attitude: she thought she should have access to her husband at all times and for whatever reason. He felt duty should come before family life.

Even his closest colleagues agreed that Edward didn't understand women. His view of them was rooted in the nineteenth century: One should always be charming to women, but they merited scant attention. Their role was to be subservient.

Diana was jealous of Charles's time and would not be put off by any royal employee. She and Adeane clashed repeatedly, at all levels. Charles repeatedly tried to bring each to respect the other's position in his life, but their antipathy was real—and deep. As one of Diana's friends remarked, "When the two of them were in a room together, you could cut the atmosphere with a knife."

"I cannot understand why you push so much paper to the Prince," Diana repeatedly told the hapless Adeane. In actuality, Charles had never displayed the same disciplined approach to state business that his mother did, and now the state papers would sometimes pile up. In the mornings, Adeane would often be kept waiting (and fuming inwardly) for an hour before he could see Charles privately to go through papers or plan the days ahead. To Adeane this amounted to dereliction of duty. The fact that the Prince was with Diana, or, more likely, with Prince William in the nursery, only heightened his concern that Diana was interfering in Charles's royal role.

For a time Adeane put up with Diana's interference. He believed that sooner or later Charles would realize that the affairs of state were suffering because he was spending too much time with Diana and William. But Diana had done a good job of convincing Charles that his wife and children had to come first. Adeane just couldn't understand Diana's hold on Charles. When his father had worked as the Queen's private secretary, he had enjoyed her complete attention to the exclusion of all else.

Charles realized what was going on and often agreed with Adeane, but he couldn't bring himself to contravene Diana's wishes. Marriage and fatherhood were still a novelty for him, and he tended to let his strong-willed wife have her own way, if only for the sake of peace. When he had to choose between Adeane and his wife, Diana won every time.

It couldn't go on that way. The tension and conflict were too great. At the end of 1984 Adeane confronted Charles. He told the Prince that if he didn't have greater access, there was no point in his continuing as principal private secretary. He pointed out that Charles was neglecting his duty to the nation. Charles understood but was afraid to upset his wife. There was a steaming row between Adeane and Diana.

Diana realized that Charles had been siding with her and yielding more and more to her demands—which meant she was given preference over Adeane. Sometimes she would relent and allow Charles to attend to his work, but she still, on other occasions, dug in her heels and demanded that Charles accede to her wishes and spend more time with her.

Humphrey Mews, a former Guards officer, joined Charles's staff as secretary after his marriage and became close to Diana. He remembered: "It was obvious Diana detested Adeane. She thought him supercilious and superior. She always felt he was looking down his nose at her. She felt vulnerable whenever he was around because of the difference in their intellect. And I think Adeane believed Diana was refusing to acknowledge her role, that of the Princess of Wales, the wife of the Prince.

"One day, Adeane knocked at the door and there was no reply. He knocked a couple more times, and there was still no reply. So he knocked even louder and opened the door. Diana was sitting alone in the room. He had mistakenly believed that Charles was with her. Diana roundly accused him of barging into her private rooms without permission. She told him to get out immediately.

"Adeane was taken aback. He began arguing with her, explaining precisely the reason he had entered. Diana's anger took over. She shouted and screamed at Adeane, ordering him out of her room. For a while he stood his ground and tried to placate her. But she wouldn't listen. She was in a fury. Eventually, white with rage at being spoken to that way, Adeane withdrew." Charles sided with Diana, and Adeane, as a man of principle, resigned.

The departure of Edward Adeane in the spring of 1985 was seen in Buckingham and Kensington palaces as a remarkable victory for the young Diana. Most people in the royal circle believed the shy Princess would crumble before the authority of men such as Adeane. But Diana had won the day, and convincingly. Overnight, those in the royal circle saw Diana in a different light. This was no weak and ineffectual bride, but a young woman of remarkable determination who had the ability to get her own way, even against the strongest adversary.

Adeane's forced departure proved that Charles was capable of being "persuaded" to do most of the things Diana wanted. However, some friends remarked that Charles had also spent his entire life seeing a woman, his mother the Queen, in command of the family, the monarchy, and the country. Perhaps he didn't understand that he had to be master in his own house—he didn't have to bow to the wishes of his wife the way his father, Prince Philip, had to.

At a dinner party days after resigning, Adeane told companions, "I am deeply distressed at what happened. I would not have resigned, but I was deeply frustrated. I did not resign because of my relationship with Charles; we could handle that together. It was because of Diana's attitude and her insistence that she should have first call on Charles's time no matter what."

Diana wasn't sorry to see Adeane leave. Dislodging the most senior aide to the Prince of Wales was no mean achievement for a young woman of twenty-three. For his part, Adeane confided, "I can't get out of this bloody place quick enough."

About the same time, Prince Charles lost another important member of his inner cabinet, one of his close aides. He had taken on Michael Colborne as secretary to his private office in 1975.

Michael Colborne was a chief petty officer who had befriended the Prince when he was serving on HMS *Norfolk*. Aboard ship, Charles was unable to find any brother officers who would treat him as one of them. But Colborne was not awed by status or position. Along with another noncommissioned officer, George Summers, he invited the Prince, half jokingly, to look in to the petty officers' mess any time for a nightcap or a chat. To their amazement, he did just that.

Charles was intrigued by Colborne and Summers, and particularly by Colborne, who was fourteen years his senior, married, with a son. The two NCOs and the Prince got on surprisingly well. Charles would regularly appear in the mess late at night, and the three would chat for an hour or so over a drink or a mug of cocoa. The Prince thoroughly enjoyed this routine, and a friendship developed. It was natural, ordinary. But for Charles, having commoners for pals was different from anything he had ever known.

Charles was fascinated by stories of how ordinary people lived. He would question them about their family lives, their homes, how they spent their holidays, and what they did on weekends. They usually told him straight, but sometimes Colborne, a man with a dry sense of humor, couldn't resist pulling the Prince's leg. He once explained to Charles, deadpan, that Wrens were not permitted to use elastic to hold up their panties but had to wear suspenders. For a while the trusting Prince believed him.

After leaving the navy, Charles did not forget Colborne, an efficient, businesslike professional seaman. He liked him as a man and admired his honesty and straightforwardness. After behind-the-scenes string-pulling, Colborne was released from the navy and worked closely with Charles for ten years as a sort of business manager. He and the Prince grew extraordinarily close, to the irritation of others in the tight-knit, mainly aristocratic, and sycophantic royal circle.

In public Colborne would unfailingly spring to the defense of the Prince. In private, face to face with Charles, he was brutally honest with him. Their relationship, say royal insiders, thrived on mutual respect. Each was mature enough to tolerate the other's flaws—the Prince's bouts of sulkiness and Colborne's moments of frustration with the protocol, jealousy, and starchiness that abounded in the closed Palace world. But even that relationship, probably the closest Charles has ever had with any member of staff and the most fulfilling, did not last. After ten years Colborne resigned, to the dismay of the Prince— and the Princess as well.

Colborne had had enough of the backbiting and bitching that went on behind the scenes in the royal household, but, more important, after twenty-three years in the navy and a decade in royal service, he wanted to see more of his wife, Shirley.

It was April 1984 when the Prince first received Colborne's notice. He was dismayed and at first took no notice of the unwelcome letter, for Charles has a habit of ignoring bad news. Colborne had to press his boss for an agreed leaving date, but although Charles wanted his friend and employee to stay, he was too proud to say so directly.

Instead, he brought subtle pressures to bear. One Palace source maintains he even phoned Colborne's wife and urged her to persuade her husband to withdraw his resignation. But Colborne was adamant, and in a typical act of generosity, Charles finally organized a well-paid senior job in December 1984 in the City of London with an old friend of his, the chairman of a big insurance company, and he and his old naval friend have never lost touch.

Of all Charles's staff members, Diana was closest to Colborne. Yet he was the only one who decided to leave entirely of his own free will. All the others were forced out by the willful Princess.

Diana would often seek Colborne's advice. She would ask him about protocol and role. She almost always went along with what he told her. Colborne was no Palace factotum, living the life of a royal toady. Diana never liked those people, never could abide having them around. Colborne spoke his mind and was honest in the advice he gave her.

When single, Charles had an inner circle of handpicked men who were his constant and closest companions. But within a couple of years after his marriage to Diana, they were all gone. Most couldn't work with Princess Diana, who showed early on that she did not want Prince Charles's leftovers. It also meant that with her own people in positions of power, she had control over the royal household. It didn't take Diana long to figure out the royal conundrum: Unless she had her own people in positions of power and influence in the Palace, she would have no control of her own life. And Diana was determined that, Princess or not, she would be mistress of her own destiny.

Diana told one of her former flatmates, "They just try to tell me what to do all the time as though I have no mind of my own." Those in the Palace soon realized they had made a monumental mistake.

One of the first casualties of Diana's campaign to assert herself was Prince Charles's valet, Stephen Barry. Barry, a

homosexual, had become Charles's valet in 1969, when
Charles and Barry were both twenty-one. Barry grew
close to Prince Charles. He loved his job and the kudos it
gave him among his gay friends in London. He was proud
of working for Charles, and for twelve years he undoubtedly did a first-class job as his valet.

He served the Prince in many ways. He was his
dresser, tended his vast wardrobe, which included caring
for the dozens of uniforms Charles had to wear. Each
morning he would select the Prince's clothes for the day
and advise him on style and color, sometimes taking hours
the night before to decide which tie Charles should wear.
During their time together, Barry bought the great part of
Charles's clothes, doing all the Prince's personal shopping.

Barry was not well paid, but he didn't care. He adored
the life he led and would do anything for his employer.

Stephen Barry traveled the world with Charles, living
his life out of a suitcase, accompanying the Prince wherever he went. His being gay was probably an advantage,
since the job was not suitable for anyone with family com-
mitments.

Stephen Barry knew everything about the Prince: his
girlfriends, his love life, his pleasures, his hates. He was
closer to Charles than even the private detective who
shadowed the Prince. Too close, thought Diana, when she
came into Charles's life.

Barry's fate was sealed that first day, when Diana realized that Stephen Barry knew more about her husband,
and his past, than she ever would. The two of them shared
many secrets—most pertinently, about Charles's love life
—which she would never be privy to. After so many years
together, a special relationship had developed between
them. But Diana wanted to be the one and only person
really close to her husband. She wanted the valet to keep
his distance and involve himself only with the care of
Prince Charles's clothes and nothing more. Diana felt that
everything else of a personal nature was a matter for her
and Charles. She also did not like the fact that he was gay.
Barry had to go.

For his part, Barry found it difficult to work for Charles
as a married man. He had been responsible for escorting
Lady Diana across London and to the country for secret
meetings with Charles. At first they were good friends.
She had needed him in those early days. She would question Barry about the Prince, about his life-style, his
moods, his work, in fact, about everything that a future
wife would want to discover. Barry found Diana far less
pretentious and far more open and friendly than some of
Charles's former girlfriends. He liked the way Diana
seemed to trust him and treated him as a friend rather
than a servant.

But after the marriage, everything changed. Diana no
longer needed the gay valet.

Barry became jealous of Diana. In a sense, she had
taken over his role, and he felt supplanted. Egged on by
friends, he decided to write a book, *Royal Service*, about
his years with Charles. To his credit, Barry did not reveal
the most intimate details of Charles's life, although he
could easily have done so. He couldn't bear to be that
disloyal to the man he had hero-worshipped for nearly all
his adult life.

Barry gave his notice to Charles three months after the
wedding. He disliked constantly visiting Highgrove because he much preferred life, particularly his weekends,
in and around London, where he could enjoy the gay
scene. Further, Diana gently eased him out, explaining
that she, as Charles's wife, would take over much of
Barry's former role. It was clear to Barry that Diana's
arrival fundamentally altered his relationship with
Charles.

In his book, he writes: "I knew I couldn't face spending
nearly all my time at Highgrove, so it seemed the appropriate moment to say farewell. I would never have resigned while the Prince was single—there would have
been no reason to do so. But now he was a married man,
and with less need of someone like me around, it seemed
a good idea to go."

Barry went out of his way to show he hadn't fallen out
with the Princess: "Diana grinned when we discussed my

resignation and said to me, 'People will say we've had a terrible row!'

" 'As long as we know we haven't, that's all right, isn't it?' I said."

But he added: "I think that perhaps she was a little relieved."

Naïvely, Stephen Barry intended no disloyalty to his Prince by publishing his book. Indeed, he had written a personal letter to Charles explaining why he had decided to write it.

Addressing the Prince as Your Royal Highness, he explained that he had told his story in book form, and not as an instant newspaper story, "so there would be no great shock or surprise . . . which might have upset Your Royal Highness insofar as not knowing what was coming next.

"It seems slightly ironic that at present there are so many books published, mostly inaccurate, about yourself and The Princess.

"Here now is an opportunity for me that will do no harm, and of course the financial side of things will provide for my future."

Reminding the Prince of Wales that his meager Buckingham Palace pension was frozen until he was sixty-five, Barry, some thirty years short of that birthday, pointed out the pension would be virtually worthless then and explained that profits from the book would give him a chance to start a business.

"I therefore was hoping that you might turn an official blind eye and take a lenient view of this matter," he wrote, concluding hopefully: "I would be only too pleased to talk to Your Royal Highness or Mr. Adeane on any point or changes in the draft," signing himself dutifully "Your humble and obedient servant, Stephen."

Charles could have pursued his indiscreet valet through the courts for his breach of confidence, but he could not bring himself to do it. But Edward Adeane, then still the Prince's private secretary, fired off warning letters to Barry, pointing out his legal duty. He reminded Barry that when he had first come to the Palace at the age of eighteen, in September 1966, he had signed a long-forgotten employment contract containing a binding confidentiality clause.

Barry was so alarmed by Adeane's letters that he made arrangements though a New York literary agent, Lucianne Goldberg, for the book to be published in the United States, where the right of free speech is far stronger than in Britain. The book was published there in 1983, despite Adeane's threats of reprisals.

Charles was badly shaken by Barry's disclosures, although at one time he joked about it. "I hear the newspapers are after you for your story of your life with me," he had teased when Stephen was about to leave royal service. "I don't know how much money they are offering you. But I wonder what they would give me for my account of my life with you."

After he left the Palace, the stylish, handsome Stephen Barry began a jet-setting life in the south of France, New York, and America's West Coast. He wasn't long able to enjoy the £250,000 his book brought in. Soon after its publication, he contracted AIDS and died in a London hospital in October 1986, at the age of thirty-seven.

During the early days of Charles's marriage, another person once important in his life also left royal employment. Oliver Everett, a brilliant diplomat with a bright future in the Foreign Office, had accepted the position of assistant private secretary to Prince Charles for a two-year tour of royal duty—a salaried position attached to the Royal Family—from 1978. The two men got on well. Everett was only a few years older than Charles, and they had much in common. Because of their love of polo they had become friends, although Everett always called Charles sir and Charles called him Oliver. Like many of Charles's aides at the time, he was both a friend and an adviser; they were far closer than the usual employer and employee. And above all, Everett was someone on whom Charles could rely in an emergency.

It was Oliver Everett who saved the Prince's life when he was playing polo in ninety-degree temperatures in Palm Beach, Florida, in 1980. Charles had dismounted at the end of a hard chukker. A moment later his legs buckled under him as he collapsed from heat exhaustion. He lay unconscious, motionless, a couple of feet from his pony. Everett ran to the Prince, grabbed a bucket of cold water used for washing down the ponies, and began to bathe his face with it. Two full minutes passed before he managed to revive Charles. He then accompanied him to the hospital.

The collapse was hushed up and reported as merely a touch too much of the Florida sun. But it was more serious than that, and Charles knew it. Regaining consciousness, the alarmed Charles found Everett at his side. Remembering what had happened, he declared, "Oliver, thank God you were here. I think I would have died. Do you realize you saved my life?"

On their return from Florida, the Queen immediately rewarded Everett by making him a member of the Royal Victorian Order. At the end of his royal tour of duty he returned to the Foreign Office and was sent as a senior diplomat to Madrid. But immediately after the engagement to Diana was announced, Charles personally begged him to interrupt his career and return to royal duty, not as an aide to himself, but as Diana's private secretary. The salary was only £16,000 a year, half his pay at the Foreign Office. Purely out of loyalty to Charles, Everett agreed.

It was a decision he was soon to regret. Diana knew that Charles and Oliver had been friends for years. She saw more than an employer-employee relationship between them, which ignited a spark of jealousy. They would go off together riding their polo ponies and holding practice chukkers in the afternoons. Diana was already unhappy with all the demands on her husband's time: the occasions when he had to get up at six A.M. to perform yet another royal duty in a remote part of Britain, the hours he spent with his private secretary. She rarely saw him. Instead of having the number one position in his life, she had been relegated to a great deal less. She often remarked, either to Charles or to Everett, "Do you have to see so much of each other?"

The royal staff believe that six months after the wedding, Diana decided that Everett was becoming too bossy toward her and that she would get rid of him in order to appoint her own secretary. It didn't help that Oliver Everett was very bright and quick-witted. He learned quickly and seemed able to cope with anything without even trying. Because he was clever, Everett couldn't seem to understand that some people—like Diana—take longer than others to learn.

Charles had asked Oliver to shepherd the Princess through royal life, to teach her everything she should know about Palace routine: what she should or should not do, to whom she should write and talk and on what subject. Oliver took to the role too enthusiastically. He tried to teach Diana everything she needed to know within a year. Diana probably needed much more time to absorb her dismaying new role and was demoralized by her inability to master Oliver Everett's lessons.

Every day Oliver sent her notes and messages, which was normal Palace routine. But instead of making them short and simple so she could understand, he would send long, detailed instructions that utterly confused Diana, who found his messages tedious and irritating. Of course Charles had asked him to leave no stone unturned, so Everett wanted to explain everything so there was no possibility of error. Charles realized that joining The Firm was daunting. The Queen and most of the royal household were not only enmeshed in the details of protocol and the correct social balance, but took the view that the Palace should always appear above the executive government, Parliament, and the Church, and in certain circumstances the law itself.

The relationship between Diana and her private secretary became strained. Often, Diana wouldn't bother to read all his instructions. And if she did, she couldn't understand them. When she made mistakes, as she did, Everett would not only point out where she had gone wrong, but would also remind her that he had already instructed her in the correct way. The more exasperated Oliver became with Diana, the more tension built up between them.

As the weeks passed, the strain grew worse. Charles interceded and Everett tried to placate the Princess, but it was too late. Diana began to object to the advice her private secretary was offering. The more she objected, the more Charles acquiesced to her. But Everett wouldn't yield to Diana. He knew his job and what he had to do, even at the expense of ruffling a few feathers. He persisted in trying to get Diana to do things his way.

Humphrey Mews recalled: "I heard about the problems between Diana and Everett. It seems extraordinary there should have been problems because for more than two years Everett had been everything to her—friend, confidant, big brother, uncle. You name it, he played the role. And she had needed him so very much.

"One example, which took place near the end of their relationship, was when Diana did not want to carry out a certain engagement which Everett knew she should attend.

"Diana told Everett that she wasn't going to do it. Everett said that she should. She refused. He tried again. She told him that no matter what he said, she was not going to take his advice. He told her that she didn't really have any option. That was the remark that broke her anger. She began shouting obscenities at him, demanding who he thought he was telling the Princess of Wales what she should and should not do. She was the princess and she would decide. And if he didn't like it, then he could get out of her life, and Charles's life, for good.

"I understand that row finally decided both Charles and Everett that there was no future in Everett's staying on at Kensington Palace as her adviser."

Diana was absolutely determined to rid herself of Everett. One day she put a huge note to Charles on the desk in his study. In large capital letters it read:

OLIVER MUST GO.

The last person Charles wanted to fire was Everett, and yet he knew that he had to move him away from Diana and get him out of Kensington Palace. Charles turned to an old friend, Lord King, boss of British Airways. "Get me Lord King," he told one of his aides.

Within minutes the phone rang. "I've got a problem, Lord King," Charles said, "and I wonder if you can help. What I want to know is how you fire a senior member of your staff?"

"Oh," said Sir John, "that's very simple, very simple indeed. What I do is summon the person, whoever he is. When he arrives at my door, I say, 'Fuck off.'"

Holding the phone, Prince Charles stood openmouthed with amazement. He did not take Lord King's advice.

Diana's objections became more heated. The disagreements became rows, many ending with Diana in tears asking Charles for help. Diana once became so exasperated she shouted at Charles, "Get him out of my life. For God's sake, get rid of him! I can't take it anymore!"

Charles faced an impossible situation. He knew that Oliver had done everything correctly, and as he had asked him to do. But the situation between Oliver Everett and Diana couldn't last. Charles knew his friend would eventually have to go. At this juncture, hoping for a good marriage, Charles was willing to do almost anything to keep Diana happy. If that meant losing a good friend and employee, so be it. After nine argumentative, embarrassing months, Oliver agreed he should resign.

Having persuaded Everett to return to royal duty after the wedding and therefore interrupting and, some say, badly derailing his highly promising diplomatic career, Charles was loath to let his old friend down. If Everett had not returned to work for the Palace, friends at the Foreign Office believed, he would have been an ambassador by the mid-eighties. Amends had to be made, so it was arranged that Everett should take over the job of librarian and assistant keeper of the Queen's archives, a prestigious back-room job usually reserved for an old, favored royal retainer at Windsor Castle, thirty miles away from Diana. Prestigious it may have been, but it was a waste of a brilliant man.

Two days before Christmas 1983, Oliver Everett bowed out. It was a sad farewell for Charles and Everett. Prince

Charles had grown to depend on his advice, especially since the death of Mountbatten. To a great extent, Everett knew Charles well, knew how he thought, what his priorities and concerns were. Everett could usually judge what Charles thought about subjects, problems, and everyday affairs, and more important, how he would react in most circumstances. He was a very useful close companion and adviser, and Charles did not want to lose him.

Charles was proud of the team he had built around himself, including Everett, Colborne, Adeane, his personal police bodyguard John MacLean, and his valet, Stephen Barry. They understood each other and worked well together. They had shown the Prince great personal loyalty, and he had returned that loyalty by putting his trust in them.

But after Diana's arrival on the scene, Charles suddenly realized his retinue had been decimated; everyone wanted to leave because they could not cope with her negativity toward them. She made all of his personal staff feel that they were intruding on the Waleses' personal life when they were simply doing their jobs.

Charles knew that Diana's demands for his time and constant attention had caused trouble. He was forever explaining that he had work to do, a position to uphold, the Duchy of Cornwall to administer, royal duties to perform, visits to make, speeches to write and deliver. But her demands never diminished.

He was at the end of his tether. At first Charles had given in to Diana's demands because she was his bride and he wanted to please her, then because she was pregnant, then because she had a newborn baby to care for, then because she was pregant again. His acquiescence seemed to make her happy for only a few days, then she would be miserable again. She also complained constantly about every one of his staff. His life had never been in such disarray.

By then, Charles had come to understand one of the basic problems: the intellectual gap between himself and Diana was almost unbridgeable. During their engagement, he had loved her and wanted her as his wife, but had been blind to everything else. Not until the first few months of marriage did he realize the new Princess was so lacking in intellect. He was amazed at her lack of interest in politics, economics, industry, in how Britain was governed. He could not comprehend why she religiously watched the soaps on television, listened nonstop to pop music, and was awed by pop stars. He didn't know what to do.

Diana had no explanation other than her feeling she was trapped in a marriage that was making her unhappy. She felt Charles always preferred to be working with his staff, or playing polo, rather than being with her. Given her feeling of being slighted, she naturally resented Charles's work and his team. Every time she persuaded Charles to get rid of a staff member, she felt a twinge of satisfaction or victory, but it was fleeting. Her jealousy was uncontrollable.

She realized Charles was unhappy, and yet she could not sit back and allow him to get on with his work and his life. They fought constantly. She wanted him to give her the love she craved, all the time. She wanted no one around who might distract him or take him away from her. She knew she was being silly, unreasonable, seeking the impossible, but she could not stop herself from acting like a spoiled child.

It only got worse. Trouble was brewing between Diana and the members of the Royal Protection Squad. In Britain, the Royal Family's personal detectives live close to their charges. The job is not rotated, with different men guarding royals around the clock. These private detectives live in the homes of royals and travel with them at all times, throughout Britain and the world. Members of the Royal Family never go anywhere—on official or unofficial business—without the knowledge or permission of their protectors. Only when the royals enter their own homes do the bodyguards give them some privacy.

One of the first detectives assigned to Princess Diana was Superintendent Paul Officer, a senior policeman who was always discreetly in attendance whenever required. But, like Oliver Everett, he tried too hard to instruct and advise Diana, so that she became nervous whenever he was around. A sensitive man, Officer worried too much, which troubled Diana, who read it as a lack of self-confidence.

Officer understood that wherever Diana went he should be with her, no matter what the circumstances. For her part, Diana felt suffocated by Officer. He was behaving like a mother hen, allowing her no personal freedom and demanding to know where she was going, even if she was moving from room to room.

To be fair, Paul Officer was only doing his job, which was becoming difficult. Diana loved to phone friends and pop out to see them without telling him. The consequences for him if some troublemaker had seen her out alone in her car were incalculable.

But at times he probably was overprotective.

One day Diana found Officer waiting outside the bathroom for her. She told him quite bluntly that she was perfectly able to go the john on her own, without being escorted. And often, when she was driving, Officer turned into a back-seat driver, telling her to do this, do that, watch this, watch that. On one occasion, Diana got so fed up that she stopped the car, got out, and told him to drive them back to the palace.

Inevitably, the job took over Officer's life. There was no time for his wife and family; his marriage ended in divorce. Greatly upset, he suddenly changed his life-style— from that of an ordinary policeman to an introverted vegetarian desperately interested in alternative medicine. Diana's trust in him disappeared. Officer sensed that moves were afoot to get rid of him, and he resigned the post.

Once again, Diana felt she had won another victory. Once again, she had gotten her way. Once again, the royal household understood that when Diana made up her mind to dispense with someone, that person would eventually go, no matter how long it took. The Princess of Wales was rapidly gaining a reputation as a hard-nosed, insensitive young woman determined to have her own way in everything, no matter whose feet she trod on or whom she upset in the process.

Not long afterward, another royal minder quit the royal couple. Inspector John MacLean did not argue with his reputation as the toughest man in the Royal Protection Squad, nor did he dispute his reputation as the untidiest. An evening jacket might create the illusion of elegance, but beneath it was a crumpled, unironed shirt. When the rugged Scot went to bed, his clothes, gun, and holster would be strewn all around him. He was a brilliant protection man. Just as he had saved the Prince from pursuit by a scantily clad young model on Bondi Beach, so he would have reacted in the face of a real threat.

Together, MacLean and Officer had shadowed Prince Charles in his bachelor days. Like the Three Musketeers, they became firm friends. They would shoot, ski (MacLean was an expert, passionate skier), and drink together informally, even if they still had to call the Prince sir. They loved their life because everything was straightforward and man to man. Suddenly, when Diana became Princess of Wales, a host of problems entered their lives.

Diana made it plain to Charles that she found MacLean untidy, uncouth, and brash. MacLean decided the fun had gone out of his job after Charles married, and by mutual agreement he quit in 1984 and became a ski instructor in Andorra, in northern Spain. Charles sorely missed him, but Diana was quite pleased to have one fewer of Charles's old friends interfering in her life.

Yet another senior minder who left was Inspector James McMasters, known throughout his career as Lucky Jim. He had served with Charles just before his marriage and, unusually, became very friendly with Diana. They had a lot of laughs together, and Diana came to rely on him; she even referred to him as "my favorite minder." Indeed, he was one of the very few people she would allow to cuddle and feed Prince William. Jim McMasters seemed to have a way with William and could stop his crying when all else failed.

Then, in 1985, the forty-six-year-old McMasters was unceremoniously and mysteriously transferred away from his duties in the Royal Protection Squad. He was promoted to inspector and posted to a suburban London police station at Croydon, then moved again and given a lowly desk job, shunted away from the glamorous and prestigious Royal Protection Squad.

Diana was distressed at his dismissal and urged Charles to intervene. He immediately called senior Scotland Yard officers to a meeting at Buckingham Palace and asked for an explanation. Someone who attended the meeting reported: "Charles was furious and opened the meeting by demanding by whose authority McMasters had been taken off royal protection duty without informing him and gaining his permission. He spoke for a couple of minutes demanding an explanation. A piece of paper was passed to Charles, who was invited to read it silently. He did, then looked around at everyone in the room and threw up his hands in despair.

"It was only known to a few people what the contents of that note were. But it stopped Charles in his tracks, so it had to be something pretty serious."

Three years later, the bachelor McMasters was caught acting suspiciously in a public lavatory and given the option of resigning immediately from the police force or facing prosecution and possible dismissal in disgrace. He quit.

In those first years of marriage some resignations and dismissals were more serious than others. There were maids and cooks and chambermaids and gardeners to whom Diana took a dislike. Charles allowed her to change the staff as she pleased. He didn't like what was going on —after all, she had dispensed with the services of some of his closest staff—but he believed he had no option but to let Diana have her way.

One of the more eccentric characters who worked closely with Charles and Diana in their early married life was a butler, Alan Fisher. He had once worked as a servant at Buckingham Palace but left to become butler and valet to Bing Crosby until the singer's death in 1977. Crosby's widow, Kathy, held him in high regard and asked Alan to accompany her husband's body back from Spain, where her husband had collapsed and died on a golf course not far from Madrid.

One weekend in November 1981, Fisher found himself in the service of Countess Spencer when Charles and Diana were staying at Althorp. He performed his duties with so much style that Diana's stepmother not only convinced the royal couple that Fisher would be right for them, but Fisher swiftly endeared himself to both Charles and, in particular, Diana. Before they left Althorp, they *knew* Alan would be right for them at Kensington Palace—even if his employment was regarded with distinct reservation by Edward Adeane and others in the household.

At first Diana loved this enormous, flamboyant character who was such a contrast to the usual servile dullards who, she felt, only stopped her from enjoying herself. He was fun to have around. He would tell risqué jokes and happily do anything she asked, even take off her boots. But although his larger-than-life personality had struck the right note in Hollywood, it was to prove his downfall in royal service. He became *too* familiar and overstepped the mark.

Fisher didn't care that Diana was now the Princess of Wales and the future Queen of England. He teased her unmercifully, swore in her presence, and made caustic comments about her within earshot. More than once he suggested that she was a very lucky girl to have become the Princess of Wales. In short, he was outrageous.

Only months after being hired, the irrepressible Fisher believed he could do and say what he liked with Diana. As Humphrey Mews relates: "The stories I heard were wonderful, and I believed they were true. Diana had welcomed Fisher as a breath of fresh air into the stuffy household Charles had built up around him. She was doing everything she could in those early years to get rid of all the cobwebs and breathe new, young life into the palace.

"But Fisher didn't realize that he could not get away with treating people the way he had before when working as butler to Bing Crosby or other well-known and wealthy, but not royal, masters.

"He would tell Diana not to be 'silly' or 'foolish.' He'd advise her what to wear; tell her she was wearing the wrong hat or the wrong dress or the wrong hairstyle. He thought he could criticize because he believed, mistakenly, that she had become a close friend because of the way she treated him. To a great extent, Diana's relationship with Fisher went wrong because, foolishly, she had become too palsy, too friendly, with him."

One day at Kensington Palace, Fisher opened the door to lunch guests of the Prince. The visitors—who included Field Marshal Sir Edwin Bramall, chief of defense staff, and Admiral of the Fleet Sir John Fieldhouse, the head of the navy—were accustomed to lunching in great houses in the company of the highest members of the realm. It was pouring. Fisher greeted them at the top of his voice: "I sincerely hope you wipe your feet properly—just like your mother taught you to."

In the end, a battle developed between Fisher and the Princess. They were out to get each other. She tried to catch him in errors, and Fisher responded by being even more insubordinate, suggesting he knew better than she how a princess should behave.

Diana decided that the time had come to get rid of Alan Fisher, and she devised a childish plan. She hid dirty glasses and then complained they were missing. In front of Prince Charles she asked Fisher if he knew where they were. Of course he didn't. A search began, and when the glasses were found, Fisher was blamed. After a few more such petty incidents, Fisher realized the end was near.

He had overplayed his hand, and the eventual outcome was obvious. But in this case it had been Diana, not Charles, who had chosen the fun-loving butler. It had been her mistake, but when she had had enough, he was given marching orders. His employment with the Waleses had lasted two years, from May 1982 to May 1984. Once again, Diana had managed to have things her way, although Fisher claimed he left "because Charles and Diana were too boring." He maintained their dinner parties were boring, most of the people they invited were boring, and he wanted to work in a more entertaining household.

Later, in 1986, their chef, Graham Newbold, quit. He had got on well with Diana until she discovered he had a liking for drink. On one occasion, after he borrowed

Prince Charles's car to go to a farewell party for one of the staff, on its return to Buckingham Palace the car was found with a dent in it, as though it had hit a wall.

Another time Diana searched for Graham so she could check the menus with him for a future dinner. She discovered him asleep on his bed and, worried that he was seriously ill, called the doctor. After the doctor examined Graham in her presence, he told her he was suffering from a hangover, which Diana thought was very funny. But in the end Newbold felt he wasn't perhaps cut out for royal duty. He quit and took a job in a smart hotel in Scotland.

Diana's most important appointment was that of Barbara Barnes as William's nanny. Barbara came to Charles and Diana with an impeccable record of service. For fourteen years she had looked after the children of Princess Margaret's lady-in-waiting, Lady Anne Tennant, and they had apparently adored her. She had a no-nonsense approach to bringing up children: plenty of fresh air and discipline, laced with a sense of humor. She seemed the perfect nanny for the modern royal mother.

But Diana wasn't the usual sort of royal mother who just handed her children over to be reared by a nanny until they were old enough to be packed off to boarding school. If Diana had one talent, it was mothering the young, and she insisted on exercising it with her children. She had never forgotten her own lonely young life and was determined the boys should have a special relationship with her.

When Prince William started to look on Barbara as his second mother, Diana became increasingly perturbed. When William was upset, he would cry out for "Baba"— as he called her—and not for his mother. The attachment of young children to their nannies is natural, but Diana was exceptionally jealous of the strong bond between Barbara and William.

When the same thing started to happen with Prince Harry, Diana decided that Nanny Barnes had to go. She, Diana, would become the children's one and only source of comfort in times of stress.

Various explanations were put forward for the departure of Nanny Barnes, but the real reason was that both William and Harry had become so close to her that whenever Barbara went on holiday, the boys became almost impossible to control and discipline. They wanted "Baba" whenever there was the slightest trouble, and Diana resented that. In effect, Nanny Barnes was fired. It was put to her that perhaps it would be better for everyone, including the children, if she left. She was given no options.

Barbara Barnes was the twenty-fourth member of the staff to leave in six years. All the dismissals and resignations were making Diana quite unpopular in the royal palace. She was experiencing difficulties not only with Charles's former employees, whom she considered "old fuddy-duddies," but also with the younger set she herself had hired.

It was becoming obvious that the source of the turmoil was Diana's inability to cope with her position as Prince Charles's wife and the future Queen.

Diana's father, Earl Spencer, innocently confirmed this problem when he told a newsman: "Diana always gets her own way. I think Charles is learning that now."

10

A Marriage in Trouble

Learning to live with another person always requires adjustments. Diana had to learn to live not only with a husband, but also with the expectations and responsibilities of the English monarchy.

One of Charles's close advisers recalled: "Diana could not get it into her head that she was no longer a free woman, able to go out whenever and wherever she wanted to. She would argue with the bodyguards, plead with them to let her go shopping on her own, or go round to see a chum on her own, or have lunch with someone. When she was told that was not possible, she would sometimes throw a tantrum. She made life very difficult for those whose job it was to protect her. She just seemed to refuse to understand that she was now the Princess of Wales and could not do what she wanted to anymore.

"Sometimes when told she could not do something on her own, she would complain to Charles, sulk and act like a spoiled child. The more she behaved in this fashion, the less respect she earned from her husband. He was appalled that his wife, the Princess of Wales, could behave in such a stubborn, childish manner.

"Diana would spend hours on the phone to her old friends, imploring them to come over and see her because she couldn't get out without her bodyguards. She understood that Charles had duties to perform, but she felt so lonely.

"At first, a number of Diana's friends would visit her, but it was rather an ordeal for them. And her old friends weren't sure they should continue to be so friendly with Diana, now that she was a Princess."

What caused the most conflict was their divergent attitudes toward duty. Diana thought Charles's duty should be to her first, his country second. Charles thought the opposite. The Queen and the Duke of Edinburgh had instilled in him that he had an honorable duty to the Crown and to the British people. His personal life had to be fitted around it. As a bachelor, that accommodation was easy. As a man married to a woman with no sense whatsoever of royal duty, it was almost impossible.

In those first few years of marriage, Diana never accepted this impasse. She naïvely believed that after the birth of their children, Charles would see that family life was more important than his "job." She was wrong, which only made her more angry and frustrated.

Time and again their arguments erupted into angry shouting matches. It was always the same argument. Diana demanded more attention for herself, and Charles reminded her of his duty. Charles hated the shouting matches; he had never been involved in such scenes and could not cope with them. He tried to placate her, tried to reason with her, whenever she became enraged. Often the scene would end with Charles walking out and Diana screaming four-letter abuse at him. When he had gone— leaving not just the room but the house—she would be in a rage of tears, often crying in her frustration. After one such screaming match Diana phoned one of her friends: "I can't take it anymore. He won't listen to reason. I don't know what to do."

One of Diana's bodyguards recalled such a row: "It was at Kensington Palace, a few months after William was born. Charles was going away hunting for the weekend,

leaving on a Friday and returning Saturday night or on the
Sunday morning. Diana was livid. She first accused him of
not telling her he was going away, then accused him of
sneaking off and leaving her and Wills alone in London
for the weekend with nothing to do. Finally she told him
that any self-respecting father would want to stay at home
with his son occasionally. Charles tried to answer each
charge rationally.

"But Diana wasn't listening. She turned on him and let
fly. I left the room in a hurry; I didn't want to hear what
was going on. As I left, I heard her call him a 'bloody
bastard.' I don't know what happened after that. But
Charles did go hunting that weekend."

It was little wonder that Diana and Charles began to
lead separate lives. Charles would not put up with such
behavior from anyone, not even his wife. When the heat
became too overbearing, Charles would fly to Scotland
and sit in peace on a riverbank and fish quietly, alone with
his thoughts and his own frustration at what he considered Diana's "intolerable" behavior.

After his navy tour, Charles had become the busiest of
all royals, carrying out more official engagements than the
rest of his family. The Queen gave him an enormous
workload, which he took on without a murmur of com-
plaint. He never shirked those duties from the moment he
quit the navy, in 1976, until his marriage began to go
wrong. Only then did he begin to question his role in life.
And after his first son, Prince William, was born in 1982,
Charles took on fewer official engagements and spent
more time with Diana and the next heir to the throne.

From the moment she discovered in October 1981 that
she was expecting a baby, Diana was determined to handle the pregnancy her own way, regardless of royal tradition. Members of the Royal Family customarily give birth
in Buckingham Palace. Everyone expected that Diana
would follow suit, but she was a modern mother-to-be
who wanted the best medical equipment at hand. Instead
of the ornate surroundings of the palace, Diana opted for

the medically superior private wing of St. Mary's Hospital in West London.

Her intransigence over the birth caused yet more differences of opinion. Charles would argue that this baby was no ordinary child, but second in line to the throne, and Diana should take that into consideration when reaching decisions. The Queen believed that the baby, like all her own, should be born in the privacy of the palace, but finally she allowed Diana to go to St. Mary's. Diana had won a significant battle with the royal establishment and the Queen herself, someone who rarely finds her views debated, let alone opposed. The Queen did suggest, however, and Diana agreed, that the famous royal gynecologist George Pinker, then fifty-seven, should take charge of the pregnancy and birth. It was Mr. Pinker* who assured the Queen that the facilities at St. Mary's were medically first-class.

Diana did not have an easy pregnancy. She had terrible morning sickness, and it went on for months. The twenty-year-old mother-to-be spent much of her time wandering around Buckingham Palace feeling very sorry for herself, listening to tapes, and watching television. The couple had been married only a few months before Diana learned she was pregnant. Naturally, her constant feeling of being unwell did not help her uneven moods. It was a difficult time for both of them. Charles tried to be a patient, understanding husband, doing everything possible to make Diana feel happy and contented, wanted and loved. But Charles wasn't a naturally loving, caring person to Diana. He had not been shown much love himself while growing up, and he found it difficult to change. Diana wanted to curl up on the sofa and watch television at night with Charles's arms around her. The last thing Charles wanted to do was to watch banal television soap operas. It made him angry that Diana—who would organize her life to make sure to see every episode of "East-

---

* In Britain, a qualified medical doctor uses the term *Mr.* upon becoming a surgeon or consultant. Thus *Mr.* Pinker.

enders" and "Neighbors"—sat and watched "such rubbish" night after night.

But Charles and Diana agreed on one thing: the importance of her pregnancy. Charles wanted to be as involved as any other father-to-be. He even took great interest in reading all the appropriate baby books. Suddenly Charles became fascinated by the whole business of pregnancy and the birth and would read the books aloud to Diana.

They were still living in Buckingham Palace, waiting for the promised apartments in Kensington Palace to be readied. Diana was desperate to move to a home of their own before the baby was born. She pushed Charles to persuade his mother to hurry the renovations at KP along. By royal standards, their new home had to be totally repainted, redecorated, and refurbished for the Prince and Princess of Wales, everything carried out with the utmost attention to detail. Diana just wanted to move in as quickly as possible. Finally, on May 17, 1982, Kensington Palace was ready, and they moved in that day. Diana, now eight months pregnant, was heartily relieved.

Like most young mothers today, Diana had been diligent about her diet and exercise during her pregnancy. She had never smoked and she stopped taking even her occasional glass of champagne or sherry. She also attended classes run by the famous Betty Parsons, a childbirth expert who had been with the Queen when her youngest, Prince Edward, was born. Betty Parsons had imparted her philosophy of childbirth to hundreds of Britain's aristocratic young mothers. She claimed there was no such thing as an unnatural birth and taught relaxation by controlled breathing, with emphasis on different forms of breathing for the various stages of labor. In Diana's final month of pregnancy, Betty Parsons was a frequent visitor at Kensington Palace, checking Diana's progress.

At seven P.M. on Sunday, June 20, 1982, Diana felt her contractions starting. She phoned Betty Parsons: "They've begun," she said, adding, "Well, I think they have." After she described the contractions, Miss Parsons suggested she go to bed. At four A.M., Diana woke with a start. She immediately roused Charles, who was lying by her side. She knew she was about to give birth.

Charles phoned his detective and St. Mary's Hospital. Mr. Pinker was alerted that Diana was on her way. Charles himself drove Diana the two miles to the Paddington hospital with a detective in the back of the car. They arrived at five A.M. With Charles holding her arm, Diana entered a side door and took an elevator to the top floor of the Lindo Wing.

Everything had been prepared. The three adjacent rooms had been cleared of patients. A screen had been put up by Diana's room, and a private telephone installed by her bedside. But there were no luxuries for the Princess, wife to the future King, who was about to give birth to the second in line. Her room was just twelve-by-fourteen feet, with an ordinary metal hospital bed, a side table, a small freestanding wardrobe, a wash basin, a small fridge, and a television in one corner. There was no private bathroom; Diana had to use the one across the corridor.

But Mr. Pinker and Betty Parsons were on hand. "Pick up your surfboard and ride it like a whale," Betty told her when her contractions became more acute. "Remember what you've been taught. Don't forget it. Doggy, doggy, candle, candle [pant, pant, blow, blow]." Whenever necessary, Betty was at Diana's side.

After several hours Mr. Pinker suggested an injection to ease the pain. Diana had wanted an entirely natural birth, but Mr. Pinker advised the painkiller, which she took.

At 9:03 that night, Diana gave birth to a baby son, weighing seven pounds, ten ounces. He had a wisp of fair, short hair and blue eyes. Diana had already decided she would breast-feed the infant. The only other decision was whether her son should be circumcised. Prince Charles had been circumcised when he was five days old, but Diana insisted that her young baby son should not be, and he was not.

Diana amazed most people by insisting on leaving the hospital and taking baby William home to Kensington Palace only twenty-three hours after the birth. Diana would have whatever help was needed, but it was unusual for a young mother to go home so quickly after delivering a first child. After such a long labor, Mr. Pinker was certain Diana would be unable to walk or move about without great discomfort for several days. But she did walk out of the hospital unaided, to the astonishment of the world's press. To journalists waiting outside the hospital for the first picture of the new royal child, Diana looked proud and happy, if tired. She was finally confident and happy in her role. She knew she had achieved an important break-through. She had produced a son, an heir to the throne. And she was still ten days short of her twenty-first birth-day.

Before the birth, Charles stayed at the hospital all day, spending time sitting by Diana's bedside, holding her hand, talking and comforting her. Two hours after the birth, he left the hospital to go to Kensington Palace to sleep. Looking elated but weary, the royal father stepped out into the street, where he found a cheering and singing crowd.

"I'm obviously thrilled and delighted," declared an excited Prince of Wales. "Sixteen hours is a long time to wait. It's rather a grown-up thing, I find," added the Prince endearingly. "Rather a shock to the system."

His new baby looked marvelous, he told the waiting press corps, who were hungry for any scrap of information about the new future King. He was fair, sort of blondish, and had the good fortune not to look like his father.

Despite the birth of a royal heir, friction between Charles and Diana continued, erupting at times into full-scale rows. One of the most public occurred in November 1982, six months after the birth of William, when Charles, Diana, and most of the Royal Family were expected to attend the solemn Annual Festival of Remembrance, in memory of those who died in the two world wars, at the Royal Albert Hall, just a couple of minutes' drive from Kensington Palace. Diana was exhausted after a sleepless night and refused to go. Charles was outraged. He insisted that she go because attendance was a royal tradition. Diana again refused. A shouting match ensued, ending with Diana in tears. Charles stormed out in a fury and went on his own. His wife had suddenly been taken ill and was unable to attend, he told everyone on his arrival at the ceremony.

Minutes after he had gone, the enormity of what she had done hit Diana. She knew it was her duty and that the Queen would be appalled if she were absent for no sound reason. She dressed hurriedly and dashed out to drive herself to the Albert Hall. Her detective, Alan Peters, spotted her heading for her car and insisted on taking the wheel. Diana eventually arrived at the hall after the ceremony had started—to the astonishment of all and the mortification of her husband.

It was an embarrassing error of judgment on Diana's part. Her chair had already been tactfully removed from the royal box. She would have done better to have stayed away. Within hours, news of her late arrival was public knowledge, and the world speculated that there was, *at the very least,* strain in the royal marriage.

As one of Charles's close officials said at the time: "It was very awkward for Charles. He would never, ever query an official engagement. If he had been told he would have to be at the Albert Hall for the next six nights, he would have gone, because that was his duty. No other reason was necessary. There was no argument, none whatsoever. He couldn't understand that anyone could query that."

Diana was unhappy in every aspect of her life. Her husband didn't pay her enough attention. She continued to feel trapped in a fishbowl, with people forever talking about her, photographing her, and watching her every move. Her only escape from the staring crowds and the press photographers was to places like Balmoral, Sandringham, and Highgrove, where she was lonely, bored, and miserable. It was a circle of unremitting misery.

· · ·

The arrival of William began a fundamental change in Diana. Motherhood not only gave her a true role, but also the confidence she needed to organize her life, that of her baby's, and, she hoped, Charles's as well. The way *she* thought they ought to be organized. Diana had at last found a worthy purpose: now her thoughts concerned the needs of her young son rather than self-pity.

Though the Prince helped her with the baby, Diana's demands on him continued to increase. She felt that she couldn't manage without Charles around her the whole time. When he refused, this led to more arguments. She repeatedly challenged his assertion that his royal duties had to come first. No matter what Charles said, she just could not understand his way of thinking.

Once the excitement over the new baby had worn off, Diana became exhausted and depressed. Her appetite disappeared, and she lost so much weight that Charles and the doctors believed she was suffering from the slimmer's disease, anorexia nervosa. She clung to Charles more and more, frequently keeping him from his royal duties. Some believed Diana was deliberately slimming too much, deliberately exposing herself to the dangers of anorexia to win her husband's attention. Now that she had a child, she wanted a proper home and her husband's company for more than a few minutes a day. She sought what every young mother wanted—to be a happy family who did things together.

Charles was baffled. He seemed unsympathetic, but in actuality it was simply that such emotional behavior was foreign to him. He had been brought up in a family in which everyone behaved correctly, no matter what. The Queen, too, was concerned about Diana, but she, like Charles, had been reared with a sense of duty that overcame all ills. Neither she nor Charles could understand Diana's problems. After all, the Princess seemed to have everything—a title, a husband, privilege, and now a child.

The friends Diana had before meeting Charles had generally faded into the background. Most had shied away once Diana joined the closed society of the Royal Family. Diana tried to keep in touch, inviting them

Charles and Diana seen at the altar in St. Paul's Cathedral, London, during their wedding.

The Prince and Princess wave from the coach that carries them back to Buckingham Palace after their wedding.

Crowd scenes around the Palace in London on the day of the
Royal wedding.

A gigantic fireworks display on the eve of the Royal wedding.

Diana, a few weeks before the birth of William, seen at a polo match at Smiths Lawn, Windsor.

The Prince and Princess of Wales leave the Lindo Wing of St. Mary's Hospital, London, with their new baby, William.

First time captured on film, Charles and Diana dancing together in their earlier, happier days during a visit to Melbourne, Australia, in 1985. Di sets a new fashion trend by wearing a necklace around her forehead. (Associated Newspapers)

Prince Charles takes part in an army rifle shooting competition at Bisley Rifle Ranges. His love for and her disgust with blood sports became a significant factor in the disaffection.

Charles and Di at a polo match at Smiths Lawn, Windsor, in June 1986, where she presented him with a prize and a kiss.

Diana with the Queen and members of the family outside Clarence House, London, on the eighty-seventh birthday of the Queen Mother, August 1987. Diana remains both awed and bored by the Queen.

A rare photo of Prince Charles seen at a polo match with his youngest son, Prince Harry, in July 1991. Charles now spends most of his time at Highgrove and away from his family.

Diana with Harry and William in ski lift during a ski holiday in Lech, Austria, in April 1991. As often happens, Charles did not accompany them.

Princes William and Harry are regular visitors to their neighborhood McDonald's near Kensington Palace, where their mother, dressed in casual clothes, takes them. They queue like everyone else and receive no special treatment. (Associated Newspapers)

Diana has become the most photographed woman in the world. Once innocent and unsophisticated, she now sets fashion news when she is seen in a new suit by her favorite designer, Catherine Walker, as she departs from Heathrow Airport for an official visit to Brazil in April 1990.

Diana and Fergie, now separated from her husband, Prince Andrew, at the Derby races at Epsom in June 1986, when they accompanied the Queen Mother and other members of the family for a day's racing.

Diana with Fergie, Prince Charles, and Prince Andrew in the Royal enclosure at Ascot races, June 1990.

Princess Diana's public appearances draw larger crowds and more media attention than Prince Charles's. Here she is on her way to attend a gala dinner held at Manhattan's Winter Garden in February 1989. She is wearing a Victor Edelstein suit.

Diana has become involved in some seventy charities, and one cause she is passionate about is AIDS. Here she is visiting an HIV project called Grandma's House in Washington, D.C., October 1990.

To show that no one gets AIDS through normal contact, Diana purposely will take a victim's hand and hold it. Here she carries one of the small children into Grandma's House.

In November 1985 the Prince and Princess made an official visit to the United States, where they were greeted on the steps of the White House by President and Mrs. Reagan.

The Royals went on to visit with then Vice President Bush and Barbara Bush at a dinner held by the British Ambassador at the British Embassy. Diana is wearing a Murray Arbeid gown and the Queen Mary Tiara.

Diana alone at a wreath laying ceremony at Arlington Cemetery.

The Prince and Princess of Wales dance at a dinner in Melbourne, Australia, in January 1988. Diana wears another Catherine Walker gown.

As part of their official duties, Diana, looking bored, and the Prince attend the Al-Magam camel races in the United Arab Emirates in March 1989.

The boredom does not end. Diana and Charles at a fashion show held at Sydney's famous opera in January 1988...

And at an official civic reception in Toronto in October 1991.

Diana with her security guard in her German-manufactured Mercedes instead of a British-made car. Her choice infuriated some Englishmen, but most forgave her. (Associated Newspapers)

In the winter of 1988, Charles and a group of friends were skiing at the Swiss resort of Klosters. They decided to ski off the track of compacted snow because it was more exciting. As they raced downhill, a wall of cascading snow suddenly roared behind them. Charles skied to one side, escaping the avalanche, but his great and good friend, Major Hugh Lindsay, was killed, and the legs of his other dear friend, Patti Palmer-Tomkinson, were shattered. Charles held himself entirely responsible for the tragedy and refused to be consoled by his wife. Major Lindsay's coffin accompanied the Royal party on the night flight back to RAF Northolt, where Charles, Diana, and Fergie are seen in mourning black.

Diana holds out her arms to the two men in her life, her sons William and Harry, above. Below, she turns her face away at a polo match in Jaipur, India, as her husband, once the man in her life, attempts to kiss her.

Diana now has a distinct spring in her step and sparkle in her eyes which her friends attribute to her satisfying, fulfilling relationship with Major James Hewitt, who served with a tank regiment during the Gulf War. Jamie, as he is known, strolls behind Prince Charles at the prize-giving of the Gulf Trust Polo Match held in July 1991 (left). Appropriately, Charles and Jamie were on opposing teams (right).

Diana alone.

around to the palace for a coffee and a chat. But obviously, they no longer had much in common. They lived in small but reassuringly homely houses and flats in fashionable Chelsea and Fulham and shopped in supermarkets and cooked their own dinners. She lived in a palace with servants to shop and cook and do everything for her. Hers was a different world, and they felt uneasy in her presence.

The couple decided a holiday in fresh mountain air might help. She and Charles went skiing in Liechtenstein, as the guests of Prince Franz Joseph, the ruler of that quaint, mountainous little principality. It was not a success. Despite appeals from Charles, Diana refused to pose for photographers, and she ended up in tears. She sorely missed her son; instead of offering a respite, the holiday was a misery.

Nearly every photograph of that time showed Diana looking thin and depressed. At the start of her marriage, the infatuated British press depicted her as the beautiful young Princess of Wales, innocent, virginal, shy, demure, sweet. But the mushrooming number of reports of so many personnel leaving the Palace, of rows, of spoiled behavior, caused the press to take a fresh look at her. They began to wonder whether a girl in Diana's position, plucked from obscurity to become the wife of the future King, should be allowed to behave with such audacity. The press argued that Diana had everything, including a lovely baby, and should either be happy or just shut up and make the best of it.

The Queen believed that Diana was near crisis. After much discussion she decided to allow Diana to break with tradition and take William with her and Charles on their first official tour of Australia and New Zealand. The concession was not easily won. For a while the tour was in jeopardy as Diana delivered a simple ultimatum to the Prince of Wales and to Her Majesty: "No baby, no visit." The Old Guard at Buckingham Palace were astonished by this show of obstinacy. Charles's secretary, Edward Adeane, was appalled. But efforts to "talk some sense into the girl" failed utterly. Never before had a member of the Royal Family embarked on an overseas tour with such a young child. Once again Diana, still only twenty-one, had gotten her own way.

The Australian tour proved a success, but when Charles and Diana toured Canada two months later, William was left behind. Diana missed his first birthday and didn't enjoy this trip nearly as much. Her own twenty-second birthday was ten days after William's. She said, "My perfect birthday present is going home. I can't wait to see William."

During those early years, Diana seemed to enjoy life only when she was with William, and later Harry, who was born in September 1984. But these were the private moments when no one, save Charles and her closest staff, saw the other side of the Princess, when she was happy, laughing, and playing with her children with the same devotion of any young mother.

Diana didn't really emerge from her depression until she was pregnant with Harry. She realized she had to pull herself together, and she was helped in no small way by her gynecologist, George Pinker. There were rumors of a nervous breakdown, but she had managed to come through it, and emerged a stronger person.

Over time, Diana had finally realized that Charles was not a perfect human being. For so long she had believed that everything he did was wonderful and above criticism. Whenever they were together, she would watch him with almost doglike devotion, eyes shining with admiration, when he was making a speech, talking to people, or just shaking hands with members of the public. When this illusion was no longer sustainable, she at last understood that she had to rely more on herself, lead her own life, and stop depending on Charles to support her emotionally.

Diana drew on two resources to develop greater self-reliance. She turned for help and advice to the man she called "Uncle Michael": Michael Colborne, Charles's navy friend, an older man who understood life and was a fount of common sense and good humor.

There was also her own character. People often compared her to her mother, Frances, who was a strong, determined, and engaging woman. Her mother had had the deep inner strength to change her life completely—even if it meant flying in the face of conventional behavior—when she recognized how unhappy she was. Diana was determined to do the same thing—to change her life, because she was miserable—for her own sake and for the sake of her children.

Around the time of Harry's birth, a mysterious transformation began to occur. The Prince and Princess began to change places.

Charles suddenly realized he was now attending the same annual functions for the sixth or seventh year in succession. He was becoming bored. Ironically, it was Diana, whom he at first despised for her negligent attitude to public duties, who began to make him examine his attitude to royal occasions and the role he played in the affairs of the nation. He read in the papers that he had no true role in life, that he was bored with his lack of a real job, that he had no ambition except in the sporting field. All he was doing was waiting, as patiently as possible, to succeed to the throne. Goaded by the press and Diana, he began to examine his life, and he didn't like what he found. He was going to have to make changes.

He also finally realized what others had seen for a long time. The girl he had married was far from his intellectual equal.

An intellectual lightweight she might have been, but Diana was the center of attention because of her position, her image as the young mother of two lovely Princes, and her looks. After the birth of her children, Diana, proud of her new slim figure, took greater care of her appearance than ever. The photographs taken before and just after her marriage contrast dramatically with those taken after William was born. She had been transformed from a pretty, round-faced young girl into an angular, sophisticated fashion plate. At last she had found something she was good at: being glamorous. She liked the way she looked, as did the entire world. Her confidence soared.

She now also had a role in life. She was the mother of the next generation of the Royal Family. For that she had become an important person in her own right. Never before had Diana felt so self-assured.

The smarter and more glamorous she became, the more the media gave her the star treatment and the more people flocked to see her. All this attention had only one effect on Charles: he became jealous.

All his life, Charles had been the center of attention. But now, Charles noted, the more beautiful and sophisticated Diana became, the more she drew the crowds. After the birth of Harry, they were now coming out, in the thousands, not to see *him* and shake his hand, but to see *her*. He remarked disconsolately, "It's only Diana they want now. I don't count anymore." A proud man, he felt slighted, even wounded.

Without realizing it, Charles had begun to be more critical of Diana. As she became more confident, he felt more vulnerable and looked for flaws in her personality and behavior, which resulted in more arguments. He began to crack jokes about her lack of intelligence. By her own admission Diana was never a good student, and she jokes about her lack of knowledge. During a royal tour overseas, when Diana banged her head on a low beam and people rushed to her, she quipped, "Don't worry, there's nothing in it anyway." She laughed off the incident. On other occasions Diana has disarmingly confessed to people she has met during her royal duties, giving them comfort when they had problems at school or training: "Don't worry, I'm as thick as a plank."

Unhappy at home and suddenly bored by what he had begun to see as his repetitious job as an official handshaker, Charles started to spend more time running the Duchy of Cornwall, his estate in the west of England and the source of his income. He has often said that if he hadn't been heir to the throne, he would have been a gentleman farmer. As he became more involved with affairs of the duchy—including a spell spent actually working the land—he found it not only an escape from the traumas of his home life, but also very therapeutic.

"Funnily enough," he reflected, "I love the work, and there's something very important about working on land, actual manual labor, mucking out cattle yards, you know, and things like that, mending stone walls and milking cows, just being in touch with the whole thing."

He was fortunate that in 1980 he had taken on John Higgs, who had just retired from one of the key United Nations agricultural agencies. Higgs had been invited to join the Prince's Council, the governing body that runs the Duchy of Cornwall, but within months the secretary, Sir Anthony Gray, became ill, and John Higgs volunteered to take his place. Suddenly Charles discovered that he had a new, trusted, older friend who knew farming inside out and on whom he could rely absolutely.

They got on well from the start. John Higgs had a deep admiration for the Prince, and the admiration was mutual. Higgs knew the latest methods as well as agricultural economics, farm mechanization, and organic farming, which struck a chord with the environmentalist Prince. The two set out to improve the duchy's finances. They worked together closely for six years, until John Higgs's untimely death.

Higgs's wife Elizabeth reports that during that time her husband became a major influence on the Prince's life. "John became a friend shortly after the death of Lord Mountbatten, and it seemed Charles needed a confidant and helper," she recalled. "There seemed no one to whom the Prince could turn at that time. John happened to be there, and they became close because the Prince became more involved in the work of the duchy and, of course, Highgrove.

"They seemed to have very happy times together, working and discussing everything in a most friendly way. Not just about farming but about everything from Third World problems to the idea of the United World Colleges.

"The Prince is a deeply caring man to his staff and has

an interest in such a wide range of matters. Perhaps, if anything, he is too caring for his own good. I think some things are very painful to him when he had to make some decisions."

John Higgs helped placate Charles concerning his relationship with Diana. On walks together they talked for hours about Diana, as well as Charles's relationship with her and the children. Higgs tried to help Charles understand how Diana felt, why she seemed unable to cope, and why she threw tantrums.

Under John Higgs, the Prince, in his six-hundred-year-old ancestral role of Duke of Cornwall, saw the vast estates, nearly one hundred thousands acres reaching out across much of southern Britain, dragged into the twentieth century and bringing in a million pounds ($1,700,000) a year for the Prince. No longer was the duchy, as some antiroyals had unfairly dubbed it, "an inefficient feudal agricultural backwater."

Each year the Prince would work as a farmhand for a few weeks, no matter how hard or dirty the work was. During those spells, the heir to the throne felt close to the land and the people. He savored this opportunity. He would often be up and out at six A.M. and worked up to fifteen hours a day.

During the years he and John Higgs were together, Charles seemed to spend most of his time involved with the duchy, particularly during 1984–85, when it became virtually a full-time job. The two men spent a good deal of time together examining new projects, reaching new decisions, and going on trips to look into farming ideas.

In 1985 John Higgs was diagnosed with terminal cancer. After he went into St. Thomas's Hospital in London, Charles would visit him frequently. There was precious little privacy, but Charles would arrive at the hospital with his detective, enter the public lift along with everyone else, and go up to the ward to see his dying friend.

The hospital visits were uncomfortable for him, especially as Higgs's conditioned worsened, but he went nevertheless, and they chatted warmly together. Near the end, Charles went to see Elizabeth Higgs to ask her if her husband would like to be knighted, a sort of last sacrament for a dying man. She thought John would be greatly touched by the idea. One day the Prince arrived at the hospital with his secretary and the ceremonial sword. In a moving ritual witnessed by his wife and daughter Nicola, John Higgs was knighted by the Prince as he lay in bed. After he died, Charles missed him greatly.

Charles had also started farming at Highgrove and had little time left for royal duties, which he began to reduce dramatically. To his friends, farming seemed to be the therapy he needed to escape the problems with Diana. Still, he always made sure there was time for polo in the summer, frequent hunting excursions in the winter, and fishing trips in Scotland. He was always present at the Royal Family holidays at Balmoral and Sandringham. All that suffered were his royal duties, which Charles had once refused to ignore.

In the last four months of 1984, Prince Charles had just fifteen public engagements, including a three-day visit to Italy. During the same period of time, his sister Princess Anne had fifty-six engagements, including a three-week visit to Bangladesh and India; the Queen had twenty-eight, including a visit to Canada; and the Duke of Edinburgh had forty-five.

People were beginning to notice Prince Charles's apparent reluctance to carry out his royal tasks. Some thought he was becoming disillusioned with the prospect of waiting to be King. He seemed to prefer to distance himself from his public royal life and become a gentleman farmer, away from his constant obligations.

There was much gossip at the Palace that there would never be a King Charles III. The Queen would reign for so long that Charles would feel he was too old to take up the crown and would pass it to Prince William instead. Charles himself had felt such tremendous frustration about his role as a powerless figurehead that he didn't want the same for his son.

It wasn't surprising that Charles became disillusioned at this time. For fifteen years he had performed the same job with no hope of a change. He had visited the same places, addressed the same societies and professional bodies, often talked to the same people at the same lunch and dinner tables. Most people's lives change and their careers alter as their interests and expertise grow, but the Prince was stuck with the same duties, year in and year out—and he was beginning to believe it was all a dreadful waste of his life.

Though Charles may have contemplated turning his back on his life and retiring to the country, he never for a moment thought about ending his marriage, whatever the unhappiness. Of course, he was more fortunate than most in some ways. Whenever the going really became tough, he—unlike most men—could get away from it all. During those difficult years, he would sometimes leave Diana and the children in London and go off to Scotland or Highgrove for a week's fishing or work on his farm and take a break from the pressures of his marriage and his overemotional, demanding wife.

Meanwhile, Diana was making her separate decisions. Having decided that her only talent other than mothering lay in looking good, she was spending more time and money making sure she did just that. She swam every day in the indoor pool at Buckingham Palace. She had secret beauty treatments at home in Kensington Palace and began to spend a fortune on her clothes. She changed her hair to a more sophisticated style that made her look more like a Hollywood star than the Princess of Wales. As her quota of "glitz" increased, she began to top magazine polls as the woman other women wanted most to look like. Soon not only her looks but her actions were more Hollywood than Buck House.

Just prior to their visit to the United States in October 1985, the couple were the subject of an attack by Tina Brown, the English editor of the American magazine *Vanity Fair*. Many people on both sides of the Atlantic described the article as "savage" and "wounding."

The piece made public much that had been whispered in Britain about the royal marriage during the previous twelve months. There were doubts about the accuracy of the research and much of it was pure gossip, but the article was sensational, bitchy, and designed to wound.

The front cover pictured Princess Diana wearing a diamond tiara and the headline proclaimed: THE MOUSE THAT ROARED.

The *Vanity Fair* piece portrayed Diana as a restless, demanding young woman and asked whether she had become a real-life Alexis from the TV soap "Dynasty." Tina Brown thought Diana was behaving like a 1940s film star, becoming increasingly disenchanted with Charles and what she considered his weird ways.

Brown saw that a curious role reversal had occurred in the marriage. Princess Diana, the once shy introvert unable to cope with public life, was emerging as the star of the world stage. Prince Charles, Brown claimed, had few friends, was mean and intolerant, and was being "pussy-whipped" by Diana into a reclusive world under the influence of a motley crew of mystics, spiritualists, and self-sufficiency freaks.

It was a nasty piece of journalism, but it contained enough uncomfortable half-truths to distress both Charles and Diana. It was a bad time for them both.

The Royal Family have little means of redress against such character assassination. By tradition they will not, except in the most outrageous circumstances, sue for libel. They just have to weather the storm or try to put out their side of the story. Charles finally decided, in a remarkably frank and revealing interview he gave to the British newspaper *The Sunday Times* later that year, to set the record straight.

In the interview he said: "I read things frequently saying, you know, I believe in this or I do that. I mean it really is quite extraordinary: as far as I can make out, I'm about to become a Buddhist monk, you know, or live halfway up a mountain, or only eat grass. I'm not quite as bad as that. Or quite as extreme."

He continued: "I try very hard to maintain as balanced an approach as I can to things. But it's very easy to be misunderstood. It's very easy to reduce one's thinking or the occasional expression one may have made to the level of absurdity, possibly through ignorance or not knowing actually what I think. . . .

"But then I think so often, don't you, that today's unorthodoxy is tomorrow's convention. I mean it does happen quite a lot, doesn't it? I know there are so many cases, for instance in science and technology, of people propounding theories and ideas which at the time are completely rejected as nonsense by the Establishment, the scientific Establishment or whatever—which later on everyone else claims they thought of at the time."

In that interview Prince Charles permitted a little more daylight than usual to fall on himself. He gave the impression of a gentle, questioning man who was by no means entirely comfortable in his royal straitjacket.

"I have," he said, "found a way of coping with life by doing straightforward physical work. Working with people every now and then, taking your jacket off and doing something, is very salutary—and therapeutic. And again it just means that you're in contact with your surroundings. I do a lot of my own gardening and I do enjoy enormously the business of actually doing the work myself."

He went on to talk of inner peace. The Prince, who seemed to have everything, spoke of how he reconciled material success and other trappings as well as how outer life was not sufficient for inner happiness.

"If we do not examine our inner selves," he said, "we are on a slippery slope, for our inner self is where it all ultimately lies."

But if that interview did much to establish in people's minds that he wasn't some mystical freak but a sensitive man who wanted to give as much to life as he took out of it, it didn't dispel the rumors which abounded about the shaky state of his marriage.

One of his closest friends recalls, "Charles worried terribly about marriage, and he would ask what happened to people who one moment were madly in love with one another and then, six months down the road, parted company forever.

"He wanted to know how people could change so dramatically toward each other and wanted to know if everyone changed so much after marriage. I told him of course people change. We talked often about marriage, not about anyone in particular, but about the state of marriage and people's relationship to each other in marriage. It fascinated him, and it troubled him because he knew that he could only have one crack at it. For him there would be no second chance. He had to get it right the first time."

But apparently he had not. During 1985 and 1986, the weekends the couple spent at Highgrove were very different from the time they had spent there when courting. Then they were so much in love they would snatch every moment they could to be together, longing for the time when they could be alone. Now, they hardly saw each other. At Highgrove Charles would spend most of his time working in the garden, while Diana sat watching videos or swimming alone in the indoor pool. They met for breakfast or a quick snack lunch, but most of the time Charles would be outside while Diana never left the house. Usually Diana would drive back alone to London after Sunday lunch, leaving Charles to return on Monday afternoon. They were leading virtually separate lives.

Even humor had become a flash point for discord. Charles thinks that Diana's sense of humor is juvenile and obvious, while Diana believes Charles is so stuffy he can rarely see the funny side of anything.

Charles sometimes complained to friends about what he considered Diana's coarse, even vulgar, sense of humor. Once the couple were lunching with Charles's old friend, the South African philosopher and writer Sir Laurens van der Post. The two men were enjoying a weighty conversation about the problem of blacks and whites living together in South Africa when Diana suddenly put in, "What's the definition of mass confusion?"

Both men were utterly nonplussed at this interruption.

"Father's Day in Brixton [a predominantly black London suburb]," Diana told them merrily. She rocked with laughter while Sir Laurens and Charles sat in stunned silence.

Charles was appalled and not a little embarrassed that

his wife could be so gauche and insensitive in front of such a guest.

"I can't believe you just said that," he finally said.

"Oh, well, if you two are having a sense of humor failure, I'll leave you to it," Diana replied, as she left the table.

On another occasion Charles and Diana were having dinner at a friend's house with several other guests, including Prince Andrew and his wife, Sarah. A friend asked them, "What smells worse than an anchovy?"

When the four of them looked blank, the man replied, "An anchovy's bottom."

Diana and Sarah collapsed in laughter, but Charles went white with anger. He couldn't believe anyone could be ill-mannered enough to tell a joke in such bad taste during dinner. He left the table, and although Diana tried to persuade him to return, he refused.

At the ball following the dinner, Diana and Charles barely spoke a word. Diana spent most of the night dancing flamboyantly with a string of young men, evidently wanting everybody, especially her husband, to see how much she was enjoying herself.

The royal marriage appeared to be heading for rock bottom during 1985–86. At this time Diana herself had no idea how she was going to come to terms with her life or her marriage. She was only a young woman and there were decades of life ahead, but she had no wish to remain a wretchedly unhappy woman trapped in a miserable union.

It was after an intimate dinner party in the spring of 1986 attended by her friend Sarah Ferguson that Diana decided to seek a possible solution to her problems in a psychic. Among the guests that night were Sarah, Prince Andrew, and Penny Thornton, the astrological guru of English aristocratic women.

During dinner, Penny Thornton, forty-two, explained that no emotional problem was insoluble if you placed your faith in the stars. She explained how she had used astrology to help save a number of wrecked marriages.

Next morning Fergie phoned Diana and told her about Penny Thornton and her claims. Diana decided to seek her help; after all, what had she got to lose? If Penny could help her, then so much the better. She would give it a try. At 11 A.M. next morning the telephone rang in Penny's $500,000 country house in Hampshire: "Hello, this is Diana. I am the Princess of Wales, and I've been given your number by Sarah Ferguson. Please can I see you?"

Penny explained that she would not be able to see Diana for a few days, but Diana persisted: "Could I come now, immediately? I could be at your house in a couple of hours."

Sensing the urgency in Diana's voice, Penny agreed, and two hours later she opened the door of her house and found a grim-faced Diana standing there, dressed in jeans and T-shirt.

Penny invited Diana in, and they sat down in the small sitting room Penny keeps for her intimate conversations. Penny calmed Diana down and began to talk quietly and positively. Diana poured out her problems, her emotional turmoil and the breakdown of her marriage. She told Penny everything. Penny explained that by using her inner psychic strengths and astrological powers Diana could face the future with confidence. It was four hours later that Diana left the house and drove back to London. She felt as though a huge load had been lifted from her mind.

Penny agreed to visit Diana the following week at Kensington Palace after she had prepared Diana's own astrological chart. It contained all of Diana's personal details, the astrological influences at the time, date and place of her birth, the influences of the moon on her personality, and the current heavenly aspects influencing her life. Being born on July 1, 1961, Diana is a Cancer. Penny also prepared a star chart for Prince Charles.

When Diana and Penny met the following week at the palace, both charts were laid out side by side on the dining room table, and Penny explained them in detail to

Diana. She explained how the planets were lined up in opposition to one another, showing a rift had developed between her and Charles—but also showing that Diana should not think of leaving Charles at that time.

Importantly, Penny told Diana that the stars also pointed to a future of real happiness, which could be built out of her present mood of despair.

Since that first visit Diana has seen Penny Thornton on a regular basis, and they often talk on the telephone. Penny slowly built up Diana's confidence, gave her a lifeline, and encouraged her to channel her energies into what astrologers call "plus mode." And it worked wonderfully.

Later, Diana confided to one of her close friends: "Penny was a revelation to me. She made me totally rethink my life. She taught me things about myself I never knew. And her suggestion I should use my own marital difficulties to channel positive ideas into helping others gave me a new direction to my life. That's why I so love my work with Relate [Britain's guidance counseling service]. I feel I can actually help other people, and that makes me feel so good inside. She has been a godsend."

One Conservative member of Parliament, Tony Marlow, even tried to force a debate in the House of Commons on the delicate question of whether Prince Charles should, by right of primogeniture, or firstborn, automatically succeed to the throne. His unfortunate marriage had brought the issue into play. Government ministers sat "stony-faced and silent," noted one observer, when this contentious topic was raised openly in the House, rather than in the more private Cabinet. No debate got off the ground, for ancient procedure in the Mother of Parliaments forbids discussion of such Royal Family issues.

Informal consideration was being given to the enormous constitutional consequences of succession in the Prime Minister's office at No. 10 Downing Street. A newspaper poll of a thousand Britons indicated that some 72 percent believed the Church should waive its rules to allow a divorce if the marriage were to break down totally, and 61 percent declared that Charles should go on to be King, even if the marriage collapsed.

The marriage was probably in worse shape than anyone knew. Determined to show her independence, Diana now often refused to accompany Charles on engagements, while the Prince seemed deliberately to ignore his young wife when they did attend functions together.

The impression was that Charles had entirely changed his approach to Diana. At first he had tried to please her in every way, when he thought her tantrums arose from her inability to settle into her new life. When the tantrums turned to stubborn independence and she started to do things her own way, Charles responded by ignoring her, leaving her to sort out her own problems.

Sometimes Charles cracked under the pressure. On one occasion in 1988, after the Royal Family met at Balmoral to discuss the working of the estate, Charles asked a chauffeur to bring the car to the front of the house to take an aide to Aberdeen. When he found a Range Rover outside, he blew his top.

"Why doesn't anyone take my instructions seriously?" he raged. "I said bring the car, so why is the Range Rover here?"

The hapless chauffeur, Simon, explained that after talking to the head chauffeur he judged the Range Rover would be better suited to the rugged journey.

Then Charles really exploded. Thumping the bonnet with his fist and kicking a wheel, he ranted, "When I say I want something done, I want it done! I don't want everyone else deciding what I want. Understand?"

Hearing the commotion outside, the Queen hurried to the driveway: "Charles, what on earth is going on?" she asked.

"My staff don't take any notice of my orders," retorted the Prince as he stormed off, scarlet with anger.

Next day, young Prince William gave a clue that his father's outbursts were becoming more frequent. Spotting Simon, the chauffeur, washing a car, Wills went up to him and said, "Don't worry about yesterday, Simon. Daddy was just in one of his moods."

At about this same time in 1988, Charles resorted to writing notes to Diana because he found they could not talk to each other, even about a topic as seemingly innocuous as their weekend plans, without ending up in arguments and rows. With written notes, he avoided the bickering, and by sending them through their respective offices, he would be sure of receiving a reply.

These written notes and verbal flare-ups were only symptoms. The cause of their troubles was more deeply rooted.

11

Princess Di Rebels

In just two years, from 1984 to 1986, Diana dramatically transformed herself from a shy, awkward young Princess into a confident, dashing young woman who would win praise from fashion experts around the world for her poise, elegance, and style.

It was almost certainly the arrival of Sarah Ferguson on the royal scene that gave Diana a radically different perspective on life.

Fergie, as she is universally known, is nearly two years older than Diana and the daughter of Prince Charles's former polo manager, Major Ronald Ferguson. Her impeccable, upper-class English background includes King Charles II as an ancestor. But unlike Diana, she had lived life to the fullest before becoming a member of the Royal Family.

Fergie breezed into the Royal Family as though she had been merely waiting for an invitation. In contrast to Diana's first few months as a royal, she took to the role with gusto. Confident, boisterous, and outspoken, she had acquired her sophistication as a result of a somewhat checkered past. "A gutsy girl," said her friends. "Too self-centered," claimed others. Like her outspoken father, who once commanded the Sovereign's Escort of the Household Cavalry Regiment, Fergie could be utterly charming. But she could also be reckless, tasteless, arrogant, and insensitive.

Her childhood had been sporty and tomboyish, and her young adulthood was not much different. Having learned to ride at a very young age, she is an excellent horsewoman, an attribute that found favor among the horsey royals. Indeed she always went riding with the Queen whenever they were at Windsor, Balmoral, or Sandringham. She is also a fearless and very competent skier, possibly because she was first put on the slopes when she was four years old.

Because of her close attachment to her father, Fergie was brought up more like a son than a daughter. Major Ferguson was proud that his younger daughter had the courage and guts of a tomboy, and he encouraged these qualities. Because of her father's position, Fergie had known the Royal Family since she was a child. She was used to meeting them at polo and didn't find them in the slightest bit fearsome or awe-inspiring, either before or after she married. And she was so outgoing it was difficult to imagine her being intimidated, even if she had never met them before.

Fergie practically grew up with the man she would marry. The rules of royal protocol and etiquette came as no great surprise to her, and in any case, she paid little attention to stuffy protocol. If she thought she could get away with it, she often did what her bubbly, outgoing personality demanded.

Fergie and Diana's friendship actually started in 1981, the year that Lady Diana Spencer married the Prince of Wales, and five years before Sarah Ferguson married Prince Andrew and became the Duchess of York. Diana had few royal companions of her own age. In Fergie, Diana found a companion, which she had always wanted and never had. She had certainly never had a friend with such formidable confidence and strength of character.

Without a doubt Fergie (Andrew detested the nickname

and insisted on calling her Sarah) possessed a more open, gregarious personality than her quieter, more diffident, younger friend. Those who know both women quickly detected that theirs was not a relationship of equals. The worldly Fergie was clearly the dominant partner. Though the Princess enjoyed higher social status, Fergie was the ringleader whenever they did anything together.

Fergie was not particularly popular among older Palace aides, who grew anxious as she appeared to influence the young Princess more and more during the early years of her marriage. There was even a suggestion that Fergie might be appointed one of Diana's official ladies-in-waiting, but that was quickly quashed.

Both Diana and Fergie had grown up without a mother, which was a strong initial link between them. Fergie was thirteen when her mother Susan walked out of her unhappy marriage to live with Hector Barrantes, a rich Argentine polo player. Susan Ferguson and Barrantes eventually married and settled down on a one-thousand-acre ranch at El Pucara, Argentina. (Barrantes died of cancer in 1991.) Despite the distance from Britain, Fergie and her mother kept closely in touch. When her daughter became engaged to Prince Andrew, the horse-mad Susan Barrantes remarked, only semihumorously, "I know Sarah met him on the polo field. But then doesn't everybody?"

Fergie's confidence began to rub off on Diana. More important, she helped Diana to relax and enjoy herself for the first time in her married life. Fergie had always had fun, whether at school, parties, balls, dinner parties, or restaurants. She enjoyed life to the fullest and decided nothing was going to change because she was to marry a Prince.

Her zest for life was infectious. Diana started to love the excitement and stimulation Fergie brought to her life. Until Sarah Ferguson arrived on the scene, Diana was starting to take life far too seriously, especially when it came to the state of her marriage and being a mother. Fergie was outgoing and friendly; she loved a laugh, a joke, or a prank. For Diana, it was like being back at school, where she had always admired and secretly envied girls like Fergie, who were the center of attention. Now Diana had a girl as her "BF," best friend.

Because of her friendship with brash, effervescent Fergie, at a time when she was beginning to see that her once adored husband was not perfect and could not give her everything she craved, Diana reached a turning point in her life. She had Fergie to thank for the change in her attitude toward her husband and her way of life—a change which was to shake and almost undermine her marriage, worry the Queen, and alarm the royal advisers.

Fergie's existence made Diana do some hard thinking. She envied her friend's independence and realized that she, too, had a life of her own to lead. Her youth was slipping by. She had met Charles when she was very young, and hardly had time to enjoy the carefree teenage years before she was saddled with the yoke of royal protocol.

Diana began to realize that the time had come for her to start enjoying life. She was twenty-five years old and needed to cast aside her feeling of immaturity and nervousness.

After the birth of Prince Harry, in 1984, people noticed that during her royal visits and functions Diana was becoming more relaxed, less formal, and easier to talk to. But inside she was still the worried, highly nervous young woman Charles had married. In 1986, the Princess of Wales confessed to actress Milly Weir at a Help the Aged benefit, "I feel so nervous every time I have to make a speech in public."

Other members of the Royal Family were quick to criticize Diana's public speech-making. Diana said, "The worst part of speaking in public is the reaction when I get back home. The family is very critical of me. They watch everything I do, and sometimes they are positively rude about me. And to my face."

For a time Diana was known as Rabbit in royal circles, because Charles and his brothers teased her that whenever she made a speech, she looked like a "frightened rabbit." The teasing only made matters worse for poor Diana.

Diana's escape from this world of duty, restraint, and criticism began after Fergie introduced her to a younger set of women who brought along their boyfriends. These young men were perhaps five or ten years younger than Prince Charles, and Diana realized that she was enjoying herself in their company. There was no heavy conversation that she couldn't understand, as there so often was at Kensington Palace dinner parties. These people made no demands on her intellect—she could just chat away about trivia. Nobody took anything very seriously. Diana could now act like a young woman. She could laugh and have the type of fun she had all but forgotten was possible after her marriage into the Royal Family five years earlier. And she could crack her own little jokes and get a laugh in return, instead of the icy looks from around the royal dinner table that often greeted her attempts to lighten the conversation.

These young men and women were full of vitality. Their dinner parties were noisy, funny, and argumentative, so different from the boring, protocol-ridden dinner parties Diana had become used to with Charles and his conservative friends.

It was Fergie who brought Diana back out into the world she had once enjoyed. Fergie and Prince Andrew loved to go out together to cocktail or dinner parties and joke around, even drink a little too much. One reason Andrew was attracted to Fergie was that she always seemed to enjoy life and have a smile on her face.

At one evening cocktail party in the summer of 1985, Diana, Andrew, Fergie, and twenty or so other young people had gathered. The evening was going swimmingly when the phone rang. It was the Queen.

The hostess shouted, "Andrew, it's your mother on the phone."

"What the hell does she want?" he asked in a loud voice.

"I don't know. I'll ask," came the reply.

A second or two later the hostess shouted, "She wants to know whether you will be home for dinner tonight."

Andrew called to her above the noise of the conversation, "Tell her no. I'm out enjoying myself."

He turned to the group around him, which included Diana and Fergie, and said, "If she thinks I'm going back to a boring old dinner at the palace she's in for a shock." Diana roared with laughter.

Diana started to enjoy alcoholic drinks, something she'd rarely done before. She started to unbend and forget the rules of etiquette which had been drummed into her by Charles and the royal advisers. She cast off her inhibitions and behaved like a normal, decidedly unroyal, person. She was no longer confined by the restrictions and protocol of Kensington Palace and the need to keep up appearances in front of the staff. She persuaded Fergie to hold more dinner parties, which she attended on her own whenever Charles was away.

The more Diana began to drink, usually champagne, the more she unwound and the more she loved her newfound freedom. Never before had she been the center of attention with young men. Before she met Charles, she had hardly had a boyfriend. She was such a shy, mousy girl that men all but overlooked her. But now she was not only a fashionable and attractive female, but also the Princess of Wales, the second most important woman in the country. She started to flirt brazenly. The men's responses gave her yet more confidence in herself and her ability to attract the opposite sex.

The life Diana had missed out on as a teenager was now reincarnated in a new setting. The spark was back in her life. But the effect her behavior had on her marriage, and on Charles, was disastrous.

Diana had begun to lead a life somewhat separate from Charles. The more she socialized with her new set of friends, the more she realized the difference between her husband and the dashing young men she met. She realized she had far more in common with these young profligates, whose idea of a good time was to laugh boisterously and throw bread rolls at each other in a restaurant or drink too much bubbly. Anything but serious conversation.

Charles and Diana started having more rows. Diana was determined to continue her newfound, hedonistic life, and damn the consequences.

In 1985 Diana confessed to a royal friend that she was decidedly fed up with the strictures Charles was trying to impose on her. "So what if he doesn't approve?" she said. "So what if he thinks my conduct is unseemly for Her Royal Highness The Princess of Wales? For once I am having fun, and all Charles can do is to try and dampen my spirits and make my life miserable. Well, I'm not going to let him."

How the tables had turned. Early in their married life, Diana had been angry when Charles left her at home and went off hunting, shooting, or playing polo. Now it was Charles who was angry. He wanted his wife to stay home in the evening instead of going off with Fergie and her friends to dinner parties.

Occasionally the Prince would accompany her, but he didn't enjoy what he considered the immature company she liked keeping. Charles had never been fond of the Hooray Henry dinner-party set who drank too much, spoke too loudly, and were notably hearty or jolly. This breed of upper-class Londoners seemed to come into their own in the 1980s. Self-indulgent, shallow, and wealthy, they drove BMWs or Porsches, frequented smart, expensive restaurants, and worked in the City. Many, including Charles, found this type obnoxious. But to Diana, they were fun when they didn't go over the top, as they were wont to do.

Diana, Fergie, the blond Australian comedienne Pamela Stephenson, and Renate, Elton John's former wife, often used to go out together to friends' houses for dinner. Diana was even beginning to develop her own repertoire of jokes and party pieces. Those around her always appreciated Diana's humor, perhaps because she was the Princess of Wales. Some found her jokes rather juvenile, but they were always received with loud laughter, which Di-

ana loved. It made her feel like one of the party. She was
wanted by the friends she was desperate to keep.

In fact, she earned a reputation for making rather
naughty, even sexy, jokes. One example of Diana's more
risqué jokes was: "What are the door straps in a Roller
[Rolls-Royce] for?" Answer: "To rest your ankles in."

In December one year Diana sent at least a couple of
naughty, rude "Christmas cards" to close friends. One depicted a car crash and asked: "Why are women so bad at
parking?" Inside was drawn a hand with the finger and
thumb narrowly spaced, and the rude caption: "Because
men keep telling them this is six inches." The other
showed a lifeguard with the heading: "What did they call
the man who swam the Channel with his arms and legs
tied together?" The answer inside read: "A clever dick."
No one knew to whom the cards were mailed.

Nor did anyone know to whom Diana was going to
send two naughty stocking-fillers when, in 1991, she went
to a joke shop in London's crowded Oxford Street and
bought a windup jumping "Jolly Pecker" and some "Fart
Powder."

Whenever there was dancing at a party, she would show
how accomplished she was, whether it was disco dancing,
rock 'n' roll, or ballroom. At first, her new men friends
were not sure whether it was permissible to invite the
wife of the future King of England to disco dance, so she
would ask them to take the floor with her. The message
soon got around that Diana loved dancing. However, she
had become so expert that she was interested only in partners who could match her skill and energy. Those few
competent enough to meet her standards discovered that
they needed stamina if they were to stand the pace. Diana
would happily dance for two hours, virtually nonstop. "It's
so good for me, it's so good for my figure," she would tell
them.

Throughout the evening Diana wore a cheeky smile
and had a sparkle in her eye. She was flirting, showing off,

and, for Diana, being downright outrageous. And she was
determined to continue.

Occasionally, her appetite for enjoyment, at the expense of Charles, went too far. At a London party in the
spring of 1986, Diana asked Charles to dance with her
when dinner was over. Charles, who hates to dance, refused. Diana was furious, her eyes ablaze. Since she
couldn't have a row with Charles in public, she stormed
off and invited a young male friend to dance. She didn't
return to the table for nearly two hours, dancing with
various partners while Charles sat and talked to others at
the table. Whenever Diana needed a drink of water or a
Coke, she asked her dancing partners to fetch them. This
incredible rebuff was a severe embarrassment to Charles.
It is unthinkable that the Prince of Wales's wife would
dance with various young bachelors for two solid hours
without returning to the table.

It was the height of rudeness, and Diana knew it, illus-
trating the enormous change that had taken place in herself and in her relationship with Charles. It was the first
time Diana, flaunting her independence to the world, had
deliberately insulted Charles in public. What amazed the
other guests was that she didn't seem to care what she
had done to Charles.

One of the most outrageous examples of Diana's devil-
may-care attitude was Prince Andrew's stag night in July
1986. Fergie believed her husband-to-be was having a
night on the town with his friends at Annabel's, London's
plushest nightclub, in Berkeley Square. In fact, she was
wrong and the joke misfired. But the prank showed the
change that had come over Diana.

Diana, Fergie, and Pamela Stephenson were at a dinner
party at the home of Jane, Duchess of Roxburghe. They
decided that afterward it would be a good gag to raid
Andrew's stag party dressed as policewomen. Fergie and
Pamela had hired the outfits from a theatrical costumer,
and the girls set off, accompanied by Diana, who enthusiastically went along for the fun.

Annabel's, an exclusive club where applicants may join
only after a vote by the club committee, is not the sort of

place in which you would expect to see a uniformed police officer. Since the two young women officers were giggling, not entirely correctly dressed, and looked slightly the worse for drink, they were immediately singled out as not to be taken seriously. (They were allowed in because the doorman recognized Fergie and Pamela.) The three went into the dimly lit bar at the back of the club and ordered Buck's fizz (champagne and orange juice). Fergie made discreet inquiries of the staff and discovered that Andrew was not at the club. By this time, Diana was wearing Pamela's policewoman's hat to try to make herself slightly less recognizable. Some of the older members were starting to take disapproving notice of the three giggling young women who appeared to be on their own.

The three were enjoying themselves tremendously by the time the astonished members realized who they were. No one said anything. The members continued drinking and talking, but secretly paid close attention to the bizarre trio, who eventually decided it would be prudent to leave before someone asked them to go. The Princess of Wales was last seen that night walking across Berkeley Square doing one of her favorite party pieces—imitating Charlie Chaplin's famous gait.

A few members of Parliament protested that action should be taken against the two young women who had impersonated police officers, which was a violation of the law. Naturally nothing was done. The newspapers thought the prank sensational, but stuffier citizens felt it was disgraceful behavior for a future Queen of England.

Charles was in despair at his wife's behavior. Despite his own taste for offbeat pranks,* he did *not* think the joke a great lark. On the contrary, he was fighting to maintain

---

* Charles's idea of pranks included jumping into a dustbin during a university sketch at Cambridge, and imitating the voices from the 1950s radio "Goon Show," starring, among others, Peter Sellers and Spike Milligan. While in the navy, he made a twenty-minute private film depicting the "Goons" training to be helicopter pilots and loved "Sod's Operas" on mess nights, when those aboard would each get up and sing songs with salacious verses.

some semblance of dignity for a monarchy that he rightly feared was being increasingly diminished by tacky stunts. He was dismayed, but Diana didn't care a jot. She told a friend, "Charles is just a stuffy killjoy."

During skiing holidays, Diana and Fergie really let themselves go. They played the royals' favorite after-dinner game, charades, but preferred more active fun, which included a lot of drinking. Sometimes they would dance in the evening. Sometimes they would sit around drinking and chatting and laughing loudly. Occasionally they would dress up in outrageous clothes and go for a walk around the ski resort. Because everyone knew the royals were at the resort, Diana and Fergie would disguise themselves and pretend to be other people. For Diana, particularly, it was a wonderful form of escapism, and she reveled in it.

Charles disapproved but was powerless to do anything about it. If he complained, Diana would tell him not to be an old fuddy-duddy. He should try to let himself go and enjoy life, as she was. The more Diana went her own way with her BF Sarah, the more Charles disapproved.

His irritation with her began to show in public. At Klosters in 1986, Diana and Fergie began shouting at each other in fun and stuffing snowballs down each other's ski suits, in full view of the press photographers. They tried to push each other over. After they both nearly fell into the snow, Charles said irritably, "Come on, come on." Diana ignored him and made as if to continue. But Fergie gave a quick glance at Charles and realized he was not amused. With a scowl from Diana, they all skied off together before the incident developed further.

During another ski holiday, Diana and Fergie were engaged in a pillow fight in their villa one evening, until Charles came along and made them stop. A friend commented, "It seemed as though Charles was acting like her father, not her husband."

Charles could not tolerate Diana's boisterous behavior and made no effort to hide his contempt. During the first three years of their marriage, Diana had hero-worshipped Charles and wanted to please him. Charles had once been her mentor, teaching her how to behave and how to become an acceptable member of the Royal Family. Now he was no longer the most dominant person in her life, and Charles was having problems coming to terms with this.

The shy teenager he had first fallen for was gone forever. That Diana—who had squirmed with embarrassment, blushing to the roots of her blond hair when a speech-maker declared in her presence she was "more beautiful than Cleopatra, Queen of the Nile"—was, like the fabled monarch, a creature of the past. Now that she had produced not one, but two heirs, she felt she had done her duty to Charles and the Queen. Now she was going to do what *she* wanted. Charles didn't know how to respond to this new, confident, headstrong woman. He didn't know what to do about the crisis which had engulfed not just his marriage, but his whole life.

Six years after their wedding, Diana spent the summer of 1987 on a round of parties and dinner dates, most of them without Charles. One day she met a handsome young City banker, Old Etonian Philip Dunne. Dunne, twenty-eight, was the son of the Lord Lieutenant of Hereford and Worcester, and had met Diana through his sister Millie. Shortly after, he was invited to join the royal party at Klosters for their winter skiing holiday. Charles wasn't happy about Dunne's being there, sensing some chemistry between him and Diana. But Charles couldn't refuse without voicing fears which would lay him open to accusations of jealousy.

The Princess held Dunne in such high esteem that she also invited him to join the royals at Ascot. Soon, the couple were seen lunching together at the sophisticated, intimate restaurant Menage à Trois, near Harrods in Knightsbridge, and at San Lorenzo's in Beauchamp Place, Diana's favorite lunchtime restaurant. As Diana and Dunne saw more of each other, his three-year romance with divorcée Katya Greenfell lost its sparkle and quickly collapsed altogether.

The gossip percolating through royal circles was sparked into active tongue-wagging when Diana attended a David Bowie concert later that year. Sharing the royal box with Diana was not the handsome Dunne, but another young upper-class Englishman, thirty-one-year-old cavalry officer David Waterhouse. Major Waterhouse, a nephew of the Duke of Marlborough, was a bachelor and an officer in the exclusive Life Guards. To judge by the way he and Diana whispered closely throughout the performance, he seemed to be enjoying a special relationship with the Princess. Seemingly unconcerned about the conclusions people might draw, Diana rested her head on his shoulder during the concert, and they danced together afterward.

The Princess was enjoying herself immensely, animatedly laughing and joking with her companion, caring little that she would be the subject of intense speculation. She seemed to worry not a jot about what people were saying, nor what she was doing to her own reputation or that of Charles and the Royal Family. She was being totally indiscreet and must have known this would embarrass, anger, and humiliate Charles.

She displayed her newfound independence at the wedding of Lord Worcester and British TV star Tracy Ward, sister of film star Rachel Ward. She and Charles attended the wedding together. But once Charles left, shortly after midnight, Diana and Philip Dunne danced together until dawn, seemingly oblivious to the other people on the dance floor.

Making a public spectacle of herself was one thing, but real consternation ensued when Diana accepted a weekend invitation to stay at Dunne's family home. Prince Charles was abroad. Diana's decision to stay the night under the same roof as Dunne, without proper chaperons, made her susceptible to gossip and innuendo and alerted the royal courtiers that Diana cared nothing about her reputation, her marriage, or the dignity of the Royal Family. To subject Charles to speculation that he was a fool, if not a cuckold, was a most glaring example of Diana's headstrong character. When the press revealed Diana's weekend visit, Britons began to ask what was really going on in the royal marriage.

Throughout the year 1987, the two grew further apart.

His wife's behavior was having a depressing effect on Charles. Charles often looked tired and worried. Instead of his customary bonhomie and good humor, he was irritable and short-tempered, even with his immediate staff, which was most uncharacteristic. There was even serious talk of possible separation—but nobody mentioned the word *divorce*. It could never be countenanced.

In October 1987, the Princess's conspicuous absence from an important wedding fueled the intensity of the growing public interest. This was the wedding of Lord Mountbatten's granddaughter, Amanda Knatchbull (who Mountbatten once hoped would marry Prince Charles) to Charles Ellingworth. Because of the special relationship between the Royal Family and the Mountbattens, all the royals from the Queen down turned out for Amanda's wedding. Except Diana.

Charles's grim face in church confirmed what was in most people's minds: his own marriage was in desperate trouble. Diana's excuse was that she was too busy packing for the couple's official visit to Berlin the next day. No one believed her. Diana never missed *her* friends' weddings. The public snub to her husband, his family and friends, and the Mountbatten family was a reminder that she wouldn't kowtow to anyone.

The executive committee of the powerful 1922 Committee of Tory backbenchers concluded in 1987 that the Royal Family was in urgent need of better advisers, and they made public their view that certain younger members should make strenuous efforts to avoid criticism.

The controversy grew, as did Charles and Diana's seeming indifference to each other. In the autumn of 1987, Charles, desperately unhappy, went to Balmoral. There seemed no one he could turn to. He was hardly on speaking terms with his father, who wouldn't have understood anyway. He didn't want to discuss the matter with any members of the family, not even the Queen Mother, with whom he had always enjoyed a close relationship. His family, brought up with such a thorough respect for duty, couldn't possibly comprehend the problem. Emotional turmoil was beyond them.

He stayed alone at Balmoral for over five weeks, shooting, stalking, and fishing, while Diana remained in London with the children. Diana continued her solitary social life. She would lunch with a girlfriend, attend small dinner parties—in private homes as before, but also, more and more, with small groups of friends in London's smart restaurants—dance at clubs, and drink.

On one occasion, after they had been separated for a month in 1987, Charles flew to London to see William and Harry at Kensington Palace. He stayed with the children while Diana went off to a London night spot to celebrate Fergie's twenty-eighth birthday with Prince Andrew, Viscount Linley, and other friends. Diana returned to Kensington Palace at midnight, and Charles left for Balmoral at six A.M. the next day. They had never seemed so far apart.

Waiting for him in Scotland was Charles's longtime friend Dale Tryon, or Kanga, as she was affectionately known. Dale had been one of the Prince's closest confidantes before he married and one of the women friends to whom he had turned for advice when he was planning to marry Diana. They were so close that Diana was offended by their friendship, and as a result Kanga was virtually banished from their circle of friends when Diana and Charles were married.

Dale was frank and honest about her attraction to Charles. She used to openly tease him that she thought him "very sexy" and "infinitely bedable." At a party in the 1970's, Dale, as a joke, grabbed Charles and, in front of everyone, marched him toward a bedroom. The couple disappeared for a few minutes, then Charles emerged from the room, smiling broadly, with his clothes distinctly disheveled. He said, "I feel as though I've been pulled through a hedge backward." Dale emerged minutes later, hurriedly adjusting her evening dress, and smiling broadly. "Mmmmm, he's wonderful," she purred.

The extroverted Dale had always been a good friend to Prince Charles. She openly told her friends, "I adore him. He's wonderful. I would do anything, anything for him, no matter what." Now Charles was facing a crisis, and

Dale Tryon was happy to help in any way. A mature, intelligent, happily-married woman, and the mother of four, Kanga understood Charles's problems. She and her husband, Anthony, stayed at Balmoral for a week. She spent most of her time talking and listening to the unhappy Prince.

Ten days later the Prince and Princess of Wales visited a flood-disaster area in Wales. They met at RAF Northolt outside London and flew together to Swansea. As they toured the area they virtually ignored each other. It had been announced that Charles would return to London with Diana, but he decided instead to fly back to Scotland immediately, without even spending a night at Kensington Palace with Diana and the children. It was evident to the world that the royal marriage was in serious trouble.

In November 1987, more in sadness than in anger, the Queen decided to intervene. The Queen is usually reluctant to interfere in the lives of her family, particularly their love lives. But this crisis was too important to the Crown. She summoned the couple to the palace for an informal talk and delineated the obvious dangers ahead if they continued warring. She reminded them that whatever their future plans might be, divorce could not be considered, even for a moment.

A member of the Royal Household, the term for the Royal Family's most senior staff members, noted: "The Queen invited both of them over for tea and a chat. But the Queen spoke directly to Charles and blamed him for whatever was going wrong in the marriage, not the Princess. The Queen did not think Diana had done anything wrong."

The Queen blamed Charles because he was far older than Diana, far more experienced in royal matters, and therefore, in her eyes, the marriage was his responsibility. Whether or not this was fair to Charles, he accepted her view that he must make more of an effort to help, encourage, and sustain Diana, since she was so clearly having difficulty settling into royal life.

Despite the Queen's appeal however, Princess Diana continued on her reckless slide toward near-scandal. She

was seen at more dinner parties where the company usually included either Philip Dunne or David Waterhouse.
But as the year wore on, Diana seemed to be seeing more
of the handsome Household Cavalry major.

Diana attended the birthday party of one of her new
friends, Jamie Keeling, at a smart Kensington pizza parlor,
where David Waterhouse was a guest. Dressed in a tight,
leopard-skin print dress, the Princess danced with two or
three young men but spent most of the evening with Waterhouse. Their farewell was noted by everyone, as they
held each other closely and kissed each other on both
cheeks. Only the night before, Waterhouse had accompanied Diana to Covent Garden to see the ballet *Sleeping
Beauty,* and they had left together in her convertible Ford
Escort Turbo.

Diana was careless of the fact that these assignations,
far from being clandestine, were taking place in full public view. As rumors grew, so did Prince Charles's distress.
He didn't have to be told by Diana, or anyone else, the
identity of the men who were escorting her so publicly
around London. Her nocturnal activities were filling the
gossip columns of the newspapers.

The tabloid press began to follow Diana whenever she
left Kensington Palace. Some of the paparazzi even
mounted a twenty-four-hour watch on her home. Officially, because of the ever-present threat of terrorism or
kidnappers, Diana is not permitted to leave her home
without a bodyguard, who is always armed with a hand-
gun. But the rebellious Diana began to flout this rule. She
would sneak away and drive her car around London. The
photographers would follow her on motorbikes with link-
ing walkie-talkie radios and mobile phones. She hated the
intrusion into her private life, but it didn't make Diana
any more discreet.

Heiress Kate Menzies had become a kind and close
friend to Princess Diana after Sarah Ferguson had introduced them. Kate, an attentive hostess, held frequent dinner parties or cocktail gatherings for her friends. Diana
was delighted to attend. At Kate's she could meet and talk
to whomever she wished in relative privacy. Briefly she

could enjoy the illusion that somehow she was just "one of the girls again."

One night in November 1987, after a party at Kate's London mews home, a paparazzo snapped Diana as she larked around with the Major. In his Audi, David Waterhouse pretended to run down Diana, who was screaming and laughing. "Stop it, stop it! You're acting crazy!" she exclaimed as Waterhouse playfully "kangarooed" his car toward her.

When photographer Jason Fraser started snapping away, Diana and her police bodyguard approached. The bodyguard pushed the photographer and began swearing. His life "would be hell," he was told, if he didn't hand over the film. But when the photographer refused, Diana took over, pleading, "I must have that film. You don't know what this could do to me."

Diana broke down in tears and sobbed. "Please, please let me have that film. No one has to know this has ever happened, do they? Not a word, please. You don't know what the whole thing is doing to me. I feel so trapped."

Diana went on, trying to control her sobbing, "I've been working hard all week, and I just don't get to go out anymore. I have got so few friends left, and this will make things worse."

Diana went on to explain. "Katie fixed up a nice evening for me. She laid on the whole thing. It's very sweet and this is the only time I've been out all week. I've got to go to Wales tomorrow and I'm so tired. I want to go to bed."

This amazing confession was a remarkable opening of the heart by Diana, who was obviously distraught. She continued, "Nearly all my friends have gone now. You don't know how it feels. You just don't know what I go through. I'm sorry, but I *must* have the film."

Fraser was so moved by the Princess's appeal that he handed his film over to the bodyguard. Meanwhile, Waterhouse had sped from the scene.

Diana dried her eyes and calmed down. "Oh, thank you. I'm so sorry. What's your name? Give me your number and we'll call you. I'm sorry to take your film but I had to have it. I promise you will get it back tomorrow."

The next day the bodyguard met Fraser and handed back the film, minus the negatives of Diana and Waterhouse. But her distress of the previous evening did not seem to instill in Diana any sense of the usefulness of discretion.

In the spring of 1989, the tenacious, watchful Fraser located his quarry again. This time the stylish Princess, in tuxedo and blue satin trousers tucked into her red boots, the casual Waterhouse in green jumper and slacks, and a small group of friends had gone to see the movie *Rain Man*, starring Dustin Hoffman and Tom Cruise, at the Princess's local cinema, the Odeon in High Street, Kensington. Prince Charles was at home at Kensington Palace, hosting a dinner for some European leaders.

While kissing good-bye in the theatre foyer, just before midnight, Diana and Waterhouse spotted the waiting photographer. Diana cut short her kiss and made a dash for her own high-powered Jaguar. Waterhouse vaulted roadside barriers in a mad dash to a friend's waiting BMW, as Fraser captured him on celluloid. The resulting photo did not flatter the Guards officer's dignity.

Minutes later Diana returned to Kensington Palace. There was little discussion with her husband that night. Around midnight, barely fifteen minutes after her return, a Rolls-Royce swept out of Kensington Palace with a backup car. Charles, alone in the passenger seat, stared straight ahead as the limousine set course for the hundred-mile drive down the M4 motorway to Highgrove House. The Princess stayed in London and attended a fund-raising lunch for a children's charity as the guest of honor. The next time the couple were together was later that same night, for the start of the traditional Easter break with the Queen at Windsor Castle.

A week later they were apart again. Diana went into a London hospital to have her wisdom teeth removed, while Charles took their two sons to Scotland for a holiday.

A flirtatious, disco-dancing, party-going Princess of

Wales was not the royal wife the public wanted. They liked their Royal Family to be worthy or courageous, like Princess Anne, who rode in the Olympics and over National Hunt fences and who did sterling work abroad for Save the Children. Seeing the Princess of Wales shouting and singing along at rock concerts and keeping company with handsome young bachelors was not in keeping with her position. Although she remained the favorite royal for the bulk of the population, some in the upper and upper-middle classes began to think her behavior vulgar.

Charles took to escaping to Scotland as often as possible. There he would fish for salmon in the rushing waters of the Dee, a sad lonely man. During the summer months he gave vent to his aggression on the polo fields, but he found himself unable to carry on his normal life unaffected by all that was happening.

He had desperately wanted a happy, trouble-free marriage. But in his search for a young, untrained bride, Charles had been swept off his feet. His ego had been boosted by the beautiful young teenager who was so plainly in love with him. The marriage he had planned for so long had disintegrated into a marriage of convenience, exactly what he had feared would happen. He knew he had to find a way out of the mess he was in and to take charge of his life again. He didn't know how.

Diana, meanwhile, knew exactly where the marriage was heading. For the rocks. She had spurned her husband, the Prince of Wales and heir to the throne, and usurped his position as the nation's favorite royal. She now realized that she could behave very much as she liked and get away with it. The fact that the marriage hadn't worked did not mean her life was going to end there. She had her two sons, her charity work, and her looks, and she was determined to enjoy her position, her privileges, and her power.

12

---◦≫≫◦≪≪◦---

Charles's Private World

Prince Charles is known for being open-minded and sympathetic to new ideas. However, his growing interest in the more spiritual aspects of our existence and his sympathy toward a way of life that embraces natural medicine, vegetarianism, organic farming and even mysticism, has led to criticism. And not a little controversy.

At one time, most ordinary Britons lumped all alternative pursuits under the vague and erroneous heading of "the occult" and believed people interested in such phenomena were a little odd, to say the least.

Princess Diana counts herself among those who believe most occult-based interests are for people who feel that investigating "extra" normal or paranormal powers might lead to a more interesting, revealing, or enlightening life. She thinks mysticism is equivalent to clairvoyancy, fortune-telling, palmistry, and crystal-gazing. She is far more down-to-earth than Charles and has been known to smile when people joke with him or tease him about his habit of talking to his flowers and vegetables to encourage their growth. On the other hand, she finds his interest in collecting antique lavatory seats odd but not totally bizarre.*

Newspapers liked to portray Charles as a crazy vegetarian health freak who meditates with gurus, but despite the ridicule, Charles's unorthodox views are having an impact. If the heir to the throne is interested in such phenomena, they must be worth a closer look.

Charles is aware that promoting his unusual views can be dangerous because so many people misunderstand him. When he was invited to learn more about the theories and practices of the British Holistic Medical Association, a healing group, he asked the association's secretary, Dr. Eric Austen, "Do people think I am a crank?"

Forthrightly asking such a question illustrated both his sensitivity to public opinion as well as his willingness to be considered eccentric. Mr. Austen's reply: "Not at all. I'm sure they think you're sensible."

Diana herself often makes quips about Charles's unorthodox ideas, describing some of his views as "cranky." Charles's friends maintain that he became involved in such subjects shortly after his marriage in 1981, when all was not going well. Others suspect he was trying to "get in touch" with his late Uncle Dickie through mediums. But in fact, Charles has always wanted to delve into the deeper, more spiritual side of life.

Charles chose an unlikely occasion to make his definitive public statement on what he saw as the meaning of life. In Vancouver, while on a tour of Canada in 1986, he waxed lyrical to an audience composed largely of lumberjacks. He told his bemused listeners:

"I rather feel that deep in the soul of mankind there is a reflection, as on the surface of a mirror, on a mirror-calm lake, of the beauty and harmony of the universe. But so often that reflection is obscured and ruffled by unaccountable storms.

---

* Charles has a fascinating collection of over thirty antique lavatory seats, which he keeps in the cellar at Highgrove. All of Highgrove's bathrooms are fitted with antique, cast-iron cisterns and antique wooden seats.

"So much depends, I think, on how each one of us is introduced to and made aware of that reflection within us. I believe we have a duty to our children to try to develop this awareness, for it seems to me that only through the development of inner peace in the individual and through the outer manifestation of that reflection we can ever hope to attain the time of peace in this world for which we yearn. We must try if we can to make living into an art itself, although it will always remain a tremendous struggle."

This remarkable speech was roundly derided in the British press. Could it be that his reference to "inner peace," which sounded so like the teaching of Buddhism, mean that Charles was flirting with other religions besides that of Christianity?

Charles has an exceptionally inquiring mind, and he is interested not only in learning about other religions but also in other less orthodox forms of spiritual fulfillment. He has sought respite from his stressful and restricting life by turning his back on civilization from time to time and going on retreats. These excursions perhaps have been most responsible for the tabloid press dubbing him "cranky," in the sense of "odd" or "flaky."

Charles has always been influenced by mentors—older, wiser men with whom he can discuss philosophical ideas. Besides Lord Mountbatten, there have been others, not infrequently derided as his "funny friends." Father Harry Williams, dean of the chapel at Trinity College, Cambridge, when Charles was a student, is among them.

Despite a thirty-year age gap, or perhaps because of it, they became good friends. Their friendship was entirely proper, but Father Williams, an ordained priest who later in life joined a monastic community in Yorkshire, caused speculation when he penned his startling memoirs.

"How profoundly glad I am for the privilege of Prince Charles's friendship," recorded the former dean, who went on to describe how, during his academic days, he had fallen in love with a number of men, noting: "I slept with several men, in each case fairly regularly."

If those memoirs had been published before Charles's

wedding—and not eighteen months later—the Prince's mentor probably would not have enjoyed so prominent a role at St. Paul's Cathedral. For Charles had made sure that Harry, from whom he had once borrowed a dog collar for one of his stage appearances ("Let's get drunk for Harry the Monk," the Prince had sung), was much in evidence. Chanted Father Williams, in a prayer he had composed for the royal marriage service: "Bless and enrich them in their joy and when, as all people must, they have to go through times of hardship and trial, give them the wisdom and strength to bring them through victoriously."

Later, when Prince Harry was born, Father Williams pointed out that any suggestion the young Prince had been named after him was nonsense. Henry, he explained, was a traditional royal name.

Charles had also had close friendships with other older, but less eccentric, sages. Among them were Lord "Rab" Butler, master of Trinity College, Cambridge, a much-respected, highly intelligent scholar; John Higgs, secretary and keeper of the Records at the Duchy of Cornwall, given the job by Charles primarily because he was an energetic thinker; Sir Hugh Casson, an eminent architect and former president of the Royal Academy; and the Prince's former English teacher from Gordonstoun, who became headmaster of Eton, Dr. Eric Anderson.

Diana cannot understand Charles's respectful relationship with some of his eccentric friends. For example, Charles had always had an ongoing relationship with Sir Laurens van der Post. Since Mountbatten's murder Sir Laurens, now in his seventies, has become an important counselor to the Prince.

The extraordinary Sir Laurens—author, explorer, mystic, and philosopher—has influenced Charles greatly over the past twenty years. Van der Post was a close friend of the philosopher and psychoanalyst Carl G. Jung, whose ideas, particularly the concept of the collective unconscious, play a major part in forming his views. But Sir Laurens is also an adventurer. His extensive knowledge of the San (formerly known as Bushmen) of Africa—who, he believes, still retain their natural psychic powers because the culture, of which they are the last survivors, existed in harmony with nature—also forms the basis of his views.

Charles accompanied Sir Laurens on a desert retreat in the Kalahari in 1987. It was their second such expedition; the first was in 1977, when the philosopher escorted Charles to the lakes of Nakuru and beyond, in the mountains of Kenya, for a ten-day trip. Their second pilgrimage took them through some of the most remote places on earth to the Xadi district, home of the Kalahari San. The Prince and Sir Laurens walked where no white man had ever been before. They spent four days in the wilderness, sleeping in tents, discussing philosophy and the meaning of life. Charles undertook the trip to "find" himself—to sort out his life, his marriage, his future, his thoughts. Apparently it was so successful that some say he then underwent a spiritual rebirth.

When asked by friends what Charles was doing, Diana replied rather disparagingly, "Oh, he's gone walkabout again in the desert. Don't ask me what he's up to. I don't know."

It is easy to see why Charles feels such empathy with the elderly mystic. Sir Laurens is a passionate conservationist, a philosopher, and an intellectual. But more than that, he is someone with whom ideas that most would dismiss as nonsense can be discussed, dissected, and debated.

Sir Laurens, to whom Charles gave the honor of being one of Prince William's godfathers, denies that he is a guru to the Prince. "He thinks for himself and doesn't need me to show him the way," he says. "We're very lucky to have a man like that. People make a great mistake if they think there are a lot of gurus whispering in his ear. The great thing is that he's a searcher—a searcher for better answers than the ones we've got. I don't see how anyone who is in search of the truth and cares about the meaning of life can avoid the immense unknown dimension of life."

Charles explained some of his views in an interview. "To me it is very interesting to see how primitive societies

—though I think primitive is a complete misnomer anyway—are the whole time subconsciously far more aware of their instinctive relationship with the things and people around them than we are in the so-called civilized world. I believe that the subconscious awareness in man is still there but buried under a mountain of . . . what?—anxieties, fears, worries, a feeling that it's something we should be ashamed of, as though rational thinking is the only acceptable process. Yet I believe instinct, sensitivity, call it what you will, is enormously important. As a result of this I am trying to teach myself to listen with an inner ear."

Listening with an inner ear has led the Prince of Wales to investigate even more esoteric pursuits. Sir Laurens believes that the Kalahari Bushmen use their powers to communicate with the dead and that we all have that capacity. Many think that Charles, too, believes it possible to reach those on "the other side," and that he tried to do so after Mountbatten died. Not with a Ouija board, as has been rumored, but through his dreams. Jung, Sir Laurens's friend, believed that dreams can be interpreted as messages from the spirit world and that the spiritual world influences everybody.

Charles keeps a notebook and pen by his bedside to write down all his dreams. Charles began to correspond with Dr. Winifred Rushforth, an expert on interpreting dreams. Diana told friends that she would sometimes awaken at night to find Charles, having put on the bedside light, sitting up in bed busily scribbling away on his notepad. At first she believed it was something he needed to remind himself about, but Charles explained it was his dreams he was trying to recall. The down-to-earth Diana found this behavior odd.

Prince Charles's notoriety relating to the paranormal really took off in the 1980s, after Mountbatten was assassinated. Stories emerged that Charles was trying to contact him using Ouija boards. The story was first published by Tom Johanson, secretary of the Spiritualist Association of Great Britain, and editor of SAGB's newspaper, the *Spiritualist Gazette*. Johanson labeled Charles the "Prince of

Psychics," a phrase Charles can't abide, and suggested that Charles was trying to convince Diana of the merits of the occult.

Tom Johanson also believes that Charles has tried to contact Mountbatten "on the other side." "Charles has told Diana that he strongly senses Mountbatten's presence," Johanson said. "In fact, after a charity ball held at Mountbatten's old home he told a friend that when he danced with Diana it was as if his uncle was guiding them around the dance floor."

Understandably, Britain's tabloid press took up the cry, and stories abounded of Charles's alleged involvement with the occult and, in particular, with Ouija boards.

However, in a television interview in 1985, Charles denied such rumors, saying: "I've seen articles saying I play with Ouija boards. I don't even know what they are. I've never seen one. I spend my entire time, apparently, trying to get in touch with Lord Mountbatten, and all sorts of other things. The answer is I don't, nor would I necessarily want to. I may as well say it, I may as well emphasize it, because I'm fed up with getting letters from people all the time saying, 'Don't touch the Ouija boards.'"

Communicating with the dead is not something that goes down well with the established Church. When newspaper stories revealed Charles's interest in the occult, the Establishment emitted predictable howls of outrage. But he received support from one influential figure within the Church, Dr. Mervyn Stockwood, the retired bishop of Southwark and no stranger to controversy himself. Dr. Stockwood revealed that he had communicated with his dead parents through a medium, and he noted: "If you cut out psychic occurrences from the Bible, you would have to cut out a great deal. It is irritating when people dismiss the whole thing as black magic or roguery."

·   ·   ·

Charles's predilection for getting away from it all to live a simple life on the land manifested itself again in 1987, when he spent three days working as a crofter on the remote Scottish island of Bernerary, in the Outer Hebrides.

The object of his visit was to compare the islanders' way of life to the farmers' in the Duchy of Cornwall. While there he cut peat, fished for prawns, planted potatoes, and rounded up lambs. Dressed in his work clothes, he was indistinguishable from everyone else. On his last night, the islanders laid on a ceilidh for him, a traditional Gaelic dance accompanied by accordion and singing.

"He had a really great time," said Angus MacAskill, who took the Prince out for prawn fishing. "Really seemed to be enjoying himself. I can tell you we were all very sorry to see him go, but I think he'll be back."

Diana could not imagine why her husband would want to visit such a backwoods place as Bernerary and stay there living the life as a peasant crofter. Diana has never understood this side of Charles and sees it as one reason they find it so difficult to live together. Diana tells her friends in a perplexed voice, "I just don't understand him sometimes, I really don't."

Charles, however, sees his activities quite simply as trying to escape his privileged role in life, and its burdensome duties, in order to learn to understand and appreciate how the most ordinary members of British society live, survive, and think. In Cornwall, Charles is a familiar figure to some of his tenants, whom he has worked with for days at a time. And like many other weekend gardeners, Charles works hard at Highgrove, where he has transformed the gardens into some of the most beautiful in Gloucestershire. This genuine eagerness, especially where hard physical work is concerned, has earned him the respect of many.

His gardening at Highgrove, which has included replanning and replanting flower beds and meadows with wildflowers, has been greatly assisted by another elderly friend—distinguished scientist, writer, and conservationist Miriam Rothschild. Dr. Rothschild, who spent a large part of her life studying fleas, is a passionate campaigner for organic farming and gardening, and she cultivates rare wildflowers at her home in Northamptonshire.

She became interested in wildflowers fifteen years ago when she noticed that many of the flowers butterflies need to feed on were disappearing, victims of chemical pesticides. She decided to cultivate her own, and her garden is now resplendent with poppies, cornflowers, buttercups, harebells, and knapweed.

She has helped Charles sow wildflowers along roadsides, on wastelands, and in his own flower beds at Highgrove. Highgrove's organic gardens are packed with flowers which attract butterflies and bees, and the surrounding meadows are full of wildflowers. She is entirely in agreement with the Prince about the necessity of preserving beautiful things: "It is spiritually important and stimulating to be surrounded by beautiful things, and we have only just noticed how much beauty has been destroyed . . . waste ground, rubbish tips and roadside verges should be planted with wildflowers," she insists.

Charles's preoccupation with his garden led to newspaper headlines like CHARLES THE MYSTIC LOON, when he remarked to a television interviewer that he talked to his plants in an effort to help them grow. He regretted making this off-the-cuff remark, since it was often cited as a reason not to take him seriously. Diana, among many others, thinks the practice is crazy. However, numbers of horticulturalists support his theory that talking to flowers and vegetables encourages their growth.

The Prince's interest in a natural life-style is reflected in his support for alternative medicine.

The British Medical Association, that traditional group of doctors utterly opposed to anything that is not orthodox, once invited Charles to be their president. They lived to regret their invitation after he began to support holistic medicine openly.

Charles is on record as saying, "I must admit that I am psychologically predisposed toward an acceptance of the value of self-help remedies such as herbal medicine, acupuncture, meditation, and special diets."

Holistic medicine—which encompasses a variety of techniques, including radionics (the psychic treatment of patients around the world through radio waves), osteopathy, chiropractic, healing, herbalism, naturopathy, and the Royal Family's particular favorite, homeopathy—strives to cure the whole person rather than just the specific ailment. The belief is that once the whole body is working well, its own healing processes are strengthened. Drugs are seen as agents that merely mask the symptoms of illness and fail to reach the root of the problem. At its best, alternative medicine works hand in hand with orthodox medicine and can be beneficial. At its worst—because there are no laws controlling its practice—it gives charlatans great opportunities.

The Royal Family are in robust health, and some may say it is because they have always believed in the efficacy of homeopathy. It is widely known that the Queen always takes along a bag full of homeopathic remedies whenever she is on a royal tour. Her endorsement, like Charles's, has increased interest in the treatment.

It was Queen Elizabeth, now Queen Mother, and George VI who first became interested in homeopathy. It works on two basic principles: (1) like cures like, and (2) the minimum dosage is to be used. That is, a substance which induces symptoms similar to the disease in a healthy person is probably stimulating the disease-fighting systems in the body, and the more a drug is diluted the more potent it becomes.

The treatments are derived from natural herbal ingredients, and together with osteopathy, homeopathy is becoming one of the more recognized forms of holistic medicine. There are six homeopathic hospitals within the National Health Service and three hundred qualified medical doctors practicing homeopathy in the United Kingdom. Even the orthodox medical hierarchy are grudgingly beginning to pay attention to it.

Charles has lately been open in his support not only of homeopathy but of all forms of natural medicine as well.

At the opening of the controversial Bristol Cancer Help Center, he said, "Remember those sometimes long-neglected complementary methods of medicine which, in the right hands, can bring relief to an increasing number of people . . . alternative treatments, especially for cancer, should not be simply dismissed as hocus-pocus."

By attending the opening of the Bristol Center, Prince Charles knowingly gave his public blessing to alternative medicine. It was a brave act when sections of the press, at that time, were insolently describing him as "loony." Some people suggest his decision to open the Bristol Center conferred upon alternative medicine the extra authority it had long been seeking, others that Charles foolishly caused fury among the medical establishment. But Charles was big enough to live with the criticism.

His interest in alternative medicine does not mean the Prince rejects orthodox medicine. Cancer specialists promptly expressed fears that he would encourage people to put their faith in bogus treatments, but that is a superficial interpretation of his beliefs. Charles thinks that orthodox and unorthodox medicine should complement each other, that there is a place for both forms.

At Bristol, patients are often being treated with the conventional cancer treatments of radiotherapy and chemotherapy, but the "alternative" treatment at Bristol—the cleansing diet, the stress-relieving techniques, the individual care, and the moral support they are provided— give them the strength to cope with the often grueling orthodox treatment.

In September 1991, the Prince highlighted the plight of cancer sufferers in a video message to launch a $35 million appeal by the Cancer Relief Macmillan Fund. He spoke movingly about the lonely plight of many cancer victims. "Some found friends avoided them, while others had to deal with a conspiracy of silence among relatives," he says. "Doctors even sometimes appeared cold and uncaring when dealing with cancer victims." The money raised though the appeal will be used to recruit 260 hospital-based cancer-care nurses.

In this endeavor, Diana has been supportive. She encourages Charles to help cancer victims in the same way she helps AIDS victims. When Charles extends the caring and compassionate side of his nature rather than the intellectual one, Diana understands him and warms to her husband. Over the years, she has tried to persuade Charles to show more kindness and compassion to all sufferers.

Prince Charles is only really happy now when he is poking his finger into pies where it is least expected. According to his staff, he often refers to himself as a "one-man NGO" (non-governmental organization) or a "single-person pressure group" or, more mundanely, a "catalyst." He talks excitedly of his battles with the Establishment and once remarked that he enjoyed "throwing a proverbial royal brick through the inviting glass of pompous professional pride."

Charles now pursues multiple campaigns, few of which Diana has much, if any, interest in. His varied targets embrace architecture, education, the environment, philanthropy, complementary medicine, the arts, and organic agriculture. In 1992, he produced a new interest, tyrophilia (love of cheese).

As a result of such complex interests, Charles has now come up with a new idea: to sell his ideas to the British public as a single concept, with the logo of a crowned C and a slogan along the lines of "An initiative of the Prince of Wales." The marketing effort, a first for the House of Windsor, will promote the Prince's main organizations, which include the Prince's Trust, the Youth Business Trust, Business in the Community, the Business Leaders' Forum, and the Advisory Group on Disability, having, among them, a combined income of $36 million a year, four hundred staff, and seven thousand volunteers. Charles has decided the time has come to give them all a higher profile.

Dealing with all these disparate activities are Charles's private secretary, Commander Richard Aylard, who joined the Prince in 1991 and looks after environmental issues; Peter Westmacott, Charles's deputy private secretary, who takes charge of education and architecture; Hugh Merrill, an assistant secretary who deals with the Prince's Trust and Business in the Community; and Belinda Harley, a former PR person whose portfolio includes the arts, health, and heritage. They read and sift through two thousand letters a week, carry out research, and prepare reports. At the end of each day, their work load ends up in a vast box of paperwork that can take Charles up to three hours to deal with.

Charles has built up this remarkable enterprise since marrying Diana in 1981, and the amount of time and effort he devotes to his activities has mushroomed remarkably. Nearly all of this work he does down at Highgrove.

At first, many thought Charles's ideas outlandish, and some called him "barking mad," but he has persisted in his ideas, accepted the criticism, made jokes about himself, and kept on with the main thrust of his crusade to tackle the important issues of the day. He no longer fears ridicule, and in 1991 he said, "I am not an expert, but I have strong feelings and not to expose them would be cowardice." His speeches are part of a strategically planned campaign to bring his presence to bear on the issues that concern him and society most in the latter part of this century. Because he is the Prince of Wales, people listen and take note.

The Prince's campaign, the outgrowth of his spiritual and philosophical development, is his response to his need to find a role, rather than idly waiting for his mother to die, which has plagued him for some years.

During the past few years Charles has become highly critical of much of modern Britain's postwar architecture, and he has lambasted the architectural establishment mercilessly, while appealing for town planners to "humanize towns and cities." In a widely quoted remark, he described one architectural scheme as a "monstrous carbuncle."

So determined was he to change British architecture

that in 1992 he launched his own London-based Institute of Architecture, which was to explore "architecture which nourishes the spirit . . . a kind of architecture based on human feeling." The institute will offer would-be young architects a foundation course in theoretical and practical aspects of design and building. As its first head, Charles chose Keith Critchlow, an architect well known for his mystical studies into the sacred geometry of buildings and his quest for the lost city of Atlantis.

In 1991, Charles turned his guns toward education, a politically explosive issue in Britain, pointing out in a speech "that one child in seven leaves primary school, aged eleven, functionally illiterate." It was powerful stuff.

More and more Charles sees himself as an agent for social change, someone who has the power to put forward his strong views and make people sit up and listen. He has gone out of his way to bring together a constantly expanding network of experts on the topics that interest him.

In 1990 he held a conference in Charleston, South Carolina, at which 120 chairmen and chief executives from around the world could discuss the environmental crisis. Declaring himself merely a "catalyst," he posed question after question, issue after issue, for which he sought written answers.

The Prince convenes gatherings of experts at regular intervals in Britain. He invites them to lunch at Kensington Palace or Highgrove, feeds them on his organic vegetables, and asks them to go away and solve a particular problem. Understandably, no one refuses his invitations.

Yet critics in Britain still maintain that Charles is a crank who indulges in unwholesome practices such as dendrological conversation (talking to trees), not to mention the anatomically inexact science of contemplating one's own navel.

Others call his environmental concerns hypocritical because he drives gas-guzzling autos like a Bentley Turbo and an Aston-Martin. His interest in philosophy is cited as evidence of a George III–style looniness. His architectural campaign is characterized as a "reign of terror." And all the time he is portrayed as a curmudgeonly, stick-in-the-mud old fogy fomenting against the youth, freshness, and glamour of the most adored royal ever, his wife Diana.

Prince Charles knows he has a long wait to become King, and he has determined that he will raise issues that will be politically impossible for him to pronounce on when he does take over the monarchy. He now feels he has a role to play, and he is doing so with all the power at his command. Princess Diana lets him get on with it. Most of the matters of principle that he brings into the open for debate are of little or zero interest to her and her coterie of friends.

13

※>>>≫≪≪≪※

The Princess of Wales: Secrets of the Queen of Fashion

It was Princess Michael of Kent, the Wales's next-door neighbor at Kensington Palace, who first noted: "Princess Diana has such a beautiful figure she would look good in a sack." The British fashion industry, a multimillion-dollar export business, knows that fact full well. Diana's good looks and fashion sense make her their most important asset, a strikingly good-looking young woman who stands 5 feet 10 inches tall, her bust and hips measure a rounded 35 inches, her waist fluctuates between 28 and 30 inches, she takes a slender 7AA shoe, and she wears a size 10 or 12, depending on the designer. (British and American sizes are comparable.)

The Princess of Wales was first hijacked by the British fashion industry in 1979, when she wore a gossamer Laura Ashley skirt to work at a Kensington kindergarten, and the Fleet Street photographers posed her backlit, exposing her legs for all the world to see. When she saw the pictures in the papers the next morning, Diana said later, "I buried my hand in my face and went scarlet with embarrassment. I felt I couldn't set foot outside again. I was showing everything."

The naïveté of that totally unprofessional pose, holding a child in her arms, won over the nation at a stroke. Here was no toffee-nosed, upper-crust member of the aristocracy, but an ordinary girl looking after children in a nursery. The British people loved it. Here was a girl that everyone could relate to and accept as one of their own. Given her background, that image wasn't quite true, but it won for Diana an army of loyal supporters who have never deserted her.

Ever since that first fateful photograph, Diana has been learning the hard way how not to duck out of a limousine when wearing a low-cut evening dress and out of a car when wearing a short skirt. But she became knowledgeable about fashion and clothes quickly for a girl who had grown up without a mother to advise her and a father who was not even remotely interested in women's fashions.

Lord Spencer said: "She has always loved dressing up. I can remember when she was a child always wanting to dress in grown-up clothes, pretending to be fashionable." Though there were maids at their Norfolk home, Diana always insisted, in her early teen years, on doing her own washing and ironing to make sure she looked smart.

When Diana Spencer burst into the limelight, she was a rather pudgy-faced, healthy-looking country girl, certainly no classical beauty. Her large nose always embarrassed her: "I hate my nose," Diana has often quipped, "it's so large. One day I am going to have my conk done." But despite many newspaper stories about her "nose bob," she hasn't yet done it. On various occasions she has also denigrated other parts of her body: "I don't like this awful mole above my top lip. I think my legs below the knee are far too thin. I would love a fuller figure, particularly up top."

No one, even those in the fashion world, predicted that Shy Di would become one of the great beauties of modern times, displayed on more magazine covers in the past decade than any other woman in the world. But she has managed to do just that.

·   ·   ·

When Diana was single, she was very much a Sloane Ranger, wearing the upper-middle-class look that girls and their mothers have propagated for the last thirty years in Britain: dark blue skirts and sweaters, with a blouse, dark blue shoes, and dark blue tights. Occasionally they would wear flowery Laura Ashley separates and, of course, blue jeans. For evening, they would put on a little black dress or a full-length skirt with a ruffled blouse. Sloanes are strong on wearability but short on flair or imagination.

The look was, and still is, more a uniform than a fashion statement. It was fine for Di, the kindergarten teacher who shared a Chelsea apartment with two or three girl-friends and lived on crisps, chocolates, coffee, spaghetti, and something on toast while biking around London to save money.

But it was not suitable for a Princess of Wales in a fashion-conscious world. The transformation from duck to swan began well before the July wedding in the following year, 1981. Her own family showed up to take her in hand. Within hours of those first pictures, her mother, Frances Shand Kydd, came to London and took Diana shopping.

It was Frances who bought Diana the blue suit, designed by Cojana Cobalt, off the peg from Harrods, that Diana wore for the famous engagement photos taken in the gardens of Buckingham Palace.

But it was her sister, Jane Fellowes, who had worked at *Vogue* as an editorial assistant, who really metamorphosed the old Di into the dashing, high-profile young woman who captured the fashion world. When Jane approached the London editors of *Vogue* and suggested they help her sister, they enthusiastically agreed. Editor-in-chief Beatrix Miller, soft-spoken deputy fashion editor Anna Harvey, and beauty editor Felicity Clark were the principal members of the task force that helped create Diana's new image and injected the fresh-faced country girl with a dose of chic.

Diana would sneak into *Vogue*'s offices in Hanover Square by the back entrance and be closeted upstairs with the special Diana team. They went through her entire ensemble, from her makeup to her perfume, her hairstyle and coloring, and her entire wardrobe, down to bras and panties—everything she would need to look the part of a princess.

One of the team recalled, "Diana would spend hours here, sometimes just looking at old copies of *Vogue*, watching the next issue of the magazine being prepared, or rummaging among some clothes that were to be used for a photographic shoot. It was while doing this that she discovered a blouse she loved, designed by a young couple hardly heard of outside the fashion world—the Emanuels."

Thus began a love-hate relationship with the famous husband-and-wife design team that has gone on ever since.

Diana was furious when she believed the Emanuels were cashing in on the success of the famous wedding dress that Diana wore when she became the Princess of Wales. "We'll see about them," she stormed to her friends at *Vogue* when newspapers alleged that the designers had revealed secrets about her dress. Diana was still angry when they presented her with a white leather photo album showing the various stages of making the dress and the final product.

She later said, "As I sat looking through the album, I felt like tearing out the pictures and bashing them over the head with the book, I was so cross."

But in fact, the Emanuels had revealed nothing, and have produced many stunning designs for Diana since then.

Vogue's task force even gave Diana hints on how to avoid embarrassment and stay elegant in the toughest conditions. Diana confessed to blushing madly whenever she was talking to "important" people, because she feared saying something foolish or naïve. She was told to stand upright and not to drop her head or look sheepish, which was her habit, and she was advised to sip some water when feeling bashful and to realize that everyone speaking to her was far more embarrassed then she was.

At first Diana could not accept the advice. She said to her roommates, "I wish I could believe what they tell me. But I still feel awful on so many occasions. At those times I still wish the ground would open and swallow me up. Charles tries to encourage me, but he's not always there."

Britain throbbed with debate and argument in March 1981 when Diana wore a strapless black satin Emanuel dress to a charity dance at London's Goldsmiths Hall and revealed a plunging display of cleavage.

Independent Television News ran a prime-time bulletin, with frame-by-frame shots showing Diana stepping from the car. Viewers were asked to judge whether young Diana had overdone the décolletage. Most people took Diana's side, dismissing the hoo-ha as nothing more than a prurient slight on the beautiful young woman.

Diana has since been more careful. She once told the Emanuels, "I am terrified that one day I might pop out of a low-cut evening dress and show everything. That would be too terrible for words. I would feel so terrible." But she hasn't done so yet.

In those early years, most of Diana's wardrobe was put together by Anna Harvey, who introduced her to Bruce Oldfield, Victor Edelstein, Catherine Walker, Murray Arbeid, Jacques Azagury, and other British designers. Later Diana turned to Caroline Charles, Alistair Blair, Rifat Ozbek, and Arabella Pollen, also all British designers. But Diana has always loved best the work of Caroline Walker and hatmaker Philip Somerville. From the outset, Diana wanted to help the British fashion industry and asked that her official clothes be purely British. It was, of course, an excellent diplomatic move that helped her win the total support of most people in the nation. Now her clothing labels read like a Who's Who of the British fashion world. Other designers Diana helped in the early 1980s included Donald Campbell, David Neil, and Benny Ong, to name but three whose careers blossomed with Diana's assistance.

Diana now goes further afield for her purchases, particularly for what she calls her "private wardrobe." She loves Chanel and Yves Saint Laurent but also buys clothes from the Italian Moschino, German Escada, and Mondi. She of course makes exceptions to not wearing foreign designs when visiting overseas. In 1987 Diana wore Escada to Germany and in 1980 wore a Chanel to France. On both occasions the host countries applauded Diana's selections.

In the past few years, however, Diana has begun to relax her hard-and-fast rule of Brits-only on British soil. She wore a striking black-and-red houndstooth Moschino jacket, teamed with a black-and-white skirt topped by a chic red sombrero for the 1990 christening of Princess Eugenie (the second daughter of Prince Andrew and Fergie). And to lay the foundation stone of the new wing of London's world-renowned Great Ormond Street Hospital, she wore a chic red Chanel jacket with gilt buttons and a filmy black pleated skirt. Both outfits were greeted with great enthusiasm by the fashion writers.

Anna Harvey has since become more than just a fashion adviser to the Princess. They are now good friends, and she simply refuses to speak about her relationship with Diana. The two young women now also share an interest in the same charity, Birthright, for the rights and care of the unborn child, of which Diana is a patron. Shy, slim, dark-haired Anna and her stockbroker husband Jonathan have three children. In 1987 she was offered the job as top fashion buyer for Harrods but preferred to stay on at *Vogue*.

For some time in the early 1980s, Diana would attend designers' catwalk shows—the renowned events where models parade on a raised platform and the guests' seat assignments reflect their current status—but on Anna's advice, private shows are now organized for Diana at Kensington Palace so she can have personal think tanks in absolute privacy. She still listens to advice, particularly from Anna, but has become increasingly secure in her own choices.

At the beginning Diana was nervous about everything, even shopping, but she soon learned to enjoy the privilege of never having to worry about money. Her only concern is not simply to look good, but to look sensational. Now she totally enjoys herself whenever she goes out shopping, spending either Charles's money, or the Crown's.

Suzy Menkes, fashion editor of the *International Herald-Tribune*, commented, "In the old days there was lots of giggling and fun and jokes whenever Di went out shopping with Anne or other friends. They would spend some time in shops simply having fun. Now it's more businesslike. Twenty minutes maximum while the business is done, and then out before the crowds begin to realize it really is Diana."

Sometimes, if Diana wants to do some serious shopping in a major store, arrangements will be made for her to arrive before opening or after the shop closes so she can take her time and choose in privacy. But more often than not, Diana will shop on impulse. She and a detective will drive somewhere in London and spend perhaps fifteen minutes. Most customers, and often the staff, remain totally unaware that it is *the* Princess of Wales.

Diana likes it that way. To nervous shop managers she says: "I don't want people to put themselves out for me. I just want to shop like everyone else. Please don't make any fuss. I'll be fine."

Harriet Jagger, senior fashion editor of British *Vogue*, has followed Diana's changing style. She said, "In the first, shy, teenage phase, Diana's main concern was quite simply having enough clothes to do the job, that she didn't appear day after day wearing the same clothes.

"Then she moved into the more adventurous, experimental phase with various styles and different fashions, using many differing designers. In this phase, in her early twenties, and in between having two children and wearing maternity clothes, she became more glamorous, sometimes floaty, but always feminine. As her hair became more blond, more chic, and her skirts followed fashion and became shorter, she earned the embarrassing title of Dynasty Di. She hated that.

"I remember one talented designer, Gini Fratini, who epitomized the feel of this time and this look. On a visit to the National Film Theatre in 1981 Diana shone demure in a bottle-green Fratini dress with a large lace collar and just a peep of lace petticoat. At first, some of the press thought it was an accident, but of course it wasn't. She had a brief affair with the puffball skirt, all the rage in the mid-eighties, and a hot little backless gold lamé number which gave her the Dynasty Di look. Her pert Sergeant Pepper military jacket with gold trimmings was pure Hollywood. She looked great.

"In this phase Diana did make a few fashion faux pas, but remarkably very few, really, when one considers that every time she steps out, a whole world of female critics are desperate to find fault and criticize. It must put her under great pressure. One such example was in 1987 when she turned up at Lancaster House for a stunning reception dressed in a dressing-gown-style outfit, giving rise to jokes that she was wearing Prince Charles's nightwear!"

Suzy Menkes created a storm of protest when she criticized one of Di's more adventurous outfits. The Princess arrived at the theatre to see *Phantom of the Opera,* in March 1987, dressed in a provocative, figure-hugging suede jacket, a short leather skirt, and lacy black tights. In a BBC interview, Menkes remarked that she was appalled that the Princess looked like a supermarket check-out girl.

Diana took the criticism marvelously. Three years later she met Suzy Menkes at a fashion party and said with a big smile, "You can be assured that little ensemble won't ever be seen again." And it hasn't been.

In the middle eighties, after Britain had suffered three years of severe recession and mass unemployment, Diana's clothes became a subject of controversy. People began to question her love of shopping and clothes. While many Britons were surviving on the basics, and some relying on the dole to exist, Diana appeared to be spending a fortune on her back.

It was claimed that her $2 million wardrobe weighed over a ton, contained over three thousand different outfits (not counting underclothes and nightwear), and barely fit into two huge walk-in wardrobes the size of very large bedrooms. Her ball gowns stretched the width of *eight* terrace houses, about fifty yards. Diana was also believed to have six hundred pairs of shoes from shops like Charles Jourdan, Midas, and Berties, and to own over four hundred hats.

In fact, virtually everything Diana decides to buy is sold to her at cost. In April 1985, when Diana seemed to be wearing a new outfit for every occasion, rumors flew that she was spending around a million dollars a year on clothes. When she flew with Charles on an official state visit to Italy, a major center of the fashion business, it was suggested that her wardrobe had cost a staggering $150,000.

Diana got back at her critics by appearing at Milan's famous La Scala for a majestic gala evening, and the most important fashion event of the year in Italy, wearing an evening dress she had worn two years before, in Canada. The old dress, a beautiful pink chiffon by Victor Edelstein, silenced the carping overnight. "That'll show them," Diana told her dresser when she sailed forth into the night to face the throngs of paparazzi.

When Diana goes on official royal tours, formally representing Queen Elizabeth II, the entire cost of her wardrobe is paid for by the Queen's Treasurer. He has a special fund which comes from the Civil List, the name given by Parliament to the money allotted yearly to the Queen to pay for upkeep, her hundreds of staff, and all the members of the Royal Family who carry out official duties on behalf of the state. In 1990 the Civil List was nearly $10 million.

Diana's private wardrobe, however, is paid for by Prince Charles, who can well afford it. The annual income from his estates, including the Duchy of Cornwall, is some $2,000,000. Out of this sum, he pays approximately 25 percent in taxes and maintains his two homes (in Kensington Palace and Highgrove, in Gloucestershire), pays for all his personal staff and the household bills, and keeps Diana the best-dressed woman in Britain.

What Diana actually spends on her wardrobe is difficult to estimate. The guesses of fashion experts range from

$100,000 to $250,000 a year, which does not include the expensive outfits she wears when representing the monarchy on overseas visits. Although her outfits are purchased from designers at cost, they still do not come cheap.

Bills are signed for by one of her ladies-in-waiting, usually her great friend Anne Beckwith-Smith, and sent to Kensington Palace for payment. In some shops, a detective will produce a Duchy of Cornwall American Express card, and the goods will be purchased instantly. The Amex card is never put through a machine to authenticate it.

Besides being a mother and royal spokeswoman, fashion is Diana's business. Expert attention must be given her clothes so that the Princess looks perfect, whether shopping, picking the boys up from school, attending a charity event, or dining at a state banquet. That task is performed by her two personal dressers, Evelyn Dagley and Fay Appleby. Every garment is carefully sprayed and pressed as it is worn, whether for an hour or a day. Then the clothes are individually packed into plastic bags and labeled with the details of where and when and on what occasion they were last worn. After each item is worn twice, it is taken to the dry cleaner. The dresses are checked for missing buttons, damaged hems, and other minute details of the Royal wardrobe.

Royal skirts are generally weighted at the hem to avoid showing too much leg in strong winds; hats are equipped with a special device to stay on in wind and driving rain; heavy bags can cause a sagging shoulder and distort a neckline; sleeves cannot be too tight, otherwise they might tear from the constant hand-shaking; a simple clutch bag is nearly always what Diana holds so she can easily accept bouquets and shake hands.

Diana admits to adding to her wardrobe every week, and usually more than once. She simply cannot keep away from the shops. She loves it and admits to it. She confessed: "Sometimes I know I shouldn't buy something but

I just can't resist it. It's a terrible temptation, and I can't stop myself."

She regards shopping as an excuse for a bit of fun, an indulgence. Once she tried on a figure-hugging Patrick Kelly sheath that she knew was far too tight and that Charles would never allow her to wear. Twirling on the sidewalk outside the shop, she asked her detective, waiting near the door, "Do you think this is too tight?"

"Yes, Ma'am," came the reply.

"Well, I'll buy it then," Diana replied with a laugh. And she did.

She prefers to buy her own underclothes. For everyday wear she usually goes to Fenwicks in Bond Street for inexpensive panties and bras. Diana also loves to wear Janet Reger's pure silk and satin lingerie. For special events, Diana splurges on expensive French and Italian underwear.

Despite it all, Diana says clothes are not a priority for her. In 1988 she commented, disingenuously, "I enjoy bright colors and my husband always wants me to look smart and presentable, but out-and-out fashion isn't my big thing at all." Perhaps one reason is that Diana is a fashion trendsetter, with the power and influence to dictate fashion rather than having to follow it.

After ten years of holding center stage, Diana, now over thirty, is not only Britain's most famous ambassador but also still the most important clotheshorse for the British fashion industry. What Diana decides to wear will be photographed, copied, manufactured, simplified, and offered in shops within a matter of days. Those who try to emulate her style may not always succeed, but what matters is that the stuff sells.

When criticism of her self-indulgence was at its height, Diana turned up at an important event in a dress she had been seen wearing on numerous occasions. One of Fleet Street's friendlier photographers asked her, "Why are you wearing that boring old frock again?"

"I suppose you would like it better if I turned up naked," Diana replied.

The photographers all laughed. "Please, please! We would love it."

Diana just smiled and went on her way.

On another occasion, goaded beyond endurance by all the fuss in the papers about her extravagance, Diana turned on the photographers: "I just can't win," she complained. "You accuse me of spending too much on my clothes or wearing the same outfit all the time. I wish everyone would stop talking about my clothes."

During the past few years, perhaps in answer to the criticisms, Diana has been offering some of her cast-off designer clothes to her sister, to Fergie, and to close friends. They are happy to accept, for most of the garments are sensational and would cost a fortune to purchase, and the women in turn hand them on to others. Fergie gratefully accepts Diana's older clothes, has them altered, wears them a few times, then gives them to her sister, Jane Makim, in Australia.

While attending an aristocratic wedding reception in the late 1980s, Diana joked: "It was amazing. I looked round the guests and discovered that a number of the women were wearing my cast-offs. I just smiled to myself and said nothing. Only two of them came up to me and confessed. But I told them to be quiet so that no one would know. It was our secret."

Diana does the same with her children's clothes. Fast-growing Harry, two years younger than brother William, wears the clothes his elder brother has outgrown. Diana believes this shows she can be thrifty and is not intent on squandering Charles's money. Besides, in Britain, upper-middle-class children traditionally wear hand-me-downs. Most of Britain's expensive, fee-paying schools even hold secondhand-clothes sales at the end of every year.

Now that Diana has turned thirty, Harriet Jagger believes she has matured and need not experiment anymore. Harriet commented: "She has changed from being nineteen to someone totally different. The designer who currently reigns supreme is the lovely and discreet Catherine Walker of the Chelsea Design Company. Diana loves her

elegance and style. They work together with two or three
principal looks that suit Diana.

"Catherine Walker is a charming and elegant dark-
haired Frenchwoman in her forties who started her company in 1977, after she had taught herself to make clothes
as a therapy after her husband died. It began as a hobby,
as something to take her mind off her husband's death,
and she built up a successful business employing more
than forty highly skilled dressmakers. Her exquisitely-
made couture clothes range from $1,000 to $10,000."

Adds Miss Jagger: "These clothes give off very clear
signals. Simple, assured, pared down, fluid, serious and
above all elegant; they say very plainly a professional
working woman with style. No one can call the Princess
'Dynasty Di' anymore or describe her as a fashion victim.
For the daytime she now dresses not to kill but to work."

Princess Diana now wears mainly Catherine Walker for
her public engagements. These are nearly always tailored,
structured clothes, created by cutting excellent fabrics in
neat, tapering lines. The suit or dress is teamed with an
accessorizing coat is complemented with a matching hat
and the finest quality leather court shoes (plain, basic
women's shoes with a heel).

A favorite Catherine Walker suit, worn to many functions, that clearly defines Diana's businesslike style is a
sophisticated cream jacket with red contrast facing and
matching skirt. Another Catherine Walker creation for
more glamorous occasions is a silk coatdress, a stunning
number in vivid, clashing shades of pink and red, fastened
on one side with large gilt buttons and topped with a
Philip Somerville cloche in matching colors.

The Princess now confines herself to a few eye-catching
prime colors, in line with royal custom, but she still has an
occasional lingering fondness for black. Detailing is now
simple and workmanlike. Gone are the fussy bows and
trimmings.

Miss Jagger argues: "If a woman wanted to copy her
look, she would need to invest in a straight tailored suit,
classic court shoes, real jewelry, and be exceptionally well
groomed, with a good figure. There are now no easy ac-

cessories to give someone the 'Diana look,' no bits and pieces. It is a total look which, of course, is very expensive to emulate."

By her own admission, Diana has become a perfectionist in her dress. If everything doesn't meet her high standards, she is unhappy and uncomfortable. In the early days of her marriage, she used to stand before her full-length mirrors, trying on outfits and discarding then, simply because she didn't feel 100 percent right. Now she is more assured and confident of her taste, and has learned to cope with looking only 95 percent right.

The off-duty Diana look is much easier for others to copy. When she drops off Harry or William at school, she is the perfect modern 1990s glamorous young mum, usually in a loose jumper and well-fitted skirt, or sometimes a smart blouse tucked into jeans with Texas boots and a baseball cap.

Diana is like most other young mothers. At home she usually dresses in jeans and a sweater or shirt. She wants to be as she was before she met Charles, and act as if she was just an ordinary mother at home with her family. The home might be a palace, she might be a princess, her husband might be heir to the throne, but Diana loves to enjoy the simple side of life with her sons.

As Diana told her sister Jane, "I just love to get home and kick off my shoes, take off my smart clothes, and get into jeans and a sweater. Then I really feel like myself, the real me."

And when she takes part in the inevitable Mother's Race at sports day, Diana makes sure to dress like most of the other mums, in a long pleated skirt. She tries to appear as one of them, not the star of the show. With all the attention trained on her, this is difficult to carry off.

Diana also tries to dress to flatter her hosts, to make that little extra effort which people always appreciate about her. This usually comes off most successfully on foreign trips. In Japan in 1986 she wore a dress with the national symbol of the rising sun. She will wear a sailor hat to a naval base and an army-style jacket to visit a British regiment. All this takes time and attention to detail, thought and hard work, but Diana knows it pays off. The people love her for it.

Diana knows full well that she has that certain je ne sais quoi, that indefinable appeal that men find instinctively attractive but which she is careful never to flaunt in her dress. Sometimes she will wear a long, light summer skirt split to the thigh to show a flash of long, svelte leg; another time a long, tapering V top reveals a little cleavage. But she never overplays the innuendo in her dress and never wears a split skirt and a hint of cleavage at the same time.

Occasionally, Diana likes to dress as if she weren't a princess. At chic Gstaad, where Charles loves to ski every winter, Diana will take herself off with a group of friends in the evening to attend a disco. Charles, of course, prefers to stay in the chalet and read or have dinner with some of his chums. Diana likes to get out there and enjoy herself in ways she cannot in Britain. Gstaad is the winter playground of the rich and famous, and Diana knows that there she can get away with being herself. She'll arrive at the disco huddled under a big coat, then reveal tight, figure-hugging trousers and a thin sweater with a hint of no bra. Then she will spend two or three hours dancing, drinking, and chatting with other members of the party.

At polo in England, which Diana now sometimes attends with the young Princes, she will show up dressed informally, like everyone else, in a bright casual frock and flat pumps. Indeed, at polo Diana probably dresses more casually than the other women, who believe they should dress up if Charles and Diana are present. Diana knows she is attending a sporting event, not a fashion show.

Diana sometimes loves to play to the press photographers, knowing the shot will appear in newspapers and magazines around the world. In 1990 she took off for the West Indies with Wills and Harry for winter sunshine, leaving Prince Charles back home in cold, damp, wintery Scotland. The paparazzi followed, taking out boats each day to stand off the beach waiting for the family to go for a swim. It was not till the second day that Diana emerged, wearing a bikini and a long, light, flowing, sexy summer skirt which made her look more like a highly sophisticated *Vogue* model on a summer shoot. The effect was stunning.

When Diana returned to the house, she said, "I hope I wasn't too naughty. But they had been waiting for so long in the hot sun that I thought they would like it." Newspaper and magazine editors around the world loved it.

Sometimes Diana will wear something the fashion world snaps up within minutes. Perhaps her most famous fashion innovation was clasping Queen Mary's beautiful emerald choker around her forehead to accompany a one-shouldered dress. The headband was stunning, and within days, this 1920s fashion was back with a vengeance.

Would Diana be more daring if she weren't the Princess of Wales? Miss Jagger believes so: "Her private wardrobe is just as enviable, in a casual way, as her working clothes. She has a great collection of frocks, bomber jackets, baseball caps, cowboy boots, shorts, and outrageous tops, but we never, or hardly ever, see them.

"But I don't think she would ever have been in the least bit 'punky,' nor do I think she would ever have worn really short miniskirts when they were in fashion. She may, though, have worn tights with short skirts, but not too short. She isn't from that sort of background."

Diana is often considered a tomboy. She used to "borrow" Charles's shirts until he complained. Now she has Turnbull & Asser make similar shirts for her at a hundred dollars each. She has worn Charles's dinner jacket for an evening out, pushing up the sleeves in a fashion trend which many young women gleefully snapped up and copied.

Diana is often seen popping into men's outfitters, not only to buy the odd sweater for Charles, but also to shop for herself. She occasionally goes into Hackett in Fulham and Paul Smith in Covent Garden and leaves with shirts, sweaters, and a silk waistcoat for herself.

And it is at men's shops that Diana purchases her nightwear. On a trip to France, in November 1988, Diana confessed, "I love sleeping in pajamas, but not that slinky, sexy lingerie for women. And I don't seem to be able to find any women's pajamas that fit well. So I always sleep in men's pajamas in the winter. And in the summer I don't wear anything in bed." Sometimes, for variety, she wears men's nightshirts.

Diana's private wardrobe is something very few know about—it is her secret passion. Only then does Diana—and her dressers and those who know her best—see the real Diana, the girl who is basically shy but would love to dress wildly.

Diana told one of her *Vogue* team: "I like dressing for myself the way I dance. I love losing myself when I'm dancing in private. People never see me dancing, not the way I really love to.

"I used to spend my time at home when I was a teenager listening to my music on my own and dancing as I wanted to, wildly, in an abandoned way. It was the only way I could express myself then, and I do the same thing now. It's wonderful therapy. And I'm telling you all this because that's the way I think about my clothes. In private I love to dress in an outrageous way. Charles hates it, of course. So perhaps might lots of people. But I love it."

One such item of personal clothing Diana loves is her really wicked pair of Hermès ostrich-print leather trousers. She has other pairs of tight leather trousers, all of which make her look extremely seductive, with her long, slim legs and her well-muscled backside, kept taut by constant swimming, which is her favorite way of holding on to her model-like figure.

It is said that Diana has become more conscious of her figure, more determined to look the super mum, more keen to be outrageously sexy in private as her relationship with Charles grew more difficult. It seems the more Charles and Diana became estranged, the more Diana threw herself into her body and her clothes.

Now, in the 1990s, Diana recognizes that she is two very different people: One is the public Princess, dressed for work, for interviews, for meeting people, for receptions, for her charity obligations. The other is the private Diana, whose life as a Princess has nothing whatsoever to do with her personal life, friends, entertainments—and clothes.

Diana, it seems, cannot win. Ten years ago she was criticized for dressing too much like a high-fashion model. Now that she is in her thirties, the designers are complaining that her dress sense has become boring.

Diana is now very, very particular about how she looks, what she wears, and what statements her attire might be making to the world. Whenever she wears something new, Diana goes through all the newspapers the next day, checking how the outfit looked. And she is happier now that most of the tabloid press in Britain, which will run a picture of her in a new outfit, are in full color.

During the late 1980s, when Diana knew her marriage was in crisis, she wanted to find a way of telling the world what her situation was. She was being criticized for her apparent high-handed attitude to her staff, for the plethora of royal sackings she had instigated, for her attitude toward Charles and the rest of the Royal Family, for her spendthrift approach to her fashion-conscious clothes mania. So Diana decided to dress for a charity evening—the royal jeweler Garrard's famous annual charity night—as Mary Queen of Scots, beheaded in 1558. Diana wore a Renaissance-style dress, with its traditional high collar, made by Catherine Walker specifically for the society fashion magazine *Harpers & Queen*. They lent it to Diana for the evening, and she looked stunning. What made the whole effect was the Mary Queen of Scots cross she wore. That night, Diana looked forlorn, a sad, lonely figure, creating through her costume precisely the picture she wished all to see.

Elizabeth Emanuel commented, "Diana is just proving that she is in tune with the times. The 1980s were a boom time for Britain, there was lots of romance and people with money to splash out on fashion. Now we are into the more serious nineties, the economies of the world aren't booming, Britain is in a long recession, and she is reflecting the mood of the people. And so she should. It would be embarrassing if Diana looked frivolous. And she has grown up. Just ten years ago she was a teenager. Now she is a mother of two growing sons and in her thirties."

Jeff Banks, one of Britain's most respected fashion experts, hosts the BBC's "Clothes Show," a weekly television program watched avidly by most young people involved in the industry, fashion pundits, and Diana herself. It is a must for chic idea-seekers. He said: "I think she is just great now. She has found the compromise between the glamorous and the practical. The royal uniform has to have a kind of formula to it, and this is the only reason she can sometimes look old-fashioned.

"The hip-length jacket with the skirt must be comfortable to wear and something she doesn't have to worry about. And that's important when you spend your entire life meeting different, and many highly critical people, and yet you must look one hundred percent the entire time. That is an incredible discipline for anyone, especially someone like Diana, who the world believes has to look stunning whenever she appears."

Jeff Banks takes note of everything Diana wears, scanning the newspapers, magazines, and television news to see her. He said: "Diana is now wearing more and more of the same clothes. For example, I have seen her wear a lilac jacket for Ladies Day at Ascot, a very important fashion date, and since then I've seen it worn with different length skirts on a number of occasions.

"And I think that is perhaps because Diana does use her favorite designer, Catherine Walker, a great deal. When someone sticks to one designer, then it is often found that a woman will recycle her clothes more often, rather than take dramatic chances all the time. Now Diana wants to be known as a workhorse, not a clotheshorse, and that's a decision she has taken. I admire her for that, refusing to slavishly, constantly change to keep ahead or abreast of the latest trend."

Diana does, however, like to feel involved with her designers. She wants to make them feel they are part of a team, her team, to make her look good, not just for her own self-esteem or her gratification, but because she is the Princess of Wales; they are all assisting to make sure the Princess looks the part.

She is on first-name terms with all her designers and helpers, and they in turn seem to enjoy, if not indeed revel in, putting together her outfits. But they are most certainly not on first-name terms with Diana. They all call her Ma'am (to rhyme with *harm*). At Christmas she always sends them cards, usually a color photograph of the family, Charles, herself, Wills, and Harry, with the official Prince of Wales crest on the outside. To her designers and helpers Diana always writes a personal note, such as "Thank you for helping design my dresses," signed simply, "Diana."

One cutter to a British designer rushed into work one morning and saw someone she half-recognized waiting at the reception desk. "Hi, how are you?" she asked in a welcoming voice.

"Oh, I'm fine, thanks," came the reply from the friendly young woman.

"What are you up to now?" asked the cutter as she waited for the lift, hardly bothering even to look at the person she was talking to.

"Oh, just the same old thing," came the reply.

It was only when shooting upward in the lift that the young cutter realized to whom she had been chatting. Her heart sank. She said, "I shall never forget. I went bright scarlet. I had been talking to Princess Diana and simply hadn't realized. I felt such a fool. A few weeks later we met again and I apologized. She just laughed and told me that I had seemed in such a rush she thought it would be fun to have a joke. So she did. She really is a good sport. When she is being fitted and chatting away with everyone, it is sometimes difficult to remember who she is. As a client she is just wonderful. Always so understanding and an absolute delight to work with."

If Diana doesn't like something, she either doesn't say anything or pulls a face, which all around instantly recognize as a "no-no." One of Diana's favorite hatters, John Boyd, has a shop in Brompton Arcade and provided her wedding-day going-away hat: small with a curvy brim and a flowing ostrich feather. She teamed it with a new pink Belville-Sassoon outfit, but the hat Diana had seen and bought on the spot months before. Boyd described the process of coordinating hats and clothes:

"We are invited to the palace and are shown a selection of clothes designs which the hats must complement. Then one will go away and come up with ideas which I hope she likes. If she doesn't approve there is usually a very quiet silence. So I come up with another idea, quickly. But, what is lovely, is Diana never makes me feel 'yuk' or embarrassed. She understands we cannot always gauge her thoughts correctly. But it is great fun trying."

Jewelry is another matter. Diana is simply not fussy about the jewelry she wears. She will occasionally dive into a costume jewelry shop like Butler & Wilson and emerge with something different, like a pair of earrings or the odd-looking brooch which she knows she can team with some of her outfits. "I don't mind if it's fake or real," she happily confesses, "it makes no difference to me."

Some cynics retort, "Well, of course it doesn't matter to Diana. She has all the jewelry she will ever need, and more."

During the past decade, Diana has acquired a formidable collection of jewelry. As Princess of Wales, Diana is frequently presented with gifts of the most sensational jewelry, some of which she loves, and some of which she would never want to wear. She also has access to the Queen's jewelry, reputed to be the most valuable collection in the world, but only for special occasions, state visits, or the more formal royal occasions. However, the Queen has given Diana "bits and pieces" as gifts.

Diana's jewelry collection began at her wedding, when the Queen gave her an emerald necklace worth a king's ransom, and a diamond-and-pearl bowknot tiara. Charles gave her an Art Déco emerald-and-diamond bracelet, which she loved. The Queen Mother gave her an enormous sapphire brooch, surrounded by diamonds; it was so heavy the brooch pulled down any bodice it was pinned to. Quite a start for a teenager in love with the man of her dreams.

Diana has two tiaras—one from the Queen and one from the Spencer family. She complained forcefully, "They either give me a terrible headache or they fall down over my forehead, pushing my hair into my eyes. I hate wearing them." Thus there are very few pictures of Diana in a tiara.

The Princess has received the gifts of extraordinary jewelry from Arab kings, sheikhs, and sultans. The "rocks" are amazing but sometimes set in designs Diana dislikes. Discreetly, she has them reset in a style she prefers. She has been given the most wonderful suites, or strings, of diamonds and sapphires; she often wears them not as intended, but as a magical fashion accessory, such as turning a sensational sapphire suite into a choker and a cascade of diamonds into a bracelet.

Despite her fairy-tale wardrobe and jewelry collection, Diana retains enough perspective to laugh at herself. Recently she was about to buy a beautiful Cartier watch in Zales, costing about $30,000, when she realized it didn't have any numbers. "Oh, I can't buy that without any numbers!" she exclaimed. "I'd never know what the time was."

What is truly surprising is that Diana managed to present this confident image to the world when her own married life was slowly disintegrating. She talked to her sisters and to her friends about the growing divide between Charles and herself with some desperation. She had tried, and failed, to persuade Charles to spend more time with her and the family, but to no avail. She knew she could do nothing about it. What she could do something about, however, was herself and her persona. And this she has achieved with panache.

14

---❖❖❖❖❖❖---

The Royal Beauty: Discipline and Nature

By 1991, Princess Diana was fed up with most of the published photographs of her, the majority of them taken by newspaper photographers and paparazzi. There had, of course been picture sessions with such "royal" photographers as Lord Snowdon, Lord Lichfield, and selected others. Still there were few photographs of herself that Diana truly liked.

She admired the work of French photographer Patrick Demarchelier, renowned for his pictures of the world's most exquisite women—both private sitters and professional models—and his apparent ability to make them all look sexy. With friends at *Vogue* and with her close friend Major Jamie Hewitt, she discussed the idea of asking Demarchelier to photograph her.

Diana was embarrassed to ask Demarchelier, fearing it would make her appear too pushy, too full of her own looks and importance. But Jamie persuaded her to go ahead. She finally asked the French photographer if he would be interested, but told him to forget that she was a Princess. She wanted simply to be photographed as a woman, as he would any model, and she hoped he would make her look great.

He agreed, and the effect was stunning. The swarthy Demarchelier decided to portray Diana in a cover-girl pose, resting her head on her hands and smiling gently at the camera.

A makeup artist and a hairdresser were brought in, just as in any cover-girl shoot. Diana wore more makeup than usual to counteract the studio lights and to bring out her eyes; her hair was ruffled in a way which Diana never chose for herself; her nails were perfectly manicured.

Demarchelier later commented. "I waived my ten-thousand-dollar fee because it was a privilege to photograph the Princess Diana. I do not believe I have ever before photographed a more beautiful woman.

"In fact, I did three totally different sessions with the Princess this year. She is very easy to photograph; she is a natural model. It is simple to make her look beautiful because she *is* a beautiful woman. After taking the photographs I showed them all to Diana and she chose the one she wanted. I understand she intends to give the pictures away to special friends."

Sarah-Jane Hoare, fashion editor of British *Vogue*, which has now twice featured shots of Diana on its cover, explained: "He likes women to look sexy, and he makes them look sexy. But unlike a number of photographers, especially those in the sixties who wanted women to look sexy because they wanted to go to bed with them, Patrick makes them feel safe. He likes people to look real. What makes his pictures of Prince Diana so brilliant is that he has underplayed her. He let her personality shine through."

Originally, Diana had no intention of publishing the photographs anywhere; they were designated solely for her personal friends. As she explained to friends at *Vogue*, "Every photo of me is taken because I am the Princess of Wales, not because I am Diana. I wanted some pictures of the real me, photographed naturally, and not because I am married to Prince Charles. I like what he did. I hope everyone else does."

However, Diana did show them to then editor of British *Vogue*, Elizabeth Tilberis. Over lunch, Liz tried to persuade Diana to allow her to use one photo on the cover. Diana refused, worried that the world would think her vain. She thought her friends would ridicule her for wanting yet more pictures when most magazines ran great numbers of photographs of her every year. By the end of lunch, however, Diana had been persuaded, with one important proviso: Liz Tilberis promised to plug three projects of which Diana is a patron—the Arts 2000 Year of Dance, the English National Ballet, and the London City Ballet—in *Vogue*.

Though naturally shy, and once lacking in confidence, Diana does now believe that she has a certain beauty, which both men and women admire. Ever since she became Princess of Wales, magazines and newspapers worldwide have published a torrent of pictures, all making the point that Diana is beautiful. Though she fears becoming conceited and vain, even arrogant, as a result, Diana still strives to make herself attractive, fit, and healthy, no matter what the monetary cost or the physical effort required. Feeling fit gives her self-confidence, and secretly she loves the attention.

A 1985 poll of British women identified Diana as the woman they most wanted to look like. In 1992, another poll came up with the same answer. It is a remarkable achievement to top the polls for over seven years, from the age of twenty-four to thirty-one. And she did it not because she is married to the Prince of Wales, but solely because of her looks.

It was not always so. The rather pudgy girl that Charles first wooed in 1980 was a plump, not exceptionally attractive, 140 pounds. But during the six months Diana secretly lived in an apartment adjoining Prince Charles's in Buckingham Palace prior to the wedding, the bride-to-be took strenuous, hour-long swims every day in the indoor palace pool. Swimming, always one of Diana's favorite pastimes, helped her to shed at least ten pounds before the great wedding day in July 1981.

In addition, royal dance teacher Lily Snipp, then a

sprightly seventy-seven-year-old, came to the palace and put her through her paces for one hour, twice a week. Lily was happy to help the fledgling Princess.

"Diana had once lived for the ballet and even had dreams of becoming a serious ballet dancer," Lily relates. "But she grew too tall for that. She loved our dance hours. Not only did they help her get fit, but they relaxed her. Diana was in Buckingham Palace, feeling trapped by her new position in life. It was very difficult for her to adapt to the situation, and I think dancing helped take her mind off everything."

But for the *new* Diana, trying to get into shape for her wedding, swimming and dancing were not enough. She forswore eating everything she wanted, including excessive pasta, beefburgers, and chips in favor of slimming salads and fish. Even when pregnant with William, Diana was determined not to put on too much weight, despite cravings for chocolate and biscuits. Diana's postpartum depression, which lasted some months, took yet more pounds off her.

Toward the end of 1982, she had dropped to an alarming 110 pounds, quite thin for a woman of her height. But she was still pounding away in the pool, pushing herself to faster and faster times as she swam at least twenty lengths every day.

Charles and her doctors worried that the young Princess might have a tendency, as did her sister Sarah, to anorexia nervosa. She was put on tonics to boost her appetite and encouraged to eat more. Ignore the strict no-fat diet and exercise routine, doctors warned her. They were taking too much out of her. (Now, several physicians feel that Diana was suffering not only from postpartum depression, but was fearful that she was losing the love and admiration of her husband.)

For the past seven years, Diana has fluctuated between 115 and 125 pounds but believes her best weight is just under 120. She keeps that weight not so much by dieting as by exercise. She is determined to keep her remarkable 35-28-35 figure, and, engagements permitting, she works at it every day.

After Harry's birth in September 1984, Diana took a breather from her fitness routine. The following summer, a picture of her walking along a beach with William while on holiday showed a tummy overhanging her bikini bottoms. "I saw myself," she said, "and went yuk, how awful I look." That picture stunned her back to her old routine.

Back home she once again swam every day and took up dance lessons again. Twice a week, dressed in her black leotard, Diana would do a strenuous one-hour workout of ballet and then tap. She always finished in a sweat.

She joined the Pineapple dance studios in central London, enjoying her weekly stretch exercises until too many people recognized her and stared as she worked out. It became unbearably difficult to concentrate or relax in the classes, so she had to find some other way of keeping fit.

She tried working out in the Buckingham Palace gym, playing music and using the Jane Fonda fitness tapes. But Diana found she needed the company and the ambience of people to encourage her.

Secretly, under the name "Sally Hastings," she went to an American-style gym—full of Nautilus machines, treadmills, step machines, weights, counterbalances, etc., which was then quite rare in London—called LA Fitness in West London. This was London's most trendy fitness factory in the late eighties, where young women were put through their paces as if it were boot camp.

Diana enrolled like any other member of the public. She filled out a detailed medical questionnaire, saying she had two children and a history of back pain, but revealed no other medical details. Her weight, height, and measurements were taken, including measurements of her thighs, calves, forearms, and biceps, so the gym instructors could judge her progress. Her heart and lungs were tested, and her blood pressure examined at rest and then again after tough exercise. Diana even took advantage of a one-hundred-dollar discount off the enrollment fee, which was part of a general offer to the public.

She was put through a strict no-frills regimen. Unlike nearly all the other London health clubs, there was no Jacuzzi, no pool, and no alcohol. Instead, the patrons were put through a grueling workout on the sophisticated $300,000 gym equipment. It was all done professionally, with instructors making sure clients did not try to over-reach themselves. Diana loved it, especially the cloak-and-dagger aspect of her secret life.

"This place may look hard, but it's an environment people work hard in and enjoy working hard," said LA Fitness manager Bruce Taylor. "Princess Diana picked this club because she knew it was the toughest one in town. She is very knowledgeable about keeping fit and knows you don't get much benefit from swimming in a tiny, kidney-shaped pool, lying around in a Jacuzzi, having a massage, and then sipping a gin and tonic."

Another reason Diana loved the gym was that it enabled her to be with other people, instead of being isolated in her ivory tower, Kensington Palace. "It's lovely just to get out among normal people and it makes me feel good to exercise and work out," Diana told one of the women at LA Fitness. "I love it."

But it was not to last. Some members tipped off the press, and in September 1990, she was photographed by a newsman leaving the gym. Her secret was out. At the next visit a horde of photographers were waiting for her. With great regret, she realized she would have to quit the club.

She next took the workouts, led by her personal trainer Carolan Brown, to Kensington Palace. Diana persuaded her to visit the palace two or three times a week. When the workouts began, the palace staff were surprised to hear loud, high-energy funk music blaring out of the room where Diana and Carolan were doing aerobic exercises, but after a while they took the wild, hour-long music sessions for granted.

Carolan, who has a degree in movement and dance from London University, says, "The Princess is in superb condition. She is a very fit woman, particularly when you consider she has had two children. She comes from what we call the well-conditioned market. She already knows about fitness and knows what she wants to work on. Our aerobics are a great way of toning up all over. Most women who come here want to firm up their backsides and the tops of their legs and the abdomen muscles, and that's what Diana wants too."

After a few months, Diana moved up to more strenuous work called stepping, a low-impact exercise where the athlete steps on and off a plastic box called a body board. Stepping really gets the heart pumping and tones the leg muscles.

"Diana's dancer's grace makes it look easy," Carolan explained, "but it's very easy to stumble off the box and fall quite hard. She is good at it, but she has taken a few stumbles as well. What's good is that she gets up again with a smile and starts right back again. But I don't treat her any differently from any others I have in my care. She wants me to help her get really fit, and that's what I'm doing."

One reason Diana seeks to be super-fit is to improve her tennis game. She had played at school and occasionally made up tennis parties when on school holidays. Though she had enjoyed the game, she never excelled at it. After the birth of Harry in 1984, Diana played an odd game at people's country houses during the summer months but had never taken it seriously. Then she realized that if she could find the right setting, she could meet and chat with people, and perhaps be allowed to enjoy the ambience of a club.

Diana yearned for the company of others. She was becoming more lonely, feeling herself drifting further apart from Charles. Typically, she wanted to be with more ordinary people, not royals or their friends, who only wanted to invite her to parties, dances, weekends, or tennis games because of her position—the Princess of Wales.

A friend suggested she join the Vanderbilt Racquet Club in London's Shepherd's Bush, without doubt the most exclusive tennis club in Britain, more exclusive even than the All-England Club, the official name of the world-famous tennis club at Wimbledon. The Vanderbilt was the brainchild of Charles Swallow, a former Harrow School history teacher, who bought the premises for $1 million in 1984. At the time, it was an ordinary indoor club with five poorly-heated courts, a sparsely-furnished bar, and shower rooms which members described as "a goddamn fridge." Swallow spent another $1 million totally refurbishing the place, which now boasts a wealth of facilities. The Vanderbilt has night courts with four different surfaces and sixteen professionals to instruct its members. There is a children's practice area, where Diana loves to take Wills and Harry. There is also a fully-equipped gymnasium, a massage room, and a beauty parlor for women. For the less energetic, there are bridge and snooker rooms and a table-tennis area. The Vanderbilt's bar serves champagne, wine, and liquor, but Diana rarely has anything but fruit juice.

The club is expensive by London standards. The initiation fee is $2,000, and the annual membership fee is $1,500. A court costs $50 an hour, and a coaching session, which Diana has once a week, costs $25. With lunches and occasional beauty treatments, Diana lays out about $11,000 a year at the Vanderbilt, but she believes it is money very well spent. She tries to visit the club two or three times a week.

The members are undeniably from the privileged classes, though money alone is not enough to make one a member. Swallow accepts only those with that certain ineffable quality of worldly belongingness. Those who qualify include not only the Princess of Wales and other aristocrats, but also an amazing cross-section of society, including people like Mick Jagger, Charlton Heston, and Steffi Graf.

Says Lady Annunziata, a London socialite and an enthusiastic member for six years: "I love it here and so, I believe, does the Princess. It's good for everyone, whether you're a brilliant tennis player or abysmal like myself. There is never a feeling that you are too bad to play here, as there is in some clubs.

"And when you play here you are never conscious of famous people being around you. Many people who come here are famous in one way or another, and that makes everyone behave naturally. It must be a lovely atmosphere for someone like Diana to relax in."

Once, after a game, Diana was having a fruit juice in

the restaurant with her partners. As she left to speak to a friend she said, "Keep my seat, please, will you?" This wonderfully natural question illustrated a charming, modest side of Diana. She simply did not assume that no one would dare take the chair of the future Queen.

Adds Sir Patrick Sergeant, a publisher, who is also a member: "What is so lovely is that you can bring the whole family here and everyone fits in and no one minds. There is no snootiness at all. Diana made it known when she joined that she wants to be treated like any other member, which was lovely for her and for everyone else as well. She seems to love the place."

In 1990, Diana once played top-ranked world tennis star, Steffi Graf, at the club. Charles Swallow explained: "Diana has always admired Steffi's play and asked whether it would be silly if she asked whether Steffi would mind giving her a game. I told her to leave it to me and I fixed it up. Steffi was only too delighted.

"Diana has come on really well since she started playing here. At first, we had to iron out some basic problems in her game because she had never received any real coaching and had picked up some bad habits. Most of the time she is coached by Rex Seymour-Lyn and has developed into a competent player. She is now an intermediate club player of real promise. She is naturally athletic, has a good eye, and plays a good game.

"And," he stressed, "I must add that she is not a fair-weather player. She plays a sweaty, punishing game and likes to keep going for a good hour. And of course she likes the exercise."

Charles Swallow watched Diana's game against Steffi Graf: "It was during Wimbledon in 1990. Of course Steffi didn't play her hardest tennis and smash the ball at her. But Diana stood up to Steffi very well and gave her a good game. I think Diana really enjoyed herself that day."

Afterward Diana, smiling broadly, told Steffi, "I hope I wasn't too awful for you, thank you very much. I think I've got some way to go yet."

Perhaps dreaming of helping to shape real champions, Diana now takes William and Harry along during school holidays at least once a week for proper coaching. They seem to enjoy their outings there, especially when they play with their mother.

Another of Diana's serious interests is dancing of any type. In October 1991, when handing out the Arts Council's Year of Dance awards in London, she said, "I love to dance. I love to jive, because it makes me feel so alive. Dance is one of my greatest loves. It is one of the best ways I know of expressing the joy of living."

She then went on, "Dance is a universal language with a unique ability to express human ideas and emotions to bring people together."

Diana, well known for her skill, danced with President Ronald Reagan at a White House dinner in 1985, and then surprised everyone by dancing, with professional ease, with John Travolta. For six weeks in 1983 she took ballet lessons at the South London Studio of Royal Ballet director, Merle Park. In December 1985, she took the stage during a charity event at the Royal Opera House, Covent Garden, with Wayne Sleep, one of Britain's best-known modern dancers, and wowed Prince Charles and the revelers with a sparkling dance display. Diana had secretly rehearsed the movements weeks before, receiving instruction from Wayne Sleep over the telephone! For the final rehearsals Wayne went to Kensington Palace, and they danced together in tracksuits to Diana's then favorite hit, "Uptown Girl" by Billy Joel.

After the performance, Wayne said, "She has rhythm, she can do high kicks, and she has a real feel for jazz dancing. The rehearsals were amazing. We had a great time together."

The whole act was a closely guarded secret, kept even from the cast. Throughout the performance that evening, Charles suspected nothing and hardly noticed when Diana excused herself and left the royal box toward the end. She dashed backstage, changed quickly into a hip-length, flimsy top with tights and ballet shoes, and waited for Wayne's signal. The audience, in tails and formal gowns, gasped audibly when Diana walked out onto the stage. Charles was amazed. Diana and Wayne danced everything from jazz to waltzes to the Charleston. They were called back eight times, and after each round of applause, Diana curtsied perfectly to the royal box. Later that night, she confessed, she had been practicing for weeks.

Dancing is yet another tragedy for the couple. Charles, unfortunately, is embarrassed at dancing in public and never dances any more than he absolutely has to. In their earlier days, Diana did all in her power to persuade Charles to dance with her, but he never wanted to. He had been taught to dance at school, and at Buckingham Palace as a teenager at lessons arranged by the Queen; as part of his royal upbringing, he had to learn the social graces. Though competent at ballroom steps, dancing makes him feel shy, awkward, and self-conscious. He describes it as "the awful exhibition" whenever he and Diana have to perform before hundreds of people to start the dancing off for the evening.

Though she hides it when dancing, Diana has one really painful physical problem. She has suffered backaches ever since Harry was born. She kept her back problem a secret until July 1991, when she told the Anglo-European College of Chiropractic, "This is undoubtedly the area I support. I have chiropractic treatment myself and have been doing so for seven years."

She believes her back first became injured when she stood for hours at official functions and engagements. It may also have been caused by her habit of picking up children on official visits. She also loves to gather up her own children, even when they became too old and too heavy.

"I just can't resist some young children," she says. "They stand before me, some with their arms stretched out. I just want to pick them up in my arms, so I do."

Ironically, recurring backache is one thing she and Charles share. He believes he first hurt his back playing polo, and that his backache has been exacerbated by continual riding, as well as the number of hours he has to stand at official royal engagements. In 1991 Charles thought he might even have to quit polo, not so much because he broke his arm, but primarily because he could not rid himself of the back pain, despite physiotherapy and chiropractic treatments.

Diana is a frequent patient at the Hale Clinic in London, where a chiropractor massages her painful back muscles. Says Medical Director Graham Heale, "It is a fairly vigorous and very precise manipulation we give for back problems. We try to move joints that have not been moved for years. If you can get them moving again, it eases the pain. The treatment involves deep pressure on the muscles to relax spasms."

Swimming is the best possible exercise to keep back muscles moving. Today, Diana, who always enjoyed swimming, even at school, happily swims most days at the Kensington Palace indoor pool, keeping fit and easing her back problem.

As a particularly health-conscious person, Diana is very aware of everything she eats and drinks. Her diet forms a vital part of her fitness program. Her typical breakfast is homemade muesli with skimmed milk or wholemeal toast with just a smear of butter. Once a week she treats herself to a chocolate croissant without butter. Most mornings she will have fresh orange juice and usually takes a fizzy multivitamin tablet to supplement her diet. Lunch is only a light single course: perhaps a lightly cooked vegetable soup or a nonfatty pudding. In the evening she eats a simple meal, perhaps fish with steamed vegetables or a salad with grilled chicken.

Diana always has her vegetables steamed, never boiled or cooked in the oven, and she prefers her chicken grilled. However, she still likes pasta. Her favorites are carbonara as well as seafood in a cream and mushroom sauce. But her meals are never heavy, and seldom include meat. When she goes out for lunch with friends to her favorite Italian restaurant, San Lorenzo's in Beauchamp Place, near Harrods, she will usually have a salad. One of her favorites is avocado and mozzarella cheese, along with a bottle of mineral water. Occasionally she will indulge in one of their scrumptious puddings from the trolley. But not too often.

Diana faces a diet problem only at official lunches and dinners—usually heavy affairs crammed with calories and carbohydrates. The hosts are always informed beforehand that Diana prefers a light meal, and her staff suggest that she not even be offered the main course.

Diana has earned the reputation of eating very little, but that is not true. She did go through that "starving" phase, but not for long. Now she exercises so much and runs about doing her official duties that she needs to take in sufficient calories to keep going.

Some of the myths about Diana's poor appetite stem from official occasions when members of the Royal Family mingle with guests at supper and cocktail evenings. Understandably, everyone wants to speak to the royals, especially Diana, who is very much in demand. Since it is difficult to chat, shake hands, and hold a plate, fork, and glass at the same time, Diana prefers to eat nothing and concentrate on the job at hand.

Guests often say after the affair, "Diana doesn't eat a thing, I never saw her take as much as a nibble." But appearance is illusory in her royal world. Diana will excuse herself for a few minutes, while her ladies-in-waiting explain that she has had a tiring day and is going to lie down for a while. In reality, Diana will retire, put up her feet for five minutes, and devour a sandwich to keep up her strength. The guests will have seen nothing.

"As beautiful as an English rose" is often used to describe Princess Diana. She thinks it highly flattering; Diana does enjoy the smooth complexion that often accompanies the saying.

But it is not simply nature's gift. Diana works at it.

She achieves her look by paying regular monthly visits to the Mayfair salon of beautician Janet Filderman. Like Diana, Janet believes in a minimal skin-care regime: light cleansing and moisturizing, supplemented with regular facials. Janet generally uses vacuum suction to remove the dead skin.

"I may not go down too well with the billion-dollar beauty industry," Janet confesses, "because I believe that 90 percent of skin-care problems are caused by beauty products or their misuse.

"We're obsessed with removing anything natural and plastering on expensive creams. Good skin relies on healthy blood. That comes from cell renewal, not a wonder cream designed in a laboratory."

Warming to her subject, Janet goes on: "This misuse is why I believe so many women have bad skin on their faces. If it was down to anything else they would have bad skin over the whole of their bodies." And she believes outbreaks of acne are usually an overall health problem that should be treated medically.

Diana's simple routine is a good wash of the face in the morning, followed by a gentle rubbing in of a cleanser, which she takes off with a tissue. Usually, she will apply moisturizer to the neck and sides of the face, leaving the central T-zone (forehead, nose, and chin), which looks after itself, totally clear. Then, Diana finishes off her morning facial with a gentle spray of warm water—and nothing more.

At night, Diana adopts a similarly light routine, gently cleansing and then applying water to keep the skin blooming. She never applies night cream, leaving the skin time to renew itself during the hours of sleep.

Unlike most women, however, Diana has a special makeup problem. She must contend with the constant glare of TV lights and powerful spotlights whenever she appears on stage. She cannot let her face swell up under the harsh camera lights or let her mascara run in the heat of the lamps. Smudged lipstick would look appalling and prove embarrassing. Whether in the freezing wind of a New York winter day or the burning heat of a Saudi desert, Diana must contrive to look fresh, glowing, and beautifully made-up. And she must make sure her makeup never hints at being overdone.

Prior to her wedding in 1981, Diana was introduced to

Barbara Daly, known as Britain's makeup wizard, whose celebrity clients include Joan Collins. One of Barbara's first actions was to persuade Diana to throw away the pink blusher she used to conceal her fine cheekbones as well as the powder-blue eye shadow that detracted, rather than enhanced, her naturally bright blue eyes.

Diana now uses blusher in subtle shades of russet and peach, to throw her cheekbones into relief, and a concealer, to hide bags under her eyes or the occasional blemishes on her usually flawless skin. She makes the vivid blue of her eyes seem even more electric with a thin shadow of blue eyeliner on the lower rim of the eye, a tip given her by Elizabeth Taylor.

Barbara Daly taught the young Diana everything she needed to know about makeup: how to blend colors with a soft brush to avoid harsh lines; how to take account of her special features, like the stronger left side of her face; and how to compensate for her distinctive nose, which has caused Diana much embarrassment during her life.

For an extra-glamorous look for special occasions, Barbara curled Diana's naturally long eyelashes and then applied blue mascara. Sometimes, Diana experiments and paints her eyelashes blue-black to match a particular outfit.

One of Diana's makeup specialties, her "Golden Goddess" look—which *Vogue* experts have described as "making strong men melt"—is achieved by preparing the inside of the eye with white pencil, then using a light blend of apricot and gold eye shadow, finishing off the mouth with gold lipstick.

Says Barbara Daly: "The Princess has discovered a great deal about what will and what won't work to give her the right look. I gave Diana all the tips I knew. Since then she has learned to be a real expert at doing her own makeup. I think she manages very well considering the tremendous pressure she is often under.

Diana loves fashion, but she also enjoys walking around bare-legged in the summer. Protocol forbids that, however, so that even with temperatures in the nineties, Diana must wear stockings to a Buckingham Palace garden party, or face a severe reprimand from the Queen.

As soon as summer arrives, Diana applies brown-tinted body makeup to her legs until the sun give them a natural, delicate tan. But she still pops into Headlines in London's Thurloe Street for leg and underarm treatments to give herself that polished look.

Her taste in perfume is simple. Her trademark scent is the subtle, floral Diorissimo for daytime. At night she prefers Estée Lauder's more exotic scents.

Caring for her hair, Diana's crowning glory, takes time and work, but she attempts to keep it to a minimum. If she must leave the palace before seven A.M. for a trip upcountry, there is no time for a complicated hairdo. But whatever Diana does to her hair, the odds are that within a matter of weeks, many women will have asked their own hairdressers to copy the latest Princess Di style.

The secret of her endearing fascination for stylists who follow her lead is that she never settles long for any particular look. Her haircuts have ranged from the dreadful, short Teddy-girl DA crop to a glamorous 1940s shoulder-length braid.

When Diana appeared looking like a 1950s delinquent Teddy-girl, Richard Dalton, who became Diana's stylist in 1985, was held responsible. But it was not his fault.

Diana herself explained later: "I had got into a rage about something, I can't remember what. I was angry and frustrated. I was standing in front of my mirror in the bedroom and suddenly had this mad urge to cut off my hair. So I did. I tried to cut off just a part of it, to make it short, less feminine. I don't know why. When I realized what I had done I phoned Richard immediately and he came round."

All Richard could do was to cut off more to balance her head. Diana had to wait weeks for it to grow out before Richard could give it a proper new style. "I've never repeated that experiment," Diana laughed.

Her fine, flyaway hair could look dull and lank without proper care. Her naturally mousy, ash color is regularly highlighted, and the roots are permed to give the hair lift and body. This also makes for a flattering femininity and reduces the harshness of her profile, which Diana frankly doesn't like. Occasionally, she treats her hair to a deep-conditioning treatment, which she believes revitalizes it, reducing the effects of swimming. Her shampoo is a camomile, and for conditioner she mushes bits of banana with other creams.

Except for special occasions, Diana's hairstyle has been more functional than feminine, to accommodate her regimen of sports and exercise. Her hair is now generally styled loose at the sides and shaped trimly short at the back. It is the most versatile possible for her life-style— unfussy and natural during the day, and yet dressy enough for evening. What Diana rejects is any style that takes time and trouble. She does not have the leisure to sit for hours in a hairdresser's chair.

But Diana does encourage good relationships with her hairdressers. She likes to feel they know her likes and dislikes. Since she was sixteen, Diana had enjoyed a good relationship with hairdresser Kevin Shanley, who worked in South Kensington, and whom she used to visit during school holidays. It was Kevin who did her hair for her first dates with Prince Charles.

"I remember her telling me one day that she had an extraspecial date and asked me to do her hair especially well," Kevin recalled. "Of course it wasn't until I saw her picture in the newspapers that I realized who that special date was that night."

Kevin fixed her hair for the famous engagement photographs at Buckingham Palace and for the most important date in Diana's young life, her wedding. But Kevin was dumped, on advice from the Palace, when he allegedly gave away all Diana's beauty secrets to a Sunday tabloid. In 1985, he was succeeded by Richard Dalton, who had taken care of the Princess's hair when Kevin was absent.

Dalton devoted the next few years to caring for Diana, on standby most days, and many nights, waiting for a call from Kensington Palace. He built his day around Diana's busy schedule, often working at seven-thirty in the morning after her morning swim, and then fixing her hair at night for the theatre, a charity film premiere, or a formal dinner.

Dalton's cuts left an unmistakable imprint on Diana's hair over the years. It was Dalton who advised her to be bold and go gold. He persuaded her to ditch her initial, hesitant highlighting, which he thought gave her a sun-bleached effect. Instead he advised her to go wholeheartedly for the blonde bombshell look. Diana loved it from the start, and so did the public. And she still does it.

But Richard Dalton, too, fell by the wayside. In 1990 he found his name plastered over the tabloids, which alleged he had promised to persuade Princess Diana to support an AIDS benefit being promoted by Dionne Warwick in London. Dalton claims he never made the promise, but Diana broke with him. She now uses different hairdressers and seems to have no particular favorite.

Charles, of course, thinks Diana spends far too much time on her looks. He severely criticizes her for making no effort to improve her mind, either through serious books or conversation, and for having no considered views on worthwhile subjects. He is further appalled that she spends fortunes on maintaining the right "image."

Diana, in turn, hates what she believes are Charles's deliberate attempts to put her down intellectually.

As far as the world is concerned, Diana has won the argument. She is the one whom magazines feature on their covers and whom the crowds yearn for.

Diana, Princess of Wales, has called upon her position, wealth, and cunning to make use of every avenue, every available talent, every method to enhance the one factor she knows will always keep her on top: her beauty. With her, it is not just the idle pastime of a spoiled rich woman. Rather it has become one of her key tools in her fight for independence and power.

15

❦ ➤➤➤⫸⫷⫷⫷ ❦

The Sensitive Princess

The young Princess of Wales unofficially came of age when she was twenty-six years old, married for nearly six years, and the mother of two young sons. That moment was a turning point in her life because she decided to become involved with AIDS, a subject that was all but shunned by "the great and the good" of British society. Overnight, Princess Diana changed from a young mum who liked to shop or listen to pop songs on her Walkman, to a mature young woman who had created a role for herself.

The metamorphosis came the day in April 1987 when Diana opened Britain's first purpose-built ward for AIDS sufferers, at London's Middlesex Hospital. *The Times* correspondent reported that, remarkably, "she did not wear any protective clothing."

At that time the average Briton knew very little about AIDS. Some believed it could be caught and passed on by touch or kissing or even hugging someone who was infected. The revelation that a royal, like Princess Diana, the mother of two young sons, one the heir to the throne, had taken such an enormous risk with a deadly disease

shocked many people. The great majority thought she was
foolish at best, and stupid at worst, to have taken such a
dangerous step. And for what? Perhaps, after all the criticism of her flippant, frivolous life-style, she wanted to
prove herself with a dramatic, headline-catching act of
bravado.

Before Diana went to the clinic that day, she had to
observe standard royal protocol. The Buckingham Palace
bureaucracy had made all the usual rigorous checks that
the cause was indeed suitable for the young Princess of
Wales. Her office sought advice from the Department of
Health and a number of independent people in the field.
Papers were written by the Department and sent to the
Palace for perusal. The National AIDS Trust was contacted and advice was sought from their senior members.
Was it advisable for the Princess of Wales to become involved?

Buckingham Palace was torn. Some of the Queen's advisers totally opposed the young Princess's becoming involved with AIDS, a taboo subject never discussed in
polite company or at British upper-class dinner parties. In
1987, many Britons condemned it as "that gay disease"
which only affected "homosexuals and drug addicts," two
groups which received very little sympathy from the chat-
tering classes, many of whom believed the victims were
reaping the harvest they themselves had sown. The advisers argued strongly that the public would be unsympathetic and warned that becoming associated with AIDS
charities could harm her position as the future Queen.
They also feared it could weaken public sympathy for the
Royal Family.

But Diana was determined. She pleaded with Prince
Charles to bring his weight to bear on her side in the
argument. Charles preferred not to get involved, fearing
his mother sided with her counselors.

"I must do something. Someone must do something,"
Diana told a close friend. She contacted charities to produce studies showing how innocent babies and young
mothers who had nothing whatsoever to do with homo-
sexuality or drug addiction had caught the disease. Armed

with this evidence, Diana returned repeatedly to the attack until she won the day.

The Palace bureaucracy reluctantly capitulated to Diana's determined arguments and pleas and officially met the senior members of the charity. The Department of Health and the Charity Commissioners had already investigated the National AIDS Trust and reported that the charity was efficient and well run. It seemed a highly reputable charity, one in which a member of the Royal Family could become involved without risk of scandal by the trustees. Only then did Buckingham Palace agree that Diana could go ahead.

Now, five years later in 1992, Buckingham Palace adopts a different attitude. Press spokesman Dickie Arbiter explained: "It's abundantly clear that Princess Diana is determined to break down prejudice about HIV. Nobody told her to adopt this cause. Everything she does is spontaneous and nothing is premeditated. It was her own decision to show the world that you could not catch AIDS by touching someone infected with it."

The Princess has gone about her new commitment with great fervor. The more she discovered about the status of AIDS sufferers, the more determined she was to push their cause.

"She was the first important person in Britain to show you can touch an AIDS victim and not catch it," says Pamela, Lady Harlech, an AIDS fund-raiser of some years. "One cannot overestimate the importance of what Princess Diana did that day. Before that no one would go anywhere near them. AIDS sufferers were treated by the general public as though they were the untouchables, that to touch them meant death.

"And when the Princess picked up a baby with AIDS in New York it took all the stigma out of it. I think that one of the things that genuinely upset Diana, to the core, was that children were getting it as well.

"Diana is genuinely interested in the cure of AIDS. I've been at various events with her where she has specifically said that at her table there should only be people who work with AIDS patients—doctors and researchers, as opposed to grandees. She is incredibly well informed."

One of Diana's close friends, Angela Serota, is also involved in helping AIDS victims. Angela, the wife of Nicholas Serota, director of London's Tate Gallery, spent months nursing Adrian Ward-Jackson, an AIDS charity worker whom Diana had come to know well from working together on various AIDS causes before he realized he had the disease.

Angela has seen Diana's compassion for people and why she stands out, far above all the other royals, in her caring approach to suffering.

"She's driven by this sense of wanting to make life change for people," Angela says. "She's got the courage to step outside what is expected of the royals and have real conversations with people. There are no barriers there when she talks to patients. She has compassion, honest compassion. I have seen her at close quarters with sufferers and she really does make a difference."

Diana is not only the royal patron of the National AIDS Trust but is involved with every other significant AIDS organization as well. She knows she is tracking new, some would say forbidden, territory. She always shakes AIDS sufferers by the hands, lingers at their bedsides for intelligent conversations, picks up little babies who are suffering the ravages of the disease, talks compassionately to the mothers of AIDS babies. When she leaves an AIDS ward, the nurses comment on the sparkle in the eyes of those she had been talking to.

"HIV does not make people dangerous to know, so you can shake their hands and give them a hug," Diana says. "Heaven knows, they need it."

Yet many people in British society protest even today: "What the hell does Diana think she's doing, getting mixed up with this lot?"

Former judge James Pickles, famed nationwide for his controversial judgments and remarks at the closings of cases he had presided over, is now a newspaper columnist. In September 1991, he wrote: "I believe her constant, high-profile, all-embracing support for AIDS victims is both wrong and highly damaging to her. Caring for blameless victims was all right, but it was dangerous for her to express the same concern for men who got the disease by indulging in sleazy, unnatural sex with other so-called gays."

Angela Serota has talked to Diana about the negative reaction to her work. "She finds it very hurtful. It's very undermining for her, but she believes it is usually out of ignorance. She knows that people doubt her motivation. I've heard people suggesting she's just doing it for the publicity. The point that must not be forgotten is that Diana does all this knowing that people are misjudging her, but she's got the sense and compassion to follow her own inner beliefs."

Angela believes that Diana's commitment to AIDS has been her making. "Because Diana was not born a royal, it has taken her some time to find her feet, and her confidence, to do what she believes in, no matter what others might think and advise. Now, she has found a cause to support, and yet the cause she has chosen is perhaps the most difficult one she could have selected from all the other high-profile charities. Whichever charity Diana had thrown herself into, she would have received amazing coverage, and none of it negative. By choosing AIDS she has shown real courage. And I believe it when she tells me that whatever happens she is going to continue."

Diana herself underscored her commitment in July 1991 when she escorted Barbara Bush, wife of President George Bush, on a visit to London's Middlesex Hospital to see AIDS patients. (In 1990, during Diana's whirlwind visit to Washington, Mrs. Bush's favorite AIDS charity benefited from half the proceeds of a glittering dinner for the Princess.) During the visit at Middlesex, Diana chatted quietly to twenty-six-year-old AIDS victim Steve, a signer for the deaf and dumb. "Anywhere I see suffering, that is where I want to be, doing what I can," she told him.

Twenty minutes later, when Diana and Barbara Bush were about to leave the hospital, nurses appealed urgently to Diana: "There is a man here who desperately wants to meet you. He only has forty-eight hours to live. Will you see him?"

Diana explained the situation to Mrs. Bush and agreed to go immediately to the man. He was in dreadful condition, his body covered with lesions, and he was unable to sit and could barely talk. Diana sat at his bedside and immediately put his hand in hers to comfort him. "How are you? I'm Diana. I've come to see you."

The man couldn't even open his eyes but tried to smile. Turning to the nurse with tears in her eyes, Diana said, "I'm so sorry. It's terribly sad." Fittingly, the man was in Broderip Ward, which Diana opened in 1987 when she launched her campaign to help AIDS victims.

Both Princess Diana and Mrs. Bush have thrown themselves into learning a great deal about the frightening disease, and doctors are surprised at the level of their understanding. After their visit to the Middlesex Hospital, Professor Michael Adler, clinical director of the AIDS unit, said, "We had a private session before the visit, and they both showed how well informed they are about the spread of the disease. You could see the way they both handled themselves that this was not just another state visit for them. They were both very interested and concerned that more should be done to combat the disease."

It is a measure of Diana's commitment that she never lets criticism prevent her from continuing to comfort AIDS victims. Some people loathe Diana for her caring, and others genuinely fear for her safety. She receives hate mail from some people who before thought she could do no wrong.

Fortunately, many people support her thoroughly. Margaret Jay, director of the National AIDS Trust, was so impressed with a speech Diana made in 1991 that she wrote to the Princess: "I believe that you are perhaps the only person in Britain that can change public perception of the disease." That is an awesome burden for a fairly inexperienced young woman to carry, especially in the face of great opposition.

Victor van Wetering, press officer for the Terence Higgins Trust, which is involved with AIDS victims, explained what Princess Diana has done: "Her attitude to AIDS has tackled the stigma and bigotry—many people thought AIDS sufferers deserved their disease, and she has helped blow that myth apart."

Some of Diana's friends believe one reason she is so committed to AIDS sufferers is that she has always moved in the social circles which AIDS has struck most prominently—fashion, the arts, the dance, and theatre worlds. She has witnessed the distressing effects of HIV on people she has known personally. One of the few people who showed Diana real warmth when she first moved into Buckingham Palace was Prince Charles's gay valet, Stephen Barry, who died of AIDS in 1986.

One person who has helped Diana to champion the cause is a remarkable woman, Marguerite Littman, the daughter of a Louisiana lawyer and the wife of an eminent London barrister, Mark Littman. From the middle of the 1980s, Marguerite Littman has transformed AIDS into a socially correct charity on both sides of the Atlantic.

Apart from organizing film premieres, parties, and charitable functions for victims of AIDS, Mrs. Littman, who still speaks with a classic Southern accent, has been credited with bringing the rich and famous to her charity. For example, she coached Elizabeth Taylor on how to "speak Southern" for *Cat on a Hot Tin Roof,* and they have remained friends ever since.

Marguerite met Diana in 1986, at another charity, Birthright. They discussed AIDS, and Diana was won over. The two are still good friends today.

Much of the caring work for AIDS patients that Diana has done since 1987 has been kept secret from the media. She became a frequent visitor to the Mildmay Mission Hospice in East London, a private hospital originally established in the nineteenth century to care for the victims of a cholera epidemic that had ravaged the slums of London. It reopened in 1985 as an AIDS center.

Chairman of the hospice, Helen Taylor-Thompson, told how Diana first came to visit: "The phone rang one day and to my astonishment it was Buckingham Palace asking if it would be all right if Princess Diana paid an unofficial, private visit. They gave us only a few days to prepare, which I understand is very unusual. The day she arrived she was suffering from the aftermath of flu, but she was wonderful, absolutely charming, and asked us so many questions about the place and the patients. She also asked if there was any way she could help."

Her visit led directly to a dying patient, Martin, thirty-three, being reunited with his mother and young sister, whom he had been too embarrassed to tell about his disease. Because Diana was coming to visit, he contacted his family and, for the first time, told them that he had AIDS and was expected to die shortly.

Helen Taylor-Thompson went on: "For the occasion he wore huge Elton John–style red plastic glasses, and Diana went straight over to him. She was laughing at his glasses, enjoying his sense of fun. She sat on his bed, held his hand, and chatted. Two weeks later I was in the official lineup for the star-studded gala performance of the film, *Dangerous Liaisons,* and was introduced to Diana. Her first words were 'How is Martin?' and I had to tell her he was near death, but said her visit had resulted in him being reunited with his family. She replied, 'So, it was like a fairy tale come true. Give him my best wishes.' Two days later Martin was dead."

Diana's gentle touch was evident in October 1990, when she visited a home for AIDS children in Washington, D.C. She met a three-year-old girl called "The First Lady" because she was the first baby admitted to the home.

Director Reverend Debbie Tate tells the story. "I saw people here wipe away their tears as Diana arrived, saw the little girl, and went over to her. Somehow there was an immediate rapport. Diana picked her up as if she was her very own child. Later Diana was kneeling on the floor, tickling her and making her laugh. The Lady asked if she could go for a ride in Diana's Rolls and Diana immediately agreed: 'Of course you can.'

"But Diana was close to tears when I explained to her that our little Lady had no idea she was shortly going to die and kept asking about two of her little playmates who had recently died. That day everyone realized the poignancy of the visit, and there were many wet eyes."

It is not only AIDS that commands Diana's attention and concern. Princess Diana is now the royal patron of seventy separate charities and has a hectic work schedule which often starts at six A.M. and is not finished until after a formal function at ten-thirty at night. That is a punishingly long day, particularly since Diana can never relax on those occasions, or put her feet up, or not show that she is interested, no matter how bored she may be or whatever else she may have on her mind. It seldom matters how the Princess is feeling personally; she knows she has a duty to perform and she does it.

In the early years after she married Prince Charles, Diana was much criticized for neglecting and being uninterested in her royal duties. No allowance was give to her youth. She first had to change her life totally, bowing to new, strict disciplines.

Criticism of Diana began to fade after the mid-1980s as she discovered that she could perform very useful and much-acclaimed work for the Royal Family, especially for good causes. She began to enjoy the praise and the respect she was beginning to earn for herself. Now, in the 1990s, Diana is the hardest-working member of the Royal Family, undertaking far more work than Prince Charles. It has even been noted that their work loads are inversely proportional, with Diana's increased number of official duties in 1990 corresponding with Charles's decreased number that same year.

Diana seldom becomes involved with her husband's good causes, since their interests are so different. However, there are occasions when they work together, like the regular rock concerts that raise funds for the Prince's Trust, the charity Charles set up to help out-of-work, underprivileged young people to start businesses. Although the Prince is not fond of rock, he recognizes that such concerts are an excellent way to attract young people and to bring in much-needed money. Diana not only loves rock music, but admits to being a little star-struck when she meets big-name rock stars.

The concerts for the Prince's Trust earn tens of thousands of dollars. The artists, who include such people as Eric Clapton, Phil Collins, and Mark Knopfler, offer their services free. Being a rock fan herself and closer in age to the concert audiences, Diana becomes personally involved in putting these spectacles together.

Attending the concerts with Charles is virtually the only occasion she can be seen in public wearing stylish, trendy, younger clothes. She has even managed to persuade the Prince to enjoy rock music a little. At the Live Aid concert, while she sang along with the crowd, he actually started tapping his handcrafted brogues to the rhythm of the music.

Diana's interest in charities began when she attended functions where Charles was the patron. She was impressed with the way the newspapers and the public reacted whenever he spoke out passionately about a particular subject. The more passionate Charles was about a charity, or a controversial subject, the more respect he was given and the more positive attention he received from the newspapers.

Diana knew she could never be intellectually persuasive or write thought-provoking speeches that intellectuals or politicians would listen to. But she did come to believe that where Charles could provide passion, she could provide compassion.

She hoped that by so doing people would start taking her seriously—to take notice of *her* when she spoke. At that time, in the early 1980s, few people did. Indeed, she was then universally regarded as a featherbrain who thought of little but fashion, babies, and rock.

Diana had always been a caring person, happy to chat with ordinary people. She hated having to talk to important people who she felt looked down at her lack of intellect. Diana was desperate to know what she could do with her life. She kept asking Charles, her advisers, her ladies-in-waiting, her girlfriends, what she could do to prove to the public that she had a job, a role, a future other than being the wife of Prince Charles and the mother of William and Harry. After much soul-searching, she decided to make caring charities her particular work.

Initially, charities devoted to babies and child welfare were singled out for her attention, but soon Diana discovered other opportunities. She decided she wanted to help young people—closer to her own age—with drug and alcohol problems, then later, AIDS victims, the underprivileged, and the young homeless.

She discussed these ideas with Prince Charles. As usual, Edward Adeane and other advisers helped plan a campaign for Diana and produced a list of good causes the Palace thought would be appropriate. Their job is to protect the image of the Royal Family and to foresee any possible criticism that might arise, and they do it very well.

Charity organizers regularly write to the Princess of Wales's office at St. James's Palace, inviting her to be their royal patron, knowing full well that Diana is the best attraction they could have. But although Diana is careful not to overload herself, she discusses the merits of each particular charity with her secretary and other advisers.

She thought hard before taking on her charities because she wanted to get it right. Diana had been married for nearly a year before she made her first choices: the Welsh National Opera (because she is Princess of Wales), the Royal School for the Blind, the Malcolm Sargeant Cancer Fund for Children, the Pre-School Playgroups Association, and the Albany, an East London community center in London.

For Princess Diana, charity work principally involves meeting and chatting with people and encouraging those responsible for fund-raising. But Diana wants to do more than that. She insists that she be allowed to meet the sick, the handicapped, or the people in need for whom the charity is raising funds. This is where the Princess of Wales is in her element.

As Diana told one of her close Palace advisers, "I much

prefer to be talking to all these poor people rather than the bigwigs I have to meet. I hate having to make small talk, because I'm so bad at it. I never know what to say."

That was some years ago. Today Diana will happily chat with everyone she meets, whether they be princes, Presidents or Prime Ministers. At the annual November meeting of diplomats in London, Diana is now the favored royal, as members of The Firm take turns chatting individually with all five hundred members of the diplomatic corps and their wives.

As Sir John Morgan, former British ambassador, puts it, "Nowadays, she is interested in everyone she speaks to. She brings the event alive in a way that the other royals simply don't. The diplomats don't want to chat with her only because she is the high-profile royal everyone loves, but because she shows the most animation and a real interest in their countries, which they find refreshing."

Diana has the knack of conducting one-to-one conversations with people. She convinces her woman listeners, for example, that far from being a member of the most prestigious family in the land, she is just another young mother with problems similar to theirs.

After AIDS, the charity Diana is most closely identified with is Birthright, of which she became patron in 1984. Birthright is the appeal arm of the Royal College of Obstetricians and Gynecologists, and its aim is to raise funds for research into problems of the unborn child, including stillbirth, infant death, and infertility.

She was invited to become Birthright's royal patron by gynecologist George Pinker, who had supervised her pregnancies and the births of both William and Harry. Diana is deeply conscious of the fact that while she had two healthy babies and trouble-free pregnancies, many women are not as fortunate.

Diana's personal identification with the charity has meant a remarkable upsurge in its fortunes. Before her support, Birthright had struggled for funds, and its valuable research had been largely ignored when it came to handing out money. Since Diana came on board, all that has changed.

Her involvement with the charity has attracted stars from the entertainment world, such as Cilla Black, the former pop star turned TV presenter; David Frost; Scottish comedian Billy Connolly; and Mirian Stoppard, former wife of playwright Tom Stoppard. Big names equal big money: they managed to raise $5,000,000 for the charity, which has helped it improve the survival rate of some categories of premature infants by up to 70 percent. Diana can feel quietly proud that the turnabout is due primarily to her enthusiasm, persuasion, and patronage.

She does not stop at fund-raising. As with the AIDS charities, she gets personally involved, visiting maternity wards and research clinics and wanting to know all about the work that is being done. Vivienne Parry, the group's national organizer, is full of admiration for Diana's work.

"The Princess has helped enormously with fund-raising," she says. "But the lift she gives to other young mums when she visits maternity wards is every bit as valuable as the extra money she brings in.

"There is something quite moving about the way she talks with the patients. Not only is she concerned about their problems, but she shows she is. She understands the joy of having a baby and the anguish if something goes wrong. She felt very lucky and privileged to have had one healthy child and another problem-free pregnancy when she visited the center." (The first time Princess Diana visited a Birthright research clinic, at King's College Hospital in London, she was eight months pregnant with Prince Harry.)

"It must have been very difficult for her seeing all the new techniques at that time," Vivienne Parry recalls. "We all felt she was rather brave because it is very off-putting to a young pregnant woman to see all the needles and transfusions. She handled it all remarkably well."

Diana keeps closely in touch with Birthright's work. In an interview with writer Suzy Menkes, she explained her interest in the charity:

"I was expecting Harry when I first agreed to become

patron of Birthright, and it seemed important to me, particularly at that time, that as Princess of Wales I should become more closely involved with a charity that involved the early detection of abnormalities of the unborn child, as well of course as the treatment of the unborn while they are still in the womb.

"There is also very interesting work being carried out on the level of blood flowing through the placenta, which is of vital importance to the health and growth of the baby. This is assessed using a new type of 'noisy ultrasound,' and I have since met several women who have been able to have healthy babies through close monitoring with this device in the latter stages of pregnancy.

"I am pleased that Birthright will be able to open many more research centers around the country. Already, for example, at Leeds a new research unit there is carrying out research on the treatment of recurrent miscarriages."

Birthright also funds research into laser treatment for cervical cancer and infertility.

Diana says, "My primary interest is concerned with the right of every mother to give birth to a healthy child, but Birthright's research covers a wide variety of distressing problems. One such area is infertility research. Today about 40 percent of infertility is unexplained, and that will be the main impetus of our next line of research. To long for a child and not be able to have one I imagine must be a nightmare."

Supporting charities concerned with drug addiction is another of Diana's concerns. She has never smoked and hardly drinks herself, but she is well aware of the health risks of both, and also particularly the dangers of taking drugs. In 1987, she became patron of Turning Point, the largest national charity in Britain helping drug addicts, alcoholics, and mental-health outpatients. This gritty enterprise, with more than 350 employees, runs over forty projects around the country, offering residential rehabilitation, day care, as well as street-level advice, information, and counseling services.

It was founded in 1964 by Barry Richards, the philanthropic son of a prosperous flour miller and a trustee of the famous Leonard Cheshire Foundation, which helped ex-servicemen from World War II deal with their problems. Richards, who died in 1991, saw the need to help alcoholics in inner London and began his community-based charity single-handed. It has never held five-hundred-dollars-a-head black-tie dinners or glittering society balls, yet it has mushroomed into a concern that assists twelve thousand people a year and has become the largest British charity of its kind, with an annual turnover of $15 million. Turning Point now receives 90 percent of its income from central government and local authority grants. Since Diana became involved, their fund-raising has more than doubled.

Once again, Diana was showing her strength in becoming involved in another "downmarket" charity, work generally ignored by other members of the Royal Family. To her great credit, Diana has changed their discreetly leaving certain charities out in the cold.

Diana has not only proved her compassion for sufferers, but has also shown the courage to take risks she believes are worthwhile. Without publicity coverage, Diana would visit clinics—some on her own without detective protection—to meet and chat with the patients in an effort to help them kick their addiction and encourage them back to health. Such risks could have ended in trouble, not only because of possible irrational attacks by those she was seeking to help, but also because of the possibility of an IRA attack or a chance meeting with an antiroyalist.

Once again, Diana's risk-taking was reported back to Buckingham Palace. When she stubbornly refused to give assurances that she would stop her secret solo visits to drug centers, the Queen herself intervened and invited Diana to one of her famous chats over afternoon tea. Her Majesty's private chats are legendary within the close confines of the Royal Family. Any member of the family may at some time find him or herself "invited" to take tea with HM, as she is called in Palace circles. In reality, of course, the invitations are not a request at all, but an order.

Diana attended but refused to back down. She argued that she was taking no risk whatsoever. She was making her visits secretly only because she believed it was less obtrusive; if she were accompanied by an escort, a detective, or a lady-in-waiting, no matter how discreet they were, the visit would be marred. If she went alone, she could be more beneficial to the patients. The Queen pressed her to take more care, but Diana would have none of it. She did promise she would try to avoid exposing herself to any danger, but did not agree to discontinue the secret trips.

The visits to Turning Point were never on the official court circular, which publishes daily information about the comings and goings of the royals. Diana also believed she would be taken more seriously by the trustees and the patients if her visits were not publicized. During her visits she got to know some of the drug addicts and alcoholics personally, one to one, and built up quite close relationships.

Diana tries to visit at least one clinic every month, and sometimes more. Deborah Newbury, Turning Point's public relations officer, cannot speak highly enough of Diana's work. "Our area is political with a very small *p*. Drink, drugs, and mental health are not popular fund-raising causes. Understandably, these causes make people uncomfortable, and they tend to sweep them under the carpet. That is why we really appreciate Diana's bravery in making a stand."

In December 1990, for the first time ever, Diana entered the turbulent waters of government policy, at the annual general meeting of Turning Point. Britain's unwritten constitution excludes the monarchy and all members of the Royal Family from any direct involvement with politics. If they do dip their toes in, there is usually an unholy row. Thus, while Prince Charles has become more socially critical during the late 1980s, he tries to draw a line between propounding certain views and interfering in government policies.

Diana spoke on the thorny issue of "Care in the Community," the Conservative government's controversial plan of emptying mental institutions and returning former inmates to community life. The policy has come under severe attack, not only from the opposition political parties in Britain, but also from many social workers and psychiatrists who believe the mentally ill should be kept in institutions because they are unable to care for themselves in the outside world. The government of Prime Minister Margaret Thatcher, however, was adamant in its belief that returning patients to community care not only was financially beneficial to the government, but also rightly allowed those patients considered well enough to reenter the community at large.

Diana's speech made her beliefs clear. "Those rosy words Care in the Community do not, I believe, convey the harsh reality faced by the mentally ill when they are released from hospital," she said in an icy tone of voice. There was immediate applause from the meeting. The Princess had had the courage to say the exact words, plainly and simply, which the vast majority of Turning Point members believe to describe the facts of the situation. Her remarks raised a storm of protest from MPs that she was involving herself in politics, but Diana refused to withdraw her statement.

So courageous has Diana become that she now visits maximum-security institutions like Broadmoor, which houses criminals with a history of violence and others having serious mental disorders. Diana asked to visit Broadmoor after the Palace received a letter from an inmate who saw her on the TV news making visits all over the country. In 1990, she spent hours touring the forbidding fortress and spoke to many of the inmates. She went directly into their cells, sat on their beds, chatted with others in open wards, and tried to hold a dialogue with them. Many asked her for help; others pleaded with her to return. She said she would, and she kept her promise a year later.

By involving herself with patients, and sometimes in group therapy discussions, Diana leaves herself open to possible abuse and even physical attack. But it never appears to worry her. In 1989 when visiting Roma, a drug project in West London, she was asked to take part in an open discussion with a number of patients.

Deborah Newbury witnessed the discussion: "A couple of the more direct addicts began attacking her, calling her a painted doll and telling her that it was no good her visiting them because she could not possibly begin to understand their problems, because of the privileged life she led in a palace.

"Diana argued back, telling them that just as they had great difficulty coming to terms with some aspects of their lives, didn't they realize that she also had had great problems coming to terms with parts of her life. Didn't they realize that they were free, and that she sometimes felt imprisoned in her palace and in her circumstances?"

Her involvement with addiction units is also a first for a member of the Royal Family. Those who have seen the Princess with drug patients are astonished at the relationships of trust and informality she strikes up in a matter of minutes. It is surprising since not only is she untrained, but has had little experience with the seamier side of life before or after her marriage.

Ted Unsworth, chairman of Turning Point, added, "It is quite remarkable how well the Princess gets on with the victims. She is not very old and has no training or experience of dealing with such people, and yet she does have the confidence to handle the situations which are thrown up in the hard-talking group therapy sessions. She is clearly a very compassionate person, in a constructive, not a sloppy, sort of way.

"I must stress that no one who has had dealings with her feels patronized, affronted, or intruded upon. She is genuinely most caring and has a great depth of understanding for the young men and women."

It was even more remarkable, he declared, when you consider that most people she speaks to are not supporters of the monarchy, and indeed, often the opposite.

Once Diana realized her involvement was really aiding drug abusers, she began to visit more and more treatment centers. Secretly, she went to the Coke Hole Trust rehabilitation unit in Andover, Hampshire, one of the few centers specializing in helping female drug addicts. Diana toured the center and talked to women who had been sexually abused as children and sought solace in drugs as teenagers. She spoke to others who had been physically abused by their fathers, husbands, or lovers. That Diana, with no experience of such horrors, could find common ground with the women was extraordinary. But she did.

Says Lorna Payne, assistant director of the Coke Hole Trust: "The Princess understood how women might be the victims of this drug abuse as an escape from some far worse fate of physical or sexual abuse. She understood that the women wanted their children with them when they were trying to kick the drugs, rather than fighting it alone with their children fostered out somewhere. As a mother of two children herself, she understood that having the children with them helped them fight the addiction for the children's sake."

During the past couple of years, Diana has begun to speak out more authoritatively about drug and alcohol abuse. She ventured into the world of controversy when, while touring Turning Point's Camberwell Alcohol Project, she spoke out against TV soap operas, saying that because much of the action takes place in pubs or over a drink, they may be influencing people to turn to drink. Even though a furor followed her remarks, many people thought what she said made sense. She did, however, admit that she was also a slave to certain soap operas, which brought a laugh.

Diana has a good sense of humor and loves a laugh. On one occasion, when Diana was visiting a home for the mentally ill in Camberwell, South London, in January 1989, she was invited to inspect the kitchens, which the staff and the inmates had spent days cleaning. Diana went straight to the large fridge and opened it. Inside was moldy food; the smell was awful. "Did you leave this for me to do?" she joked. But the room was full of red faces.

Another occasion for laughter was the charity film launch in London of *When Harry Met Sally*. Diana attended dressed in a perfectly stunning outfit, a fabulous, skintight, red-and-gold gown. She loved the film and could hardly contain herself at the simulated orgasm scene in the café, especially the pay-off line when the old woman tells the waitress: "I'll have what she's having." Afterward the Princess said to the stars, Billy Crystal and Meg Ryan, "That was wonderful entertainment, but so naughty, it was terrific." The evening raised more than $100,000 for Turning Point.

Diana doesn't take exception when people put her down, as long as it is carried out in a friendly way. The brilliant, temperamental violinist Nigel Kennedy took part in a charity concert which Diana was attending. During his solo, the unshaven young fiddler openly teased Diana over the microphone. "It's fantastic that you're here to-night listening to all this classical music, and that you have got over your Duran Duran thing [her favorite pop group for years]." The audience held their breath at such audacity and looked at Diana in her box. She just smiled, giggled, and took it in her stride.

One of the main reasons Diana has thrown herself en-thusiastically into social work is that, although for a time she enjoyed being a glamorous superstar, she has since grown increasingly uneasy about her image as just a royal clotheshorse. She decided to show the world there was more to her. Now, the more closely involved in people's problems she finds herself, the more rewarding she finds the work. She hopes that finally she is overcoming her image as beautiful but shallow.

In 1988, Diana told a friend, "People who *really* know me understand there is more to me than that. The glamor-ous star is a role I have to play. And I hope I'm getting better at it. But I care about a lot of other things, and I can do a lot of good. And that can be more satisfying than anything."

Diana believes that becoming a mother moved her to-ward causes concerning child welfare. One of the latest charities of which she has become patron is the Child Accident Prevention Trust, which campaigns against dangerous toys and seeks to educate people about the perils of accidents to children in the home.

In a speech at Christmas 1988, she warned parents not to turn the holiday into a tragedy by buying dangerous toys. "I ask everyone buying something for a child this Christmas to ensure it is totally safe. Objects which grown-ups take for granted can become a major hazard." She promised to have her own household fitted with the latest line in safety gadgets. She is deeply aware that it might have been *her* five-year-old who was given a dangerous teddy bear one day, or, who was scarred for life after pulling a kettle of boiling water over himself.

Not surprisingly, one of the first organizations of which Diana became patron was Dr. Barnado's, a charity which cares for orphaned and abandoned children. She learned much about Barnado's from Bruce Oldfield, whom she knew well and who had firsthand knowledge of the organization. One of Diana's favorite dress designers, Oldfield makes frocks for Joan Collins, Jerry Hall, and Bianca Jagger, among others. He now has a salon in fashionable Knightsbridge. But he spent his childhood in a foster home and at Barnado's children's home. Says Oldfield, "The heavy-handed rules and regulations at Barnado's turned some kids delinquent. But they made me stronger, self reliant, and—on the surface, confident."

Diana often visits Barnado's homes to spend time with the children. Dr. Bill Beaver, a director, has come to know the Princess quite well. He often talks to her about the problems the home has, and she surprises Barnado's staff with her knowledge of child care.

He said, "Since she became our patron and spent time with us, we have often been taken aback by her quick brain. The trouble is that she has this gooey image, and people expect to see something sweet that has just stepped out of a chocolate box. But when you see her in action talking to people, you get a surprise.

"She is not just a figurehead president. She has this astonishing concentration of mind and cuts straight to the heart of a problem. Top industrialists come and see us and don't show the same, high-level understanding of our problems. Her questioning is incisive, and she does seem to have a remarkable grasp of the social services.

"She has turned compassion into action, and that is a good central faculty to develop. A future Queen of England could hardly have a better training. She has more knowledge of new and different ways of helping the handicapped than 90 percent of the population."

Another patronage Diana took up early on was the British Deaf Association. She delighted the young people there when she told them, through a staff member, that she would try to learn sign language before she visited them again.

Bernard Quinn, British Deaf Association General Secretary, said: "We sent her a video on how to learn to communicate, and after daily half-hour sessions for two weeks, she mastered it. The next time she visited she had the confidence to try it out in front of everyone who knew the sign language perfectly, and she was brilliant. We were very surprised. That shows amazing dedication and determination, particularly when you realize her enormous work load. It also says a lot for her character."

Princess Diana's determination to help those charities shunned by many others also extends to overseas causes. Shocked by the gruesome effects of leprosy on children, Diana agreed to become patron of the Leprosy Mission. Immediately she set about her new cause with her customary courage and good sense.

In November 1989 Diana visited the Sitanala Leprosy Hospital, set on the outskirts of the jungle in Indonesia. She had never been confronted by lepers before and knew only that she had to do something to counter the superstition and bigotry that had shrouded the disease for centuries.

Informally dressed in cool cotton to beat the steamy ninety-four-degree heat wave, she was photographed shaking hands with a patient who had a huge smile on his face. She sat on the beds and leaned against the bare iron bed rails as she chatted to other patients. Altogether she shook hands with 100 of the 550 patients that day, and though hardened TV crews blanched at the disfigured limbs and skin discolorations of the sufferers, Diana was moved only to sympathy.

As always, it was the children that nearly brought tears to Diana. A hospital doctor said, "She did so much more than she had to. She need only have shaken their hands and moved on, but she sat on their beds and listened and talked to them. Then she joined the children in a game of bowls, which they loved. She brought happiness and smiles to those children."

Diana did exactly the same a few months later when she toured Nigeria in February 1990. She visited the leper hospital at Malai in Borno State and deliberately shook hands with every sufferer as the cameras rolled.

Kate Dawson, a British doctor at the hospital, said afterward, "The Princess has helped so much. She has shown by being so open and natural with them that lepers are not a threat to anybody."

The Reverend Jim Findlay, former director of the Leprosy Mission, was full of praise for Diana: "The whole point is that this simple act of shaking hands was making people realize that leprosy is not contagious. You cannot catch it by touching a victim. The disease is in fact only mildly infectious, and most people are immune to it anyway."

By becoming the royal patron of the Mission, the Princess had taken on an organization which works in more than thirty-three countries with a $12 million budget. It cares for five hundred thousand victims worldwide, many of whom are children under thirteen years of age.

Another one of Diana's special charities ironically involves marital breakdown. She has sat in on numerous therapy sessions with struggling young couples. It must have been something of a shock for warring couples to find Princess Diana joining them in their private counseling sessions, listening to detailed, intimate accounts of their marriage. Sometimes Diana attended sessions with sex therapists openly discussing problems with young couples.

Diana takes no part in the proceedings. She sits quietly at the back of the room, listening and learning about people's problems. Afterward, she usually discusses the session with the therapist in private, in order to gain an understanding of the psychology behind the therapy.

As Diana's own marriage fell apart, the more personally involved she became with Relate, the charity once called the Marriage Guidance Council. Diana knows that in Britain today more than one-third of all marriages end in divorce, yet she has never discussed her own marital difficulties with anyone while visiting Relate centers across Britain. If she or Prince Charles has ever taken advice from marriage-guidance counselors, it is a closely guarded royal secret. Perhaps in her visits to these centers, Diana has identified her own problems in other case histories. But there is no record of her seeking any advice for herself.

On many occasions, Diana overruns her time in trying to help people. One private meeting with a woman with two young children who had been abandoned by her husband went on so long that worried aides eventually tapped on the door, to check that everything was all right.

The Princess finds the work at Relate so fascinating that when she is touring different parts of the country, she will often drop in at a local branch and spend an hour or so talking with the counselors. She likes to know what the principal problems are of the people who come to Relate, and the success and failure rate of the service.

One of Relate's marital sex therapists, Margaret Brown, said, "Princess Diana is a truly warm person, and that comes across when she is talking about people and their problems. She may look glamorous and appear like a film star when you see her on television, but when you talk to her, one to one, she is a totally different person. She cares for people and shows it."

Diana's instinctive understanding of such problems surely has much to do with her own experience as a child of a broken home. She is also pleased to have found something she is good at which doesn't require academic skills, but only, as Relate counselors told her, "warmth, openness, and an ability to listen and communicate."

Most, but not all, of Diana's support goes to caring charities. She is also a patron of a handful of arts groups and the London City Ballet, of which she is such a keen supporter she sometimes watches their rehearsals. She patronizes another ballet company as well. When Princess Margaret retired as patron of the London Festival Ballet —now the English National Ballet—she suggested that Diana take over. Diana was delighted, since her interest in ballet is genuine and long-standing. Indeed, she goes to a weekly ballet workout class in London.

Diana sees her arts charities as fun. It's the caring causes, and the pursuit of better health, that she holds dear to her heart. She has been known to preach good health to the people she meets, simply because she believes some people abuse their bodies by drinking and smoking too much. She has agreed to become patron of the British Lung Foundation, which fits in with her healthy approach to life.

Diana is very antismoking and has been known to be severe with those who indulge. Once, when visiting a lung cancer ward, she spotted a patient's mother surreptitiously holding a cigarette. The Princess, who was shocked by photographs of cancerous lungs, asked the woman rather sharply, "What are you doing with that cigarette?"

"Nothing," stammered the hapless woman, with the full force of royal disapproval directed at her.

"You're lying," replied the Princess. The squirming victim afterward vowed to give up smoking now that Princess Di had admonished her.

Diana works very hard for her causes. In a single morning she will perhaps visit three or four different charities during a royal tour. In October 1991, for instance, she went up by train from London to Birmingham and began by visiting the local Relate center, talking to staff and couples for two hours. She also talked for twenty minutes to members of the Women's Survivors' Group, a pioneer scheme to help those abused as children.

From there, she went by car twelve miles away to launch, as patron, a $20-million national appeal for the Foundation for Conductive Education, a new national center which cares for cerebral palsy victims, particularly children.

Diana toured their present headquarters and sat with the palsy victim children, many of them suffering from Down's syndrome, to watch a slapstick show by the Birmingham Royal Ballet. Two children sat on her knees during the show, and a blind three-year-old tugged at Diana's skirt, demanding to be picked up. Diana complied.

Three hours later, she was off to another part of the city to visit Drugline, which receives seven hundred distress calls a month from addicts. Drugline offers information, and hands out free syringes and condoms, to intravenous drug users to stem the spread of AIDS.

Diana spent two hours talking with the clinic staff, along with addicts who visit the center. Having been up since six A.M. for the journey north, she returned home before seven P.M., just in time to read a bedtime story to Harry. That evening she changed into jeans and a sweater and spent the evening curled up on a sofa, alone, watching television.

Most people worldwide know Diana through glossy photographs showing her in stunning outfits or holidaying with her children. But she hopes people are beginning to realize that she works, energetically and for long hours, on behalf of many charities. Perhaps at long last the public will recognize that the Princess of Wales is more than an upper-class young mother who spends her time watching soaps or playing with her children.

As the Wales's Chief Royal Press Officer Dickie Arbiter put it, "The Princess doesn't want to be continually identified with fashion. She has other much more important interests to be involved with, such as her work for charity.

She wants the press to concentrate on that, not on her latest outfit."

Diana is determined to keep up her charity work, especially for those victims who tend to be shunned by the world. She has grown into a royal who truly cares.

16

❖❖❖

The Royal Children: Parents' Clash of Views

Diana's first pregnancy, from September 1981 to June 1982, was a major turning point in her position within the royal household and in her relationship with Charles. Within a matter of months Diana had been transformed from a young woman hopelessly in love to a mother-to-be who wanted, and demanded, that things be the way she wanted them. During the first months of her pregnancy Diana discovered that when she pushed at a door she had believed was locked, it somehow swung open.

Those at the Palace who witnessed the emerging mother could not believe the rapidity of the change. "We knew that one day Diana would become a bitch, but not that quickly," said one of Diana's close advisers, who spent the first three years of her marriage helping and advising her but today prefers to remain anonymous.

He continued, "Never had we witnessed such a change in someone at the Palace. We were worried from the beginning because the marriage seemed so totally one-sided. Before the marriage, and immediately afterward, Diana literally worshipped the ground Charles walked on.

There was no balance, no give-and-take in the relationship.

"On one side was a serious man in his early thirties, mature for his years, who was flattered that a beautiful young woman with a sense of fun made him feel happy and young and was so in love with him. On the other side was a totally inexperienced young woman who thought her man was perfect, handsome, intelligent, witty, who could make no mistake in her eyes. It was a recipe for disaster."

It was during those first months of her pregnancy that so many of Charles's former advisers and servants left—quit their jobs or were fired. Diana has never indicated why she so disliked Charles's former employees and advisers and was so determined to get rid of them all. But she made very little effort to conceal her dislike, and sometimes contempt, for them.

Her close adviser added, "Much of the time there was very little reason why someone would end up leaving, or find himself fired. It was as though Diana was determined to install her own employees with allegiance to her—and who had no loyalty to Charles, despite the fact that he was not only the heir to the throne, the future King, but allegedly master of his own household.

"That was a position Diana wanted for herself. With disdain she had seen how the stepmother she hated, Raine, had taken over her father, emasculated him in her eyes, and totally run the household and the entire Spencer empire. In her teens at the time, she had hated the arrival of the bossy Raine, but she had learned from her that control of the household gave a woman incredible power.

"Unfortunately, Charles did not have the strength of character to counter her determination. Within months Charles had lost many of his trusted employees and much of his authority in the household. It was tragic to see, but although his closest advisers tried to give him the strength and courage to take command of his home, his wife, and his household, it became increasingly obvious that Prince

Charles was becoming the second most important person in the relationship."

"She who rocks the cradle rules the world" was a saying that Diana knew only too well. But Charles, the rest of the Royal Family, and their loyal courtiers had no idea Diana would be so ruthless in carrying out that maxim. If not the world, Diana most certainly was determined to rule her home and the palace.

When she returned from the hospital after the birth of William on June 21, 1982, Diana immediately put into practice all she knew about children. She had been like a mother to her baby brother. She had helped with her sisters' two young children and had worked in London as a nanny herself and at the kindergarten.

Diana herself had been brought up by a succession of nannies who had taken charge away from her own mother. She would have none of that. From the start she was to be in command of the nursery. The nannies and the nursery maids were there to take orders from her.

Before the arrival of baby William, Diana had decided that, contrary to royal tradition, she would nurse the baby. She adamantly told her doctor, Mr. Pinker, "I shall of course be breast-feeding for as long as possible. I believe it is a very important part of bonding between mother and child." The matter was never raised again.

Diana announced that she had no intention of returning to her royal duties until she was sure William was old enough to be left without being affected. She had grown up without a mother for much of her life, and she was determined that would never happen to her children.

Both Diana and Charles agreed that their youngsters were going to lead normal lives for as long as possible. Both wanted their children to grow up in a close family environment, and Diana took great delight in changing William's diapers, a task no future Queen had ever undertaken in the past. William was going to have a close, loving relationship with his mother, come what may.

Diana was shocked when Charles described his routine as a baby. He would sleep in a room next to his nannies, on a floor separate from his parents. The nannies would feed him during the night; they would wake him at seven A.M., then feed, bathe, and dress him. He would be taken down to see his mother for thirty minutes before being taken back upstairs again. Later in the day he would perhaps have another thirty minutes with his mother before being brought upstairs for the night. Charles pleaded that his old nanny, Mabel Anderson, be employed to look after William Arthur Philip Louis, the second in line to the throne, but Diana would hear none of it. When Charles persisted, Diana stamped her foot, shouting, "No, no, no!"

A few months after William's birth, Charles went on record about his views on bringing up babies: "I believe in simple old-fashioned values, not in the changing fashions in child-rearing. There were some experts who were very certain about how you should bring up children, but then, after twenty years, they turned round and said they'd been wrong. Well, think of all the people who followed their suggestions."

Ironically, one of those experts Charles was speaking of was Dr. Benjamin Spock, a distant relative of Diana's family. Diana would have none of Charles's old-fashioned nonsense. Instead, she put a discreet advertisement in *The Lady* magazine, where aristocratic women traditionally looked for their nannies and housekeepers. No one, of course, knew the discreet, two-line classified ad came from Charles and Di.

After two or three interviews, Diana decided on Barbara Barnes, a mature woman of thirty-nine, the daughter of a forestry worker who came with a splendid recommendation from her former employer, Lord Glencomer, husband of Princess Margaret's lady-in-waiting, Lady Glencomer.

Glencomer said of Nanny Barnes: "She has a natural way with children. She has a genius for bringing out the best in them. They are never bored. She has all the traditional values to the highest degree but is perfectly up to date."

She was employed, she later discovered, primarily because she saw her job as helping Princess Diana, not taking charge herself.

It was a sign of Diana's growing independence and sense of power that she chose a nanny who didn't wear a uniform and had no formal training. In effect, Diana was confronting the Royal Family, the establishment, and the nursing profession by selecting Barbara Barnes. Nanny Barnes did not regard the royal nursery as her kingdom. She was the first nanny to an heir to the throne not to have two footmen and two housemaids to help her, although she did have one nursery maid, Mrs. Olga Powell, an experienced nurse in her late fifties.

The first few months with baby William were idyllic for both Charles and Diana. Charles was happy to defer to Diana in whatever she wanted for herself and the baby. He sought to show that he understood the enormous pressures a young mother experiences and wanted to help in every way. He had read all the baby books and knew, duty permitting, that he wanted to be a real father to William, not someone who visited the nursery occasionally to discuss with the nanny the progress of the young heir, as had been the case with himself.

Charles doted on his young son. He would hold baby William, occasionally bottle-feed him, even change his diaper on the odd occasion, if only to make clear he was willing to look after his son like any other ordinary father. One of Charles's great pleasures was to take a bath with baby William. The boy splashed and kicked in the water as his father held him, with Diana looking on, laughing as they enjoyed themselves in the tub.

Diana realized that she had found what she had missed ever since her mother and father had broken up. She finally had a home and a family. It spelled security, warmth, love, everything she had always secretly yearned for and had never been able to find. Now that she had found it, she was determined to keep it.

But it was not to be.

Diana threw herself and her love totally into the child and implored Charles to do the same. She became besotted with William in the same way she had been with Charles during their early days. She wanted her husband to spend more time with her and William at home. She didn't want the nanny there. She wanted Charles to be near her, to encourage her, sustain her, tell her how wonderful she and the baby were. She became upset when Charles had functions he had to attend, meetings he had to chair. And she grew increasingly angry whenever Charles reasoned with her that he had his duties to perform. Once Diana screamed at Charles in a voice that could be heard outside the nursery, "Go off and leave us then. We can manage without you."

Charles was hurt, bemused, and baffled. He couldn't understand how someone could be so emotional and unreasonable. He realized that women sometimes experienced postpartum depression, and he asked Mr. Pinker to come and chat with her. But to no avail.

Diana's behavior became increasingly odd. She was so determined to do everything herself for baby William that she was putting herself under enormous pressure. She wanted to organize everyone and everything, inside and outside the nursery. It seemed at first that nannies and maids were superfluous. Not surprisingly she became exhausted and depressed. Her mother's milk began to dry up, and William was sometimes fed by bottle, which Diana hated. She wanted to nurse her baby, come what may. She felt something of a failure because William needed more milk than she could give.

She clung more to Charles, demanding he stay with her night and day, for the sake of the baby. She told Charles that she could not eat when he was away, and she begged him to stay home. With Diana Charles was patient and understanding, soothing and gentle, but he put his foot down when he had work to do. It was his duty to the nation, to the Queen, to himself. In Charles's book, duty came before everything else.

Finally, six months after William's birth, Charles went to the Queen and explained the situation to her, including Diana's irrational behavior. He was at a loss at what to do. The Queen called in Mr. Pinker, and psychiatrists were consulted. But Diana wanted nothing to do with psychiatrists. All she wanted was Prince Charles and William for herself and everything would be fine.

It was suggested that a holiday might help Diana get over her irrational behavior and depression. Perhaps it would help if they could relax and spend time together. Diana loved to ski, so they went skiing in Liechtenstein, in January 1983. The holiday was a misery for Diana. She hardly ate during the week's break and rarely ventured onto the slopes. One night Diana broke down in tears, moaning, "I want to go home to William. I want my baby." Charles was desolate. He had no idea how to comfort and console his young wife.

They had been married less than two years, yet the magic between them had all but evaporated.

She and Charles even argued over the choice of godparents for William. Diana wanted young people, friends of theirs, but the Prince was adamant. When the baby was christened in the Music Room at Buckingham Palace, on August 4, 1982, the eighty-second birthday of the Queen Mother, the only godparent near twenty was Tally, the Duchess of Westminster, who had married Britain's richest landowner, the Duke of Westminster in 1978. They had a baby daughter, Lady Tamara, and Diana and Tally would often chat on the phone about their babies, comparing notes.

The two other godmothers were Princess Alexandra and one of the Queen's senior ladies-in-waiting, Lady Susan Hussey. The godfathers were Lord Mountbatten's grandson, Lord Romsey, King Constantine of Greece, and, amazingly, Charles's friend the author and philosopher Sir Laurens van der Post, who was then seventy-six years of age.

Godparents are usually young enough to help bring up a child if the parents should die, not old enough to be the baby's great-grandfather. Of course if anything should happen to Charles and Diana, the Queen and the rest of the Royal Family would step in to raise the two boys. But being a royal godparent is a distinct privilege and gives the godparent some right of access to Charles and Diana as well as the opportunity to build a relationship with the Princes.

Loved and cherished by Diana, Charles, and Nanny

Barnes, young William became a fast developer. As Diana put it, "I believe in giving babies lots of love and cuddles, and talking to them. It helps them develop much more quickly."

When William was just a year old, he managed to press a button on his nursery wall while staying at Balmoral in Scotland. The button was an emergency panic button which sent a direct signal to police headquarters in Aberdeen, some fifty miles away. Armed police raced to Balmoral, sealed off the grounds, and approached the house with great caution before they realized everything was fine. Only then was the culprit discovered.

On another occasion William toddled through an infrared alarm beam in the walled garden of Kensington Palace, bringing a squad of armed police racing to the scene. Nanny Barnes was highly embarrassed, and Prince Charles apologized profusely.

William was into everything, including trouble. He loved to put things down the toilet, including his toys, Charles's shoes and slippers, as well as Diana's makeup, soaps, and toiletries. William's other passion was breaking everything he could lay his hands on. Diana referred to him as "my little hooligan." Charles called his son "Willie the wombat."

In January 1984, Diana found herself pregnant for the second time. She was then twenty-two, Charles thirty-five. Charles was absolutely delighted, but Diana wasn't sure whether her beloved William, then twenty months old, would be able to cope with the arrival of a new baby. He had, of course, been the absolute center of attention from the moment he was born.

Once again Diana had a difficult pregnancy, suffering from morning sickness. She quipped, "Charles is so excited about the new arrival. But if men had babies, they would only have one each."

However, the pregnancy did seem to coincide with her return to better health. She knew she had to get a grip on herself, eat properly for the unborn baby, and start to do her pregnancy exercises once again. Though she felt physically awful for the first seven months, she finally conquered her postpartum depression. It had taken her nearly two years.

During her second pregnancy, Diana showed her mettle. She continued to carry out her royal duties until a couple of months before the baby was due. Baby Harry—whose full name is Henry Charles Albert David—was born on Saturday, September 15, 1984, just nine hours after Charles had driven Diana to the same ward in the same London hospital, the Lindo Wing in St. Mary's, where William had been born.

The next morning, Charles arrived, along with William and Nanny Barnes. Diana had asked that William be able see his baby brother as soon as possible, to create a bond between them. William ran down the hospital corridor, ahead of Charles and his nanny, when he saw his mother standing at the doorway of her hospital room. Diana scooped him into her arms and kissed him. Then she took him over to show off his baby brother, sleeping in his cot by her bed.

At two-thirty the next afternoon, less than twenty-four hours after giving birth, Diana left the hospital, waving to the crowds who clapped and cheered her departure. Charles drove her and baby Harry back to Kensington Palace, and then went on to play a game of polo at Windsor, celebrating afterward with an impromptu champagne party with his polo pals from the back of a Land Rover.

Playful William wanted to hold his young brother whenever possible. At the christening of baby Harry at St. George's Chapel, Windsor, three months later, William was annoyed, and showed it, that he wasn't allowed to hold the baby. Lord Snowden shot the family christening pictures. His crew were appalled at William's behavior. Snowdon's assistant commented, "Every time he did something naughty everyone, including Charles and Diana, roared with laughter. No one admonished him, even though he was being a thorough pest."

The christening was shown on nationwide television as part of the Queen's annual Christmas broadcast. William was seen chasing his cousin Zara Phillips, the daughter of Princess Anne and Mark Phillips, around the legs of the

Archbishop of Canterbury. The viewing public loved it. It showed that the Royal Family behaved in private much like other families.

Princess Diana was nearly always lenient with her children when they were young, and there was many a raised eyebrow among those who came into contact with the children. People were surprised that they were not better behaved and more disciplined. But the young Princess, who was never disciplined herself, was continuing to get her own way.

When young Harry was christened, royal watchers were surprised to see Diana victorious again. The Old Guard was out; Diana's idea of younger people had prevailed. This time the godparents included Lady Sarah Armstrong Jones, Diana's former flatmate Carolyn Pride, and Lady Cece Vestey, the second wife of Charles's polo-playing pal, the meat baron Lord Vestey, all in their twenties, along with Prince Andrew, artist Bryan Organ, who had painted an informal portrait of Diana, and a young farmer, old Etonian Gerald Ward. The christening party was a total snub for the traditionalists, who believed inheritance and social position were the paramount criteria of personal worth, as well as for Princess Anne, who was famously not chosen and, in return, boycotted the event.

Diana had not been allowed the godparents she wanted for William, but this time she strongly fought royal tradition. Even during her pregnancy, she argued that since she had gone along with the Royal Family's selection for William's godparents, it was only fair that she should name the next baby's godparents. Charles knew that the Queen would not approve. Being godparents to royal children was not to be taken lightly. The Queen wanted Establishment people, relatives of the Royal Family, or aristocrats; if commoners were chosen, the argument ran, the position would be devalued.

But Diana was adamant. Charles persuaded the Queen that allowing Diana to select some, but not all, the godparents would help produce some harmony in the difficult marital relationship. Diana drew up a list of prospective godparents which he could submit to the Queen for ap-

Arriving in Egypt on their honeymoon.

Diana's most important appointment was Barbara Barnes, seen here holding Prince Harry. Barnes seemed to be the perfect nanny for the Royal children. But when William and Harry began to look on her as their second mother, Diana decided Barnes had to go.

Edward Adeane (above), the Prince's private secretary, and
Stephen Barry (right), the Prince's valet, two of the many aides
and servants to Prince Charles who lost their positions because of
Diana's need to be in charge of the Royal household.

Above, Highgrove, where Charles spends much of his time, and, below, Kensington Palace, where Diana and her sons reside.

Their marital bliss would eventually end and Charles would turn his attention to women he knew before he met Diana. Here he is seen, five years after his marriage, with Lady Dale Tryon, whom Charles called Kanga. She has always adored him and, with her effervescent personality, helps him relax.

Charles's great love is Camilla, shown here with her husband, Andrew Parker Bowles, and their two children, Tom, nine, and Laura, five, at Buckingham Palace after he received the Order of the British Empire from the Queen. Twenty years ago, when Charles was twenty-three, he fell in love with Camilla. Marriage was far from his mind and he went to sea with the Royal Navy. Camilla did not know his intentions and six months later married Charles's good friend. Now that the Prince's own marriage has disintegrated, Camilla often comes to comfort him in his loneliness.

Diana, disaffected, began to flirt with other men. In June 1987, she caused a public row with Charles when, at a wedding reception, she spent the evening dancing with Philip Dunne. During one dance, she kissed him on the cheek and ran her fingers through his hair. Later he married filmmaker Domenica Fraser, seen here soon after their wedding in 1989. During the hour-long ceremony, the Princess sat in the front pew of the church.

Another handsome young man, Major David Waterhouse, the nephew of the Duke of Marlborough, had frequent dates with Diana, taking her to parties, dinner, the theater, ballet, and cinema. Charles would remain at Kensington Palace and carry out his Royal duties. Diana and Waterhouse are seen here at a David Bowie concert, their heads together. Often, after their dates, they would part with a kiss.

Tanned and tousle-haired, Princess Diana poses in her bikini on board King Carlos of Spain's yacht in Majorca, 1988.

proval, carefully choosing candidates who would be considered responsible, God-fearing people, but who were also friends of hers. The Queen, wanting Diana to understand that she could not simply do what she wanted without the approval of the head of the family, objected to two names. Diana submitted two more names, and the list was agreed upon. Diana had ridden rough-shod over Charles's demand that the godparents be people of intellect and mature years.

Following the birth of Harry, Princess Diana once more appealed to Charles to stay close to her and their two sons. Once again, she felt insecure. In an effort to placate his wife and fearing that she might once again suffer postpartum depression, Charles went along with her pleas and stayed around Kensington Palace.

By late 1984, the Queen, Prince Philip, and the tabloid newspapers began to realize that Charles was neglecting his royal engagements. In the four-month period following Harry's birth, Prince Charles carried out only a dozen engagements, less than a third his usual number. In the same time span, his sister Princess Anne had fifty-six engagements, and Prince Philip forty-five. His parents gave Charles a severe talking to, reminding him that he had an obligation to the nation above and beyond the duties he owed to his wife and family. He had to make sacrifices. He had no other choice, and no excuses would be brooked for not carrying out those obligations.

Charles had neglected his royal duties after the birth of William, and Prince Philip believed that it would be the same, if not worse, with the second son. So angry was he with his son that it was a full five weeks after the birth of Harry that Philip deigned to visit his new grandson. This infuriated Diana, who felt she was being unfairly blamed. But Diana did not share Charles's filial obedience to his parents. She believed that Charles's first duty was to her, their sons, and their family, not the throne.

Charles, feeling more and more trapped between his repetitive royal duties and his demanding wife, began to retire to the country and the therapy of farming.

Diana hoped, and believed, that sooner or later Charles

would snap out of his doldrums and return to her and the family, like any normal married man going through a mid-life crisis.

The public began to see a young, good-looking Princess, who had done her duty by producing two healthy sons as heirs to the throne and who was having a rough time in her marriage. They believed she was married to a Prince who had lost his way in life and who appeared to be abandoning not only his royal duties, but also his young wife and his two sons, in favor of his country estate and the polo field.

During 1985 and 1986 Charles retreated more and more to the peace and quiet of Highgrove and set up his office there. He moved his papers and his books and some of his immediate staff away from the turmoil of Kensington Palace and the woman he found it increasingly impossible to live with.

Diana and Charles drifted apart during those two years and Charles appeared deliberately to distance himself from Diana. He had tried and failed to placate her, even to understand her, and he hated the arguments which always seemed to end in rows and violent language. Charles hadn't the stomach for such a relationship.

For her part, Diana's moods swung from anger, frustration, and despondency to a determination to get on with her own life—and leave Charles to go his own sweet way. It was in those years that Diana realized she had to find a role for herself. She discovered the more she threw herself into charitable work and royal duties, the more she enjoyed her life and found herself fulfilled.

Diana was most grateful that she had her sons. She realized that the love she had once had for Charles she now openly directed toward Wills and Harry. She found herself openly critical of Charles, and often, when they were together, she found herself criticizing, chastising, and berating her husband. But the more she did so, the more she drove Charles away from herself and the Princes.

By 1987 Diana had become the undisputed mistress of Kensington Palace. The staff, the secretaries, the officials, and the servants realized that Diana had taken over the reins of power and that she was to be obeyed. Diana found that being the mother of the two young Princes gave her far greater authority than ever before, and people began to ask her all the questions of the household that had previously been deferred to Charles. She was in charge, and she liked the power.

Schooling caused major disagreements between Charles and Diana. Charles wanted William and Harry to start their academic life at home, with a governess teaching them the rudiments of reading and writing, the same way he and Diana had been taught in their early years. Diana, who had worked in a kindergarten, opposed the idea. She believed that mixing with other children was the best way for children to be brought up. In addition she wanted her sons' school experiences to be as normal as possible.

Once again, Diana had her way. She went about finding the most suitable schools within a five-mile radius of Kensington Palace and produced all the prospectuses for Charles. She even produced articles by educators showing that a small school would be better for Wills's development than being taught privately at home.

After much discussion, William was sent to a private nursery school run by a Mrs. Mynors in London's Notting Hill Gate, where several of Diana's friends sent their children. Mrs. Mynors talked to all the parents and those who lived near the school in a bid to minimize the fuss and interference with the royal children.

Charles and Diana sent a letter to all the Fleet Street editors, requesting that after the initial photo session for William's first day at school, William and the school be left alone. On his first day of term, in September 1985, over a hundred fifty photographers, cameramen, and reporters turned out. On the second day there were none.

During the first term William proved to be rather a handful. His police detective, who spent the day at the school trying to be as unobtrusive as possible, would often have to intervene in playground fights. "Now, now William, that's not the way to behave," he would say when William became too demanding or boisterous.

William earned the nickname Basher Wills for the way he would charge around the playground, and sometimes during lessons, hitting other children. Some parents believe the stories of William's wild ways were exaggerated, but the nickname stuck. Naturally, Wills did take some time to settle down. He obviously realized that he was someone different, if not special. Educators believe that most children in his situation would have been somewhat confused.

Everything was done to ensure that three-year-old William would be treated like the other fifty children at the $1,200-a-year kindergarten. The teachers and the children called him plain William, and he was given no special treatment or privileges by the staff. The children, who were between two-and-a-half and five years old, were never told who William was. The parents of the other children were asked to refer to him only as William and to take no special interest in him. Occasionally, however, young Wills would pull rank: "My Daddy's better than your Daddy, because mine's a Prince." Still, Mrs. Mynors later commented, "His classmates hardly know who he is. Sadly, that won't be the case at the next school he goes to."

The school did not expect the sort of behavior Wills occasionally exhibited. At one birthday party, he flew into a rage when told to sit down like everyone else. He threw his jelly (English for Jell-O), ice cream, and sandwiches on the floor, shouting that he hated them all. He demanded to go home. When one of the nannies made him pick up the mess, an angry William shouted at her, "When I'm King I'm going to send my knights around to kill you." When Diana was informed, she scolded him and told him if he behaved like that again he would be punished.

Diana began to worry that William, and even baby Harry, were becoming over-fond of Baba, as they called Nanny Barnes. Diana always tried to return home to KP in time to bathe or read a bedtime story to the children, but often she was late, only to find Nanny Barnes had put them to bed and kissed them good night. Diana was unnerved when both boys, if hurt or unhappy, instinctively called for Baba and not Mummy. Diana could not tolerate this situation.

It was decided that Miss Barnes would leave a few days after William started his new school, in January 1987. Buckingham Palace tried to maintain that her departure was nothing out of the ordinary, but the public was not fooled. Miss Barnes had no other job to go to, and there was no replacement nanny.

Diana had mistakenly assumed there would be no problem with the two boys. But there were many tears and tantrums in the nursery after Baba left. The boys could not believe that their Baba, the person they loved and adored, had simply left them, never to return.

One excuse Diana gave for firing Nanny Barnes was that William was not well-enough disciplined, and she laid the blame squarely at the door of Barbara Barnes. William seemed to get into all sorts of mischief, to the point that Diana didn't like him to appear too often in public for fear he would misbehave.

But she had never allowed Nanny Barnes to discipline William on the spot. Diana insisted that Miss Barnes report any misdemeanor to her first so that she could decide what reprimand or punishment the young Prince should receive. Of course, that arrangement did not work in practice. William would be naughty but could not be scolded or reprimanded until much later. By then young Wills would have totally forgotten what he had done wrong and why he was being punished.

Diana is not a disciplinarian, but she does believe in punishing the boys when they are rude or disobedient. Usually they are put in a corner or sent to their rooms, but on occasion they are also smacked on the bottom, but only with the bare hand, and never with a slipper or cane. Generally, Diana believes in verbal reproofs, telling them they are naughty rather than actually punishing them.

On occasion, however, the world has seen Diana whacking Wills on the bottom. Once, at school, she caught hold of him and smacked his bottom after he had hit another child. On another occasion she gave him a short, sharp slap on his behind after he climbed into a police car and began playing with the radio-telephone. She also made Wills, who was only three, apologize to the officer.

When he was four, as a special treat, William was allowed to watch his father play polo at the Guards Polo headquarters in Windsor Great Park. He had wanted to watch earlier that season but was told he would have to wait until he was older and better behaved. Wills promised to be good.

But from the moment Diana arrived at the royal enclosure, there was trouble. Wills kept asking: "Where's Papa?" "Can I have a drink?" "Can I have an ice cream?" and "Who's that?"

Diana threatened Wills that he would be taken back to Windsor Castle if he didn't behave, sit still, and watch the game. Wills tried but couldn't. Within thirty minutes Diana picked him up, popped him into a car, and drove him straight back to the castle. His afternoon's fun ended in tears.

Wills was growing up fast. It was time for his first proper school. Once again, Diana took control of the situation and asked for a list of appropriate schools within a five-mile radius of the Palace. Before any decision could be taken, however, the Royal Protection Squad had to be consulted. The squad required a school which they would find easy to keep watch over and which had some security. After discussion with Charles, Diana decided on Wetherby, a school of 120 boys, ranging in age from four-and-a-half to nine years, which emphasized discipline and good manners.

Lord Freddie Windsor, the son of Prince and Princess Michael of Kent, had attended Wetherby and had been very happy there. He had sung in the choir, done well at exams, and had the most perfect manners for a nine-year-old. Far more important to Prince Charles was the fact that the nephews of Camilla and Andrew Parker Bowles had also been educated at Wetherby. They were full of praise for the school and its headmistress, Miss Blair Turner.

A few weeks later Diana told other parents, "Wills is settling down really well at his new school. He's already opening doors for ladies and he's calling men sir, so I hope he will soon prove a perfect little gentlemen."

Others were not so sure. One was Bob Geldof, the scruffy Irish pop star. One day Geldof arrived at Kensington Palace, dressed in his customary jeans and sneakers, to talk to Prince Charles about food aid to Ethiopia. Wills was there with Charles.

"Why do you talk to that man?" asked Wills, pointing at Geldof, whose face had the usual amount of stubble.

"Because we have work to do," Charles replied.

"He's all dirty," William said.

Geldof replied, "Shut up, you horrible little boy. Your hair's scruffy too."

Cheeky William answered back, "No it's not. My mummy brushed it."

Meanwhile, Diana was having problems finding a replacement nanny for Barbara Barnes. One was accepted until it was discovered that she was a Roman Catholic. A polite letter informed her that she could not have the position. Her employer explained, "How could a man who is one day going to be head of the Church of England employ a Catholic nanny for his children? Of course you couldn't possibly get the job."

The need to employ an Anglican nanny shows how strongly the Queen and the Establishment still feel toward the Church, even in these days of great ecumenicism.

Eventually, Ruth Wallace was offered the job. A forty-year-old State Registered Nurse, Nanny Wallace had been working next-door at Kensington Palace apartment as nanny for Princess Michael of Kent. Princess Michael was annoyed; she believed in the unwritten rule that mothers did not poach other people's servants, particularly nannies. Rather condescendingly, she commented, "Well, Diana does need all the help she can get. And Ruth is highly

competent. Who can blame her for wanting to work for
the Princess of Wales?"

Diana relented on discipline. Nanny Wallace would be
allowed to punish the boys if she found it necessary, including the odd smack on the bottom. But she was still
required to inform Diana of any poor behavior. Fortunately, Wills was having his energies sapped by a tough
school schedule for a five-year-old. He was attending
school from nine A.M. till three-thirty P.M. five days a week
plus taking extra lessons. He was taking "Fun With Music" instruction at a cost of $100 extra per term on top of
the $1,500-per-term fees. He also attended music classes
in North London each week. In addition, there were football and swimming lessons and, once a week, tennis lessons at the Vanderbilt Club with his mother. On
weekends there was horse-riding instruction on his own
pony, which Charles had bought him.

Charles hopes that both his sons will share his passion
for riding, and he would dearly love to form a junior polo
team when the boys are teenagers in which all three
would play. To her credit, despite her own great fear of
riding, Diana has not discouraged her sons from horses.
However, she demands professional instructors, and although Charles does not always wear a crash hat when
practicing his polo strokes or schooling his own polo ponies, Diana insists that the boys wear theirs whenever
they get on a horse. She is absolutely strict about that: no
riding hat, no riding. And she is angry with Charles for
setting such a bad example to younger riders by forgoing
his helmet.

Young Harry followed in his brother's footsteps and began
school at Mrs. Mynors's kindergarten in September 1987,
when he was just three. Both Charles and Diana had been
happy at the way the school had controlled William's exu-
berant spirits, as well as giving him a basic grounding in
education. Harry, a much more gentle and shy child,
seemed to settle in better than his high-spirited elder
brother.

Young William's behavior improved and he had a successful time at his pre-prep school, Wetherby. Then he made a giant step for a little boy. At age eight, he was sent to a boys' boarding school, Ludgrove preparatory school in Berkshire, in September 1990. It is a small (190 boarders), exclusive institution set in 130 acres of beautiful countryside fifty miles from London, with fees of $12,000 a year. Charles and Diana chose it on the recommendation of the Duke of Kent, who was not only an old boy, but who had also sent his son Frederick there. Wills will stay there until he is thirteen, when he will take his Common Entrance examination, which all boys must pass to gain access to Britain's fee-paying public school system.

Charles and Diana have not yet decided which public school Wills and Harry will attend. The choice will depend, to a certain extent, on the boys' academic capabilities. Diana is certainly not keen that either boy go to Charles's old school, Gordonstoun, in Scotland.

Charles was not happy during his early years at Gordonstoun and would prefer his sons to have a more academic education than he had there. If the boys are sufficiently capable, Charles wants them both to attend Eton, for one particular reason: Eton's headmaster, Dr. Eric Anderson, was Charles's English teacher at Gordonstoun and is a man Charles much admires. Today, twenty-five years after leaving Gordonstoun, he remains friends with Dr. Anderson.

However, if Dr. Anderson believes the royal children will not be able to keep pace with their classmates, then it is likely that Wills and Harry will attend either Marlborough, Winchester, or Radley. Since this will be the most important phase of their preuniversity schooling, Charles will make the final decision. He has no intention of allowing Diana, with her decidedly poor academic career, to become involved.

Since going to Ludgrove, young Wills has quieted down appreciably. In his first term there he was repeatedly taunted about being "Basher Wills," but he dealt with this maturely: he turned the other cheek and did not respond violently. William is now a far cry from the young tearaway whose favorite toys were plastic weapons—machine guns, rifles, pistols, and swords—often used against his brother.

William and Harry love to go shooting with their father in Scotland. At first they would just stand around with toy guns and imitate Charles. But by age seven, Wills was helping the beaters drive the pheasant and partridge toward the waiting guns. Diana does not approve of shooting, nor does she approve of Charles's taking his sons shooting, but he insists, and the boys enjoy the sport immensely.

One of Diana's friends who also has young children said, "Diana tried to stop Charles taking William shooting, but Charles put his foot down. He said it was a man's sport. He had always enjoyed it, and he didn't see why William should not be allowed to try his hand at everything, whether it was hunting, shooting, or fishing. William has already tried his hand at fishing with his father but found it rather boring. Charles said that the boys could have their choice when they were older. If they didn't like it, they didn't have to shoot or fish. Diana could not win that one, but she is trying to persuade the younger boy, Harry, not to shoot."

Although much quieter, Harry exhibits a more daredevil spirit than his elder brother, particularly when skiing or riding his pony. William tends to take ski slopes more gently, like his mother, while Harry, even at age six, would charge down the mountains fearlessly, like his adventuous father. Harry is the same when riding, always prepared to have a go at a jump, or a small hedge, without fear. William is more correct in his approach to riding and more stylish, but both boys enjoy it immensely. It is the same with their BMX (off-road) bikes, which they love to ride whenever they can. They ask for the bikes to go wherever they go, at Highgrove, Windsor, Sandringham, Balmoral, and even on holidays. Once again, Harry seems to go faster and more wildly on his bike than does his big brother. But they have a great deal of fun screaming around the estates, watched by their police bodyguards through binoculars.

The family argument over hunting continues. It erupted again when Prince Harry announced in December 1991 that he wanted to go hunting with his father. Harry is a keener rider than Wills—and many say more proficient—quite capable of riding to hounds, but not, of course, taking the stone walls and hedgerows that the huntsmen tackle. Diana objected to her son being taken on a hunt with the object of killing foxes. She didn't mind drag-hunting, because there was no killing involved.

She told Charles she thought hunting "barbaric" and pleaded with him not to involve the children. Charles refused. A few weeks later, in December 1991, Charles and Harry rode to hounds, but not hunting foxes. Instead, they went on a hare hunt, but the object was the same: the killing of live animals.

Young Harry, meanwhile, continued in Wills's footsteps, enrolling at Wetherby in September 1990. Both boys have been treated at all their schools as though they were ordinary pupils, with no privileges. Of course, from Wetherby onward, the other children have known who they are, that their Mum and Dad are the Prince and Princess of Wales. The boys have had to accept some teasing as a result, but are still treated and disciplined like any other child.

Like any mother, Diana suffers real trauma when either of her sons, whom she openly adores, is injured. In June 1991, William was accidentally hit on the head with a golf club by another boy, on the nine-hole golf course at Ludgrove. He was struck above the left eye and suffered a depressed fracture of the skull. He was rushed to the nearest hospital at Reading, and then transferred to Great Ormond Street in London for an operation.

Diana was in tears when she arrived at his bedside at the Reading hospital, racing above the speed limit, with a police escort, through the forty miles of heavy traffic from London. Charles arrived fifteen minutes later, having driven from Highgrove in his 120-mph Aston-Martin.

Diana took command of the situation, not Prince

Charles. He argued that Wills should be taken immediately to Nottingham's Queen's Medical Center, a hundred miles away, which had impressed him greatly when he was treated there after breaking his arm playing polo. But Diana would have none of it.

"Don't be silly. That's miles away. The best place for William will be Great Ormond Street. Don't you agree, Doctor?" she asked.

"That would be a sensible move," the surgeon replied.

Charles tried to intervene, but Diana wouldn't let him: "Oh, shush," she said. "Listen to the doctors, they know best."

The surgeon said, "I would advise he be taken to Great Ormond Street, Sir."

Diana turned to Charles. "You heard what the doctor said. Fix it."

Then she walked out of the room and left Charles to organize the details.

This exchange was symptomatic of the relationship between the two royals by June 1991, revealing the extent to which Princess Diana had become the more powerful, dominant person within the marriage. She now treats her husband with very little respect and gives his opinions little weight. The fact that Charles has accepted the position, never questioning his wife's authority concerning the children, is also revealing. It has taken just ten years for the near-total role reversal to come about.

Diana accompanied Wills in the ambulance on the forty-five-mile drive from Reading to London's Great Ormond Street Hospital for Children, while Charles followed in his Aston-Martin, driven by his detective.

Diana stayed at the hospital while Wills underwent a seventy-minute operation to relieve the pressure on the brain, caused when a small piece of bone was forced inward. Charles left to go to Kensington Palace before the operation was half over, staying just forty-two minutes with his son. Diana never left the hospital, sleeping the night in an adjoining room, while Charles went to the opera that evening and later took the overnight train to Yorkshire, two hundred miles away, to attend an environmental conference on the Yorkshire Dales the following day. As one tabloid newspaper asked Prince Charles the next day on its front page: WHAT KIND OF DAD ARE YOU?

The newspaper's editorial asked: "Was not Charles's place beside his anguished wife, Princess Diana? And could he not spare more than a measly forty-two minutes to visit his son and provide some comfort for his wife? In public affairs, the Prince is a most conscientious man. He obviously wants to use his authority for the public good. But inevitably his influence will suffer if, however unjustly, he appears to give more attention to our rural heritage than to his own son. Had he behaved solely as a concerned father in a family crisis, he would have earned and deserved new respect and even affection."

Diana continued her lonely bedside vigil the next day, sitting much of the time holding Wills's hand and talking quietly to him as he recovered from the operation. After an eighteen-hour stay at the hospital, Diana went home, but only to take a bath and change before returning to the hospital two hours later. Charles meanwhile earned black marks from child psychologists for carrying on his royal duties. Not only had he left his distressed wife alone with her tears, but also his son and heir in his hour of need. Charles returned to the hospital after six P.M. the next day, just in time to say good night to Wills.

Diana attended only one engagement during the seventy-two hours William was in the hospital. She visited mentally handicapped and deaf patients at Springfield Hospital in South London, and that only because the patients had been preparing for her visit for months and would not have understood if she had canceled, or postponed, the visit. But she returned to Wills's bedside immediately afterward.

Charles's twenty-four-hour absence was the second time he had failed to provide emotional support for Diana or his sons when the children were sick. In 1988, young Harry, then three, was rushed to hospital for a hernia operation. At that time, too, Charles left Diana to cope with the family crisis and keep the hospital vigil, while he decided not to return from his painting holiday in Italy. In fact, Harry had suffered a painful twisted testicle, which, unless operated on very speedily, can mean a young boy's losing the testicle. Fortunately, Harry was fine and returned home twenty-four hours after the operation.

Diana was angry at Charles on both occasions. She could not understand how a responsible father could leave his sons in such circumstances when they needed his love and attention. She accuses Charles of behaving exactly as his father Prince Philip was with him—cold and distant. Charles's upbringing was marked by formality and restraint, devoid of almost any emotional support. The Queen is more openly affectionate with her dogs than she was with her children. The hospital incidents proved to Diana once again that her life more resembled that of a single mother than that of a properly married woman with two children to bring up. And in the arguments she sometimes still has with Prince Charles, she never lets him forget that.

Diana suffers when separated from her two sons, which happens when she accompanies Prince Charles on official royal engagements overseas. Each time she is abroad she always comments that she is dying to return home to see Wills and Harry.

She tries desperately to make up for those separations by attending functions at the boys' schools, such as sports days and end-of-term plays. Every year Diana has taken part in the annual Mother's Race at Wetherby, with photographers always on hand to see her racing to the winning post, cheered on by her son William.

And when either of the boys needs extra comforting, Diana allows them to sleep in her bed. When they feel better, they are returned to their own bedroom, next to that of their nanny's. Diana always has been very physical with her boys, totally unlike the way Charles was treated by his father and his mother, who were never seen to hold or cuddle or kiss Charles when he was growing up. Diana believes it important that the boys hug and kiss her, both in private and public. Many photographs show Wills and Harry cuddling with their mother. Charles, on the other hand, is never seen touching his sons. He treats them more as little men, not young children.

Diana encourages her sons to read books and used to take them to the Early Learning Centers in London, shops tailored for children from three months and up. She doesn't approve of them watching too much television.

"Harry has become a little square-eyed boy," Diana complained when chatting to other boys at Dr. Barnado's charity lunch. "He comes home after a hard day at school and loves to slump in a chair in front of the TV." She is not overly worried, however, because when Harry gets to Ludgrove, when he is eight, watching television will be strictly limited.

So far, Diana has always totally supervised the boys' clothes, decking them out in nothing unusual or flashy. She likes plain, no-nonsense clothes for the boys, including jeans and, on occasion, sneakers. On formal occasions they have to wear gray suits, with shirts and ties, and lace-up black shoes. Diana happily dresses Harry in Wills's hand-me-downs. As mentioned earlier, in upper-middle-class and aristocratic families in Britain, it is the "done thing" for younger children to wear hand-me-downs. Diana also believes it is a good idea for children to learn to respect their clothes.

Diana is not too proud to alter and repair their clothes. She confessed to Betty Saunders, a parishioner who was watching the Royal Family return from church at Sandringham: "Look at the boys' trousers. Every time I let them down, they grow and I have to let them down again."

Princess Diana is not overly fussy about what her sons eat, but she does insist that they have vegetables with their main meals. She does not like them to eat sweets or chocolate between meals, but does not forbid it. For breakfast they usually have muesli, toast and marmalade, and orange juice, or sometimes a boiled egg with toast. Lunch is their main meal of the day. Tea will be accompanied by biscuits or fruit cake and something light for supper, like an omelette or pasta. However, Diana firmly opposes any foods containing additives and won't let the children have fizzy drinks, which she believes are bad for them. Although Diana is strict about her own, near-vegetarian diet, she allows the boys as much meat as they like. A special treat is a take-away McDonald's or a pizza.

Diana tries to give Wills and Harry the sort of conventional, ordinary upbringing that most upper-class British children receive, despite the extraordinary circumstances of being royal Princes. She understands the pressures the boys must face, especially at their respective schools, but she tries not to let that influence their upbringing.

With William at boarding school, Harry gets lonely when he returns to Kensington Palace when school finishes at four. He is often invited to play at the homes of his classmates; then he is picked up in a chauffeur-driven car and taken back to KP for supper and a bath before going to bed at eight. Diana is strict about bedtime. She still reads to Harry most nights and gets him to read books on his own. After fifteen ninutes she gives him a kiss good night, switches off the light, and softly closes the door.

During school holidays, Diana tries to keep the boys busy and interested. Most weekends she takes them to visit their father at Highgrove. There they ride and fish and go for walks with her. They love playing football and hide-and-seek in the gardens. At home at KP, they usually get up around eight, often in the care of their nanny when Diana must leave for a royal visit somewhere. However, she tries to cut down on her official engagements when the boys are home from school.

They usually go swimming, have a tennis lesson, or travel to Windsor for riding lessons. Sometimes they invite friends over to play or go to other people's homes. She allows them to go to the cinema once a week, but she doesn't approve of their sitting for hours watching TV or too many videos. Occasionally they're allowed to stay up to watch a video or film, but Diana usually makes sure Harry is in bed by eight and William by nine.

.   .   .

During the past couple of years, Diana has frequently accused Charles of running away from being a real father, claiming he has turned his back on the young Princes to live a separate life at Highgrove and abandoning her to the life of a single mother.

Charles refutes these charges, but there are those who believe that, unable to cope with Diana, he has in fact turned his back on Kensington Palace and sought refuge in the country. Of course Diana knows that Charles has also sought refuge in the arms of another woman, and that continues to hurt her.

17

※≫≫≪≪

A Time of Trauma for Di

Scandal is a word few people wish to be associated with. Because of the power and position of the Queen and her immediate family, however, scandal seems to stalk them.

Two traumatic experiences, both involving Charles, engulfed Princess Diana at the beginning of 1988. Both would profoundly affect her and her deteriorating marital relationship. One was a fatal skiing accident in which a close friend died; the other concerned the forced resignation of the Prince's polo manager, Major Ronald Ferguson, father of Fergie, Diana's best friend.

The Royal Family try at all times to uphold absolute standards of propriety. Ideally, they prefer to appear in newspapers and on television only when making speeches or performing public duties. They are well aware, as are their courtiers, that the public wants a Royal Family beyond approach or reproach, and that adverse publicity jars their place as the country's first family.

For members of the family itself, avoiding salacious publicity is not difficult, since most behave with natural, judicious dignity. Those on the fringe, however, not born royal but linked through marriage or other ties, have been responsible for some very unwelcome publicity indeed.

Dickie Mountbatten had urged Prince Charles to sow his wild oats and then find a young virgin to marry and train, because he recognized how gossip and scandal can undermine the monarchy. Many of the young ladies Charles had courted were not suitable for the position of Princess of Wales because they had "been around," Palace language signifying that they were not chaste. Charles could not marry someone who had "been around" because she would one day be Queen and because the British tabloid press would have a field day ferreting out all the poor girl's former boyfriends, dates, and lovers, causing no end of embarrassment to the bride-to-be, her family, Prince Charles, and the entire Royal Family.

Diana's own life had been scandal-free, but the lives of her parents were not.

Diana's mother, Frances, had been branded an adulteress who had abandoned her four young children. Even her own mother, Lady Fermoy, had turned against her. At that time, Diana told her nanny, Mary Clarke, "I'll never ever marry unless I really love someone. If you're not really sure you love someone then you might get divorced. I never want to be divorced."

The ski tragedy occurred on March 10, 1988, at the Swiss resort of Klosters, when an avalanche killed Charles's great and good friend Major Hugh Lindsay and shattered the legs of Patti Palmer-Tomkinson.

Charles's guests included Lindsay, whose wife had remained in England because she was expecting a baby in two months' time, as well as Charles and Patti Palmer-Tomkinson, all expert skiers who loved skiing off-piste— off the track proper—because it was more exciting than the piste's compacted snow. That day, his party, against the advice of the resort authorities, had decided to leave the piste and tackle the alternative Wang run, one of the most dangerous in the mountains around Klosters. As they raced downhill through beautiful, deep powder, their

Swiss guide, Bruno Sprecher, heard the avalanche and then saw the massive wall of snow cascading down toward them. He immediately screamed, "Go, Sir, go, Sir, go!" at the top of his lungs. Charles looked behind him and skied as fast as he could to the side away from the avalanche, but he saw Patti and Hugh disappear as the gigantic cloud of snow enveloped them.

Charles was utterly distraught. Tears streamed down his face as he frantically dug at the snow with his hands, trying to free Patti. He kept repeating the same two words: "responsibility, responsibility, responsibility" and "control, control, control." He was in a state of shock.

Back at the ski cabin that night, Charles remained in shock as he phoned the Queen to tell her what had happened. Diana had not gone skiing with Charles that day. She was a close personal friend of both Lindsays, and she spent the evening trying to console Charles and Patti's husband, Charles Palmer-Tomkinson.

Later Diana told friends, "That was a terrible night. I tried to get close to Charles, tried to get him to eat and sleep but he couldn't. I had never seen him so angry with himself and so devastated by anything. He held himself utterly responsible for what happened. I felt for him, but I couldn't really help him. It just made me feel useless. I should have been able to console him, but he didn't want to listen."

Only once before in his life had Charles been so emotionally crushed: the assassination of his beloved Uncle Dickie Mountbatten. The death of Hugh Lindsay was the second devastating trauma in his life. Once again, he was unable to cope. In some ways this death proved even more traumatic for Charles than Mountbatten's, because he held himself totally responsible.

Everyone in the ski party was there at his invitation, and by tradition, his guests defer to him about where and when to ski. Although he had consulted with Charles Palmer-Tomkinson and Hugh Lindsay about leaving the piste after being told not to, the final decision was his. Even today, years later, he still feels guilty and believes he will never be able to erase this tragedy from his memory.

Trained to bottle up all emotion, Charles has rarely been able to show his feelings. No matter how angry or cross, Charles will seldom react with an open, emotional response, but instead will go off alone to ponder his thoughts and to try to control his anger and frustration. This was how he handled the Klosters tragedy.

When the Klosters tragedy struck, Diana realized she would never really understand or "get near" Charles. During the previous six-and-a-half years of their marriage, she had blamed herself for being unable to draw him out during periods of stress. Now she saw that his only way of dealing with problems also forced them further apart. Charles could do nothing to sustain a loving, understanding relationship, the lifeblood of a good marriage.

Diana told a few close friends how very difficult it was for Charles to say "I love you." She explained that he seemed frightened, even terrified, to use those three words. He seemed to believe that to show emotion, whether privately or publicly, was a weakness, a betrayal of his very soul, leaving his inner thoughts vulnerable to penetration by others. Yet she had yearned for him to say he loved her repeatedly, to give her the support and confidence she so desperately needed in the early days of their marriage. When Diana realized with a shock that Charles couldn't express his love, even when things were going well between them, and also couldn't change, their relationship only grew worse.

Back in England, Diana spent the next few months trying to comfort Sarah Lindsay, whom she had come to know when Sarah worked in the press office at Buckingham Palace. Diana visited her every week, before and after the birth of the baby, who was named Alice Rose. Charles asked to be a godfather. Sarah agreed, and shortly afterward, the Prince set up a substantial trust fund for the baby girl.

Diana had always been a good friend of Hugh Lindsay's as well. It was Hugh whom Diana and Fergie had jabbed unceremoniously in the backside with their umbrellas at

Royal Ascot only the summer before. When the startled Major had spun around, he smiled when he recognized his "attackers."

A year after Alice was born, Diana still visited Sarah Lindsay frequently, making sure she wanted for nothing and spending hours trying to lift her out of her depression. It was Diana who encouraged Sarah to return to her press office job at the palace.

Today Patti Palmer-Tomkinson has forty steel screws and six metal plates built into her legs, and she cannot walk unaided. She is happy to be alive and stoutly refutes any suggestion that Charles was to blame, although a good deal of sensational newspaper coverage following the accident speculated that the Prince was "reckless" and "lacking in judgement."

Three months after the tragedy, Judge Hanspeter Kirchhofer, who was in charge of the inquiry into Major Lindsay's death, announced that Prince Charles and his ski party were to blame for causing the avalanche. "By deliberately leaving the marked slopes and skiing off-piste, the six-member group placed itself in great danger." But, he added, "In such a case, even if there are deaths or serious injury, it is not possible to charge individual members with negligence."

The official findings were a relief to the Royal Family, but not to Charles. He told Patti later that he was responsible because it was his ski party and he should not have allowed any of them to take that off-piste run.

The tragedy in the snow had nothing in common—other than Charles—with the sensational event that was about to envelop the Prince and Princess: a distasteful and very public sex scandal. Though some found the affair more comic than catastrophic, neither Charles nor Diana was among them. For a man who could number his true friends on the fingers of one hand, the outcome would be the loss of another valued friend.

The news hit the streets around ten P.M. on Saturday, May 17, 1988. A timely phone call alerted Charles that the story was about to break, so that, shaken and angry, he was at least prepared.

The People newspaper splashed a giant headline across its front page: WORLD EXCLUSIVE. The article, which was to ruin Ronald Ferguson's life and cast him into a royal limbo, was titled: FERGIE'S DAD AND THE VICE GIRLS. Inside were four pages devoted to the story, embellished with a photograph of the Prince of Wales's polo manager sneaking out of a seedy massage parlor. The package, skillfully presented for the delectation of the tabloid's nine million readers, lacked nothing in impact.

"Fergie's father, Major Ronald Ferguson, is living a secret double life," proclaimed *The People*. "To the outside world he is a friend to the Queen, polo manager to Prince Charles, confidant to Princess Diana, and one of the royal circle's most colourful characters.

"But attractive young prostitutes working at a high-class London brothel called the Wigmore Club know another Major Ferguson. He is one of their most valued, regular customers.

"The galloping major pays blondes, brunettes and redheads for sexual services—and even rewards his favorite girls with gifts of perfume."

The explicit account of Ferguson's antics sent a shudder through Buckingham Palace. Quite apart from the sordid implications, there was also a snobbish aspect: gentlemen of Ferguson's social standing were supposed to belong to proper *gentlemen's* clubs—long-established London clubs distinguished by their elegant smoking rooms, fine libraries, leather-bound armchairs, and masculine aura. The Wigmore Club was little more than a seedy, back-street massage parlor.

The newspaper maintained that many of the girls working at the Wigmore were prostitutes, with criminal records and pimps as boyfriends. It went on to suggest that Major Ferguson had left himself open as a possible target for blackmail.

What surprised the paper's reporters and many readers was that Ferguson had not only enrolled at the club under his own name, but that he openly bragged to the girls that he was the Duchess of York's father and a close friend of Diana and Charles.

What outraged the Queen's advisers and friends most of all was that Ferguson had brazenly continued to visit the brothel after his daughter had married Prince Andrew, and while Fergie was expecting her first child.

Initial reaction to the disclosures was swift. "I would expect Major Ron's resignation [as polo manager] to be on the Prince of Wales's desk within twenty-four hours," asserted one dismayed polo player, a friend of the major and a confidant of the Royal Family. "And I would expect it to be accepted. Even though Ron has grown very close to Charles over the years, if he does not quit of his own volition, the Prince will not be able to protect him in the end. He has committed the unpardonable sin: he has touched the family with the taint of scandal."

Just a week before *The People* story, Ferguson, for the best of motives, had displayed his questionable taste when he turned up at a charity show hosted by Dame Edna Everage (the character created by Australian comedian Barry Humphries) dressed as an aged punk rocker, wearing a puce Mohican wig and black leather Hell's Angel jacket, replete with swastikas and silver chains.

Foolishly, and unbelievably, Major Ferguson had ignored warnings in the months prior to his public exposure from more than one of his friends. They had seen scandal coming as whispers about his philandering spread. "Ronald had grown too big for his riding boots," one commented. "He was loving the limelight of being part of the Royal Family proper, and he thought he was the cat's whiskers. He had become a celebrity in his own right and began to think he had some divine protection. But he wasn't as universally popular as he imagined, particularly in those selfsame royal circles."

Diana for one. Despite Diana's affection and friendship with Fergie, she disliked Major Ferguson intensely, finding him seedy. For reasons she was hard put to articulate, she could not bear his touch, and whenever polo or some social or family occasion drew them together, Diana carefully contrived to keep her distance. "I don't know why, but the man gives me the creeps," she confessed to a friend years before the Wigmore Club visits became public.

Ronald Ferguson belongs to one of Britain's elite army families. His father commanded a Life Guards regiment in 1940. Born in 1932, Ferguson was educated at Eton, one of Britain's most exclusive public schools, and then at Sandhurst—the Royal Military Academy—before joining the Life Guards. He ended his twenty-year career as a major, a rather low rank considering his connections and family background. Major Ferguson also held the privileged appointment of commander of the Sovereign's Escort of the Household Cavalry, which closely attends the Queen's coaches on ceremonial occasions.

Polo is his consuming passion. It was in the rich and aristocratic world of polo that the major became a dominant personality and a close friend of the Royal Family, particularly Charles. Major Ferguson captained England and, as a result, became very friendly with Prince Philip. The two men often played on the same team before age and arthritis forced Philip to give up the game. When the teenage Charles decided to take up polo, Ferguson became one of his tutors.

Since first becoming Prince Charles's unofficial master of polo in 1973, the major has always gone to great lengths to point out that his role was "voluntary, unpaid, and part-time." For years, Charles and Ferguson played on the same team, and the major helped and advised not only the Prince's game, but also his purchase of the all-important polo ponies.

Later, Ferguson became Charles's polo manager and, others would say, even a friend and confidant, yet another of the older-men father figures whom the Prince habitually turns to. On one occasion Charles took Ferguson on a round-the-world trip lasting many weeks, visiting Australia, Thailand, Tanzania, and the United States. People wondered whether Ferguson was a member of the official royal party or simply a hanger-on.

Such was his influence that he even vetoed Charles's dinner guests on a trip to the United States, as Charles turned to him to select who would and would not dine with him. In fact, on that particular tour, Charles hardly made a decision without first consulting the major, whom he considered an experienced man of the world.

Ferguson's personal life had long been in disarray. He had a reputation as a ladies' man, so it could have been no surprise when in 1974 his wife Susan left him for the handsome Argentine polo player Hector Barrantes (who later died of cancer). Sarah was just thirteen when her parents separated, and Ferguson was mainly responsible for bringing up Sarah and her elder sister Jane. Both girls became expert riders and each day would help exercise their father's top-grade ponies. Through him they came to love the game of polo as well as the social life it introduced them to at a young age.

After the breakup of his marriage, Ferguson, who had always prided himself on his fitness and physique, courted a string of society ladies, including Diana's own mother, Frances. He was eager to marry again. According to Diana's younger brother Charles, Ferguson asked Frances—then married to Peter Shand Kydd—to marry him, but she turned him down. In 1977, Ferguson married another Susan, this one the striking daughter of a wealthy Norfolk farmer who was fifteen years his junior, and had three children.

In 1985, just prior to Fergie's marriage to Prince Andrew, there was talk that Ferguson's second marriage was in difficulty. But during the month prior to the wedding, Major Ron was ebullient, giving interviews to every newspaper and magazine and reveling in the celebrations. He seemed utterly at home posing for pictures with the Royal Family.

The Ferguson scandal created a furious debate in Britain, and even more important, among the members of the royal household. Charles was determined to keep the Royal Family as far removed as possible from the situation. Firing Ferguson would be tantamount to saying that the Royal Family was involved. Since it was a personal and private matter, and since Ferguson held no office of profit under the Crown, Charles, and the advisers at

Buckingham Palace, believed they could stand aloof. To a remarkable degree they succeeded.

Diana disagreed passionately. She was torn between her friendship and support for her best friend Fergie and the distaste she felt for Major Ferguson personally. She urged Charles to sack Major Ron and show that he, as Prince of Wales, would not tolerate such outrageous behavior among his close, personal friends. Diana was also outraged that any father could act in such an insulting and discreditable manner when his own daughter was pregnant with her first child.

When Charles wanted to stop the discussion, Diana shouted at him, "How can you do nothing when he acts in such an insulting way toward the Royal Family? You must fire him to show what you think of such a man's behavior."

Despite her demand that Ferguson be publicly disgraced, Diana did not get her way. The very afternoon of the day the story was published, Ferguson turned up, as if nothing had happened, at Smith's Lawn, the area within Windsor Great Park where the Guards Polo Club plays by permission of the Queen, who owns the park. Diana insisted that Charles cut the Major dead, signaling to the members of the club and the media his disgust with his polo manager. But Charles was seen talking to him. A few weeks later, the Queen attended a polo match at Windsor and was televised shaking hands with Ferguson, leaving the nation amazed at such a swift royal pardon. But all was not as it appeared.

The furor continued. Exactly a week later, Diana showed precisely what she thought of the major's behavior. She drove to Smith's Lawn with William and Harry to watch a polo match and present the prizes. She had been there barely fifteen minutes when Major Ferguson began to walk toward her. She quickly collected her two sons, put them in her Jaguar XJS, and drove off at speed, leaving the major standing, looking lost. The deliberate snub was intended to show all Ferguson's polo friends, the press, and the public at large, how she felt. From that time on, Diana has never been seen speaking to Major Ferguson.

The pressures resulting from Ferguson's sexual antics fell on Charles. From every quarter, and from the Prince's closest advisers, as well as the headstrong Diana, it was argued that Ferguson would have to go, despite his family connection. If not, it would appear that Charles condoned his behavior. Because of the media and public opinion, Charles had been dragged into the sordid affair simply because Ferguson was a close associate. Charles knew he could not turn his back on the problem and ignore it.

Charles decided to see what would happen. Perhaps Ferguson would do the decent thing and resign, or seek a pardon, and surely apologize for the embarrassment to Charles and the Guards Polo Club, of which the Prince is a member. But Major Ferguson remained silent. A month later, he issued this statement: "I look after Prince Charles's polo affairs and I will continue to do that. It is absolute nonsense to say I'm being forced to quit."

But forces were gathering against the errant major. It was suggested that he resign his position as chairman of the Hurlingham Polo Association, the sport's highest authority throughout the world. In a fifteen-minute speech, Ferguson resolutely defended himself, insisting that he had done nothing illegal. He survived a committee vote, but only by seven to six, and the deciding vote was his own.

Shortly afterward the Guards Polo Club committee met without him to consider whether he should be asked to resign from his position as deputy chairman. The vote was a six-six deadlock. He had survived again. But at the end of the 1988 season, the same committee met and first discussed a management consultant's confidential report on the running and finances of the club. Then, when Ferguson left to play a game of polo, the committee voted not to reelect Major Ferguson to his fifty-thousand-dollar-a-year position. When Ferguson returned, he was handed a letter informing him that his contract would not be renewed for the following season. The decision, he was told, had been unanimous.

Ferguson's career was rapidly coming to a halt. He had joined the Guards Club in 1955 and had worked tirelessly to improve the club and the game of polo in Britain. He had been the club's deputy chairman for twelve years. On the last day of the season, his remaining supporters listened to a eulogy from a commentator and then broke into "For he's a jolly good fellow." Sarah turned up to support her father and stayed till the end. There was no sign of Charles.

Major Ferguson's removal was a classic example of the power of the monarchy. No one needed to do anything. In case of scandal, the guilty person usually resigns forthwith. If there is any doubt about the severity of the offense, the matter will be discussed among the Queen's senior courtiers, who decide the person's fate. The Queen will be told beforehand how the royal advisers intend to deal with the problem, and she will usually respond with something like "That seems a good idea" or "Perhaps that is being a little unfair."

The same holds true for employees of Prince Charles. It is considered undignified for the monarchy to become involved with the unsavory. It is all done on their behalf. Often nothing is said to them, for the courtiers know from experience how the Royal Family will react to any given situation.

The Prince of Wales played polo with the man who had broken the rules and had been found out; the Queen proffered her hand in public as if nothing untoward had occurred. Nothing was said officially or unofficially about the matter to Ferguson directly by anyone, certainly not by any royal advisers to the Queen or Prince Charles. But he was doomed all the same.

Because Ferguson was so stubborn, his removal from office, and therefore from close proximity to the heir to the throne, took longer than usual in such circumstances. Traditionally, after someone so blatantly breaks the unwritten rules of social conduct, his immediate resignation is accepted, much cant is uttered, and the offender leaves with praise heaped upon him. But Major Ferguson genuinely believed that because of his royal connections, he could ride out the storm. In the end, he had to be forced out.

Today, Major Ron Ferguson is employed at the Royal Berkshire Polo Club, in charge of arranging sponsorship deals, at a salary of sixty thousand dollars a year.

The departure of Major Ron also brought home a lesson to Diana which she was not to forget. Diana had not understood how the complicated machinations of the Royal Family's power actually function. She had wanted public and instant disgrace, but the monarchy's subtle approach was a perfect example of how they wield their power—effortlessly, calmly, and without the smallest public display. The results are inexorable.

18

Di's Defeat, Di's Victory

At the age of twenty, Lady Diana Spencer was the bride
of the decade, cheered by millions at her wedding. She
was besotted by Charles, and he was infatuated with her.

But the young bride could not cope with being imprisoned, as she saw it, in Buckingham Palace and Sandringham or desolate Balmoral. No longer an ordinary
person, she was now a member of the Royal Family and
the wife of the Prince of Wales, heir to the throne. She
understood all this, but she could not truly accept its consequences.

After their glamorous, sun-drenched honeymoon, she
found it hard to live within the stuffy atmosphere of the
Royal Family on holiday. To Diana, their life-style was out
of a 1930s black-and-white film about the aristocracy:
walks on the estate, hunting before lunch, stalking the
odd deer, fishing for hours, and set times for lunch and
dinner, when everyone sat in regulation dress having boring discussions in which Diana was too frightened to say a
word.

Everyone, even the Queen, tried to put Diana at ease,
encouraging her to feel like one of the family. They des-

perately wanted to make the young Princess feel comfortable, wanted, and loved, to enjoy their life with them. But she couldn't.

Someone who attended the occasional dinner at Balmoral recalls the typical conversation:

"Diana, tell me, what have you done today?" the Queen would say.

"Not very much, Ma'am," came the reply.

"Did you enjoy yourself? How did you amuse yourself?" the Queen would ask with a half smile.

"Well, I went for a walk but it was rather cold. I watched some television," Diana would answer.

"Well, tell us how are you settling down here, at Balmoral?" the Queen persisted.

"Very well, thank you," Diana would say.

That exchange would be followed by silence, as the Queen perceived that she was making no headway with Charles's bride. Diana told her sister that she was always petrified that the Queen was going to talk to her. Her mind just seemed to go blank whenever the Queen asked her anything.

"I just felt so foolish," Diana said. "I know she is trying to be kind, but I sit through meals hoping she won't ask me any questions, so I won't have to feel embarrassed."

Charles also sought to make his bride feel at home, but the divide between them was never bridged. Diana wanted Charles to be like any other young husband: to spend time with her, to indulge her whims, protect her, sit with her and enjoy simple pleasures such as watching television together. She somehow expected them to listen to pop groups together, to have people her own age whom she found interesting and simpatico around for supper. It was a life far removed from any Charles had expected, and one he found impossible to comprehend, let alone engage in.

Their love for each other had certainly been real. Charles was flattered that such a youthful, attractive girl like Diana had fallen hopelessly in love with him and apparently worshiped the ground he walked on. She was amazed that someone like the Prince of Wales could find her stimulating enough to contemplate marrying.

Certainly there had been passion in their lives, particularly those months together after they became engaged and Diana secretly lived in Buckingham Palace, not far from Charles's personal suite of rooms. That passion helped them survive those first months in the cold of Scotland, when Diana felt so cut off from her real world.

Their problems were aggravated during her first pregnancy, when Diana made constant demands on Charles's time, insisting he put her before his royal duties. The arguments became rows, with Diana first shouting, then screaming at her husband in frustration and anger. Charles put her tantrums down to the pregnancy and tried to be the understanding husband. But it proved difficult; he couldn't understand her hostility, especially when he was trying to be so understanding and helpful.

Diana's life changed dramatically as she became the world's number-one cover girl. Her confidence bloomed as the press and the British people adulated her for her looks and style. The more confident she became, the more capable she seemed, managing on her own without Charles's support. At first, Diana had been unable to do anything without her husband's encouragement and assistance. But after the birth of Harry in 1984, the emerging, confident Diana realized that she was a person in her own right: she was the Princess of Wales, whom everyone wanted to meet and associate with.

Her looks, her clothes, her smile had won her great affection from the nation. But Diana also realized that people would soon enough demand more from her than a slim figure and fashionable clothes. Her decision to throw herself thoroughly into charities was very shrewd, turning out far more successfully in terms of public relations than she could ever have hoped. It cemented her relationship with the people, making her the most favorite royal, surpassing by far the nation's affection for her own husband, the heir to the throne.

Never before had Charles been second best, and he didn't like it. It came home to him during a 1983 visit to

Canada with Diana. When he emerged from the car by himself, the crowd groaned. They wanted Diana. He tried to make light of it, but deep down it hurt. Suddenly he had a rival.

As a former aide to Prince Charles said: "People who came to work for the Waleses realized quite quickly that you were either on his side or hers. You couldn't support both of them. There was no middle course. Charles believed if people came to work for him as Prince of Wales, he was the employer to whom they should look for advice and orders.

"He is known, to a great extent, as a charming male chauvinist who recognizes women as attractive helpmates but, except for his mother, not as intellectual or working equals. In the early days it worked perfectly, Diana being only too happy to play the Eliza Doolittle to Charles's Professor Higgins.

"But everything changed as Diana's confidence grew. As she matured, gained in popularity and stature, she was no longer willing to play the adoring wife, content to sit and listen in awe to her husband's views and opinions."

According to those people in whom Charles still confides, rivalry between them was not the primary reason for their dwindling passion toward one another.

As one of Charles's advisers, who has known him since 1976, commented: "Prince Charles could not take Diana's tantrums, her arguments, and her screaming matches. She would say the most awful things to him when she was angry, and would not apologize afterward. He could not understand why she behaved like that when he had given her his total support for the role she had to play as the Princess of Wales.

"Charles gave her everything she wanted. When she wanted a new car, he bought her one. When she wanted a new hi-fi or whatever, he bought it. When she wanted holidays, they went on them. Whatever she wanted she was given. Charles wanted a quiet life, but he has never had a quiet life with Diana.

"It just became too much for him. He began to escape from her, then realized he was a much happier man the more he was away. He spent more and more time at Highgrove, until it became his first home and he began to use Kensington Palace as a hotel when he was in London."

It was by accident that Charles at first found himself living apart from Diana. She was determined to spend as much time as possible with the young Princes at Kensington Palace. Diana felt it important that she see the children last thing at night and, if possible, first thing in the morning, so nearly all her royal engagements were organized so that she could return to London at night.

Since Charles's royal duties often necessitated an overnight stay, he found he was spending nights away from the palace, often at Highgrove, before going on to another engagement. Sometime in 1986, he realized he enjoyed the seclusion and privacy of Highgrove and his own solitary company. And, by this time, he had discovered his passion for gardening; he loved pottering about his beloved vegetable garden at Highgrove, talking to his vegetables and herbs, encouraging them to grow. Charles began to lead a more distant life, away from his family and Diana. He spent more time at Highgrove, more time hunting in the winter and playing polo all summer, and more time attending to the affairs of the Duchy of Cornwall.

Diana's escape from her world of duty and restraint began after Fergie, who become her new "BF" sometime in 1985, introduced her to a younger set. Diana realized she enjoyed herself in their company; there was no heavy conversation that she couldn't understand, unlike at Kensington Palace dinner parties. She could just chat away about trivia, laugh, enjoy even risqué jokes, and have the fun she had all but forgotten after her marriage into the Royal Family five years earlier.

Diana talked to her sister Sarah and her close friends about her relationship with Charles. Toward the end of the 1980s, she realized that her marriage was all but over. She and Charles had drifted apart, and her husband made little effort to rescue the situation. She hoped that Charles would come back to her, that their marriage would get back on track, but it never did. The good times became fewer.

One of the reasons Diana became so closely involved with Relate, Britain's marriage-guidance service, was her hope that by attending sessions, she might learn something about her own marriage. She tried to talk to Charles about their marriage, but he would usually end the discussion by walking away. More often than not, the talks would conclude with Diana in tears, having lost her patience and her temper at what she believed was the pigheadedness of her husband.

People hardly noticed, but the couple began to take separate holidays in the late 1980s. Charles would go to Switzerland for a few days' skiing or to Tuscany to paint or to Scotland for weeks at a time. Diana would fly to a beautiful Caribbean island for a week in the sun, take the Princes skiing, or snatch a few days on a European beach with her sons. When the boys were younger there were pictures of the family together, holidaying on a sunny European beach, usually as guests of King Carlos and Queen Sophie of Spain. But Charles never looked comfortable playing sand castles. He always preferred swimming in a rough sea, not lazing around on a sun-drenched beach, which Diana loves.

Sometimes their coldness to each other is apparent. One such occasion occurred in Paris, in November 1988. A romantic dinner during a trip down the Seine on a *bateau mouche* was organized, but the evening proved a disaster. As the band played "I Love Paris" and other sentimental love songs, the air was tense. Although Charles and Diana sat close to each other and conversed animatedly with those around them, they never once looked at each other throughout the evening. For two-and-a-half hours they floated around Paris and, one aide reported, they actually never said a word to each other. They seemed to be inhabiting different worlds.

Police Constable Andrew Jacques was assigned to the Royal Protection Squad in 1987, when he was just twenty-three. His job was to guard the Prince and Princess of Wales whenever they were at Highgrove, and to keep an eye on the Gloucestershire estate when they were away. Jacques became friends with not only the permanent staff at Highgrove, but also with the royal couple's staff whenever the Waleses visited their country house.

For four years Police Constable Jacques knew everything that went on between Charles and Diana, their staff, and their children. In March 1991, Jacques quit his thirty-thousand-dollar-a-year job as a cop, fed up with the life and the police force, and talked about the breakdown of the royal marriage. Most members of the Royal Protection Squad sign confidentiality contracts never to reveal what they see or discover about the Royal Family, and the contract can never be abrogated.

However, Jacques, a married man himself, told all to Britain's mass tabloid newspaper, the *Sun*, shortly after he quit the job: "Basically, they now lead two totally separate lives. And, in reality, they have two separate homes as well."

He went on to detail their 1991 life-style: "Prince Charles has moved everything, lock, stock, and barrel, to Highgrove, while Diana lives full-time at Kensington Palace in London. Charles has even moved some of his staff to Highgrove.

"Diana goes to Highgrove occasionally at weekends to take Wills and Harry to see their father. She arrives on a Friday night and leaves early on Sunday to take the two boys back to London and prepare them for school the following day. But even when they are on holiday from school she still only stays for the weekend."

Jacques had more compelling revelations. "The couple now have separate bedrooms at Highgrove. She sleeps in a big four-poster and he uses an old brass bed he brought down from Kensington Palace.

"From what I have seen, their marriage has changed enormously since 1987. Originally they seemed quite happy, like any other married couple. But during the past year or so they seem to want as little contact as possible with each other. They never smile, laugh, or do anything together. Most weekends Charles seems to spend locked away in his walled vegetable garden while Diana stays inside with the children. And Charles has banned the boys from his private garden, where he grows all the produce for Highgrove, in case they harm his treasures, his vegetables. The only time they meet is at mealtimes, and very often that ends in a blazing row for all the staff to hear."

Jacques outlined the typical Highgrove weekend in 1990, when Diana would drive down to visit Charles with Wills and Harry. "At about five-fifteen P.M. on a Friday evening the four cars arrive with Diana in the first one, followed by her detective, then the children in their car followed by another detective. In the early days Diana would always wave and smile to me and others when she arrived. Now she sits stony-faced, looking ahead. And Charles is never there to greet them at the door. If he's working in the garden he doesn't even stop to wave or shout hello.

"At five-thirty P.M. Diana goes up to her bedroom, leaving the two boys with the nanny while she watches the TV soap 'Neighbors.' Charles has banned television from Highgrove and refuses to let the boys watch it, but Diana got around the ban by putting a portable TV in her bedroom, which is out of bounds to Charles.

"After the thirty-minute 'Neighbors' program, Diana will often go outside, in the summer months, to play with the boys. Sometimes they will play cricket or mini-golf while the detectives also play to make up the numbers. Charles never joins in such innocent fun.

"At seven P.M. the butler Paul rings a bell to call the family to high tea. If the weather is fine they will eat out on the patio which Charles designed. They will eat something like pasta and salad, all the salad ingredients having come from Charles's garden. Di is usually silent, picking at her food, while Charles talks to the boys about school or what they have been doing in London. But it is not a happy, friendly family atmosphere. It is dull and starchy.

"After high tea the boys may be allowed to play outside for a while. Charles will go back to his gardening, and

Diana will usually go to her small, private sitting room and listen to tapes while having the odd glass of wine or champagne. Charles hardly ever drinks nowadays, but Di occasionally likes a tipple. Charles has quite a substantial wine cellar at Highgrove and only keeps it for guests. Diana will sometimes sneak down there and nick a bottle without Charles knowing.

"I've seen Diana in her sitting room dancing away like crazy as she listens to the music. When she does that she turns up the music really loud so it can be heard all round the house, and even outside. It's as though she is daring Charles to complain or ask her to turn down the funky music. She doesn't mind who sees her dancing; she seems to love the attention of people watching her. She doesn't bother to draw the curtains.

"Bedtime for the boys can be real trouble. They just refuse to come when called and run off. Charles takes not the slightest notice and leaves Diana to put them to bed. Di gets the detective to round them up. Sometimes they have run off and security alarms go down at the local police station. They can be really naughty and disobedient. It can take up to thirty minutes to get them in on a lovely summer's night. In the end Diana comes to the front door and shouts in a really loud voice to the boys, 'Come in right now or you will be in trouble!' That usually makes them come running.

"Charles usually stops gardening at about eight P.M. and goes into his study to ready his private papers or listen to opera or classical music. Diana usually goes up to her bedroom and watches TV, listens to music, reads, or telephones friends. Although Diana and Charles used to share the master bedroom suite, nowadays it is only used by Diana at weekends. Charles has moved his favorite brass bed from London and installed it in his dressing room, which has now become his bedroom as well.

"Charles's room is very masculine with only three embroidered cushions on the bed. There are no feminine touches at all. It's very bare, but he does still keep his battered old teddy bear and a Womble [a cartoon character portrayed as living on London's Wimbledon Common] on his bed. Di's bedroom is absolutely hers. She has brought down forty or fifty of her cuddly toys and propped them all up on a sofa in the room. I think the only reminder of the two of them Diana has in her room is a giant pair of padded slippers which have the pride of place by her bedside. They are shaped like two single beds with Spitting Image puppets of Charles and Di peeping out of the top.

"Charles's bedside table is usually empty and untouched, but Di's has a stack of glossy magazines like *Vogue, Tatler* and *Country Living,* as well as a well-thumbed copy of the Relate guide to marital problems.

"Charles usually goes to bed fairly early during the week, but when Diana is at Highgrove he often stays in his study until two A.M. before retiring."

Saturdays are just as bleak for Charles and Di. Jacques went on: "Diana and Charles go their own way. Charles is up with the lark and goes down to his favorite breakfast, stewed rhubarb which he has grown in his garden. Then he puts on his Wellington boots and heads out to his walled garden. No one will see him for the rest of the day. No one, family, friends, or staff, is allowed into his garden without permission. It has a seven-foot-high wall surrounding it and a gate which he locks. And he hates to be disturbed.

"Diana gets up at about seven A.M. and goes for a twenty-minute swim in the indoor pool. She swims with grim determination, as though she is working out her frustration as she powers through the water. Then she usually changes into a tatty cotton tracksuit, sticks her hair under a baseball cap, and jogs two-and-a-half miles around the estate with her detective following. After a shower she will breakfast alone on orange juice and muesli while the boys are being given their food. Then they are taken off to the local pony club for riding lessons.

"As soon as the boys have gone, Diana will usually take off by car to shop in Cirencester, accompanied of course by her detective. There are only a few shops in the town. It is basically a small, typical English market town, but she seems to love to get away and shop on her own. Everyone recognizes her of course, and most people nod or say hello. She loves to chat with the shop assistants, passing the time of day. And the people love it. It seems to be Diana's favorite part of the whole weekend. She loves the attention. She never seems to buy anything very much. I think she goes to escape the atmosphere at Highgrove. It's a sense of freedom. She can't do that in London; otherwise she would stop the traffic. But here she's known and they all love her.

"Virtually no one visits Highgrove anymore when Diana and Charles are there together. During the week of course, when Charles is on his own, his friends Camilla Parker Bowles and Patti Palmer-Tomkinson pop over frequently.

"Diana will sometimes wander alone around the garden. but never in the walled garden. Sometimes she will sit on the front doorstep, up to an hour at a time, waiting for the boys to come home from riding or whatever. I have seen her sit there, with her head in her hands, looking lonely and desolate. Sometimes she seems a very sad person.

"On Saturday evening the family will have another meal together, but the conversation will usually be stilted and forced, as on the previous night. Sometimes Charles will tell the boys to behave themselves, if they are being naughty at table. He does insist on proper table manners from the boys, and urges Diana to set a good example. And the procedure of the Friday night will be followed again, with Charles and Diana not seeing each other after supper. Once again Diana will go to her room at about nine P.M. and Charles to his study.

"Sunday mornings is meant to be a family breakfast, but it rarely is. Charles goes down to a late breakfast and waits for Diana. But she swims for her statutory twenty minutes and again jogs around the estate before showering and coming down to breakfast. That delay seems to infuriate Charles. It seems that most Sunday mornings they end up have a blazing row which the whole house can hear. Diana screams at Charles and he tries to quiet her.

"Sometimes Di will storm out of the house, shouting at her detective to leave her alone, and she will go for a half-hour walk in the woods. Then she returns, seemingly in a cold fury, throws her bags in the car and races off, without once looking back. The children, the nannies, and the detectives follow on as soon as everyone is in the cars. Sometimes Charles will say good-bye to the children, but not always."

As a Christmas present in 1990, Diana surprised Charles with an old-fashioned, crown-shaped lamppost for his garden hideaway. The present was in fact quite sensible, as Charles had been using a battery-powered flashlight when working in the garden at night. But there were other thoughts in Diana's mind. One, she thought it a very good joke at Charles's expense, and two, she wanted to remind him in an amusing way that she feels he spends far too much time in his garden and not enough time with his sons. Understandably, one of Diana's principal points of contention, and often the cause of many a heated argument, is that Charles wants Diana and the children to visit him at weekends at Highgrove and then spends most of the time ignoring them.

During one such weekend row in the autumn of 1990 Diana screamed after Charles as he left the dining room, "If you go on behaving like this I will never come down here again. You can spend your whole bloody life in your bloody garden if you want."

Charles does try to interest his sons in gardening, his obsession. He bought them both miniature trowels and forks and gave them small patches of garden to grow their own vegetables. The two boys lose interest fairly quickly, which irritates Charles. They prefer to play around the estate or take riding lessons.

July 1991 was a special month for Princess Diana, marking both her thirtieth birthday and her tenth wedding anniversary. Her birthday fell on July 1, and she spent it alone in London, while Charles stayed at Highgrove.

Nothing could have illustrated more clearly to the world that the royal couple were indeed leading separate lives. Looking radiant and happy, Diana went to the Savoy Hotel in London to a lunch in aid of a children's hospice. There was a birthday cake with thirty candles, ten thousand balloons, and five hundred guests, many of them from the world of show business Diana loves. The Princess's favorite pop star, Phil Collins, serenaded her with three of his hits, including her favorite, "A Groovy Kind of Love."

Earlier, the band of the Grenadier Guards played a medley of tunes to herald her arrival, but Phil Collins revealed that Diana had banned him or the Guards from playing or singing "Happy Birthday." Diana was heaped with flowers and birthday cards as she arrived at lunch and quipped, "How did anyone know it was my birthday?"

Asked how she would be spending her birthday evening, Diana replied, "I will be spending it having a drink with the only man in my life—Prince Harry." (William was away at school.)

But it was Diana's choice to be alone on her thirtieth birthday. Prince Charles had sought to organize a gala thirtieth birthday party for her, but she had refused. He looked forward to buying her a special birthday present, but she would not tell him what she wanted. She said she didn't want a present, didn't want any special celebration.

It had all been so very different when Prince Charles turned thirty, back in 1976. The Queen had thrown a magnificent, riotous party for her eldest son at Buckingham Palace, and the champagne had flowed till three-thirty the next morning. Every kind of music was played virtually nonstop, and the Queen was heard to say, "Well, that was some party." She had footed the bill for the three hundred fifty guests, who included not only thirty members of the Royal Family but many of Charles's former girlfriends. That was the sort of party Charles wanted to give for Diana, but she was not interested.

An aristocratic friend of Charles explained: "Charles asked Diana again and again if she would let him organize a party. He even thought of arranging a surprise party. But Diana let him know, in no uncertain terms, that she would just not turn up. She was adamant. But no one knows why she was so obstinate. It's a mystery.

"Charles knew only too well how this would be read. Everyone would know that Diana was going out of her way to state to the world that their marriage was now a sham, that they were together for the sake of the children and the fact that they cannot divorce. So, this was her way of showing they do in fact lead separate lives. It is all very sad.

"People are suggesting that there is a cause for concern. All that is now past. For all intents and purposes the marriage is now over. Full stop."

Charles spent Diana's landmark birthday resting quietly at Highgrove and then held a small fund-raising drinks party at the house in aid of the Tetbury Church Restoration Fund. Later, Charles took the royal train to Edinburgh where, the next morning, he attended the installation of the Knights of the Thistle at St. Giles Cathedral.

It was not what the nation expected for Diana's thirtieth. Many Britons believe the stories of the unhappy marriage are fiction: the Prince and Princess might have the usual marital difficulties, but basically they are happy together; they both love the children and only their royal duties keep them apart so much. Those who believe the marriage is happy think Charles should have thrown her an enormous party because everyone loves the Princess.

Diana was at the height of her popularity at that time. In a poll conducted in July 1991, she was voted the most favored member of the Royal Family. Another poll in the *Sunday Mirror*, carried out three days after Diana's birthday, revealed that only 15 percent of the respondents thought they should divorce, 60 percent said no, and 25 percent weren't sure. In apportioning responsibility for their separate lives, 15 percent blamed Charles. Diana was blamed by 5 percent, both by 28 percent, and the remaining 52 percent did not know. Although 23 percent believed Charles had chosen the *wrong* partner as his bride, 66 percent said he had chosen the right person.

The poll also asked the delicate question of whether Charles and Diana should consider having another baby to help heal their marriage: a resounding 80 percent said no.

Monday, July 29, 1991, was their tenth wedding anniversary, and the nation wondered whether the royal couple would celebrate it together.

Charles and Diana were apart most of the day before. Charles had stayed the night at Highgrove and then drove alone to attend a breakfast at the Dorset mansion of close friends Simon and Annabel Elliott. Charles's friend Camilla Parker Bowles, Annabel's sister, was there, but her husband Andrew Parker Bowles was not. Charles then took off for Windsor to take part in the year's biggest polo event, the Cartier International, attended by more than twenty-five thousand people who hoped to see the couple together. Diana preferred staying at Highgrove with Wills and Harry rather than being seen with her husband. After the polo bash and a glass of champagne, Charles drove down to Highgrove for the evening with Princess Diana and their children.

For their great anniversary day the couple spent little time together. They were, in fact, never seen with each other in public the whole day. Princess Diana stood in for the Queen at the Queen's Review of the Royal Air Force College at Cranwell, flying by helicopter the hundred and fifty miles from Highgrove to Sleaford in Lincolnshire, the RAF base where Charles had learned to fly twenty years before. That afternoon she returned by chopper to Highgrove, where she and Charles spent the rest of the day together. There was no party, no drumroll. They had no special celebration dinner but ate a simple supper with Wills and Harry. Charles did insist on opening a bottle of champagne, but hardly a drop was drunk.

The following day, Luciano Pavarotti tried his utmost to

rekindle the magic in their marriage when they both attended a special charity night in Hyde Park. More than one hundred thousand people crowded into the park for the festival of opera, but the heavens opened and the entire audience, including Charles and Diana, were soaked to the skin as torrential rain poured down throughout the concert.

Pavarotti deliberately sang his passionate arias directly to Charles and Diana as they sat huddled under umbrellas and plastic sheeting in the front row. Both of them loved his music. They reveled in the night and seemed to be enjoying themselves immensely. They spoke intimately together; they touched each other's hands. Charles tried in vain to protect Diana's legs from the lashing rain. They seemed more companionable than they had in months, if not years. Afterward they went to the Hyde Park Hotel for a champagne celebration with the great tenor. Pavarotti said, "Diana was charming. She looked magnificent, even though she was wet through. It was a marvelous night. I'm proud I made Charles and Diana happy again."

Their rekindled love seemed to gain strength when Charles and Diana took the Princes and others on a Mediterranean cruise during August 1991. Greek oil billionaire, eighty-year-old Ioannis Latsis, lent them his extraordinary boat, the *Alexander*. At four hundred feet, it is the world's second largest privately owned yacht. Charles invited friends and relatives to join them, including Princess Alexandra and her husband Sir Angus Ogilvy; his cousin Lord Romsey and Lady Romsey, with their three children, Nicholas, Alexander, and Leonora; and ex-King Constantine of Greece, his wife Anne-Marie, and their children, Theodora and Phillipos.

It was a wonderful, sun-drenched cruise. Most days the yacht dropped anchor at beautiful deserted coves so the royal party could go ashore. The children played on the beaches while the adults enjoyed lovely barbecues. Diana swam and bronzed her body every day, and Charles found time to do some painting and reading. At night, after the children had been put to bed by their nannies, there were drinks in the sunset and delicious dinners.

But those close to Charles believe he invited so many others along to prevent any arguments between himself and Diana during their cruise. Though the yacht was large, it was still impossible for a couple to have a raging argument without people hearing. Charles knew it was a simple way of ensuring a fairly trouble-free two weeks.

During the cruise, Diana became attached to Lord Romsey's five-year-old daughter Leonora, who the year before had been rushed home from holiday suffering from cancer. After four major operations, chemotherapy, and radiotherapy, the doctors believed she had conquered her illness. Not long after returning to London, Leonora fell ill again. Most days Diana would visit her in St. Bartholomew's Hospital, sit on her bed, and hold her hand as she willed her to stay alive.

A ward sister said, "It was very moving to see them together. The Princess read to her, played games, or simply sat on the bed holding hands and talking to her. And Diana never showed any signs of sadness during the visits. She would tuck Leonora in with a good-night kiss before she left. Diana knew Leonora was dying. During Diana's last visit she sat on the bed talking to her as Leonora was fading fast. It was so sad; we couldn't hold back our tears. Diana left her with a long kiss and turned, the tears streaming down her face."

But the apparent newfound love was not to last. From late September to the end of October 1991, the couple spent nearly the entire time apart. Diana went alone on a royal visit to Pakistan for five days and then stayed in London attending official engagements. Some weekends she managed to escape to Highgrove with the boys. Charles, meanwhile, was in Scotland on holiday, stalking deer, fishing in the River Dee, walking, riding, and relaxing at Birkhall, a guest house on the Balmoral estate. He never traveled south to see Diana or the Princes. Nor did Diana bother to see Charles or other members of the Royal Family on holiday in Scotland. Diana, of course, has never liked the Royal Family get-togethers in Scotland, but not to see each other at all for so long gave the wagging tongues yet more evidence of disharmony.

Further, Camilla Parker Bowles, accompanied for some of the time by her husband Andrew, did go to Birkhall to spend part of Charles's holiday with him.

In the past, royal advisers tended to dovetail their respective diaries so that major events or speeches would not clash. Since 1988, these advisers sensed that Charles and Diana had become rivals, and gradually they were told simply to go ahead and not bother to cross-check the schedules.

One day in 1991 Charles, who had been preparing a major speech on education in Britain, discovered to his horror that, at about the same time on the same day, Diana was making one of her rare major speeches, on her favorite subject, AIDS. Charles was furious. He had spent weeks making sure his speech on education would be received as a major contribution on a subject of considerable political debate in Britain. But as a result of the overlapping schedules, media attention was divided between the two—precisely what Charles had wanted to avoid. Charles won the duel with Diana in the majority of papers and in all the quality broadsheets and TV. But Diana was the major star in the tabloids.

During the Gulf War of 1991, the two clashed head on. Diana wanted to visit the troops, knowing her appearance would be a great boost to the British soldiers and airmen as well as a magnificent public relations gesture for herself. She also knew that her new male friend, Major Jamie Hewitt, would be there with his tank regiment. Charles insisted, as Prince of Wales and Colonel-in-Chief of various British regiments, including two in the desert, that he be the one to visit the front line. Both flew out to Saudi Arabia, but the Princess was kept away from the war zone so she could not steal Charles's thunder. The maneuver worked. The royal seen on the TV screens back home supporting the British troops was the Prince, not the Princess.

In 1991, a newspaper filmed the couple at a few public engagements together and invited psychologists to analyze the couple's behavior. One psychologist observed, "The emotional temperature is very, very cold. There's nothing there, not even at the most basic level. It seems as if she is trying to cut him out of the picture entirely, to pretend he isn't there. It's not the sort of behavior one would expect from a close, happily married couple living normally as man and wife."

The more the matrimonial experts examined the royal marriage, the bleaker the conclusions. As Maria Molett of the Marriage and Counselling Center put it, "If this was an ordinary couple coming to see me, I frankly don't think they'd have a very good chance of making it. The trouble lies in their disparate backgrounds. He is a university graduate, she is a high school dropout."

As the two of them have gradually grown apart, so the people around them have changed. Not only their staff and advisers, but their friends as well. Now they are a couple divided by their friends.

Diana loves easygoing dinner parties in fashionable restaurants and small supper parties in private homes, with music in the background and lots of laughs and convivial chitchat. She has many pals, including her three old flatmates. Ten years after wedding bells for Diana broke up the gang at Coleherne Court, the Princess saw the last of her former flatmates marry. Virginia Pitman, thirty-two, married banker Henry Clarke, thirty-two, at Chelsea's Register Office in August 1991. Virginia had moved into Lady Di's apartment in South Kensington at Christmas 1980, joining Carolyn Pride and Ann Bolton.

Carolyn's husband, William Bartholomew, runs an upper-crust mobile disco, trucking all the gear for a disco—CDs, tape machines, loudspeakers, and a disk jockey—to various venues ranging from private homes to outdoor marquees. He is often asked to provide music at parties Diana attends.

Anne Beckwith-Smith, now forty, has been a stalwart friend and supporter and Diana's principal confidante since those first heady days when she was dating Charles. Anne remains her stalwart friend and advisor and the person Diana turns to in moments of crisis. Catherine Soames is the ex-wife of one of Charles's best friends, Lord Nicholas Soames, a Tory Member of Parliament.

Catherine was with Di in the Klosters ski chalet the day Hugh Lindsay was killed. They still have quiet, intimate lunches together, and Di was on hand to comfort her when her marriage broke up.

Kate Menzies, the same age as Diana, has been a good friend for years and frequently provides a place for Diana to hide in London when she gets fed up with the confines of Kensington Palace. Kate will tell her to "pop around" for coffee or a chat, or will arrange a small supper party at a moment's notice, inviting whomever Diana would like to see. For some time Kate's house became a home away from home for Diana.

There is Julia Dodd-Noble, known as Di's court jester and nicknamed Crown Jules, a friend of both Diana and Fergie; she is always a fun pal for Diana.

In contrast, Prince Charles's friends are mainly people who share his interests in the great issues of the day: architecture, education, the world of art, the opera, and the green issues which Charles strongly advocates. Diana has not the slightest interest in most of Charles's concerns or friends. She has often told Charles he is "boring," a description that wounds him.

Since their fairy-tale marriage began to crumble, Charles has turned to some of his former girlfriends for emotional support. When she first read stories that Charles was seeing some of his old flames, Diana bridled. But she has tried to come to terms with her husband's spending time with other women. Charles needs their respect and affection, and they are happy to provide it.

As described earlier, the one woman who has undeniably given Charles the greatest support, both before and since his marriage, has been Camilla Parker Bowles. Everyone who sees them together detects the empathy between them. Other women he sees from time to time include the bubbly Australian, Lady Dale Tryon.

There is also Jane, Duchess of Roxburghe, thirty-seven, sister of the Duke of Westminster, who was divorced in 1990 because of her husband's adultery. Janie—a Debutante of the Year and considered one of the most eligible, wealthiest, and prettiest young heiresses in the land, and a fitting bride for a future King—was once romantically linked with Prince Charles. She has remained close to Charles. Since her divorce, she has visited Charles at Highgrove, and he has often been to her new home, a six-bedroom Georgian house near the River Tweed on the Scottish border, where she now lives with her three children.

Princess Diana does not mix with Charles's many friends and not only leads a life separate from Prince Charles, but also seems to have grown ever more distant from other members of the Royal Family as well as from her own Spencer relations.

Diana never got on with Princess Anne, who is ten years older. From their first meeting, the two women seemed to rub each other the wrong way. Diana could not take Anne's direct approach and sense of humor. Anne, of course, is a most forceful woman and is regarded as the strongest personality of the Queen's four children. She has also proved to be the most prodigious worker among the Royal Family, clocking up tens of thousands of miles every year as she visits all parts of the world as patron of the Save the Children Fund. But others, besides Diana, bridle at Anne's direct approach in everything she does, from tackling a tough jump while steeplechasing or speaking her mind on every subject she sees fit.

Though they don't get along, it still came as a shock to the Royal Family when Diana refused to have Anne stand as godmother to either Wills or Harry. Charles had wanted his only sister to be godmother to one of the boys, but Diana simply put her foot down and refused. Without doubt it was a deliberate snub, and Anne took it as such. Princess Anne returned Diana's snub by deliberately not attending Prince Harry's christening in December 1984. She was also letting Charles know that she was appalled that he hadn't got the strength to stand up to Diana.

Since then, the relationship between the two women has remained icy. Anne and Diana hardly ever speak to each other and are always seated apart at dinners and other royal get-togethers.

The Queen could have done much to keep the pressure

off Diana during those first troubled years, but, unfortunately, Diana has never had any rapport with her mother-in-law. Although Kensington Palace is only a five-minute car ride from Buckingham Palace, the Queen has very rarely visited since Diana and Charles moved there in 1982.

The Queen has made only one fleeting visit to Highgrove. Shortly after the birth of Prince Harry, the Queen flew by helicopter to the country estate, walked through the house and up to the nursery, where she stayed for just fifteen minutes before flying off again for London.

The conversations between the Queen and Diana still hardly ever get past "Good morning, Ma'am" and the reply, "Good morning, Diana. How are you?" Diana always says, "Thank you, I'm well Ma'am," and the Queen moves on. Occasionally Diana will be invited to go riding with the Queen when she is taking her holiday at Sandringham. Diana dreads the invitation because she dislikes riding, but the Queen has insisted: "Don't be silly. You'll be perfectly safe with me." And dutifully Diana changes into riding clothes, puts on her crash hat, and goes for a walk on horseback, never a trot, canter, or gallop.

Like Prince Charles, the Queen is a country person at heart and would have loved to live in the country and look after her dogs and horses. The Queen usually has her thirteen corgis around her feet at all times, whether in London, Sandringham, or Balmoral. She recognizes them all as if they were her children. She knows their names, their likes and dislikes, and their temperaments—and corgis can be very objectionable little dogs indeed. They are temperamental, they fight with each other, and they often snap at people's heels for no reason. After dogs, the Queen likes horses, not only to ride, but also to breed and race. She has always been by far the most enthusiastic royal race-goer. There is nothing more she prefers than a day at the races or chatting to her trainers about her horses in training. And, of course, she likes to win.

It is not entirely in jest that the Queen's advisers say: "Her Majesty's priorities are dogs, horses, people, in that order." The state of her children's marriages would seem to confirm this observation.

Neither has Diana had much of a relationship with her father-in-law, Prince Philip. The distance between the two may have been due to Charles's own cool relationship with his father. Charles often complained that his father never acted like a real father should, helping, encouraging, and advising rather than demanding, from a young age, that he stand on his own two feet.

The only member of Charles's immediate family that Diana has got on well with is Prince Andrew, who married Sarah Ferguson. Andrew and Diana have a similar sense of humor, enjoy the same young, slightly irreverent people, and prefer to have a laugh rather than engage in serious conversation. Some royal advisers believe that a marriage between Diana and Prince Andrew would have had a far greater chance of success than the marriage of Diana and Charles.

Diana, Princess of Wales, future Queen of England—if Charles ever becomes King—is a most unusual young woman. Basically separated from her husband and most of her royal in-laws, she has yet managed to carve out an empire for herself and to this day remains the most popular member of the Royal Family.

Without a formal education, she has cleverly side-stepped or vanquished all her opponents and made herself the head of Kensington Palace and its staff. She loves and is close to her sons, one of whom will someday be King—if the monarchy survives.

Diana has set herself on a path of compassionate charity work, which brings constant accolades from the British public. She is considered one of the world's style-setters in fashion and beauty.

But Diana, at age thirty, is plowing a lonely furrow. She is cut off from her own parents, has decided that her marriage to Charles is over in all but name, and has no close friends. Her best friend, Fergie, has fled the Royal Family. Frightened of her mother-in-law, wary of her other relatives by marriage, Diana prefers to keep her distance, which only compounds her loneliness.

Diana is like a stage actress who receives her lifeblood from the applause whenever she steps outside. She is a star who responds with a dashing smile and a warm spirit. But when the curtain comes down, Diana retreats most nights to the loneliness of her sitting room at Kensington Palace, where she watches television and nibbles a TV snack before going to her empty bed.

To relieve the monotony Diana has a few special male friends, including some handsome young bachelors whom she sees from time to time, but not every night. She loves to flirt. It not only gives her confidence and makes her feel sexy, but it helps to overcome her feeling of inadequacy at being repulsed by the man she once loved, her husband Charles. One particular friend is Major James Hewitt. Friends comment that today Diana has a distinct spring in her step, a sparkle in her eyes, and a heartfelt vibrancy when she talks to strangers on her official visits. They attribute this sense of well-being to her having a satisfying, fulfilling relationship with Jamie, which sustains and contributes to her emotional stability.

She adores her two sons, but she also knows that one day her sons will leave her to make their own way in the world. Diana has told strangers that she would like a daughter, but that prospect now seems most unlikely.

Willful, dogged, and headstrong, Diana refused to bow to her husband's wishes for her to play the dutiful, loving wife to the heir to the British throne. In the space of ten years she has seemingly emasculated her husband and, in the process, taken over the palace for herself and exiled him to his country estate.

At the same time, Diana knows that she can never divorce Charles, never have an open relationship with another man, never live the life of a happy, married woman surrounded by her family. She is fearful of her lonely future, desperate to keep her friends, to be liked, to be wanted, to be loved for herself and not because she is the Princess of Wales.

The irony of Diana's life may well be that because of

the breakdown in her relationship with Charles, she will never be Queen. As mentioned earlier, in private Charles has let it be known that if his mother lives for another twenty years, he may decide to renounce the throne in favor of Prince William and live a quiet country life.

He is enjoying his newfound position as champion of the people, critic of the Establishment. He knows that once integrated with Europe, the Britain of the next century, will become a far different society.

Diana knows that she must make the most of life, while she still has her sons, her beauty, her fitness, and her hold on the public. The once shy young woman has become synonymous with royalty. If there is a contest with Prince Charles in that arena, she appears to have won.

But at what price?

In the process, she has all but lost her husband, his love and companionship, and may have quashed forever his chance for the British throne, which had been the goal of his entire life.

Diana and Charles are no longer the magical couple of a decade ago. Diametrically different in temperament, passion and interest, they remain tragically joined in a marriage torn asunder, condemned to live separate, unloving lives to the end of their days.

19

❯❯❯❮❮❮

Further Troubles

The opening of the year 1992 brought yet more traumas for Diana. First came the separation of the Duke and Duchess of York, followed closely by the death of Diana's beloved father, Earl Spencer.

Prince Andrew, the third child of the Duke of Edinburgh and Queen Elizabeth, is fourth in line to the throne, after Charles and Charles's two sons. The dramatic failure of his marriage to Sarah "Fergie" Ferguson in March 1992, after less than six years together, brought great anxiety and concern to the Queen and her close advisers. After so much speculation about the marriage of Charles and Diana, the breakup of the Yorks' marriage was the last thing the House of Windsor needed.

For some time the Buckingham Palace staff had murmured of escalating tiffs, rows, and fiery language emanating from the east wing of the palace, where Andrew and Fergie had their London apartment. During the past year, as the screaming grew more and more heated, many heads were shaking, wondering as to how it was all going to end. And yet, so intently had Britons of all stations been scrutinizing Charles and Diana, the separation of

Andrew and Fergie hit the country, in the midst of an election campaign, like a thunderbolt.

The Queen well knew that Andrew would be difficult for anyone to live with. Her favorite child, the action-man naval officer, is headstrong, arrogant, conceited, a man's man who believes women like strong, forceful men—and that is the image and reality of Andrew's character. He spent most of his married years at sea with the Royal Navy, leaving Fergie to bring up their two daughters as best she could.

Those who know him and his set well consider Andrew a thoroughly boorish, spoiled young man. His idea of sophisticated high life is to throw bread at a dinner party; and his favorite film is *Terminator,* which he has seen innumerable times. He and Fergie seemed well matched because both are hotheaded, emotional types, driven by libido, and lacking in any impulse control. His tabloid nickname, "Randy Andy," accurately reflects the primacy of his sexual drive.

The Queen believed that since Andrew is a close heir to the throne, Fergie should never have married him unless she intended to stick with it through thick and thin. She had personally interceded and believed she had persuaded her bubbly, wayward daughter-in-law to calm down, take things gently, and try to reconcile her differences with Andrew, to no avail.

In any case, the Queen felt the couple should have patched up their differences and developed the self-discipline to overcome their disabling emotional drives. What she found truly appalling was Fergie's willingness to break up her family and cut all ties between the Royal Family and her two daughters—Beatrice, three, and Eugenie, two—who are fifth and sixth in line to succession.

The reaction of the Queen and her advisers to the Yorks' separation was remarkably angry. One indication of her fury was that Buckingham Palace let it be known that courtiers had never considered Sarah Ferguson "royal" material, worthy of belonging to the House of Windsor, and that while she was acceptable as a fling, Andrew never should have married her.

Unlike most mothers-in-law, however, the Queen had further reasons for anger and sadness. She feared for the British monarchy itself. Two of her four children were separated; her own sister, Princess Margaret, was divorced from Lord Snowden. The world wondered how the marriage of Charles and Diana would devolve. The Queen's efforts to instill in her children the idea that family is of vital importance to the moral health of the nation and that the Royal Family should set an example to the people had clearly been of no avail.

In addition, the Queen feared Fergie's abandonment of the Royal Family might give Diana the confidence to follow suit, a decision which, in the context of the family's marital history, could shake the very foundation of the monarchy. She knew that Diana had considered leaving Charles on previous occasions and could well do so again.

As news of the Yorks' breakup flashed around the world, the French newspaper *France Soir* talked darkly of a curse on the House of Windsor. Britain's *Sunday Times* commented: "The fear now is that the marriage of the Waleses could go the way of the Yorks, and for much the same reasons. If that happened, the British monarchy would indeed be in peril. For it would have run out of other royals to marry, yet failed to have found commoners prepared to stick with it. To go from Queen Mother to a collection of single-parent mothers cannot be a future the monarchy relishes. In such circumstances British royalty would face the prospect of extinction by atrophy."

It appears that the royal strategy of permitting their offspring to marry nonroyals has failed. Throughout Europe, the royal families used to intermarry, thus avoiding the need to school spouses in the unspoken rules of the game, with its constraints, disciplines, and responsibilities. All that necessarily changed as the pool of eligible partners from foreign royal families dried up after World War I. But commoners, even aristocratic commoners, face overwhelming difficulties in accommodating to the demands and duties of royal life. After ten years, Diana is still having difficulties coming to terms with many of the constraints placed on her as a royal.

The Queen knew that Diana had at times contemplated walking out on Charles because she, too, felt she had come to the end of her tether and simply could not take any more pressure. Once, in 1986, Diana turned to her newfound friend Fergie and blurted out her feelings and frustrations about marriage to Charles. Fergie told Diana not to pack her bags but to try to improve the situation. She finally persuaded the Princess to see an astrologer who might shed some light on the future and give her hope. Diana heeded Fergie's advice and, after several visits to an astrologer, decided she must consider the consequences of any change on her sons. She would give her marriage another chance and try to come to terms with her life and role as the Princess of Wales.

At a private lunch between the Queen and Fergie, in February 1992, the Duchess of York told the Queen that she had tried everything to keep the marriage together, but felt she could no longer do so, particularly in the face of the hostility from both the press and the Palace courtiers. She blamed the press and Palace officials for ganging up on her and breaking her spirit; she could not survive living in a fishbowl for the rest of her life. She had thought long and hard about sticking to the marriage but felt she simply could not do so.

The Queen understood the reason Fergie gave for quitting the Royal Family: she could not survive the pressures of royal life. Fergie felt that the royals had abandoned her to sink or swim in a situation for which she was totally untrained and unprepared. Attacked by the press for her independent spirit and for her lack of fashion sense and royal dignity, Fergie believed the Royal Family offered her no support in her search for a role to play.

What distressed the Queen most was Fergie's disregard for her responsibilities to her marriage, to the Royal Family, and particularly to her two young daughters. Fergie seemed not to have considered the difficulties the two girls will face, being raised by a single mother who had exiled herself from the protective embrace of the royals.

The Queen did not trouble herself with the possibility that the Duchess might have had an affair with Texas mil-

lionaire Steve Wyatt, the son of a man convicted of man-
slaughter. Wyatt, thirty-six, was a good-looking, serious,
athletic young man with a mahogany suntan who did not
smoke, drink, or take any form of drugs. He was a great
dancer and talker. Young women found him mesmerizing
when he spoke of karma, astrology, divinity, and other
New Age subjects—interests dear to the heart of Sarah
Ferguson.

She met him on November 2, 1989, when she was five
months pregnant with Princess Eugenie and on an official
visit to the British Festival at the Houston Grand Opera.
Her official hostess was Lynn Sakowitz Wyatt, heiress to
the Houston department store and wife of oil billionaire
Oscar Wyatt, who adopted Steve and his brother Douglas
when he married their mother. Lynn Wyatt introduced
her son to the Duchess at their Houston mansion.

Despite her pregnancy, Fergie and Steve spent much of
the evening dancing together, and when not on the dance
floor, talking nonstop. It was a real-life fatal attraction.
That single meeting dramatically changed Fergie's attitude toward Andrew, her marriage, and her future life.
She found Steve so intensely fascinating that she was not
able to get him out of her mind over the next two years.

Back in London, the two continued to see each other.
Steve was brokering deals in his stepfather's oil business
in London. His office was in St. James's, close to Buckingham Palace. Fergie invited him to the palace for lunch and
for dinner at Windsor Castle; she arranged for him to
attend balls at Buckingham Palace celebrating various
royal birthdays: the ninetieth birthday of the Queen
Mother, the fortieth of Princess Anne, the thirtieth birthday of Prince Andrew. She also arranged at least six get-
togethers for herself, Steve, and Prince Andrew. Steve has
always said he was a good friend of Andrew's.

Alarm bells began to ring in 1991 when Wyatt escorted
Fergie to a London dinner party to which he had not been
invited and sat down next to her, uttering the immortal
words, "Mah woman and I sit together."

But the affair, which seems to have been platonic, came
to a head in early 1992 when a house cleaner in Wyatt's

rented London apartment accidentally discovered a set of innocent photographs of Wyatt and Fergie in Morocco. They had gone there together on vacation in 1990, along with her children and the American actress Priscilla Phillips. At first Andrew considered the pictures a joke, but when shown more embarrassing photos of the same vacation, he was furious and took the whole thing as a personal rebuff, an insult to his manhood, and an attack on their marriage.

The picture that really hurt the Prince showed Wyatt lovingly holding a smiling baby Bea. Andrew, who had spent most of his married life at sea, felt Wyatt was usurping his place as head of the household. In the past, whatever had gone wrong could be more or less patched up. The Wyatt incident was something Andrew could not forgive or forget. He began spending his leaves from the navy shooting or playing golf. It was the beginning of the end.

Other than Diana, whom Fergie had advised five years before in her despair, Fergie had few people to turn to besides her father, the disgraced Major Ron, and Wyatt himself. All of a sudden, she felt, the Palace courtiers were rejecting her and deliberately indicating that she was no longer to be trusted or treated as a member of the Royal Family. In time, the icy treatment would have melted away, but Fergie could not take the pressure.

Diana did all in her power to calm and placate Sarah. But Diana herself was conflicted because the courtier Fergie considered most hostile was Sir Robert Fellowes, the Queen's secretary and Diana's own brother-in-law, married to her elder sister Jane. The Duchess of York, who had come to fear Fellowes's tongue-lashings, nicknamed him Bellows.

Within hours of the Queen's official announcement of the Yorks' separation, on March 20, 1992, the Queen's respected press secretary, Charles Anson, attacked Fergie with almost personal abuse. He told the BBC that the Duchess of York had deliberately ordered media leaks, that she had personally employed a high-powered public relations firm, and that her behavior showed that she was not fit to be a member of the Royal Family.

The specific behavior Anson criticized occurred when Fergie flew back to London from the United States with her father, Major Ron Ferguson. On that commercial flight, she put a paper bag on her head, stuck her tongue out through a hole in the bag, and then pelted her father with bread rolls and sugar lumps. All this in full view of a number of British journalists, who had never seen royals behave so crassly.

The day after he attacked Fergie, the Queen ordered Charles Anson to make an unprecedented, humiliating public apology to the Duchess and to herself, for the criticisms themselves as well as for suggesting that the criticisms had been endorsed by the Queen. Anson said, "I have apologized to the Queen, and both Her Majesty and Her Royal Highness have been kind enough to accept these apologies."

Charles Anson did not deserve the full responsibility for the attack on the Duchess. It is known that he had been briefed not by the Queen, but by her private secretary, Sir Robert Fellowes, the man who had spent so much of the last two years criticizing Fergie and subjecting her to enormous psychological stress. The Queen, of course, knew who was to blame, and within days, bets were being laid that both Anson and Fellowes would be sacked after a respectable period of time had elapsed.

Diana tried to help the unhappy Fergie, and when all else failed, encouraged her to seek the help of an astrologer, a medium, and a psalmist. Steve Wyatt persuaded her to turn to a mystic healer.

Fergie tried them all in her desperation. The most famous was Madame Vasso, a Greek mystic healer who practices New Age philosophies such as the healing power of the pyramid. Fergie would go to her home in London and sit on a little stool under a blue glass pyramid while Madame Vasso tried to drain away all of her tensions. To no avail. The Duchess could not take the strain and felt her brain would "explode" if she did not get out altogether.

Fergie realized she would be cut off and treated as American divorcée Mrs. Wallis Warfield Simpson had been treated nearly sixty years earlier. When Edward VIII abdicated in 1936 for her sake, the wrath of the royal Establishment came down on her with a vengeance. She was never allowed to return to Britain, not even for a private visit, until after the death of her husband. Fergie, of course, will not be exiled, but she will be ruthlessly cut out of all Royal Family events. Within minutes of the official announcement from the Queen in March 1992, Fergie had become a nonroyal.

She is now a single mother, but responsibility for her daughters' schooling and their future will be taken out of her hands and become the responsibility of the Queen, their grandmother.

The British public have never cared much for the Yorks. All the recent opinion polls have shown them to be the least popular royals. Many singled Fergie out for taking unfair advantage of her position, accepting free holidays and free flights, and not setting a good example. Most people went even further and said she should not be supported by tax monies (the Yorks receive $400,000 a year from the Civil List, administered by the Queen).

Yet there are those who now feel that the irrepressible Fergie, whom so many welcomed to the Royal Family as a "breath of fresh air," may have been hard done by. In her final interview before the separation was announced, at Buckingham Palace in the summer of 1991, an emotional Fergie remarked: "You're always on show and you've just got to accept that. I so often just want to get away. To get away from the system and people saying no you can't, no you can't, no you can't. That's what the system is."

She went on: "This life I lead isn't for real. Modern life isn't the pomp and circumstance of Buckingham Palace . . . I cannot stick to the guidelines because . . . we are not being real. I think I'm managing to keep as normal as

I physically can. . . . It is very difficult to get any privacy . . . in fact, I don't have any.

"If I get a bad press, if I'm perceived to be a person I'm not, all I can do is keep my head down and get on with my work."

She ended the interview with these sad words: "At the end of the day you die alone . . . and as long as you're kind, and you get up in the morning and you're happy to look at yourself . . . and you're straightforward and thank God for everything you do . . . because He knows. And the journalists can write what they want to write."

Everything, every word Fergie that spoke that day reiterated the pressures, the strain, and the stress that Diana, too, has sustained since joining the House of Windsor in July 1981. It is truly remarkable that Diana has been able to withstand the exhausting, sometimes torrid, and often unfair, pressure from the Palace, the Royal Family, and the press during those years—and has emerged a woman of strength and character.

Diana, too, has had to cope with the stress of a disintegrating marriage and a husband who she believes hasn't the stomach for marriage or the will to tackle the problems of the marriage jointly. Diana believes Charles has opted out of the marriage by setting up his alternative home at Highgrove, away from the children, away from the limelight, away from the stress of married life. She cannot forgive him for that.

Yet Diana, who began her married life a naïve, unsophisticated teenager, utterly unprepared for royal discipline, somehow managed to survive. She was certainly unprepared for the royal fishbowl world in which the press ruthlessly chips away at every mistake, every lapse of judgment, every moment of not being on one's best behavior due to exhaustion or simple pique. Fergie succumbed to the incessant stare; Diana tamed it.

.   .   .

The second harrowing shock in the space of a few weeks, at the end of March 1992, hit Diana while she was skiing with Prince Charles and their sons in Lech, Austria. It was the first family holiday in the snow for three years. They had been in Lech only three days, and Charles had been with them for only a few hours. With the family were Kate Menzies and Catherine Soames, as well as Viscount Linley and Laura Fellowes, Diana's eleven-year-old niece. Newsmen reported that Diana seemed happier than she had been for some time.

On March 28, after a morning of snowball fights and skiing in the bright sunshine, followed by lunch in a private chalet, Diana, Charles, Wills, and Harry returned to the Hotel Arlberg just before three P.M. for their regular swim in the hotel pool.

Diana was called to the phone in their suite in an annex. It was Laura's father, Sir Robert Fellowes, Diana's brother-in-law and the Queen's private secretary. He broke the news: Earl Spencer had died an hour before, alone in his hospital room. Diana turned white, put down the phone, and went to her room, where she wept uncontrollably. Her father, sixty-eight, had entered Humana Wellington Hospital, in St. John's Wood, North London, with pneumonia on Sunday, March 21, and appeared to be making a good recovery. Diana had seen him there twice, the last visit on Wednesday, the day before she was due to fly to Austria, to reassure herself that he was fit and well. She had left for her skiing holiday in good spirits.

Prince Charles was outside in the snow, playing around with the two Princes. Dressed in a white bathrobe, Diana went to the balcony and called down, "Charles, I've just taken a call. Daddy's dead."

Immediately, Charles called to one of the police bodyguards to look after the boys as he dashed inside to comfort Diana. After Diana had composed herself and bathed her eyes, the boys came up, and while Charles stood by, Diana told them that their grandfather, whom they hardly knew, had died. Shortly afterward, Charles took the boys back onto the slopes to distract them and to allow Diana privacy to call her sisters back in England. Later that evening, Charles took the boys to the dining room for supper so she could be alone with her grief.

Earl Spencer's son and heir, Viscount Althorp, twenty-seven, works as a TV interviewer with TV-AM in London. The day after their father died, Diana's brother* said, "My father had been in a very good condition and improving all the time. It came as a great shock to my stepmother and the whole family to hear he had had a massive heart attack. He died instantly. There was no pain. It appears that the stroke he suffered in 1978 left his heart bruised on both sides. Because he had been in such good spirits and was due to leave hospital in a matter of days no one from the family was with him at the end."

Diana and Charles, unable to take a scheduled flight, flew back to London two days later, leaving their sons at Lech in the care of their nanny, Jessie Webb, two Royal Protection bodyguards, and the others in the party. Diana's eyes were red and puffy from crying.

The funeral was Wednesday, April 2. Diana was driven from London in her new red Mercedes sports car, arriv-

---

* Diana and the little brother she "mothered" as a baby have always got on well. She is now more likely to spend time at Althorp with her two sons during school holidays.

Charles, dubbed "Champagne Charlie," married Victoria Lockwood, a professional model, now twenty-six, after a six-week courtship in 1989. They have a daughter, Kitty, born in 1991, and Charles said he was delighted to be able to tell his father, just days before he died, that they were expecting twins in August 1992. In January 1991, a British tabloid discovered Charles spending a weekend in Paris with Sally Ann Lasson, a magazine columnist, but since then, Charles and Victoria have been the picture of contented togetherness.

Victoria and Diana have much in common, though they are not close. Victoria, the daughter of a civil servant, was brought up in Putney, London, managed to achieve only four O levels, and after attending secretarial college, achieved her ambition of becoming a model. She is shy and doesn't like country life; she doesn't like walking, riding, or shooting. But unlike Diana, she doesn't even like tennis or driving a car, and she has little interest in clothes; she prefers unflattering, stretched-out jerseys and leggings in dull tones. Victoria doesn't even like cooking; it is husband Charles who cooks most of their meals as well as happily changes their daughter's diapers. When she was single, her interests were wine bars, pubs, and discos.

ing at the same time that Charles touched down on the lawns at Althorp in his helicopter.

From Althorp House to the tiny nearby village church, Diana shared a car in the cortege with her two sisters, Lady Jane Fellowes and Lady Sarah McCorquodale. The twelfth-century church of St. Mary the Virgin, in Great Brington, commemorates generations of Spencers, including the first Sir John Spencer, who bought Althorp House in 1508 and was buried at the church in 1522. Diana and Charles sat together in the choir stalls alongside the new Earl and Countess. Throughout the simple service, Diana seemed forlorn, careworn, and on the verge of tears, looking down most of the time, her eyes hidden by the brim of her hat. Opposite the Prince and Princess were Raine and Viscount Lewisham, her son from her first marriage. Earl Spencer's first wife, Frances Shand Kydd, Diana's mother, did not attend. On a beautiful but simple bouquet of white lilies and sweet peas, Diana's handwritten card read: "I miss you dreadfully Darling Daddy, but I will love you forever . . . Diana."

After the service, Diana approached her stepmother, the woman from whom she had been estranged for so long, and put out her arms to comfort her. They walked together, Raine trying valiantly to smile, trying to obey the wishes of her husband, who had said, years ago, that he wanted no sadness at his funeral, and Diana, biting her lower lip as she fought back the tears. They were two women united in their grief.

Raine moved immediately into the lovely, $2.5 million five-story Regency town house in Mayfair which had been purchased earlier for the time of her widowhood. She said, "I could never go back to Althorp, now my husband is gone. There are too many memories of the happy years we spent there together. It would be too distressing to go back."

The new, ninth Earl Spencer, Diana's twenty-seven-year-old younger brother Charles, is inheriting, besides the title, the bulk of the family fortune, estimated to be

between $1 and $1.5 million, as well as 8,500 acres of
Althorp farmland in Norfolk and a further 5,000 acres in
Warwickshire and Norfolk. The estate also carries crippling debt along with death duties that are expected to
top $7 million.

And, of course, he will inherit Althorp House itself.
Many connoisseurs judge that Raine has ruined the beautiful stately mansion, not only by stripping it of many
artworks to sell, but also by her tasteless alterations and
redecorations. One cruelly compares it to "an Arab's gin
palace in South Kensington."

Relations between the different Spencer generations
had worsened as time went on. Even before Johnny died,
Diana hardly ever took her children to visit her family
home in Northamptonshire. At the 1990 Spencer Christmas party for the grandchildren, Diana took along Wills
and Harry but uttered not a single word to her stepmother, who managed to smile serenely throughout the
afternoon. Diana also forbade William and Harry to call
Raine "Grandma," although she encouraged the children
to call Lord Spencer "Grandpa."

The real issue that divided the Spencer family and pit-
ted Diana against the father she loved was the treasures of
her ancestral home, the beautiful and historic Althorp
House. The Princess was at the center of the storm that
began escalating in the late 1970s and bedeviled relationships between Lord Spencer and Raine, on the one hand,
and Diana, her sisters, and her brother on the other. It
involved what remained of the family treasures.

In 1976, when Raine Cartland married Johnny, who
had only recently come into his inheritance, she decided
that Althorp must pay for itself. She began her regime by
opening the house to the public and installing a souvenir
shop. The children were embarrassed: droves of people
walked through their home and bought cheap trinkets,
while Raine took tickets and served tea and cakes. They
were particularly mortified upon seeing their father, the
man they had revered, with a broom in his hand sweeping
the cobbles.

The marriage of Diana to Prince Charles in 1981 gave

Raine even greater opportunity to cash in on the family name. Althorp had always attracted a steady stream of visitors, but after the wedding, about 40,000 people a year tramped along the plush carpets peering at Diana's home.

Worse yet, Raine's enemies claimed, despite pleas by the four Spencer children, the glories of a once-great house had been systematically sold to raise cash. Art experts believe she sold off about a hundred paintings, including all but three of the unique collection of Van Dycks.

Diana and her siblings decided that perhaps the only way to stop the plunder of the family treasures was to shame their father by going public. They knew they would be washing their upper-class dirty linen in public, but they were incensed. In 1987, *Harpers & Queen,* a society magazine, published an attack on the elder Spencers' activities, ending with an imagined sequence of young Charles eventually wandering the empty corridors, looking at bare walls, and asking where all the treasures had gone.

The British newspapers were full of praise for Diana's father in their obituaries. Most wrote of "the quiet courage of Princess Diana's father," and all recalled the close affection between the two when she was growing up. They also recalled his words when told that Diana was to marry the Prince of Wales: "All I ever wanted for her was to marry the man she loved, and she does love Charles."

Now Diana is very much alone in the world. But she is very powerful. With Princess Anne separated and the Yorks planning to divorce, she would seem to hold the future of the monarchy in her hands. The extraordinary aspect of the Yorks' sundering is that the Queen was unable to keep them together, even if only in a pro forma relationship. Andrew is, after all, fourth in succession to the throne, and his divorce can only weaken the monarchy. The Queen was able to rein in Diana on the question of William accompanying the Prince and Princess to Canada and on the choice of Harry's godparents. Now with

Diana's the only intact marriage among her offspring, what can the Queen muster up should she and Diana disagree on an issue, whether a question of British-made goods or decorous behavior?

But perhaps Diana will never choose to exercise the power she holds. She seems to have grown up on the job. After her rebellious period of liberation from the strictures of Palace protocol, when Fergie introduced her to new friends and led her into a series of highly visible pranks, Diana drew back, realizing that the British public did not admire Fergie and her own reputation could be damaged. The Princess has learned to use all the resources available to her. When life didn't happen as she expected, she took in what did happen and changed either herself or her circumstances. She watched Raine take command of the Spencer household, and she eventually took command of Kensington Palace. She saw her own mother radically change her life when she was miserable. Diana did the same. Diana is now adept at using the media for her own purposes, as when she cast herself as the abandoned wife on her thirtieth birthday. She was an unhappy, motherless child, and she used that lesson to become, and be portrayed as, the dedicated mother of the two Princes.

Diana is exceptionally photogenic, and she genuinely cares about people, having suffered herself over the years. She has used these assets and experiences well. She works to look her best at all times, and she has thrown herself into her charity work, which she takes very seriously and for which she is much admired. Her picture sells magazines and newspapers, the people she meets on her royal duties adulate her, and she has created a role for herself in the world for which she can be very proud.

As for material things, the Princess need never worry about money. She has all the clothes she could want as well as jewelry, as many dinners in chic restaurants as she can eat, a new car when she feels like it, and the chance to meet virtually any movie or stage star she wants.

Are the rewards of her position enough to compensate for the constant scrutiny of her every move by the media and the general public, as well as almost certainly never having a stable, companionable home life? For Fergie, the rewards were insufficient.

For Diana, as for most people, life has always been a series of unexpected challenges. Thus far, despite periods of initial defeat, Diana has usually, with a combination of luck, resourcefulness, and energy, risen to make the best of a situation. Indeed, she has been able to turn defeat into victory. Will she be able to continue this pattern as her looks begin to fade, her sons leave home, the attention of the public becomes wearying, and she finds she is lonely?

One day, perhaps in ten or twenty years' time, Diana will sit by the side of her husband in Westminster Abbey as he is crowned King. She will then be Queen of England. After the fanfares and trumpets, the magnificent ceremony, the royal procession through millions of cheering people, Diana will return to her palace apartment and watch it all again on her television that night—alone with her thoughts of what she has achieved and what might have been.

$\Longrightarrow\!\!\gg\!\!\ll\!\!\Longleftarrow$

Afterword

In May 1992, Diana went on an official royal visit to Cairo—and arranged that she should be pictured, looking innocent and all alone, in front of the pyramids. It was the perfect photo opportunity, coming just days before the books would appear alleging how lonely and sad Diana's life really is.

It was perfectly stage-managed. Diana was suitably dressed for the occasion in a sand-colored safari top and culottes, and as the cameras clicked she gazed at the stunning grandeur of the Sphinx. She walked closer toward the pyramids with Dr. Zahi Hawass, director of the pyramids plateau. Without any fuss, her personal detective walked up to Dr. Hawass and gently ushered him away to one side. That meant Diana could be pictured—for all the world to see—standing in front of the Egyptian pyramids, once again without her husband, totally alone. It was the message of loneliness that she wanted to send to the world. Nobody there doubted that the photo opportunity was intended to convey that message to the British public. Ironically, those journalists and photographers who covered that visit to Egypt reported that they had never known Diana to exude such confidence and to be in such control.

That summer, the royal marriage appeared to be heading for a legal separation, and possible divorce, when details began to emerge of two new books being published in America and Britain.

Serialization of this book, *Diana: A Princess and Her Troubled Marriage*, caused an upsurge of interest in the royal couple when it revealed Charles and Diana had been virtually living apart for four years, and that Charles was having a close, personal relationship with one of his old flames, Camilla Parker Bowles, herself a married woman with children.

Within days another book, *Diana: Her True Story*—written by Andrew Morton, a former royal watcher of the tabloid *The News of the World*—was serialized in the prestigious Sunday *Times*. That series included claims that Diana had tried to commit suicide five times and an allegation that she had suffered from bulimia for the last nine years. But many who were close to Diana, as well as other responsible royal watchers, believed the claims made in the book were exaggerated.

What caused the furor in Britain was the suggestion that Diana had given her tacit approval to the Morton book by giving family and friends authority to speak to the author. It was understood that both Diana's brother, Charles, the new Earl Spencer, and her sister Sarah, who used to date Prince Charles in the late 1970s, had contributed information about Diana's early life. This suggestion was given further credence as family photos of Diana as a teenager were given to the publishers of the Morton book by her father, the late Earl Spencer, who gave them on the understanding that the publishers would donate $150,000 to Diana's favorite charity.

It was said that Diana had encouraged people to talk about her problems to show the world what a rotten married life she was having with Prince Charles. In that way she hoped, so the argument ran, to win the sympathy of the British people, who would feel sorry for her, a princess trapped in a loveless marriage.

There were other reasons put forward. One was that Diana allowed her friends to say how deeply depressed she was because that was the only way she could bring attention to the fact that Charles was having a relationship with Camilla: in other words, Diana was jealous of "the other woman" in her husband's life. Some believed that Diana felt that if the whole world knew she and Charles were living separate lives, then great pressure would be put on Charles to give up Camilla, for the sake of the throne and their two sons.

If Diana wanted her story to be the main part of the book, then her friends did Diana proud, for the Morton book reveals Prince Charles as selfish and arrogant to a degree that few women would tolerate, as well as showing how his behavior hurt poor Diana. It does seem Diana's friends, acting on her behalf, tried to hit Charles where it hurts most.

However, the present book arrived in the stores at the same time and provided a counterweight to the "poor Di" stories in the Morton book. It told the truth of the early days of the marriage, when Diana spent much of the time behaving like a spoiled brat, shouting, screaming, swearing, and demanding her own way on all occasions. Indeed, there are some who have been close to both Charles and Diana who believe that Diana brought a great deal of the loneliness and misery on herself—that in reality Diana's behavior in the early years of her marriage, the behavior of a spoiled young woman, drove her husband away from her, away from their home, and into the arms of another woman.

The revelations about Charles and Camilla did create outrage among a section of the British public, who responded by sending mountains of hate mail to Camilla. The strong-willed woman, who was forty-five in July, was understandably "distraught" at the hundreds of letters arriving at her home about Diana's anguish. A friend of Camilla's commented: "The letters are all blaming her for damaging the royal marriage. It seems very unfair. There has never been anything improper in their relationship, despite what people may think. She has been there for Prince Charles when he needed her, like any good friend. Some of the letters have been disgusting and very rude. Many of the letters say that Princess Diana is a goddess and how dare Camilla do anything to upset or hurt her or damage her happiness. No doubt Diana will take great pleasure in all this."

While the hype behind the Morton book suggested that Diana permitted the book to be written, it does not mean she read the text or approved it after it was written. Unfortunately for her, much of what appears in Morton's book, the book that was meant to hurt Charles and win sympathy for her, was found to be too one-sided.

It was the five alleged suicide attempts, one with a lemon slicer, that caused so much alarm—and disbelief. It appears that the only person Diana confided to in detail about her alleged suicide attempts was James Gilbey, a friend who went into hiding as soon as the revelations became known. Gilbey, thirty-five, who claimed he had known Diana for fourteen years, is an Old Etonian and former car dealer whose business went bust in 1991 leaving debts of around $1 million.

Diana's closest friend of many years, Carolyn Bartholomew, who is the same age as Diana, commented: "The Princess has never, ever, made any comments to me about suicide." That is extraordinary. For Diana not to confide in her best friend, her close friend of many years, about any suicide attempt at any time but to go and reveal all to a man, a man who was never as close to her as Carolyn, seems beyond belief.

Days after the Morton book hit the stores Princess Diana was reported to have severed contact with Gilbey—he is no longer welcome at royal residences and was struck off the privileged list of people given direct access to Diana. A senior security officer at Kensington Palace said, a few days after the book was published: "James Gilbey's name has been on the Approved List for years. It isn't now." The Approved List was established years ago to give Diana's relatives and friends easy access to her at

Kensington Palace. This select group is permitted to telephone her directly and visit her royal residences with minimum security checks. But no one is simply allowed to pop around without first phoning and being given permission. Nor do their phone calls go directly through to Diana. They are always made via a switchboard operator.

The sacking of Gilbey from Diana's close circle of friends, however, was the only official royal reaction to the revelations about the royal marriage. Many expected that the Queen's press officer might make a statement denying the wild claims in the Morton book. But the Royal Family doesn't work like that. It never has. The reason is that if the royals were to start to deny the hundreds of scandalous, libelous stories written about them every year, there would be a never-ending stream of denials emanating almost daily from Buckingham Palace. And, if the Palace were to deny say one or two books, or stories about members of the Royal Family, people might come to the conclusion that all the other stories written about them were true. It would be an impossible task.

Just as the world was being informed in this book of Charles's close relationship with Camilla Parker Bowles, the Queen went out of her way to give a remarkable show of royal approval to Camilla. The Queen and Camilla were sitting just yards away from each other in the exclusive royal enclosure at a Guards Polo Club match in Windsor Great Park in June. Also in attendance were Camilla's husband, Brigadier Andrew Parker Bowles, and their eldest son, Tom, seventeen, who is Charles's godson. There were only about twenty-five other people in the royal enclosure. Charles, however, wasn't there; he was playing polo at Cowdray Park, forty miles away. The Queen leaned forward and waved to Camilla, and Camilla waved back. The Queen had no need to give that little sign of approval; she could have quite easily ignored Camilla without being rude or offensive, for there were many people there. It showed to the world that Camilla was not being cut off by the Queen for her "friendship" with the heir to the throne, but rather the opposite.

The Queen had been asked before the match, sponsored by the cigarette firm Dunhill's, whether Camilla should be invited with her husband, Andrew, and son Tom into the royal enclosure. It would have been perfectly proper, as the couple were actually invited to the polo match by Dunhill's, for them to remain in the area reserved for Dunhill guests. But the Queen wanted to show that her friendship with the couple, whom she has known for more than twenty years, was on-going and that nothing that had occurred had in any way altered that friendship. No one would have been the wiser, and no one would have drawn any conclusion, if the couple had remained in the guests enclosure. It would have been perfectly normal.

For the Queen to make a show of her friendship with Camilla, to do so in public, meant the Queen wanted the world—and in particular the press and the media—to witness her support for Camilla. She knew it would make headline news in the tabloids the following day. And it did.

Later in the privacy of the royal pavilion, during the interval between matches, the Queen went even further. She singled out Camilla and, in front of her other guests, went over to her and the two were left alone to chat away together for five minutes, while they drank their tea and ate cucumber sandwiches. By doing that, the Queen was showing her close friends, advisers, and everyone else on the royal social scene that Camilla was a well-liked, respected, and welcome guest at court and was not to be shunned or ostracized over the fact that Diana considered her to be the "other woman" in Prince Charles's life.

Diana did not attend the polo match. But she was not amused when she read of the Queen's attention to Camilla in the following day's newspapers. In fact, a friend inside Kensington Palace reported: "Diana read the paper, getting more and more angry. She then threw the paper down and stormed off, spitting with venom. I don't know what she was saying under her breath, but it wasn't nice."

As the world waited to see what would happen to the royal marriage, there were urgent discussions inside Buckingham Palace between the Queen and Prince Charles. Although, as I have explained earlier, I had known that Charles and Diana had been living apart for about four years, no one in the outside world realized to what lows their marriage, and their love for one another, had sunk. Until this book was published, most people had read in newspapers and magazines, allegedly written by royal experts, that the royal couple had occasionally had their differences, their tiffs, that there had been problems in the marriage, that Diana did sometimes feel trapped by royal protocol. But no one realized the couple lived separate lives in separate homes.

However, I had known for some time that Charles and Diana had reached an arrangement that has been going on now for, more or less, four years. They had grown accustomed to having their separate lives and had seemingly come to terms with it. Diana had even come to terms with Charles's relationship with Camilla and her jealousy toward the other woman, as she found a new lease on life, enjoying the attentions of handsome young Guards officers. But the revelations caused such a furor throughout Britain that there was instant talk of a divorce. One reason people believed a legal separation was a probability was only months before it had been revealed to a shell-shocked Britain that the Duke and Duchess of York were separating, and they had been married only a few years. A number of royal watchers believed Charles and Diana, too, were headed toward divorce.

But divorce does not seem to be in the cards, at least for the moment. The Queen certainly does not want the Royal Family, which she believes should set an example of good family tradition for the nation, to be rocked by yet another marriage breakup. Already Princess Anne has divorced, Prince Andrew is separated and is expected to divorce after two years of legal separation, and Charles's marriage is a sham. That leaves the Queen's youngest child Edward, and he shows no sign of wanting to settle down and marry. That is a very poor record for the first family to show their fifty-five million subjects, who look to the Royal Family for moral guidance and as an example of family life!

There are many in Britain today, particularly republicans, who believe that every marriage breakup among members of the Royal Family, and not just the immediate family, is another nail in the coffin of the British monarchy. And these marriage failures among her children undoubtedly hurt the Queen personally, as well as causing her acute embarrassment as the head of the Royal Family.

Prince Charles does not want a divorce either. He believes that, for the sake of the monarchy, he and Diana should soldier on, living their separate lives, and that for the sake of William and Harry, they should try to get on as well as possible when they are together—as well as for the sake of the nation, who want to see Charles, Diana, Wills, and Harry as a happy young family, the epitome of what a happy family should be.

Charles believes they should appear for all their official royal duties together, they should continue their overseas official royal visits together, they should be seen with their children together. He believes that their marriage cannot be saved, at least not in the foreseeable future, but that they should be adult enough to understand there has been a tragic breakdown and that their unique position as the future King and Queen means they cannot separate as any other couple can, for their duty to the nation must surpass their own personal feelings toward each other. Charles understands the discipline and the obedience to duty that as a member of the Royal Family one has to accept, whatever happens in one's own life. But does Diana?

Princess Diana is the wild card. She did agree before she became engaged to Charles, in those blissful, love-filled happy days in 1981, that the two of them could never divorce, ever. She accepted that as a part of the marriage to the heir to the throne. Charles believes that Diana should, and must, keep to that agreement.

However, Diana's mother walked out of her marriage, in her early thirties, leaving her husband to cope with three daughters and a very young son. Ironically, Diana's marriage seems to mirror her mother's in many respects. Both were very young women when they married older men. Diana's mother was only eighteen when she married; Diana was twenty and very immature. Diana's mother appeared to want a far more fun-loving, social whirl of a life, parties and dinners with the London social set, than did her husband, who was blissfully happy in the depths of the English countryside, living the life of a gentleman farmer. Charles and Diana have similarly conflicting tastes.

The Queen and Prince Charles know all that, and they both wonder. Could Diana follow the example set by her own mother and walk out in exactly the same way? She has often been so depressed and so unhappy that perhaps she could.

There are very sound reasons why Diana will stay. She loves being the Princess of Wales; she loves being the center of attention; she loves being the most photographed woman in the world; she loves her privileged life. And there are other reasons. Diana does want to be the next Queen of England, no matter what she sometimes seems to suggest. And she does care, she cares very much, about the effect a separation, and perhaps ultimate divorce, might have on the sons she adores above all else. There is no question whatsoever that Wills and Harry are very, very important to Diana. And that is what does not make sense about the book that Diana allegedly wanted published. Would she really want her two young sons to know their mother tried suicide five times and suffered from an eating disorder for many years? I can't believe Diana would want that, or that she would want to put her sons in the position of having to defend their mother against such accusations from their classmates and young friends.

Diana was to rage once again at the Royal Family's attitude toward Charles's friendship with the Parker Bowleses during the summer of 1992, after the books had been published. It was at Royal Ascot, the most social racing event of the year, when Princess Anne went out of her way to show she was a good friend of Camilla's husband, Andrew. Twice, Princess Anne invited Camilla's husband Andrew to accompany her on the public walks from the royal box to the paddock to look at the horses before they went out onto the race track. Anne could not have made the public more aware of their friendship, and what that meant in terms of royal protocol, than she did. And Princess Diana viewed it all. She stayed in the royal box, high above the paddock, and watched as Anne and Camilla's husband twice made the few-hundred-yards walk to and from the paddock. Anne knew full well that the rest of the nation would see that picture and the story the following day, when the tabloid press would comment on her public friendship and splash the picture of Anne and Camilla's husband walking together.

At the Ascot meeting Charles accompanied Diana—but it was a charade for the public and the photographers. Diana and Charles arrived together to great applause and cheers from the thousands of racegoers, who wanted to support them during a troubled time when their lives and their marriage had been exposed to the full glare of publicity. The couple left together in Charles's open-top Aston-Martin, Diana waving to the cheering crowds who saw them off. But a mile down the road Charles stopped the car, and Diana got out and jumped into her waiting chauffeur-driven Jaguar as Charles roared off with his police escort. Diana was driven back to Kensington Palace, while Charles went off to play polo.

There was a most poignant moment for Diana that day, as she rode down the center of the racecourse in an open carriage. During Royal Ascot week there is a tradition, going back decades, that the Royal Family drive down the center of the course in open horse-drawn carriages before racing starts every day. They are greeted by the thousands of racegoers, who raise their top hats and cheer wildly as members of the Royal Family wave back, smiling at the applause and the enthusiastic reception. In 1992 Diana accompanied the Queen Mother in one carriage, while the Queen was accompanied by Prince Philip and Prince Charles.

Standing among the general public, with the tens of thousands of others watching the royals glide past, was Fergie with her two children, Bea, four, and Eugenie, three. Fergie and her two daughters waved at their grandmother, the Queen, and their grandfather, Prince Philip. Fergie, no longer an integral part of the Royal Family, had not been invited to join the royal party at Ascot. She was now an outsider.

Yet only the year before Fergie, the Duchess of York, the wife of Prince Andrew, had herself ridden in one of the open carriages down the course. Diana, who saw Fergie and the two toddlers in the crowd, and waved to them, would have seen the significance. She would have realized that if she did decide to separate from Charles, if she did decide to quit the Royal Family, she would receive exactly the same treatment. It must have been a sobering thought.

Prince Andrew, who was undoubtedly very involved with Fergie when they married, was deeply upset when, the following day, the tabloids showed the pathetic, rather sad trio of his wife and his daughters waving to the Royal Family as they swept by in their carriages. So the next day Andrew joined them and held baby Eugenie on his shoulders to wave at her grandparents so the world would see that he was not deserting his estranged wife and children. And the royals all waved back.

Throughout the summer the pressure on Diana continued to cause concern and anxiety. Thousands of people, far more than usual, turned out whenever Diana was attending a function. Some carried banners proclaiming "We love you, Diana." It became too much for her.

Opening a cancer hospice near Liverpool in northwest England, Diana cracked. Hospice Chairman Bill Davidson told her: "Your presence here today gives much pride and joy to us all. May God bless you, and may you always remain just you." Those words of comfort and sympathy touched a raw nerve; at first Diana looked at the floor and blushed; then her lips began to tremble. She fought hard to control her emotions, biting her lip in an effort to hold back the tears. But as she walked out after the short, official ceremony she heard the well-wishers calling and cheering her and was unable to hold back the tears; her face contorted; her eyes glazed with tears and she broke down and wept. She was hurried into her official car, where she sobbed uncontrollably as she was driven away.

Tens of thousands of people turned out for the Trooping of the Colour that weekend—an annual event when the Queen reviews one of the Guard's regiments at Horse Guards Parade, a mile from Buckingham Palace. Uncustomarily, the Queen Mother, now ninety-two, sat beside Diana, who appeared subdued and quiet. The Queen Mother seemed to keep an eye on Diana that day, occasionally chatting to her, giving her support and encouragement.

Later, with other members of the Royal Family, Diana appeared on the balcony of Buckingham Palace to wave to the people. The crowds seemed to have one message for her, chanting "We love you, Diana" as she waved. It was the same balcony where Charles had kissed her on the day of their fairy-tale wedding, eleven years before. The occasion wasn't lost on those who turned out to cheer her. And Charles, too, was there, dressed in full military ceremonial uniform. But the two, so close and so happy back in 1981, seemed cold and distant with each other. On this occasion, it seemed most of the cheers were for Diana, who the people believed needed their support during her time of crisis.

In an effort to help Diana, Stephen Twigg, a therapist, masseur, and guru who deals in controversial holistic therapy, spoke out saying that Diana had now recovered from the gorging and vomiting disease that had racked her for years. Twigg, forty-one, claimed he had treated Diana once a week for the past three years. He told the Sunday *Express*: "She is now ready to take charge of her life for the first time. She has never been healthier, never been stronger emotionally nor more able to deal with the turbulent events of her life. Diana's in perfect shape. The idea that she is ill, unstable in some way, emotionally unbalanced is nonsense." Twigg revealed: "Diana had reached a very low point indeed. Her experiences in life, the consequential view she had acquired of herself and the world, had left her feeling helpless and disabled. Intensely painful emotions and thoughts, muscular tension, digestive problems, and other physical problems. The effect was a journey on a downward spiral."

Twigg claimed he had "cured" Diana by providing her with a framework of techniques in mind and body therapy to overcome her problems. Within days, however, Diana's press secretary officially announced that Twigg had been fired. In a terse statement he said: "Mr. Twigg is no longer attending the Princess of Wales. We are releasing no further details."

In an effort to heal the rift, and so the whole world would see, the Queen arranged a Mediterranean holiday cruise for Charles and Diana, a cruise similar to their dream honeymoon, when they sailed the Mediterranean for two weeks in peace and quiet. Within days, however, details began to emerge that Charles and Diana would be sleeping in separate cabins, and the tongues began wagging again.

Shortly after the holiday the nation was rocked by the revelation of old tapes of a conversation allegedly between Diana and her erstwhile confidant, James Gilbey. People could call in to a newspaper to listen to a recording of the tapes. Most people believed the conversation was indeed between Diana and Gilbey, but nonetheless support for Diana continued, particularly among women.

The world will continue to watch with fascination the progress of the royal fairy-tale that went so disastrously wrong. Unfortunately, however, this royal soap opera is real, not one that we can turn off and then watch something else. This tragedy involves real people and two young, innocent children. I believe that both Charles and Diana are to blame for the breakdown of their marriage—but apportioning blame won't help the marriage. I am convinced, however, that their marriage is now over, finished, and for good. For the sake of the children, however, they must try to be polite, kind, and understanding to each other and forget the traumas and rows of the past, if they are going to remain legally together.

If they do stay married—and I believe they will because duty calls—then both Charles and Diana will have to learn to compromise and respect each other and stop the stupid rows and arguments that still rage whenever they spend an hour or two together, because that must cause distress and anxiety to their sons.

It does seem that Charles has found another woman, Camilla, to whom he has become very close, and it is likely that Diana will find another man to whom she can turn for love and support. The Queen would totally understand such an arrangement, as long as all was kept discreetly low key and out of the public eye.

Diana may not have the love of her husband; she may not have the respect of the Royal Family; but she has the love, the respect, and the loyalty of most of the British nation, of which she is one day likely to be Queen. That is what she must hold on to, protect, nourish, and savor. If she manages to do so, Diana will become the Queen the nation will not only respect but genuinely love.

Index